Karen B

Ital

Charming Inns & Itineraries

Written by

CLARE BROWN

Illustrations by Barbara Tapp
Cover Painting by Jann Pollard

Karen Brown's Guides, San Mateo, California

Karen Brown Titles

Austria: Charming Inns & Itineraries
California: Charming Inns & Itineraries
England: Charming Bed & Breakfasts
England, Wales & Scotland: Charming Hotels & Itineraries
France: Charming Bed & Breakfasts
France: Charming Inns & Itineraries
Germany: Charming Inns & Itineraries
Ireland: Charming Inns & Itineraries
Italy: Charming Bed & Breakfasts
Italy: Charming Inns & Itineraries
Mexico: Charming Inns & Itineraries
Mid-Atlantic: Charming Inns & Itineraries
New England: Charming Inns & Itineraries
Pacific Northwest: Charming Inns & Itineraries
Portugal: Charming Inns & Itineraries
Spain: Charming Inns & Itineraries
Switzerland: Charming Inns & Itineraries

With Love
to
My Best Friend, Bill
With Love and Gratitude for
Many Miles of Memories

Cover Painting: Londra Palace, Venice.

Editors: Karen Brown, June Eveleigh Brown, Clare Brown, Kim Brown Holmsen, Iris Sandilands, Nicole Franchini, Lorena Aburto Ramírez, Tony Brown.

Illustrations: Barbara Tapp.

Cover Painting: Jann Pollard.

Technical support: Michael Fiegel, Lynn Upthagrove, William H. Brown III.

Web Designer: Lynn Upthagrove.

Maps: Susanne Lau Alloway—Greenleaf Design & Graphics and Michael Fiegel.

Inside cover photo: W. Russell Ohlson.

Distributed by Fodor's Travel Publications, Inc., 280 Park Avenue, New York, NY 10017, USA.

Distributed in the United Kingdom by Random House UK, 20 Vauxhall Bridge Road, London, SW1V 2SA, England, phone: 44 20 7849 4000, fax: 44 20 7840 8406.

Distributed in Canada by Random House of Canada Limited, 2775 Matheson Blvd. East, Mississanga, Ontario L4W 4P7, Canada, phone: 905 624 0673, fax: 905 624 6217.

Distributed in Australia by Random House Australia, 20 Alfred Street, Milsons Point, Sydney NSW 2061, Australia, 2066, phone: 61 2 9954 9966, fax: 61 2 9954 4562.

Distributed in New Zealand by Random House New Zealand, 18 Poland Road, Glenfield, Auckland, New Zealand, phone: 64 9 444 7197, fax: 64 9 444 7524.

Distributed in South Africa by Random House South Africa, Endulani, East Wing, 5A Jubilee Road, Parktown 2193, South Africa, phone: 27 11 484 3538, fax: 27 11 484 6180.

A catalog record for this book is available from the British Library.

ISSN 1533-4627

Contents

Icons Key

This year we have introduced the icons listed below in the guidebooks and on our website (*www.karenbrown.com*). These allow us to provide additional information about our recommended properties. When using our website to supplement the guides, placing the cursor over an icon will in many cases give you further details.

❄	Air conditioning in rooms	🍴	Restaurant
☕	Breakfast included in room rate	🏊	Swimming pool
	Children welcome	🎾	Tennis
	Cooking classes offered		Television
CREDIT	Credit cards accepted		Wedding facilities
	Dinner served upon request	♿	Wheelchair friendly
☎	Direct-dial telephone in room	🏌	Golf course nearby
	Dogs by special request		Hiking trails nearby
	Elevator	🏇	Horseback riding nearby
	Exercise room	🎿	Skiing nearby
♈	Mini-refrigerator in room		Water sports nearby
🚭	Non-smoking rooms	🍇	Wineries nearby
P	Parking available		

Introduction

Of all the countries in the world, there is none more magical than Italy: it is truly a tourist's paradise—a traveler's dream destination. No one could be so blasé, that within Italy's narrow boot there would not be something to tantalize his fancy. For the archaeologist, there are some of the most fascinating and perfectly preserved ancient monuments existing today, just begging to be explored. For the gourmet, there is the finest food in the world. For the outdoors enthusiast, there are towering mountains to conquer and magnificent ski slopes to enjoy. For the lover of art, the museums are bursting with the genius of Italy's sons such as Michelangelo, Leonardo da Vinci, and Raphael. For the architect, Italy is a school of design—you are surrounded by the ancient buildings whose perfection still inspires the styles of today. For the history buff, Italy is a joy of wonders—her cities are veritable living museums. For the wine connoisseur, Italy produces an unbelievable selection of wine whose quality is unsurpassed. For the adventurer, Italy has intriguing medieval walled villages tucked away in every part of the country. For the beach buff, Italy's coastline and lakes hold the promise of some of the most elegant resorts in the world. For the religious pilgrim, Italy is the cradle of the Christian faith and home of some to the world's most famous saints. The miracle of Italy is that all these treasures come packaged in a gorgeous country of majestic mountains, misty lakes, idyllic islands, wonderful walled villages, and gorgeous cities. In addition, the climate is ideal and the people warm and gracious. Italy is truly a perfect destination.

About This Guide

This guide is written with two main objectives: to describe the most romantic hotels throughout Italy and to tie these hotels together with itineraries that include enough details so that you can plan your own holiday. This introduction explains how to use the guide and also touches upon what to expect while traveling. After the introduction the main part of the guide is divided into three sections: itineraries, hotel descriptions, and maps. The itinerary section outlines itineraries with sightseeing suggestions along the way; the hotel description section gives a comprehensive list of recommended lodgings (appearing alphabetically by town); the map section has 14 maps to help you pinpoint each town where we suggest a place to stay. The pertinent regional map number is given at the right on the *top line* of each hotel's description. To make it easier for you, we have divided each location map into a grid of four parts—a, b, c, and d—as indicated on each map's key.

We have personally inspected each place that we recommend and describe its ambiance and merits in our write-up, which is followed by an illustration and practical information such as address, telephone and fax numbers, rates, etc. Our choices are strictly based on hotels we think you would most enjoy. Frequently we hear, "I don't care where I stay— I'm rarely in my room except to sleep." If this is your true philosophy, then this book is *not* for you. To our way of thinking, where you stay weaves the very fabric of your trip and your choice of hotels is of absolutely prime importance. Not that the hotel needs to be expensive: a moonlit dinner on the terrace of a simple inn can be as memorable as dining at a fancy hotel—sometimes even more so because the owner is there to pamper you. The recommendations in our guide vary tremendously: some are grand hotels—fit for a king and priced accordingly; others are simple, inexpensively priced hotels tucked away in remote hamlets. We include them all if they have personality, romantic charm, and antique ambiance.

About Itineraries

In the itinerary section of this guide you'll be able to find an itinerary, or portion of an itinerary, that can be easily tailored to fit your exact time frame and suit your own particular interests. If your time is limited, you can certainly follow just a segment of an itinerary. In the itineraries we have not specified the number of nights at each destination, since to do so seemed much too confining. Some travelers like to see as much as possible in a short period of time. For others, just the thought of packing and unpacking each night makes them shudder in horror and they would never stop for less than three or four nights at any destination. A third type of tourist doesn't like to travel at all—the destination is the focus and he uses this guide to find the perfect place from which he never wanders except for daytime excursions. So, use this guide as a reference to plan your personalized trip.

Our advice is not to rush. Part of the joy of traveling is to settle in at a hotel that you like and use it as a hub from which to take side trips to explore the countryside. When you dash too quickly from place to place, you never have the opportunity to get to know the owners of the hotels and to become friends with other guests. Look at the maps in the back of this guide to find the places to stay in the areas where you want to travel. Read about each hotel in the hotel description section of this book and decide which sound most suited to your taste and budget, then choose a base for each area you want to visit.

MAPS

Each itinerary is preceded by a map showing the route and each hotel listing is referenced on its top line to a map at the back of the book. To make it easier for you, hotel location maps are divided into a grid of four parts—a, b, c, and d—as indicated on each map's key. All maps are an artist's renderings and are not intended to replace detailed commercial maps. We use the *Michelin Tourist and Motoring Atlas of Italy,* a book of maps with a scale of 1:300,000 (1 cm = 3 km). We also find the regional Michelin maps very useful and we state which Michelin 400-series map each hotel's town is found on in the hotel description. To outline your visit to Italy you might want to consider the one-page map of Italy, Michelin map 988. Italy hotel maps in this book can be cross-referenced with those in our companion guide, *Italy: Charming Bed & Breakfasts*. We sell Michelin country maps, city maps, and regional green guides (sightseeing guides) in our website store at *www.karenbrown.com*. Another fine choice is The Touring Club Italiano map set, in an easy-to-read three-volume format divided into North, Central, and South. Even the smallest town or, better, *localita* is listed in the extensive index.

SIGHTSEEING

Ideas on what to see and do are suggested throughout the six itineraries. However, we just touch upon some of the sightseeing highlights. There is a wealth of wonders to see in Italy, plus, of course, many local festivals and events. Before you leave, check with the tourist office for further information targeted at exactly where you plan to travel. And, once on the road, make it a habit to always make your first stop the local tourist office to pick up maps, schedules of special events, and sightseeing information. Even more important, before you drive out of your way to see a particular museum or place of interest, check when it is open. As a general guideline, most museums are closed on Mondays except for the Vatican museums, which are closed on Sundays (except for the last Sunday of the month). The most important museums now have continuous hours and either have a full- or half-day schedule but do not close for a few hours and then reopen. Smaller museums are usually open until 2 pm. Outdoor museums usually open at 9 am and close about an hour before sunset. Most monuments and museums close on national holidays—see "Holidays" on page 18. *NOTE*: To save waiting in line for hours to buy entrance tickets, buy tickets for major museums in advance from travel agencies, hotels, or tobacco shops.

About Hotels

BASIS FOR SELECTION

This guide does not try to appeal to everyone. It is definitely prejudiced: each hotel included is one we have seen and liked. We visit hundreds of hotels and choose only those we think are special. It might be a splendid villa elegantly positioned overlooking one of Italy's romantic lakes or a simple little chalet snuggled high in a mountain meadow. But there is a common denominator—they all have charm. Therefore, if you too prefer to travel spending your nights in romantic old villas, appealing chalets, dramatic medieval castles, ancient monasteries, converted stone cottages, and gorgeous palaces, we are kindred souls.

For some of you, cost will not be a factor if the hotel is outstanding. For others, a budget guides your choice. The appeal of a simple little inn with rustic wooden furniture beckons some, while the glamour of ornate ballrooms dressed with crystal chandeliers and gilded mirrors appeals to others. What we have tried to do is to indicate what each hotel has to offer and describe the setting, so that you can make the choice to suit your own preferences and holiday. We feel if you know what to expect, you won't be disappointed, so we have tried to be candid and honest in our appraisals.

CREDIT CARDS

Whether or not an establishment accepts credit cards is indicated in the list of icons at the bottom of each description by the symbol . We have also specified in the bottom details which cards are accepted as follows: AX–American Express, MC–MasterCard, VS–Visa, or simply, all major. *NOTE:* Even if an inn does not accept credit card payment, it will perhaps request your account number as a guarantee of arrival.

DECOR

It is difficult to find hotels in Italy furnished in a simple style. Italian hotels frequently reflect a rather formal opulence and tend toward a rather fussy decor. There are some exceptions. In a few instances (which we note in the hotel descriptions) the hotels are decorated with a more rustic ambiance using country antiques, but this is not the norm. When antiques are used, they are very often the fancy, gilded variety.

GROUPS & AFFILIATIONS

There are two well-known groups of hotels to which many of the hotels in this guide belong. The Romantik Hotels group is an affiliation of charming small hotels that are managed by the owner and are usually located in a historic building. You can recognize the hotels that belong to this group because they have the word Romantik preceding their name. The Relais & Châteaux group is an affiliation of luxurious small hotels that are very expensive, with extremely high standards of excellence. You can tell which of the hotels in our guide belong to this group because we have noted *Relais & Châteaux* in the hotel's bottom information. These associations impose their own criteria for selection and membership standards and have established a reputation for the particular type of property they include.

ICONS

Icons allow us to provide additional information about our recommended properties. When using our website to supplement the guides, positioning the cursor over an icon will in many cases give you further details. For easy reference an icon key can be found on the last page of the book.

We have introduced these icons in the guidebooks and there are more on our website, *www.karenbrown.com.* ❋ Air conditioning in rooms, ▣ Breakfast included in room rate, ⚡ Children welcome, ♨ Cooking classes offered, ▤ Credit cards accepted, ☎ Direct-dial telephone in room, ⛰ Dinner served upon request, ⚐ Dogs by special request, ⛃ Elevator, ⚡ Exercise room, ⚱ Mini-refrigerator in room, ⊗ Non-smoking rooms, P Parking available, ❞ Restaurant, ≋ Swimming pool, ⚡ Tennis, ▨ Television, ✿ Wedding facilities, ♿ Wheelchair friendly, ⚓ Beach nearby, ⚑ Golf course nearby, ⚡ Hiking trails nearby, ⚡ Horseback riding nearby, ⚡ Skiing nearby, ⚡ Water sports nearby, ⚑ Wineries nearby.

RATES

In the hotel section in the back of the book each listing shows a rate range that reflects the approximate 2003 high-season nightly cost in euros for a room for two persons including tax, service, and Continental breakfast. (Where quoted separately, breakfast prices are per person.) Breakfast included is confirmed in the list of icons at the bottom of each description by the symbol ▣. Rates do not reflect higher prices for various special holiday periods. There are a few hotels where breakfast and one other meal (either lunch or dinner) are included in the rate and, if so, this too is noted. Please use the rates given only as a general guide because each hotel has such a wide range of price possibilities that it is impossible to project with complete accuracy. Be sure to ask at the time of booking exactly what the price is and what it includes (breakfast, parking, etc.) so that you won't be in for any unpleasant surprises—sometimes rates increase after this book goes to print. When you plan your holiday, check the current exchange rate on our website, *www.karenbrown.com*, or at your bank.

HOW TO ECONOMIZE: The price for a room in Italy has soared in the last few years. However, if you study carefully the rates given in the back of this guide, you can still find a few bargains and can plan your trip using one of the less expensive hotels as your hub from which to venture out each day. We also publish *Karen Brown's Italy: Charming Bed & Breakfasts*, which makes an ideal companion to this guide. The maps in both are similar, making it easy to choose a place to stay from either book. Not only can you save money by sometimes choosing a bed and breakfast for a night's accommodation, but you can also enjoy the experience of staying where you have the opportunity to know your host and fellow guests. We highly recommend choosing a combination of places to stay from both books.

For those of you who want to squeeze the most value out of each night's stay, we have several other suggestions:

1) Travel off season—spring and fall are usually lovely in Italy and the hotels often have less expensive rates.

2) Ask for a room without a private bathroom—some hotels have very nice rooms, usually with a washbasin in the room, but with a shared bathroom down the hall.

3) Ask if there is a weekly rate—frequently hotels offer a price break for guests staying a week or more. If traveling with children, ask if there is a special family suite at a lesser price than separate rooms.

4) Ask about rates with meals included. For a stay of three days or longer, many hotels offer a special rate including meals: MAP (Modified American Plan) means two meals a day are included; AP (American Plan) means three meals a day are included.

5) Last, but not least, is the most important way to save money: stay in the countryside instead of in the cities. We cannot stress enough how much more value you receive when you avoid the cities—especially the tourist centers such as Rome, Florence, Milan, and Venice. Of course, stay right in the heart of town if you are not watching your budget,

but if you are trying to squeeze the greatest value from your euro, choose hotels in the countryside and take side trips to visit the more-pricey tourist centers.

RESERVATIONS

People frequently ask, "Do I need a hotel reservation?" The answer really depends on how flexible you want to be, how tight your time schedule is, in which season you are traveling, and how disappointed you would be if your first choice is unavailable.

It is not unusual for the major tourist cities to be completely sold out during the peak season of June through September. Be forewarned: hotel space in Rome, Florence, Milan, and Venice is really at a premium and unless you don't mind taking your chances on a last-minute cancellation or staying on the outskirts of town, make a reservation as far in advance as possible. Space in the countryside is a little easier. However, if you have your heart set on some special little hotel, you certainly should reserve as soon as your travel dates are firm. Reservations are confining. Most hotels want a deposit to hold your room and frequently you cannot get a refund if you change your plans. So it is a double bind: making reservations locks you into a solid framework, but without reservations you might be stuck with accommodations you do not like. During the height of the tourist season, some small hotels accept reservations only for a minimum of three or more nights. However, do not give up, because almost all of the hotels that have this policy will take a last-minute booking for a shorter period of time if you call along the way and there is space available. For those who like the security blanket of having each night pre-planned so that once you leave home you do not have to worry about where to rest your head, several options for making reservations are listed on the following pages.

It is important to understand that once reservations for accommodation are confirmed, whether verbally by phone or in writing, you are under contract. This means that the proprietor is obligated to provide the accommodation that was promised and that you are obligated to pay for it. If you cannot, you are liable for a portion of the accommodation charges plus your deposit. Although some proprietors do not strictly enforce a cancellation policy many, particularly the smaller properties in our book, simply cannot afford not to do so. As a courtesy to your hosts, in the case of cancellation, please advise them as soon as possible. Similarly many airline tickets cannot be changed or refunded without penalty. We recommend insurance to cover these types of additional expenses arising from cancellation due to unforeseen circumstances. A link on our website (*www.karenbrown.com*) will connect you to a variety of insurance policies that can be purchased online.

When making your reservations, be sure to identify yourself as a "Karen Brown traveler." The hotels appreciate your visit, value their inclusion in our guide, and frequently tell us they take special care of our readers, and many offer special rates to Karen Brown members (visit our website at *www.karenbrown.com*). We hear over and over again that the people who use our guides are such wonderful guests!

RESERVATIONS BY E-MAIL: This is our preferred way of making a reservation. All properties featured on the Karen Brown website that also have e-mail addresses have those addresses listed on their web pages (this information is constantly kept updated and correct). You can link directly to a property from its page on our website using its e-mail hyperlink. *NOTE:* In any written correspondence be sure to spell out the month since Europeans reverse the American system for dates. As an example, in Italy 4/9/03 means September 4, 2003 not April 9, 2003.

FAX: If you have access to a fax machine, this is a super-efficient way to reach a hotel. The majority of hotels in Italy have fax numbers, which we have noted in the back of the book under each hotel listing. Do not forget to include your fax number for their response. Although most hotels can understand a letter written in English, at the end of this introduction we provide a form written in Italian with an English translation. Photocopy it and use it when you fax your reservation request. See comments under "E-mail" above, and the "Telephone" paragraph below for instructions on how to fax.

TELEPHONE: Another way to make a reservation is to telephone. You can have your answer immediately, and if space is not available, you can then decide on an alternative. The cost is minimal if you dial direct —ask your local operator when to call for the lowest rates. Also consider what time it is in Italy when you call (even the most gracious of owners are sometimes a bit grouchy when awakened at 3 am). If you are dialing from the United States, the system is to dial 011 (the international code), then 39 (Italy code), then the city code (do *not* drop the 0 in front of the city code), and then the telephone number. Almost all of the hotels have someone who speaks English. The best chance for finding the owner or manager who speaks English is to call when it is late afternoon in Italy (Italy is six hours ahead of New York). Be aware that Italy's telephone numbers are constantly changing, so if you cannot reach a hotel, ask for operator assistance.

TRAVEL AGENT: A travel agent can be of great assistance, particularly if your own time is limited. A proficient agent can expertly handle all the details of your holiday and tie them together for you in a neat package—including hotel reservations, airline tickets, boat tickets, train reservations, ferry schedules, and theater tickets. For your airline tickets there is usually no service fee (unless you are using some kind of discount coupon), but the majority of travel agencies do charge for their other services. Talk with your agent about fees and be frank about how much you want to spend. If your travel agent is not familiar with all the small places in this guide (many are so tiny that they appear in no other major publications), you can loan him or her your book.

UNITED STATES REPRESENTATIVES: In the back of the book there is a page giving information on KB Travel Service, a company that specializes in Karen-Brown-recommended hotels and "mini tours." Also in the back of the book you'll find information on Hidden Treasures of Italy (HTI), a company that can arrange reservations for any hotel in this book. Telephone numbers are given for both companies. If you are interested, call to check on the services offered and the fees.

RESTAURANTS

If the property has a restaurant and serves meals to non-guests, we have indicated this with the symbol ⑂ in the list of icons at the bottom of the description.

WHEELCHAIR ACCESSIBILITY

If an inn has *at least* one guestroom that is accessible by wheelchair, it is noted with the symbol ♿. This is not the same as saying it meets full disability standards. In reality, it can be anything from a basic ground-floor room to a fully equipped facility. Please discuss your requirements when you call your chosen place to stay to determine if they have accommodation that suits your needs and preference.

Introduction–About Hotels

About Italy

AIRFARE

Karen Brown's Guides have long recommended Auto Europe for their excellent car rental services and we are now very pleased to introduce their air travel division, Destination Europe, to our readers. An airline broker working with major American and European carriers, Destination Europe offers deeply discounted coach- and business-class fares to over 200 European gateway cities. It also gives Karen Brown travelers an additional 5% discount off its already highly competitive prices. You can make reservations online via our website, *www.karenbrown.com*, (click "Discount Airfares" on our home page) or by phone at (800) 223-5555. When phoning, be sure to use the Karen Brown ID number 99006187 to secure your discount on the lowest prices they currently offer.

BANKS

Banking hours are Monday through Friday from 8:30 am to 1:30 pm and 3 to 4 pm, with some city banks now opening on Saturday mornings. Cash machines accepting U.S. bank cash cards and credit cards are widely distributed throughout Italy. An increasingly popular and convenient way to obtain foreign currency is simply to use your bankcard at an ATM machine. You pay a fixed fee for this but, depending on the amount you withdraw, it is usually less than the percentage-based fee charged to exchange currency or travelers' checks. Be sure to check with your bank or credit card company about fees and necessary pin numbers prior to departure. *Cambio* signs outside and inside a bank indicate that it will exchange traveler's checks or give you cash from certain credit cards. Also, privately run exchange offices are available in cities with more convenient hours and comparable rates.

CURRENCY

All pricing, including room rates, is quoted in euros, using the "€" symbol. The euro is now the official currency of most European Union countries, including Italy, having completely replaced national currencies as of February 2002. Visit our website (*www.karenbrown.com*) for an easy-to-use online currency converter.

DRIVING

CAR RENTAL: Readers frequently ask our advice on car rental companies. We always use Auto Europe, a car rental broker that works with the major car rental companies to find the lowest possible price. They also offer motor homes and chauffeur services. Auto Europe's toll-free phone service from every European country connects you to their U.S.-based, 24-hour reservation center (ask for the card with European phone numbers to be sent to you). Auto Europe offers our readers a 5% discount, and occasionally free upgrades. Be sure to use the Karen Brown ID number 99006187 to receive your discount and any special offers. You can make your own reservations online via our website, *www.karenbrown.com* (select Auto Europe from the home page), or by telephone (800-223-5555).

DISTANCES: Distances are indicated in kilometers (one kilometer equals 0.621 mile). As you drive through the countryside, you will be astonished at how dramatically the scenery can change in just an hour's drive.

DRIVER'S LICENSE: A current license from your home country is valid for driving throughout Italy if you are on holiday. However, when renting a car, certain age limits apply. Please check on the age limit policy with the car rental company.

GASOLINE: Gas prices in Italy are the highest in Europe, and Americans often suspect a mistake when their first fill-up comes to between $45 and $80 (most of it in taxes). Most stations now accept Visa credit cards, and the ERG stations accept American Express. Besides the AGIP stations on the autostrada, which are almost always open, gas stations observe the same hours as merchants, closing in the afternoon from 12:30 to 4 and in the evening at 7:30. Be careful not to get caught running on empty in the afternoon! Many stations have a self-service pump that operates on off-hours (€10 or €20 accepted).

ROADS: The Italian roads are nothing short of spectacular, including some of the finest highways in the world. In fact, the Italians are absolute geniuses when it comes to their engineering feats (which actually is not such a surprising fact when you consider what a fantastic road system the Romans built 2,000 years ago). Nothing seems to daunt the Italian engineers: you would think the mountains are made of clay instead of solid rock, the way the roads tunnel through them. Sometimes a roadway seems endlessly suspended in mid-air as it bridges a mountain crevasse. Names of roads in Italy are as follows:

Autostrada: a large, fast (and most direct) two- or three-lane toll way, marked by green signs bearing an "A" followed by the autostrada number. (See "Toll Roads" below.)

Superstrada: a one- or two-lane freeway between secondary cities marked by blue signs and given a number. Speed limit: 110 kph.

Strada Statale: a small one-lane road marked with S.S. followed by the road number. Speed limit: 90 kph.

Raccordo or *Tangenziale*: a ring road around main cities, connecting to an autostrada and city centers.

ROAD SIGNS: Before starting on the road prepare yourself by learning the international driving signs so that you can obey all the rules. There are several basic sign shapes: triangular signs warn that there is danger ahead; circular signs indicate compulsory rules and information; square signs give information concerning telephones, parking, camping, etc. Yellow signs are for tourists and indicate a site of historical or cultural interest, hotels, and restaurants. Black-and-yellow signs indicate private companies and industries.

TOLL ROADS: Italy has a network of super expressways that makes any spot in the country an easy destination by car. Once you are on the toll roads, you can go quickly from almost any area of Italy to another, but be forewarned—these toll roads are expensive. However, every cent is well spent when you consider the alternative of creeping along within a maze of trucks and buzzing motorcycles, taking forever to go only a few kilometers. Use the toll roads for the major distances you need to cover, and then choose the small roads when you wish to meander leisurely through the countryside. Toll roads are mystifying until you learn the system—even then it is confusing because just when you think you have the operation down pat, you find it varies slightly. This is the most common routine: first follow the green expressway signs toward the toll road. Sometimes these signs begin many kilometers from the expressway, so be patient and continue the game of follow-the-sign. Each entrance to the expressway handles traffic going in both directions. As you enter into the tollgate, there is usually a red button you push and a card pops out of a slot. After going through the toll station you choose the direction you want to go. As you leave the expressway, there is a toll station where your ticket is collected and you pay according to how many kilometers you traveled. (If you lose your card, you will have to pay the equivalent amount of the distance from the beginning of the autostrada to your exit.) Tolls on Italian autostrade are quite steep, ranging from $15 to $28 for a three-hour stretch, but offering the fastest and most direct way to travel between cities. A *Viacard*, or magnetic reusable card for tolls, is available in all toll way gas stations for €20–€50, or a MasterCard or Visa card can now be used in specified lanes (the lines for these automatic machines are always the shortest).

ELECTRICAL CURRENT

If you are taking any electrical appliances made for use in the United States, you will need a transformer plus a two-pin adapter. A voltage of 220 AC current at 50 cycles per second is almost countrywide, though in remote areas you may encounter 120V. The voltage is often displayed on the socket. Even though we recommend that you purchase appliances with dual-voltage options whenever possible, it will still be necessary to have the appropriate socket adapter. Also, be especially careful with expensive equipment such as computers—verify with the manufacturer the adapter/converter capabilities and requirements.

FOOD & DRINK

It is almost impossible to get a bad meal in Italy. Italians themselves love to eat and dining is a social occasion to be with family and friends. Restaurants are bustling not only with tourists, but also with the Italians who dawdle at the tables long after the meal is over, chatting and laughing with perhaps a glass of wine or a last cup of coffee.

You soon get in the spirit of the game of deciding which kind of restaurant to choose for your next meal. The selection is immense, all the way from the simple family trattoria where mama is cooking in the kitchen to the most elegant of gourmet restaurants with world-renowned chefs. Whichever you choose, you won't be disappointed. The Italians are artists when it comes to pasta, seen on every menu and prepared in endless, fascinating ways. Some restaurants offer a set-price tourist menu *(menu turistico)* that includes soup or pasta, a meat dish with vegetable, dessert, and mineral water or wine. A tip is usually included in the price, but it is customary to leave some small change.

Wine, of course, is offered with every meal. You rarely see an Italian family eating without their bottle of wine on the table. Unless you are a true wine connoisseur, we suggest the regional wines and if you ask your waiter to assist you with the choice, you flatter him and discover many superb wines.

Some of the most popular wines that you see on the Italian menus are: Chianti, a well-known wine produced in the Tuscany area south of Florence; Marsala, a golden sweet wine from Sicily (a favorite of Lord Nelson); Soave, a superb light white wine produced near Venice; Orvieto, a semi-sweet wine from the Umbria region near Assisi; and Est Est Est, a beautiful semi-sweet wine produced near Rome. The story that we heard about Est Est Est is lots of fun and perhaps even true. It seems that many years ago a wealthy nobleman was traveling south. Being a true gourmet both of food and drink, he sent his servant before him to pick out all the best places to eat and drink along the way. When the servant neared Rome he discovered such a divine wine that all he could relay back to his master was "Est, est, est," meaning "Yes, yes, yes." Today you will think the same about most of the wines you enjoy in Italy — the answer is still "Yes, yes, yes!"

HOLIDAYS

It is very important to know Italian holidays because most museums, shops, and offices are closed. National holidays are listed below:

New Year's Day (January 1)
Epiphany (January 6)
Easter (and the following Monday)
Liberation Day (April 25)
Labor Day (May 1)

Assumption Day (August 15)
All Saints' Day (November 1)
Christmas (December 25)
Santo Stefano (December 26)

In addition to the national holidays, each town has its own special holiday to honor its patron saint. Some of the major ones are listed below:

Bologna–St. Petronio (October 4)
Florence–St. John the Baptist (June 24)
Milan–St. Ambrose (December 7)

Palermo–Santa Rosalia (July 15)
Rome–St. Peter (June 29)
Venice–St. Mark (April 25)

The Vatican Museums have their own schedule and are closed on Sundays (rather than on Mondays as is the case with all other National museums), except the last Sunday of each month when admission is free of charge.

INFORMATION SOURCES

Italian Government Travel Offices (ENIT) can offer general information on various regions and their cultural attractions. They cannot offer specific information on restaurants and accommodations. If you have access to the Internet, visit the Italian Tourist Board's websites: *www.italiantourism.com* or *www.enit.it*. Offices are located in:

Chicago: Italian Government Travel Office, 500 N. Michigan Ave., Suite 2240, Chicago, IL 60611 USA; tel: (312) 644-0996, fax: (312) 644-3019. (Mail, fax, or phone only.)

Los Angeles: Italian Government Travel Office, 12400 Wilshire Blvd., Suite 550, Los Angeles, CA 90025, USA; tel: (310) 820-1898, fax: (310) 820-6357.

New York: Italian Government Travel Office, 630 5th Ave., Suite 1565, New York, NY 10111, USA; tel: (212) 245-4822, fax: (212) 586-9249.

Montreal: Italian Government Travel Office, 1 Place Ville Marie, Suite 1914, Montreal, Quebec H3B 2C3, Canada; tel: (514) 866-7667, fax: (514) 392-1429.

London: Italian State Tourist Office, 1 Princes Street, London WIR 8AY, England; tel: (020) 7355-1557, fax: (020) 7493-6695.

Sydney: Italian Government Travel Office, Level 26, 44 Market Street, Sydney NSW 2000, Australia; tel: (61292) 621.666, fax: (61292) 625.677.

Rome: ENTE Nazionale Italiano per il Turismo (Italian Government Travel Office), Via Marghera, 2, Rome 00185, Italy, tel: (06) 49711, fax: (06) 4463379.

PROVINCES

Italy is divided into Provinces, which appear in abbreviated form in addresses. Some of the provinces you are likely to see and their abbreviated codes are as follows:

AG	*Agrigento*	AL	*Alessandria*	AN	*Ancona*	AO	*Aosta*
AR	*Arezzo*	AP	*Ascoli Picino*	AT	*Asti*	AV	*Avellino*
BA	*Bari*	BL	*Belluno*	BG	*Bergamo*	BN	*Benevento*
BO	*Bologna*	BZ	*Bolzano*	BS	*Brescia*	BR	*Brindisi*
CA	*Cagliari*	CE	*Caserta*	CH	*Chieti*	CZ	*Catanzaro*
CO	*Como*	CS	*Cosenza*	CR	*Cremona*	CT	*Catania*
CB	*Campobasso*	EN	*Enna*	FE	*Ferrara*	FG	*Froggia*
FI	*Firenze*	FO	*Forli*	GE	*Genova*	GO	*Gorizia*
GR	*Grosseto*	IM	*Imperia*	IS	*Isermia*	LA	*Latina*
LC	*Lecco*	LE	*Lecce*	LI	*Livorno*	LT	*Latino*
LU	*Lucca*	MS	*Massa*	MN	*Mantova*	MI	*Milano*
MO	*Modena*	ME	*Messina*	Mc	*Macerata*	MT	*Matera*
NA	*Napoli*	NO	*Novara*	NU	*Nuoro*	OR	*Oristano*
PA	*Palermo*	PC	*Piacunga*	PE	*Pescara*	PD	*Padova*
PR	*Parma*	PV	*Pavia*	PG	*Perugia*	PS	*Pesaro*
PI	*Pisa*	PT	*Pistoia*	PZ	*Potenza*	RA	*Ravenna*
RI	*Rieti*	RM	*Roma*	RN	*Rimini*	RO	*Ravigo*
SA	*Salerno*	SI	*Siena*	SO	*Sondrio*	SP	*La Spezia*
SR	*Siracusa*	SV	*Savona*	TA	*Taranto*	TE	*Teramo*
TR	*Terni*	TO	*Torino*	TS	*Trieste*	TN	*Trento*
TV	*Treviso*	VE	*Venezia*	VC	*Vercelli*	VR	*Verona*
VI	*Vicenza*	VT	*Viterbo*				

REGIONS

Italy is divided into 20 regions. A map showing the location of each region is found in the back of the book in the map section. Below is a list of the regions and their capital cities.

REGION	CAPITAL CITY	REGION	CAPITAL CITY
Abruzzo	L'Aquila	Marches	Ancona
Apulia	Bari	Molise	Campobasso
Basilicata	Potenza	Piedmont	Torino
Calabria	Catanzaro	Sardinia	Cagliari
Campania	Naples	Sicily	Palermo
Emila-Romagna	Bologna	Tuscany	Florence
Friuli-Venezia Giulia	Trieste	Trentino-Alto Adige	Trento & Bolzano
Lazio	Rome	Umbria	Perugia
Liguria	Genova	Valle d'Aosta	Aosta
Lombardy	Milan	Veneto	Venice

SECURITY WHILE TRAVELING

The Italians are wonderful hosts. It seems every Italian has a brother or cousin in the United States, and so the warmth of camaraderie is further enhanced. In spite of the overall graciousness of the Italians, there are instances where cars are pilfered or purses snatched, but this happens all over the world. Just be cautious. Watch your purse. Don't let your wallet stand out like a red light in your back pocket. Lock your valuables in the hotel safe. Don't leave valuables temptingly exposed in your car. Never set down luggage in train stations or airports, even for a minute. In other words, use common sense. *NOTE:* Whenever you travel to any country, it is wise to make a photocopy of the pages of your passport showing your picture, passport number, date, and where issued. With this photocopy in hand it is much easier to get a replacement passport.

SHOPPING

Italy is definitely a shopper's paradise. Not only are the stores brimming with tempting merchandise, but also their displays are beautiful, from the tiniest fruit market to the most chic boutique. Each region has its specialty. In Venice items made from blown glass and handmade laces are very popular. Milan is famous for its clothing and silk wear (gorgeous scarves, ties, and blouses). Florence is a paradise for leather goods (purses, shoes, wallets, gloves, suitcases) and also for gold jewelry (you can buy gold jewelry by weight). Rome is a fashion center—you can stroll the pedestrian shopping streets browsing in some of the world's most elegant, sophisticated boutiques. You can buy the very latest designer creations and, of course, religious items are available, especially near St. Peter's. Naples and the surrounding regions (Capri, Ravello, Positano) offer delightful coral jewelry and also a wonderful selection of ceramics.

For purchases over €155 an immediate cash refund of the tax amount is offered by the Italian government to non-residents of the EU. Goods must be purchased at an affiliated retail outlet with the "tax-free for tourists" sign. Ask for the store receipt **plus** the tax-free shopping receipt. At the airport go first to the customs office where they will examine the items purchased and stamp both receipts, and then to the "tax-free cash refund" point after passport control.

U.S. customs allows U.S. residents to bring in $400-worth of foreign goods duty-free, after which a straight 10% of the amount above $400 is levied. Two bottles of liquor are allowed. The import of fresh cheese or meat is strictly restricted unless it is vacuum-packed.

TELEPHONES—HOW TO MAKE CALLS

The Italian phone company (TELECOM) has been an object of ridicule, a source of frustration, and a subject of heated conversation since its inception. Although more modern systems are being installed, it remains one of the most archaic and costly communication systems in the developed world, though touch-tone phones are now found in parts of the major cities. Telephone numbers can have from four to eight digits, so don't be afraid of missing numbers. Cellular phones have saved the day (Italians wouldn't be caught dead without one) and are recognized by three-digit area codes beginning with 3.

IMPORTANT NOTE: All calls to Italy need to include the "0" in the area code, whether calling from abroad, within Italy, or even within the same city, whereas cell phone numbers have dropped the "0" in all cases.

Dial 113 for emergencies of all kinds—24-hour service nationwide.

Dial 116 for Automobile Club for urgent breakdown assistance on the road.

Dial 118 for Ambulance service.

Remember that no warning is given when the time you've paid for in a public phone is about to expire (the line just goes dead), so put in plenty of change or a phone card. There are several types of phones (in various stages of modernization) in Italy:

Regular rotary phones in bars, restaurants, and many bed and breakfasts, which you can use *a scatti*, meaning you can pay the proprietor after the call is completed.

Bright-orange pay phones, as above with attached apparatus permitting insertion of a *scheda telefonica,* reusable magnetic cards worth €5–€25, or coins.

NOTE: Due to the ongoing modernization process of telephone lines, phone numbers are constantly being changed, making it sometimes very difficult to contact hotels (many times they are not listed under the property's name). A recording (in Italian) plays for only two months indicating the new number. If you are calling from the United States and your Italian is not up to par, we suggest you ask the overseas operator to contact the Italian operator for translation and assistance.

CALLING HOME: Calling overseas is very expensive from Italy. In addition, hotels usually add a hefty surcharge to telephone calls charged to your room. The best bet is to use one of the many available international telephone cards. With these you can make a local call within Italy and be connected with your home operator. When you arrive home, the cost appears on your telephone bill. Ask your local telephone company what access number to use.

TIPPING

Hotels: Service charges are normally included in four- and five-star hotels only. It is customary to leave a token tip for staff.

Restaurants: If a service charge is included, it will be indicated on the bill, otherwise 10–15% is standard tipping procedure.

Taxis: 10%.

TRANSPORTATION

BOATS: Italy has gorgeous islands dotting her shorelines, a glorious string of lakes gracing her mountains to the north, and romantic canals in Venice. Luckily for the tourist, the country's boat system is excellent.

All of Italy's islands are linked to the mainland by a wonderful maritime network. The many outlying islands sometimes have overnight ferries that offer sleeping accommodations and facilities for cars. The closer islands usually offer a choice—the hydrofoil that zips quickly across the water or the regular ferry that is slower. Italy also offers you an enchanting selection of lakes. One of the true highlights of traveling in Italy is to explore these wondrous lakes by hopping on one of the nostalgic ferry boats that glide romantically between little villages clustered along the shorelines. Again, there is usually a choice of either the hydrofoil that darts between the hamlets, or the ferry that glides leisurely across the water and usually offers beverage and food service on board. The boat schedules are posted at each pier, or you can request a timetable from the Italian tourist office. *NOTE:* These little boats are punctual, to the minute. Be right at the pier with your ticket in hand so you can jump on board during the brief interlude that the boat stops at the shore. If at all possible, try to squeeze in at least one boat excursion—it is a treat you will long remember.

TRAINS: Italy has an excellent network of trains. The major express trains are usually a quick, reliable way to whip between the major cities. In contrast, the local trains stop at every little town, take much longer, and are frequently delayed. Each train station is well organized. There is almost always an information desk where someone speaks English who will answer any questions and advise you as to the best schedule. There is another counter where you purchase your tickets. Still a third counter is where seat reservations are made. We strongly recommend purchasing your train tickets in advance: it is quite time-consuming to stand in two lines at each train station, only to find—particularly in summer—that the train you want is already sold out. You can purchase open tickets in the United States. However, it is almost impossible to purchase seat reservations in advance (except for major European routes). Go ahead and buy the open tickets, and then you can either purchase your seat reservations locally, or else pay the concierge at your hotel to handle this transaction for you. Seat reservations cannot be made just before getting on the train—it is best to make them as far in advance as possible. *NOTE:* Your ticket must be stamped with the time and date **before** you board the train; otherwise, you will be issued a €20 fine. Tickets are stamped at small and not very obvious yellow machines near the exits to the tracks.

The Eurailpass, which allows travel for varying periods of time on most trains throughout Europe, is valid in Italy. However, if you are going to travel exclusively in Italy, buy instead an Italian Rail Pass. These bargain passes which must be purchased outside of Italy include the *Tourist Pass* and the *Flexi Pass*. The *Tourist Pass* is available for unlimited travel for a period of 8, 15, 21, or 30 consecutive days. The *Flexi Pass* allows you to choose the number of days you want to travel within a month. You can buy the *Flexi Pass* for 4 days, 8 days, or 12 days of travel. All of the Italian passes can be bought for either first- or second-class travel. *NOTE:* In the summer when rail traffic is very heavy, unless you make dining car reservations in advance, you might not be able to have the fun of eating your meal en route. If you have not made these reservations, as soon as you board the train, stroll down to the dining car and ask to reserve a table.

If you plan to travel by train throughout Europe, you can research schedules and fares and purchase tickets and passes online. (Note that many special fares and passes are available only if purchased in the United States.) For information and the best possible fares, and to book tickets online, visit our website, *www.karenbrown.com*.

TRANSFERS INTO CITIES: Travelers from abroad normally arrive by plane in Milan, Florence, Rome, or Venice and often pick up their rental car at the airport. However, if your first destination is the city and you plan on picking up your car after your stay, approximate transfer rates are as follows:

MILAN

From Malpensa to city by taxi (70 min)	€75
From Malpensa to Cadorna station by train (every 30 min)	€8
From Malpensa to central station by bus (every 20 min)	€12
From Linate to city by taxi (20 min)	€31
From Linate to city by bus (every 20 min)	€3

Introduction–About Italy

ROME
From Da Vinci to city by train (every 30 min)	€8
From Da Vinci to city by taxi (45 min)	€47–€62

VENICE
From airport to city by waterbus (1 hour)	€10
From airport to city by private waterbus	€77
From station to city by waterbus (15 min)	€5
From station to city by private waterbus	€72

FLORENCE
From airport to city by taxi (30 min)	€36

WEATHER

Italy is blessed with lovely weather. However, unless you are a ski enthusiast following the promise of what the majestic mountains have to offer in the winter, or must travel in summer due to school holidays, we highly recommend traveling in spring or fall. Travel at either of these times has two dramatic advantages: you miss the rush of the summer tourist season when all of Italy is packed and you are more likely to have beautiful weather. In spring the meadows are painted with wildflowers. In fall the forests are a riot of color and the vineyards are mellow in shades of red and gold. Although the mountains of Italy are delightfully cool in summer, the rest of the country can be very hot, especially in the cities. *NOTE:* Many hotels are not air-conditioned. Those that are sometimes charge extra for it.

WEBSITE

Please supplement this book by looking at the information provided on our Karen Brown website (*www.karenbrown.com*), which serves as an added dimension to our guides. Most of our favorite properties are featured on the site (web participation is a hotel's choice) and on their web pages you can usually link to their own websites for even more detailed information and directions. You can also link to their e-mail, so that making reservations is a breeze. Also featured on our site are comments, feedback, and discoveries from you, our readers; information on our latest finds; post-press updates; contest drawings for free books; special offers; unique features such as recipes and favorite destinations; and special savings offered by certain properties.

WHAT TO WEAR

During the day informal wear is most appropriate, including comfortable slacks for women. In the evening, if you are at a sidewalk café or a simple pizzeria, women do not need to dress up nor men to wear coats and ties. However, Italy does have some elegant restaurants where a dress and coat and tie are definitely the proper attire. A basic principle is to dress as you would in any city at home. There are perhaps a few special situations: the churches are still very conservative—shorts are definitely inappropriate, as are low-cut dresses. Some of the cathedrals still insist that women have their arms covered. It is rare that a scarf on the head is required, but to wear one is a respectful gesture. If you have an audience with the Pope, then the dress code is even more conservative. The layered effect is ideal. Italy's climate runs the gamut from usually cool in the mountains to frequently very hot in the south. The most efficient wardrobe is one where light blouses and shirts can be reinforced by layers of sweaters that can be added or peeled off as the day demands.

HOTEL RESERVATION REQUEST FORM IN ITALIAN

HOTEL NAME & ADDRESS—clearly printed or typed

Vi richiediamo la sequente prenotazione:
We would like to request the following reservation:

> Numero delle camere con bagno o doccia privata   _____
> *Number of rooms with private bath or shower*

> Numero delle camere senza bagno o doccia   _____
> *Number of rooms without private bath or shower*

> Data di arrivo _____   Data di partenza _____
> *Date of arrival*   *Date of departure*

Vi prego inoltre de fornirmi le seguenti informazioni:
Please let me know as soon as possible the following:

> Potete riservare le camere richieste? Si / No
> *Can you reserve the space requested? Yes / No*

> I pasti sono compresi nel prezzo? Si / No
> *Are meals included in your rate? Yes / No*

> E necessario un deposito? Si / No
> *Do you need a deposit? Yes / No*

> Prezzo giornaliero   _____
> *Price per night*

> Quanto e necessario come deposito?   _____
> *How much deposit do you need?*

Ringraziando anticipatamente per la gentile conferma, porgo cordiali saluti,
We thank you in advance for your confirmation,

YOUR NAME & ADDRESS—clearly printed or typed (your fax number if pertinent)

Florence

ITINERARY SECTION

*Highlights by
Boat & Train-or Car*

*Romantic Hilltowns
of Tuscany & Umbria*

*Mountain &
Lake Adventures*

*Rome to Milan
via the Italian Riviera*

*Highlights
of Southern Italy*

*Exploring the
Wonders of Sicily*

31

Colosseum, Rome

Italian Highlights
by Train & Boat – or Car

Legend:
- ● Overnight stops
- ○ Sightseeing
- ▬ ▬ Itinerary route
- ··· Boat

Italian Highlights by Train & Boat—or Car

Island of Burano, near Venice

If you delight in the freedom of following a whim to explore a back road, this itinerary can easily be duplicated by car. However, the thought of Italian expressways sometimes intimidates even the bravest breed of tourist, so we have given you the formula to see the highlights of Italy either way—by public transportation or by car. An aversion to driving does not mean that your *only* alternative is the confining structure of a package tour. Italy can be seen splendidly by train and boat. This is a glorious way to travel and has many advantages: everyone can watch the scenery instead of the road, you can enjoy a glass of wine with lunch, and you arrive rested and ready to enjoy the sights. Perhaps the best advantage of all is that while using public transportation, you make friends. Perhaps there is just a smile at first, then maybe the sharing of a piece of fruit, and later comes the admiration of each other's family photographs. Somehow barriers break down on a long journey and the universal warmth of friendliness—at this the Italians are masters—spans any language barriers. Please be aware however that if you choose to travel this way, you must travel lightly—when burdened by heavy suitcases, the charm of public transportation quickly diminishes!

This itinerary covers some of the most famous destinations within Italy. For a short holiday it is impossible to include all the places of interest. However, following this route easily provides you with a glimpse of some of the highlights of Italy and will tempt you to return quickly to delve more deeply into the wonders that Italy has to offer. This itinerary is woven around towns that are conveniently linked by public transportation. Of course, if your time is extremely limited, this itinerary lends itself well to segmentation. If you cannot travel with us all the way, then choose what fits into your schedule and what most appeals to you.

In the following itinerary approximate train and boat times have been included. Please note that these are given only as a reference to show you how the pieces of this itinerary tie together. Schedules are constantly changing, so these must be verified. Also, many boats and some trains are seasonal, so be very meticulous in making your plans.

ORIGINATING CITY   MILAN

This highlight tour begins in **Milan**, a most convenient city since it is the hub of airline flights from many parts of Europe and has non-stop air service from the eastern and western United States. Also, Milan is strategically located for trains arriving from all over Europe—trains rush into its busy station via the Gotthard, Simplon, and Bernina passes. However, it is not location alone that makes Milan an ideal starting point—although frequently bypassed as an enormous industrial city of little tourist interest, Milan has, at its core, a truly charming old section. Be forewarned: not only is this a major city, but it also hosts many merchandise fairs, so hotel space is often limited and rates are very expensive. After being a pedestrian center for many years, the heart of Milan is now open to cars. The city is divided into four quadrants and you cannot drive from one quadrant to another without backtracking to the central ring road. If you are arriving by car, it is very important that you know where your hotel is located and discuss with the hotel staff how to approach the city.

Duomo, Milan

While in Milan you must not miss visiting the **Duomo**, the third-largest cathedral in the world. There is no denying the beauty of the interior but best of all is the exterior, so take an elevator or the stairs to the roof where you can admire the view and examine at close hand the statues that adorn this gingerbread fantasy.

Facing the Duomo is one of the world's most beautiful arcades, the forerunner of the modern shopping mall, but with far more style. Even if you are not a shopper, be sure to just browse and have a cup of tea in the **Galleria Vittorio Emanuele**. In this Victorian-era fantasy creation, there are two main intersecting wings, both completely domed with intricately patterned glass. Along the pedestrian-only arcades are boutiques and beautiful little restaurants with outside tables for people watching.

After more than two decades of controversial restoration, Leonardo da Vinci's famous mural, **The Last Supper**, is once again on view in the church of **Santa Maria delle**

Grazie. The mural, which covers an entire wall of the church, has been a problem for many years mainly because Leonardo experimented with painting onto drywall rather than employing the more usual fresco technique of applying paint to wet plaster. In an effort to prevent further damage, air filters, special lights, and dust-absorbing carpets have been installed, and the small groups of visitors are limited to a stay of 15 minutes. It is vital that you make an appointment in advance: from the USA call 011-39 (Europe, 00-39) 0289-421146; from within Italy, (199) 19 91 00. The unilingual Italian-speaking reservationist will make you an appointment and give you a confirmation number. Arrive at the church about 15 minutes before your appointment, confirmation number in hand, and pay cash for your ticket.

Milan's other great claim to fame is **La Scala**, one of the world's most renowned opera houses. In addition to wonderful opera, other types of performances are given here. If it is opera season, try your best to go to a performance; if not, try to get tickets for whatever is playing. It is such fun to watch the lights go down and the curtains go up in this fairy-tale-like theater with row upon row of balconies rising like layers on a wedding cake. Tickets are sold in the ticket office located around the left-hand side of the theater.

DESTINATION I   SIRMIONE

Sirmione is located on Lake Garda. The station where you need to disembark is in the town of Desenzano, which is on the main rail route between Milan and Venice. There are many trains each day between Milan and Venice, but not all stop in Desenzano. One we suggest runs as follows:

    1:10 pm depart Milan Central Station by train
    2:21 pm arrive Desenzano

When the train arrives in the ancient port of **Desenzano**, you can take a taxi to the pier where hydrofoils, steamers, and buses leave regularly for Sirmione. However, although it is more expensive, we suggest you splurge and take a taxi directly to Sirmione (only about 10 kilometers away). This is definitely the most convenient means of transportation since you are taken directly to your hotel.

Sirmione is a walled medieval village fabulously located on a tiny peninsula jutting out into **Lake Garda**. This peninsula seems more like an island because it is connected to the mainland by just a thread of land. To enter the ancient town, you first cross over a moat, and then enter through massive medieval gates. Unless you are one of the lucky ones with a hotel confirmed for the night, you cannot take your automobile inside the town walls, since only pedestrians are allowed through the entrance. But if you have hotel reservations, stop near the entrance at the information office where you are given a pass to enter in your car or taxi.

There are several hotels in the heart of Sirmione, but the most glamorous choice, the **Villa Cortine Palace Hotel** (formerly a private home) is located in a parklike estate on the outskirts of town. The entrance is absolutely Hollywood. You ring a bell at the impressive gates which then slowly swing open, allowing you to wind your way up through the truly beautiful park to the hotel crowning the small hill. For those looking for an inexpensive place to stay, the **Hotel Grifone** is an excellent choice and although the rooms are simply decorated, they are spotlessly clean and the restaurant is extremely charming. A good choice in the moderate price range is the **Hotel Sirmione**, which is conveniently located next to the pier where the boats dock.

From any of the above hotels it is an easy walk to the dock in the center of town where you can study the posted schedule to decide which boat you want to take for your day's excursion. You can glide around the lake all day and have a snack on board, or get off in some small jewel of a town and enjoy lunch at a lakefront café. There is a choice of transportation: either the romantic ferry boats or the faster hydrofoils.

There are some **Roman ruins** on the very tip of the Sirmione peninsula which can be reached either on foot, or, if you prefer, by a miniature motorized train that shuttles back and forth between the ruins and the village.

NOTE FOR TRAVELERS BY CAR: Sirmione is an excellent choice for a place to stay if you are traveling by public transportation. However, if you are traveling by car, consider staying in **Gargnano**, **Gardone**, or **San Vigilio**—these towns are also located on Lake Garda and offer a rich selection of places to stay.

DESTINATION II   VERONA

There are trains almost every hour that cover the half-hour journey between Desenzano and Verona. But if it is a beautiful day, it is much more romantic to incorporate sightseeing into your transportation and take a boat and bus instead of the train. If this appeals to you, the following gives an idea of how this can be done.

  10:20 am depart Sirmione by ferry
   2:20 pm arrive Riva

You can have lunch on board the ferry or else you can wait until you reach the medieval town of **Riva**, located on the northern shore of Lake Garda. The outdoor terrace overlooking the lake at the **Hotel Sole** (just across from where the ferry docks) provides a serene luncheon setting. The interesting ancient core of Riva is small, so it doesn't take long to stroll through the old city.

After lunch and a walk through the old part of town, leave Riva by bus for Verona (buses run every 15 minutes in summer), tracing a scenic route along the eastern shore of the lake.

When you arrive in **Verona**, you are in for a treat. This is a town that is all too frequently bypassed by the tourist, but what a prize it is. This medieval gem is the perfect city to explore on foot. Buy a detailed map and be on your way.

Definitely not to be missed is the **Roman amphitheater**, one of the largest in Italy. This dramatic arena, dating from the 1st century, has perfect acoustics and hosts operatic performances in summer. As you continue to wander through Verona's enchanting streets, you discover many delights, including the **Piazza delle Erbe** (Square of Herbs), which is the old Roman forum where chariot races used to take place. Follow your map to nearby 23 Via Cappello to find the 13th-century **Capulets' Palace** and the balcony where Juliet rendezvoused with Romeo. Another colorful square, the **Piazza dei Signori**, features a stature of Dante in its center and 12th- and 13th-century buildings. The **Castelvecchio** (Old Castle), built by Congrande I Scaligerbuthe in the 14th century, houses an art museum with paintings, sculptures, jewelry, and armaments. The 14th-century **Ponte Scaligero** (Scaliger Bridge) links the Castelvecchio with the opposite side of the river. The **Cathedral**, dating from the 12th century, is well worth a visit to see its fine red marble columns and richly adorned interior. Just across the river from the heart of the old city, visit the old **Roman theater** where performances are still held in summer.

Verona has several good hotels to complement her marvelous sights. A favorite in the heart of the city is the **Hotel Gabbia d'Oro**, which is brimming with charm and conveniently located near all the places of interest. If you are traveling by car, you have the option of choosing a hotel in the countryside outside of Verona where you get more value for your money. Hotels we suggest in the area are in **Pedemonte** and **Gargagnago**.

Amphitheater, Verona

Italian Highlights by Train & Boat—or Car

When you are ready to leave Verona, there is frequent train service to **Venice** so the following departure time is just a suggestion. *NOTE:* As you approach Venice, be sure not to get off the train at the Venice Mestre station, but instead wait for the next stop, the Santa Lucia station (about ten minutes further).

2:33 pm depart Verona Porto Nuova station by train
3:55 pm arrive Venice, Santa Lucia station

As you come out of the front door of the train station, you find that the station is directly on the **Grand Canal**. It is a few short steps down to where you can board a boat to take you to your hotel. The **vaporetti** are the most popular means of transportation and are a very inexpensive means of getting about the city. They are like boat buses that constantly shuttle back and forth from the train station to St. Mark's Square. If you have a lot of luggage you might want to consider a watertaxi. The **motoscafi** (watertaxis) cost about €50 but deliver you right to the door of your hotel, provided there is a motorboat dock (noted in the hotel description). The third choice of transportation is the **gondola**, but these are much slower

St. Mark's Square, Venice

and very expensive, so save your gondola ride for a romantic interlude rather than a train connection. If you arrive in Venice by car, keep in mind that some hotels offer a special rate at the Tronchetto garage. Check with the hotel about parking and transfers when making your reservation.

Venice has many hotels in every price range. If you want to splurge, consider the very expensive, very sumptuous, **Gritti Palace**, a former home of the immensely wealthy Doge Andrea Gritti. If you are on a more limited budget, one of our favorites is the intimate, family-operated **Hotel Flora**. It is superbly located and a gem in its moderately priced category. These and other excellent choices of places to stay in Venice are described in detail in the back of this guide. The closest boat stop to each hotel is given in the bottom details so that you know where to disembark if you come by canal from the train station. *NOTE*: For a few of the hotels, you need to change boats at the San Marco boat stop.

Glass Blowing, Island of Murano

Venice has so many sights—marvelous restaurants, beautiful boutiques, and fascinating little alleyways to explore—that you could happily stay for weeks.

Of course, you must savor the incomparable ambiance of **Piazza San Marco** (St. Mark's Square). Late afternoon is especially romantic as music wafts across the enormous square, courtesy of the tiny orchestras entertaining visitors as they enjoy an aperitif. A colonnaded walkway encloses the square on three sides, forming a protected path for window-shoppers at the beautiful boutiques and fancy cafés. The fourth side of the square is dominated by the **Basilica di San Marco** (St. Mark's Cathedral), richly endowed with gold and mosaics. The church dates back to the 12th century when it was built to house the remains of St. Mark. Next to the church rises the 99-meter-tall **campanile** (bell tower) where in the 15th century priests were suspended in a cage to repent their sins. If you are in the plaza on the hour, watch the two Moors strike the hour with their huge bronze hammers as they have for 500 years. To the right of the basilica is the **Palazzo Ducale** (Doge's Palace), a sumptuous fantasy of pink and white marble—open now as a museum. The Palazzo Ducale faces on to the **Piazzetta**, a wide square opening onto the Grand Canal. The square's nickname used to be the *Piazzetta Il Broglio* (Intrigue) because in days of yore, only nobles were allowed in the square between 10 am and noon, at which time the area buzzed with plots of intrigue. Adorning the center of the square are two granite columns, one topped by the Lion of St. Mark and the other by a statue of St. Theodore.

There is no better way to get into the mood of Venice than to join the crowd at St. Mark's pier as they climb aboard one of the ferries that ply the city's waterways. It is a real bargain to board the vaporetto and enjoy the many wonderful palaces bordering the Grand Canal. In addition to exploring the canals that lace Venice, you can take ferries to the outlying islands. Go either on your own or on a tour to the three islands: **Murano** (famous for its hand-blown glass), **Burano** (famous for its colorfully painted fishermen's cottages and lace making), and **Torcello** (once an important city but now just a small village with only its lovely large church to remind you of its past glories).

Another all-day outing by boat is to take the **Il Burchiello**, named for a famous 17th-century Venetian boat. From March to November, this boat departs Tuesdays, Thursdays, and Saturdays at 8:45 am from the Pontile Giardinetti pier near St. Mark's Square and travels the network of rivers and canals linking Venice and Padua. (The schedule might change, so verify dates and times.) This little boat, with an English-speaking guide on board, stops at several of the exquisite palaces en route. Lunch is served and there is time for sightseeing in **Padua** before returning to Venice by bus. Reservation office: Siamic Express, Via Trieste 42, 35121 Padua, Italy, tel: (049) 66 09 44, fax: (049) 66 28 30.

A favorite pastime in Venice is wandering—just anywhere—exploring the maze of twisting canals and criss-crossing back and forth over some of the 400 whimsical bridges. One of the most famous, the **Rialto Bridge**, arching high over the canal, is especially colorful because it is lined by shops. Also much-photographed is the **Bridge of Sighs**, so named because this was the bridge prisoners passed over before their execution.

Although all of Venice is virtually an open-air museum, it also has many indoor museums. Two excellent ones are both easy to find near the Accademia boat stop. The **Galleria dell'Accademia** abounds with 14th- to 18th-century Venetian paintings. Within walking distance of the Galleria dell'Accademia is the **Peggy Guggenheim Museum**, featuring 20th-century art. The paintings and statues were the gift of the now-deceased wealthy American heiress, Peggy Guggenheim. The lovely museum was her canal-front home.

DESTINATION IV   FLORENCE

Ponte Vecchio, Florence

There are several direct trains each day from Venice to Florence: however, in summer, space is at a real premium, so be sure to reserve a seat in advance. Some of the express trains must have prior seat reservations and require a supplemental fee. *NOTE:* During the busy season, if you want to dine on the train, it is necessary to make advance reservations when you buy your ticket.

11:45 am depart Venice, Santa Lucia station (reservations obligatory)
2:42 pm arrive Florence

When you arrive in **Florence**, take a taxi to your hotel. There are outstanding places to stay in every price range either in the heart of Florence or in the nearby countryside. Study the hotel descriptions in the back of the guide and you are sure to find accommodations to suite your personality and budget. Be aware that during tourist season hotel space is very tight, so to avoid disappointment, make your reservation as far in advance as possible.

Be generous with your time and do not rush Florence—there is too much to see. You must, of course, pay a visit to **Michelangelo's** fabulous **David** in the **Galleria dell'Accademia** located just off the **Piazza San Marco**. During your explorations of Florence, you will cross many times through the **Piazza della Signoria**, located in the heart of the old city. Facing this characterful medieval square is the 13th-century **Palazzo Vecchio**, a

Palazzo Vecchio, Piazza della Signoria, Florence

stern stone structure topped by a crenellated gallery and dominated by a tall bell tower. It was here that the *signoria* (Florence's powerful aristocratic ruling administrators) met for two months each year while attending to government business. During this period they were forbidden to leave the palace (except for funerals) so that there could not be a hint of suspicion of intrigue or bribery. Of course, you cannot miss one of Florence's landmarks, the **Ponte Vecchio**. Spanning the Arno in the heart of Florence, this colorful bridge is lined with quaint shops just as it has been since the 14th century.

Don't miss the fantastic museums and cathedrals—the world will probably never again see a city that has produced such artistic genius. Florence's **Duomo** is one of the largest in the world. The cathedral's incredible dome (over 100 meters high) was designed by Brunelleschi. Climb the 464 steps to the top of the dome for a superb view of Florence. The **baptistry** has beautiful mosaics and its bronze doors by Ghiberti were said by Michelangelo to be worthy of serving as the gates to paradise. The main door shows scenes from the life of John the Baptist, the north door shows the life of Jesus, and the east door shows stories from the prophets of the Old Testament. The **Uffizi Museum** (housed in a 16th-century palace) is undoubtedly one of the finest museums in the world. You can make advance reservations at the Uffizi Museum but you must prepay for the tickets by postal wire in euros (tel: 055 29 48 83) or call Hidden Treasures (888) 419-6700. Also, do not miss the **Pitti Palace** with its fabulous art collection, including paintings by Titian and Raphael. *NOTE:* In addition to regular hours, museums stay open during June, July, August, and September until 11 pm.

Be sure to buy a guidebook and city map at one of the many magazine stalls and study what you want to see. We just touch on the many highlights. Florence is best appreciated by wandering the historic ancient streets: poke into small boutiques; stop in churches that catch your eye—they all abound with masterpieces; sit and enjoy a cappuccino in one of the little sidewalk cafés and people watch; stroll through the piazzas and watch the artists at their craft—many of them incredibly clever—as they paint portraits and do sculptures for a small fee. End your day by finding the perfect small restaurant for delicious pasta made by mama in the back kitchen.

There is an excellent train service from Florence to Rome. It is probably best to take one of the midday trains—this allows you to enjoy lunch as you soak in the beauty of the Tuscany hills flowing by your window. Remember that you need both seat and dining reservations.

> 12:01 pm depart Florence via train
> 1:55 pm arrive Rome, Termini station

As the train pulls into **Rome**, you feel overwhelmed by its size and confusion of traffic, but once you settle into your hotel, you realize that Rome is really not as cumbersome as it looks. The ancient part of the city is manageable on foot—a fabulous city for walking with its maze of streets and captivating boutiques just begging to be explored. We recommend many places to stay in this expensive city. The ultra-deluxe, family-owned and -managed **Hotel Hassler**, just at the top of the Spanish Steps, is a superb choice. If you prefer to be at the bottom of the steps, another fabulous hotel is **The Inn at the Spanish Steps**. But you do not need to spend a lot of money—there are many less expensive places to stay recommended in our hotel descriptions section that are excellent and equally well located.

"She Wolf" with Romulus and Remus

According to legend, Rome was founded in 753 B.C. by Romulus, who, along with his twin brother, Remus (whom he later conveniently "did in"), were suckled by a "she wolf." Although a far less colorful story, historians concur that it was the Etruscans who first settled here and gave the city its name. By the time Christ was born, Rome controlled the entire Italian peninsula plus many areas around the Mediterranean.

Rome is bursting with a wealth of fantastic museums, ancient monuments, spectacular cathedrals, gourmet restaurants, beautiful boutiques, colorful piazzas, whimsical fountains, inspiring statues, theater, and opera—the city itself is virtually a museum. You cannot possibly savor it all. Either before you leave home or once you arrive in Italy, purchase a comprehensive guidebook and decide what is top priority for your special interests. There are many stalls along the streets as well as bookstores throughout Rome

Vatican—Swiss Guard

where guidebooks are available and every hotel has brochures that tell about sightseeing tours. If there are several in your party, a private guide might be money well spent since he will custom-tailor your sightseeing—with a private guide you squeeze much more sightseeing into a short period of time.

To even begin to do justice to Rome's many wonders, this entire book would need to be devoted to its sightseeing possibilities. However, we cannot resist mentioning a few places you must see.

You must see the **Vatican City** which includes in its complex **St. Peter's Basilica**, the largest church in the world. The original construction was begun in the 4th century by Emperor Constantine over the site of St. Peter's tomb. In 1506 Pope Julius II began plans for the new cathedral, which took over 100 years to build. It is no wonder the complex is so utterly breathtaking—all of Italy's greatest Renaissance artists were called upon to add their talents—Bramante, Raphael, Sangallo, and Michelangelo, to name just a few.

The Vatican is a miniature nation tucked within the city of Rome. It is ruled by the Pope, has its own flags, issues its own postage stamps, has its own anthem, mints its own coins, and even has its own police force—the Swiss Guard who still wear the uniform designed by Michelangelo.

Fronting the cathedral is the **Piazza San Pietro**, a breathtaking square designed by Bernini. It is so large that it can hold 400,000 people (making the square a favorite place for the Pope to address large audiences). A double semicircle of columns encloses the square, so perfectly designed that the columns fade into each other, giving the illusion that there is a single row. In the center of the square is a towering ancient Egyptian obelisk—adorned, of course, by a Christian cross. As you stand at a distance, the Piazza San Pietro forms a visual frame for the cathedral.

To fully appreciate all the Vatican City has to offer, you could easily spend two days, one in St. Peter's Basilica and one day in the **Vatican muscums**. The Basilica is like a museum. Not only is the structure magnificent, but the vast collection of works of art inside are almost unbelievable: imagine gazing at such masterpieces as the **Pietà** (the ethereal sculpture of Mary holding Jesus in her arms after the crucifixion, carved by Michelangelo when he was only 25) and the **Baldaccchino**, the bronze canopy over the papal altar created by another master, Bernini. Also, be aware when you gaze up at the double-columned dome, that this too was designed by Michelangelo.

St. Peter's Basilica, Rome

The **Sistine Chapel** alone is well worth a trip to Rome. Savor the breathtaking beauty of its ceiling painted by Michelangelo. In addition to St. Peter's Basilica and the Vatican museums, the gardens and the rest of the Vatican can be visited, but only on guided tours. If you are interested, inquire at the *Ufficio Informazioni Pellegrini et Turisti* in St. Peter's Square. *NOTE:* The Vatican museums are closed on Sundays, except for the last Sunday of the month when they are open free of charge.

Vatican City, as spectacular as it is, is just one small part of what Rome has to offer. You must see the gigantic **Colosseum**, the entertainment center for the citizens of ancient Rome. Here 50,000 people gathered to be entertained by flamboyant spectacles that included gladiatorial contests, races, games, and contests where Christian martyrs fought against wild beasts.

Another landmark is the **Forum**. It is difficult to make out much of this site because it is mostly in ruins, but at one time this was the heart of Rome. Once filled with elegant palaces, government buildings, and shops, it teemed with people from throughout the known world.

My favorite building in Rome is the **Pantheon**. It is difficult to imagine that this perfectly preserved jewel of a temple dates back to 27 B.C. Step beyond the heavy bronze doors which open into a relatively small, beautifully proportioned room lit only by light streaming in from an opening in the top of the dome.

No trip to Rome would be complete without a stroll down the **Via Veneto**, lined by fancy hotels and luxury boutiques. There are also many outdoor restaurants where a cup of coffee costs almost as much as a meal in a simple trattoria. However, along with your coffee, you are paying the price for the fun of people watching along one of Rome's most elite avenues.

While walking the back streets of Rome, you find many picturesque squares, usually enhanced by a fountain adorned with magnificent sculptures. Especially popular is the **Trevi Fountain** where tourists go to throw a coin—assuring that they will return to Rome.

Rome has many festivals including the **Festa de Noantri** (Our Festival), which starts on the third Sunday in July. It takes place in Trastevere, which is transformed into the venue of a village fair with stalls, open-air taverns, band music, and theatrical shows throughout the neighborhood. The event is wrapped up with fireworks over the River Tiber.

The **Spanish Steps** are definitely a landmark of Rome. Topped by the twin spires of the Church of the Trinity of the Mountains, the wide avenue of steps leads down to the **Piazza di Spagna** (Spanish Square). This large square is highlighted by the **Fountain of Baraccia** (Fountain of the Boat), a masterpiece by Bernini. The steps are usually crowded both with tourists who come to capture the moment on film and vendors who lay out their wares to sell.

Leading from the Piazza di Spagna, the **Via Condotti** is an avenue lined by shops and boutiques selling the finest of merchandise. Branching off the Via Condotti are the narrow lanes of **Old Rome**, again featuring exquisite small boutiques.

When you are ready to relax, walk to the **Villa Borghese**, a splendid large park in the center of Rome that

Spanish Steps, Rome

originated in the 17th century as the private gardens of the Borghese family. Stroll through the park watching the children at play. If you are not saturated with sightseeing, there are many museums to see in the park. One of the loveliest is the **Museo di Villa Giulia**, a museum in a pretty villa that features artifacts from the Etruscan era.

DESTINATION VI   SORRENTO

You could spend weeks discovering the museum that is Rome, but if you have time to add a few more highlights, venture farther south to include Sorrento and Capri. There is frequent train service from Rome to Naples and from there it is a short hydrofoil ride to Capri. However, for the adventurous it is fun to include Pompeii and Sorrento en route to Capri. Please note that this makes a long day of travel and takes some manipulating of schedules, but the rewards are great.

You need an early start to accomplish a tour of Pompeii on your way to Sorrento, but this is a must. How could you be so close without visiting this intriguing city of the Romans that was destroyed, yet preserved forever by the ashes of Vesuvius?

   9:15 am depart Rome, Termini station
  11:58 am arrive Pompeii, Main station

You arrive in **Pompeii** at the Main station, but you depart from Pompeii at the Villa d'Misteri station, located just across from the main entrance to the archaeological site. Since it's no fun to lug your suitcases around while you do your sightseeing, take a cab from the Main station to the Villa d'Misteri station where there is a place to check luggage, then just walk across the street to the main gate of Pompeii. There is a nice terrace restaurant by the entrance and also a café inside. If you want to do your own touring, you can buy a guidebook in English from a stall, or else you can negotiate with one of the licensed guides for a personal tour. You may have heard that the earthquake of 1980 destroyed much of Pompeii. It is true that many of the sites were damaged, but now almost everything has been reconstructed.

An aura of mystery lingers in the air as you wander the streets of Pompeii. All visitors are touched by this ancient city of an estimated 25,000 inhabitants, which in one day became frozen for all time. Probably there is nowhere else in the world where you can so vividly step back in time. Much of what you see today has been reproduced, but the reality is pure. Plaster was poured into molds formed by the lava that demolished the buildings and buried so many families that fateful day. Thus it became possible for latter-day archaeologists to reconstruct houses and make reproductions of people and pets. Walk through the town along the sunken streets crossed by high stepping-stones, strategically placed so that pedestrians did not get their feet wet on rainy days. Be sure not to miss some of the reconstructed villas that allow you a glimpse into the daily life of long ago. The **Casa del Fauna**, a fine example of how the wealthy lived, has two inner courtyards and several dining rooms. The **Casa del Poeta Tragico**, a more modest home, has a sign in mosaic saying *Cave Canem* (beware of the dog). At the **Villa di Giulia Felice** you see the example of an entrepreneur—in addition to using it as a private villa, the owner rented out rooms, had shops on the ground floor, and operated an adjacent bathhouse. If traveling with children, you might want to go alone into the **Lupanare** (Pompeii's brothel) where there are erotic paintings on the walls. At the **Terme Stabiane** you see a sophisticated underground water-heating system.

There are many more places to visit than those listed above. As you explore Pompeii, there is no need to watch the time. There is a narrow-gauge train departing from the Pompeii Villa d' Misteri station about every 20 minutes for the half-hour scenic journey to Sorrento.

When you arrive in **Sorrento**, stay at the **Grand Hotel Excelsior Vittoria**, a romantic old villa at the center of town in a prime cliff location overlooking the harbor. The hotel's once-perfect grandeur is perhaps a bit faded, but as you sit on the terrace in the evening and watch the sun turning the bay to shades of red and gold, the atmosphere is perfect. There is also a pool for relaxing and sunning. Sorrento, a medieval town with a maze of narrow streets, sits on a bluff overlooking the sea. From the center of town, a road twists down to the harbor from where ferries ply the Amalfi coast and go to Capri.

When it is time to leave Sorrento, there is excellent service by either hydrofoil or ferry to Capri. The following schedule is a suggestion:

   3:45 pm depart Sorrento by hydrofoil
   4:10 pm arrive Capri

Your hydrofoil arrives at the **Marina Grande**, a small harbor filled with colorful boats and edged by brightly painted shops. When the boat docks, you find hotel porters on the pier along with carrier services that go to all of the hotels. They relieve you of your luggage and take it directly to the hotel of your choice, freeing you to take either a mini-bus or the funicular to the main town of Capri, which is located on a flat saddle of land high above the sea.

There are many charming places to stay on **Capri**. Since this is a very popular tourist destination, the hotels are generally expensive, but the ones we recommend are all very special. Some are located in the heart of town, others a short stroll away—read our descriptions and choose one that suits you.

Capri has many wonders. The most famous is its submerged cave, the **Blue Grotto**, which can be accessed by boat when the seas are calm. Large boats begin leaving the harbor every day at 9 am for the short ride to the entrance to the grotto, where you are transferred into tiny rowboats. The earlier you go the better since the seas are calmer in the morning. The excursion is an adventure in itself. As you approach the tiny cave opening, it seems impossible that there is adequate room for a boat to enter, but suddenly the sea surges forward and in you squeeze. Like magic, you see it—the mysterious, stunning blue light reflecting from some hidden source that illuminates the grotto. The cost isn't great, but be aware of the system: You pay for a ticket for the motorboat that takes you to the cave, and then you pay again, on site, to the oarsman who skillfully maneuvers his little rowboat through the hole and into the grotto. It is appropriate to tip

Marina Grande, Capri

your boatman—he will do his best to make your short ride memorable and quite probably serenade you within the cave.

Capri is a superb island for walking. As you stroll the trails, all your senses are treated by the fragrant flowers, the gorgeous vistas of the brilliant blue waters, and the sound of birds luring you ever onward. There are many spectacular walks. Follow the trail winding down the cliffs to the small harbor **Marina Piccola**, located on the opposite side of the island from the ferry dock. At the Marina Piccola there are lovely views of the shimmering aqua waters as you make your way to the small beach where you can enjoy a swim before your return. Instead of walking back up the hill, take the little bus that delivers you quickly back to the main square.

Another absolutely spectacular walk—although a long one of at least 45 minutes each way—is to Emperor Tiberius's Palace, **Villa Jovis**, perched high among the trees on the cliffs on the western tip of the island. This is the grandest of the palaces left by Tiberius. Although it is mostly in ruins, you can easily appreciate its former magnificence as you climb about exploring the ruins of the terraced rooms. From the palace there are stunning panoramic vistas: you have an overview of the whole island and can watch the ferries shuttling back and forth to the mainland. A much shorter walk, but one equally as beautiful, is to the **Cannone Belvedere**. This path guides you near delightful private villas hidden behind high walls (you get glimpses through the gates) and on to a promontory overlooking the sea.

Another excursion is to **Anacapri**, the only other town on the island, to visit the **Villa San Michel**, a lovely villa overlooking the sea that was the home of the Swedish scientist Axel Munthe. His residence is now open as a museum. Anacapri is a bit too far to walk easily but buses leave regularly from the main square in town.

During the day, Capri is swarming with tourists on package tours who descend like a swarm of locusts from the constant stream of hydrofoils and ferries. You might surmise that in the evening the activity subsides, but it isn't so. The tour groups leave at dusk but then a new group of people emerges from the secreted villas and fancy hotels. Guests in chic clothes and fancy jewelry stroll the streets—both to see and be seen.

When the real world calls and you must leave Capri, there is frequent ferry or hydrofoil service back to Naples. From Naples, you can take a train to Rome or a plane to your next destination.

Romantic Hilltowns
of Tuscany & Umbria

FLORENCE

San Casciano
Montefiridolfi
Passignano
Greve
Panzano
Castello di Volpaia
Castello d'Albola
Reggello
Castello di Meleto
Castello di Brolio
San Gimignano
Castellina
Volterra
Radda
Gaiole
San Sano
San Leonino
Monteriggioni
San Gusmè
Montebenichi
Castelnuovo Berardenga
Arezzo
Polvano
Castiglion Fiorentino
Cortona
SIENA
Sovicille
Pretale
Abbazia di Monte Oliveto Maggiore
Sinalunga
Petrignano
Lake Trasimeno
Perugia
Assisi
Montefollonico
Montalcino
Poggio Antico
Pienza
Montepulciano
Solomeo
Torgiano
Fattoria dei Barbi
Monticchiello
Cetona
Colle San Paolo
Città della Pieve
San Quirico d'Orcia
Castelnuovo dell'Abate
Bagno Vignoni
Bevagna
Montefalco
Canalicchio di Collazone
Orvieto
Todi
Spoleto
Monteluco
Bagnorégio
Farnese
Civita di Bagnorégio
Terni
Lake Bolsena
to Rome

Rome

○ Orientation/Sightseeing
✻ Suggested hotels
– – Itinerary route

57

Romantic Hilltowns of Tuscany & Umbria

Assisi

Nothing can surpass the exquisite beauty of the countryside of Tuscany and Umbria—it is breathtaking. If you meander into the hilltowns any time of the year, all your senses are rewarded with the splendors that this enchanting area of Italy has to offer. Almost every hillock is crowned with a picture-perfect walled town; fields are brilliant with vibrant red poppies; vineyards in all their glory and promise lace the fields; olive trees dress the hillsides in a frock of dusky gray-green; pine forests unexpectedly appear to highlight the landscape. As if these attributes were not enough, tucked into the colorful villages is a treasure-trove of some of the finest small hotels in the entire world. If this is still not sufficient to tempt you away from the normal tourist route, remember that the food and wines are unsurpassed.

If you are including Florence in your Italian holiday, allow time to treat yourself to a special adventure. Save at least a few days to slip away from the city and into the country. Perhaps you won't have time to follow this entire itinerary, but at least sneak in a few days. You will be well rewarded with a wealth of memories that will linger long after you return home. The following itinerary makes a southern loop from Florence. Along the way are three suggested stops—one in Umbria, one in southern Tuscany, and one in the famous Chianti Classico region of Tuscany. Plan to spend a minimum of several days in each hub. However, if you don't have enough time to do this, don't dash from place to place but limit your stay to the one location that most appeals to you and make that your base, taking side trips from there.

ORIGINATING CITY   FLORENCE

Your journey begins in **Florence**. Allow enough time to savor this marvelous city but, if you are reluctant to leave, be consoled: there are many treats in store for you in the delightful hilltowns that surround it. Magnificent art is not confined to the city limits of Florence and you will see impressive cathedrals and beautiful works of art throughout the neighboring areas. On pages 44–46 we offer sightseeing suggestions for Florence.

DESTINATION I   UMBRIA

Pacing: To truly appreciate the beauty of Umbria, it is best to spend at least three nights in the area. The two major towns, Assisi and Spoleto, both have excellent hotels and either one would make an excellent base of operations. However, if you prefer smaller towns, you can also find marvelous hotels in beautiful small villages in central Umbria such as Bevagna, Todi, Armenzano, Canalicchio, Montefalco, Solomeo, and Colle San Paolo. Any of these would make an excellent place to stay while exploring the area. See Map 10 for towns with recommended hotels.

As you depart from Florence you are bound to run into a lot of traffic, but it is easier leaving the city than entering it since there are many signs to the expressway. Follow signs that lead to the A1 and take it south toward Rome. About 65 kilometers after leaving Florence you come to a turnoff to **Arezzo**, located about 10 kilometers east of the highway. Arrezo has a rich history dating back to the Etruscan era, but is not as quaint as some of its smaller neighbors. It is well known as one of the largest gold centers in Europe and has many shops selling gold jewelry. Arezzo is also famous for its antique fairs, which take place in the Piazza Grande on the first Sunday of every month. Arezzo was the birthplace of Guido Monaco who around the year 1000 devised musical notes and scales. One of Arrezo's famous inhabitants was the powerful 14th-century poet Pietro Aretino who took great glee in writing scandalous poetry about the rich and famous. Aretino's greatest skill was gentle blackmail, extorting great sums from princes and popes who paid him not to expose their indiscretions in poetry.

From Arezzo follow S71 south to **Cortona**, a gem of a walled town terraced up a steep hillside covered with olive trees and vineyards. Stop to enjoy the atmosphere of this medieval town: its narrow, twisting, cobbled streets, jumble of small squares, lovely boutiques, excellent restaurants, and colorful buildings are delightful. The heart of the town is the **Piazza della Repubblica**, the main square, which has many narrow streets feeding into it. If you are up for walking, climb the twisting streets to the old fortress standing guard over the town.

Leaving Cortona, continue driving south on S71 toward **Lake Trasimeno**. In about 9 kilometers you come to a four-lane expressway that skirts the lake's northern shore heading east to **Perugia**, a large medieval city surrounded by ramparts. An important Umbrian city since Etruscan days, the old town has at its heart the **Piazza IV Novembre**, a beautiful square with an appealing fountain, the **Fontana Maggiore**, built in the late 13th century. Although Perugia is rich in history, it is surrounded by modern development and does not exude the romantic appeal of some of the other hilltowns such as Cortona.

St. Francis of Assisi

Continue east, following signs to Assisi on the S75 and the heart of Umbria. By now you will probably be ready to stop for the day so head on to the town you have chosen as your hub for sightseeing.

There are many places to see while in this area of Umbria.

SUGGESTED SIGHTSEEING:

Assisi: Of all our sightseeing destinations in Umbria, Assisi is one of our favorites. Built up the steep slopes of Mount Subasio, this magical city is a tribute to St. Francis. Although he was born into a family of wealth, after several visions in which Christ appeared to him, St. Francis left his privileged life. He was obviously a person with a deeply poetic soul and his tender teachings of reverence for the beauties of nature and kindness to all animals and birds still appeal to us today. To remember your visit, you might want to buy a statue of St. Francis to bring home. You will find statues in all sizes and price ranges in the many shops.

Even if it were not for the lingering memory of the gentle St. Francis, Assisi would be a "must see" for it is one of the most spectacular hilltowns in Umbria. Perhaps there are a few too many souvenir shops, but this is a small price to pay for the privilege of experiencing such a very special place. The town walls begin on the valley floor and completely enclose the city as it climbs the steep hillside to the enormous castle at its summit. Assisi with its maze of tiny streets is a marvelous town for walking (you must wear sturdy shoes) and it is great fun as you come across intriguing little lanes opening into small squares. When you stop to rest, there are breathtaking vistas of the lovely Umbrian fields stretching out below.

Along with many other historic buildings, Assisi's most famous monument, **St. Francis's Basilica**, was severely damaged by an earthquake in September 1997. However, almost all of the repairs have now been completed and the town looks remarkably "back to normal." The basilica, which also houses a monastery, faces onto a large square bound by columns forming vaulted covered walkways. In addition to the monastery, there are two basilicas—upper and lower. Both are adorned with excellent frescoes that were unfortunately damaged by the earthquake. Also while in Assisi, visit **Santa Chiara** (St. Clara's Church). Clara, a close friend of St. Francis, founded the Order of St. Clares. Go into the church to view the lovely frescoes of Santa Clara and her sisters. Part of the enjoyment of Assisi is just to stroll through its narrow, cobbled streets—the whole town is like a living museum. If you have time, hike up to the **Rocca Medioevale**, an enormous 14th-century fortress perched on the hillside overlooking the city. From here you have a magnificent bird's-eye view of Assisi and beyond to the enchanting Umbrian countryside sweeping out to the distant hills.

If you want to use Assisi as your hub, look in the hotel section in the back of the book where we have recommend a selection of many charming places to stay.

Bevagna: Bevagna is an enticing, intimate, charming walled village, founded by the Romans. In addition to just enjoying the allure of the town, there is much to see including a stunning 19th-century opera house, the beautiful San Michele church, well-preserved mosaics in the old Roman baths, and a paper press making paper just as it has been for centuries. We recommend a lovely small hotel here called **L'Orto degli Angeli**. If you don't stay overnight, stop by for a meal.

Montefalco: Montefalco, located 7 kilometers from Bevagna (see above) is a walled town that crowns a hill with sweeping views of the Umbrian countryside. The town is a maze of small, narrow streets. For sightseeing, the main draw is San Francisco, a church now converted into a museum that displays some of the finest work of Benozzo Gozzoli, including the fresco *Life of St. Francis*. Just outside the walls, within easy walking distance of the center, we recommend a delightful, family-managed hotel, **Villa Pambuffetti**.

Spoleto: Not only is medieval Spoleto dramatically perched atop a hill, but it also has an almost unbelievable bridge dating from Roman times. This **Ponte delle Torri**, spanning the deep ravine between Spoleto and the adjoining mountain, was built over an aqueduct existing in the 14th century. This incredible engineering wonder is 230 meters long and soars 81 meters high. It is supported by a series of ten Gothic arches and has a fort at the far end as well as a balcony in the center. The 12th-century **Cathedral** in Spoleto is also so lovely that it alone would make a stop in this charming town worth a detour. The exterior of this very old cathedral, with its beautiful rose window and intricate mosaics, is truly charming. Although a great sightseeing destination at any time of the year, Spoleto is very popular in late June and early July when it hosts the world-famous Spoleto Festival, featuring great music, dance, and theater. During the festival season rooms are usually more expensive and almost impossible to secure so should be booked far in advance. We suggest two outstanding hotels, the **Hotel Gattapone** and the **Hotel San Luca**, both right within the city walls, plus the **Villa Milani** just minutes away. Also in the immediate area you will find the highly recommended **Eremo delle Grazie** in Spoleto-Monteluco and **Le Logge di Silvignano** in Spoleto-Frazione Silvignano.

Todi: This adorable small town crowning a hilltop like icing on a cake is one of our favorites. No, there isn't much to see—it is the town itself that is so picturesque. It is just fun to wander the twisting cobblestone streets, enjoy the medieval ambiance, and stop to enjoy a cappuccino in one of the sidewalk cafés.

Torgiano: Torgiano, in the center of a rich wine region, has a lovely small wine museum. You would never dream that such a tiny town could boast such a museum, but it is not a coincidence: the Lungarotti family owns the vineyards for many kilometers in every direction. Signor Lungarotti furnished the museum with artifacts pertaining to every aspect of wine production from the earliest days, creating an interesting and beautifully displayed collection worthy of a detour by anyone interested in wines. The family also owns a delightful hotel in the center of town, **Le Tre Vaselle**. A charming spot for lunch or an overnight stay, Le Tre Vaselle has the sophisticated ambiance of a country manor house and an outstanding restaurant.

DESTINATION II   SOUTHERN TUSCANY

Pacing: You will need at least three nights in the lower region of Tuscany to explore the stunning small towns that dot the hillsides, visit fabulous monasteries, and sample some of Italy's finest wines. There is a wealth of towns with incredibly lovely hotels in the area—look on Map 9 for towns with suggested hotels and choose one as your base for sightseeing.

When it is time to leave Umbria, drive to Spoleto and take the scenic S418, which twists west for 25 kilometers through beautiful hills to the E45. Turn north on E45 for about 21 kilometers and turn west on S448, following signs to the A1 and Orvieto. When you come to the A1, don't get onto the freeway, but instead follow signs to Orvieto. *NOTE*: If you haven't already visited the picture-perfect town of Todi (see description above), this would be a good time to do so as Todi is located near the junction of E45 and S448 and is well signposted.

Since **Orvieto** is a bit south of the sightseeing suggestions that follow, it would be an efficient use of time to stop now to see this intriguing town. Orvieto is spread across the top of a hill that drops down on every side in steep volcanic cliffs—you wonder how the town could ever have been built! Drive as far as you can up to the town, park your car, and proceed on foot. Have a good map handy because you pass so many churches and squares that it is difficult to orient yourself. Continue on to Orvieto's center where a glorious **Duomo** dominates the immense piazza. You may think you have seen sufficient stunning cathedrals to last a lifetime, but just wait—Orvieto's is truly special. It is brilliantly embellished with intricate mosaic designs and accented by lacy slender spires stretching gracefully into the sky. Also of interest in Orvieto is **St. Patrick's Well**, hewn out of solid volcanic rock. Pope Clement VII took refuge in Orvieto in 1527 and to ensure the town's water supply in case of siege, he ordered the digging of this 62-meter-deep well. It is unique for the 70 windows that illuminate it and the two spiral staircases that wind up and down without meeting.

Duomo, Orvieto

If you have time after visiting Orvieto, consider a side trip to **Civita di Bagnorégio**, located to the southwest of Orvieto. If you are a photographer and love picturesque walled villages, few can surpass the setting of this small town. Take the N71, which twists west from Orvieto toward Lake Bolsena. Stay on N71 for about 20 kilometers and then turn left, heading to Bagnorégio. Go into town and follow signs to Civita, which crowns the top of a steep, circular-shaped, rocky outcrop. There is no road into the village—the only access is by walking over a long, narrow footpath that bridges a deep ravine. Once you arrive, you will find a few shops, some Etruscan artifacts, a church, and a restaurant. However, the main focus is the town itself with its narrow arcaded alleyways and a dramatic 180-degree view of the desolate, rocky canyons that stretch out around the town with a haunting beauty.

After your excursion to Civita di Bagnorégio, return to the A1 and heard north to the hotel you have chosen as your base of operations. Look on Map 9 for towns where we recommend places to stay. A great choice is **La Frateria di Padre Eligio** in Cetona, an intimate hotel housed in a 13th-century convent founded by St. Francis. Also, we love the deluxe **Locanda dell'Amorosa** in Sinalunga, the **Relais alla Corte del Sole** in Petrignano, the **Romantik Hotel Villa di Montesolare** in Colle San Paolo, and the **Relais Magi** in Città della Pieve.

If wine is your primary interest, **Montepulciano** makes a superb location for accommodations since it sits in the heart of a rich wine-producing area. We recommend several hotels here including two owned by the Savini family, the **Montorio**, just outside the city walls, and, a few kilometers away, the delightful **Villa Poggiano**. Not far from Montepulciano, still in the wine-producing area, **Hotel Relais Il Chiostro di Pienza** in Pienza and the nearby **L'Olmo** are excellent choices.

During your stay in lower Tuscany, there is much to see and do. Below we recommend some of our favorite spots.

SUGGESTED SIGHTSEEING

Loop Visiting Wineries, Abbeys, and Quaint Villages: The area of Tuscany that lies south/southeast of Siena is famous for its superb wines. A great bonus is that these vineyards are in one of Italy's most picturesque regions, filled with quaint villages and amazing abbeys, thus making your adventures even more enchanting. Whereas Chianti Classico wine is renowned in the area between Florence and Siena, the vineyards farther south also produce some of the mostly highly regarded wines in the world, the most famous of these being **Vino Nobile**, grown near Montepulciano, and **Brunello**, grown near Montacino. There are many wineries open to the public where wine can be tasted and purchased. Some of these are free, others charge a nominal fee. As you drive through the countryside look for signs reading *Cantina* (wine shop) or *Vendita Diretta* (direct sales).

We suggest a loop that covers some of our favorite wineries, medieval towns, and picturesque abbeys. It would be impossible to squeeze everything in this itinerary into one day unless you rush madly from place to place. Therefore, if your time is limited, don't stop at each place suggested but just choose a few of the sightseeing suggestions below that most appeal to you. But better yet, take several days and follow the itinerary in its entirety, covering a small section each day at a leisurely pace.

This loop begins in **Montepulciano**, a rare jewel of a walled hilltown that not only oozes charm in its narrow, cobbled streets but is also center stage for the delicious Vino Nobile di Montepulciano. This wealthy town was home to many aristocrats who built magnificent palaces here. The heart of the city is the **Piazza Grande** where you find the dramatic 13th-century **Palazzo Comunale** accented by a stone tower. Also facing the square is the picturesque **Palazzo Contucci**, fronted by a charming Renaissance well decorated with the Medici coat of arms and highlighted by two stone lions. Leading off the Pizza Grande are small streets that crisscross the town, connected by staircases.

A masterpiece you absolutely must not miss when visiting Montepulciano is the **Temple of San Biagio**, a stunning church located on the west edge of town. You can walk from town, but it is a long way down the hill and then back up again, so you might want to drive, especially in hot weather. Made of creamy travertine, the church's façade is extremely picturesque and its elegant interior is equally lovely—nothing cluttered or dark but rather light and airy, with fine marble pastel-colored walls.

Within Montepulciano there are many boutiques, restaurants, and cantinas selling wine. Our favorite wine shop here is an extremely special one, the very old **Cantina del Redi**, located just down the street from the Piazza Grande with its entrance next to the Palazzo Ricco. Once you enter, an ancient staircase leads ever deeper into the hillside, passing rooms filled with huge wooden casks of wine. When you finally reach the lowest level, you wind your way through more casks until you arrive at the cantina where you can sample and purchase wine. When finished, you discover that you have descended quite a way down the hillside and the main entrance to the winery faces onto a lower terrace.

Another of our favorite wineries, **Dei**, is just a few kilometers outside Montepulciano's city walls. What is especially fun about this winery is that it is family-owned and managed by the lovely daughter, Maria Caterina Dei, who still lives in the beautiful family villa on the property. Maria Caterina is passionate about wine and with great professionalism can explain about the production of the Dei wines, which have won many awards. Before taking over the family's vineyards, the multitalented Maria Caterina trained in music and the theater, and sometimes she entertains the guests during wine tours. There is a fee for tours, depending upon what is requested. Lunches and wine tasting can be prearranged. Call in advance for tours: Dei, Villa Martiena, Montepulciano, tel: (0578) 71 68 78.

Leaving Montepulciano, take the S146 west toward Pienza. After driving about 3 kilometers, take a small road on the left marked to **Monticchiello**. You soon arrive at a sweet, tiny, picture-perfect walled town whose allure is its unpretentious, non-touristy ambiance. Park your car in the designated area outside the main gate. As you enter through the gate, you will see on your left **La Porta**, a charming restaurant with an outside terrace sitting on the town walls—a great place to stop for lunch. As you stroll through Monticchiello (it won't take you long), take a look inside the 13th-century church where you will see a beautiful altarpiece by Pietro Lorenzetti. *NOTE*: Just a few kilometers outside of Monticchiello we recommend a superb small inn, **L'Olmo**.

From Monticchiello, continue on the back road to **Pienza**. This is one of our favorite walled hilltowns in Tuscany, a real gem that mustn't be missed. The town is perched on the top of a hill and is pedestrian-only so you need to park your car outside the walls. It is no wonder that the town is so perfect even though so tiny: it was here in the 15th century that Pope Pius II hired a famous architect, Bernardo Rossellino, to totally redesign the town where he was born, making it into a masterpiece. You will find many restaurants if you are inclined to dine. If you want to stay overnight, we recommend the **Hotel Relais Il Chiostro di Pienza**, whose terrace has a spectacular view of the countryside.

Leaving Pienza, take S146 west to **San Quirico d'Orcia**, a very attractive small medieval town with a lovely Romanesque church. If you stop to see the town, you must not miss its lovely garden, called **Horti Leonini**. An entrance about a block from the main square leads into a tranquil Renaissance garden, originally designed as a beautiful resting place for the pilgrims who stopped here on the road to Rome. This cool oasis with clipped box hedges and shade trees makes an interesting stop. If you are hungry, the Osteria del Leone makes a good choice for lunch.

From San Quirico d'Orcia, head south on S2 for about 6 kilometers and watch for a small road to the right leading to **Bagno Vignoni**. This is a most unusual, very small town, known for the curative value of its hot sulphur springs. In the center of town, you find what would have been the town square made into a huge sulphur bath built by the Medicis. The pool is surrounded by picturesque medieval buildings which complete the interesting scene.

Leaving Bagno Vignoni, don't continue on the S2, but take S323 directly south for 12 kilometers and then turn right following signs to Montalcino. In a few minutes you come to **Castelnuovo dell'Abate** where, just a few minutes outside town, you will find the superb Romanesque **Abbey Sant'Antimo**, whose origins date back to the 9th century when it was founded as a Benedictine monastery. The abbey—a simple, pastel-pinkish stone church serenely set amongst fields of olive trees—makes a beautiful picture. Try to arrive at 11 am or 2:45 pm when the Benedictine monks, clad in long, pure-white robes, gather at the altar to chant their prayers in Latin. This is a haunting, beautiful experience.

The singing lasts only a short time, and the times might vary from the ones we mention above, so to confirm the schedule call (0577) 83 56 59.

Leaving Castelnuovo dell'Abate, drive north on the road for Montalcino. In a few minutes you will see a sign to the **Fattoria dei Barbi**. Turn right and follow a small road up the hill to the Barbi winery, an excellent winery to visit. It is extremely pretty with many gardens and a charming cantina where you can sample the vineyard's fine wines and purchase wine and other gift items. Its restaurant serves wonderful meals made with only the freshest products, accompanied, of course, by their own wines. Free tours of the winery are given hourly from 10 am to noon and 3 pm to 5 pm. Tel: (0577) 84 82 77, *www.fattoriadeibarbi.it*.

After your visit to the Fattoria dei Barbi, continue north for 5 kilometers to **Montalcino**, which is world-famous, along with Montepulciano, for its superb wine, Brunello di Montalcino. There are many places in town where wine can be tasted and purchased. In addition to wine, the town is famous for its fine honey, which can be purchased in many of the shops. Montalcino is fun for wandering—it is not large and you can in no time at all cover the area within the walls by foot. On the east edge of town is an imposing 14th-century fortress.

From Montalcino, head south on the road to Grosetto for a little over 3 kilometers to another of our favorite wineries, **Poggio Antico**. Excellent tours are offered and, of course, you can also sample the superb wines. These tours are very popular so you should reserve in advance at (0577) 84 80 44. For dining, the winery's Ristorante Poggio Antico serves outstanding Tuscany cuisine. Reservations for the restaurant are also highly recommended—tel: (0577) 84 92 00.

After visiting Poggio Antico, retrace your way north to Montalcino and continue on for 9 kilometers to where the road intersects with the S2. Turn left here, going north toward Siena. In 10 kilometers, turn right on S451 and continue for another 10 kilometers to the **Abbazia di Monte Oliveto Maggiore**. Founded in the early 14th century by wealthy Sienese merchants as a Benedictine retreat, this fascinating abbey is well worth a detour.

Be prepared to walk since you must park your car and follow a long path through the forest to the abbey's entrance, which is through a gatehouse crowned by a beautiful della Robbia terra cotta. Once through the gate, you continue through the woodlands to the huge brick complex. After visiting the church, it seems you could wander forever through the various hallways. Before you get too distracted, however, ask directions to the cloister because you don't want to miss this marvel. Here you find 36 frescoes depicting scenes of the life of St. Benedict, some painted by Luca Signorelli, others by Antonio Bazzi.

In the region around the abbey you will come across an entirely different type of landscape, called the *crete*. Here, tucked among the green rolling hills, you unexpectedly come across bleak, canyon-like craters, caused by erosion. These are especially out of character as the surrounding scenery is so soft and gentle.

From Abbazia di Monte Oliveto Maggiore, weave your way through the small back roads to Montepulciano. Follow signs to San Giovanni d'Asso, then Montisi, then Madongino, then **Montefollonico**. Take time to stop in Montefollonico because this is another "sleeper"—a quaint, small, medieval walled town that is fun to explore. For the gourmet, there is a superb restaurant on the edge of town called **La Chiusa**, which also has rooms for overnight guests (see description in the back of the book).

From Montefollonico, go south on S327. When you come to the S146, turn left to complete your loop back to Montepulciano.

DESTINATION III   CHIANTI CLASSICO WINE REGION

Pacing: We recommend a minimum of four nights in the heart of Tuscany's Chianti wine region, which stretches from Florence south to Siena, though you could blissfully spend a week or more in this idyllic area that lives up to every dream of Tuscany—hills crowned by picture-perfect villages, towns wrapped by medieval walls, straight rows of towering cypresses, romantic villas, ancient stone farmhouses, vast fields of brilliant poppies, forests of pine trees, vineyards stretching to the horizon. Take a look at Map 8 in the back of the book, study the towns where we recommend hotels between Florence and Siena, then choose a hotel that captures your fancy to use as your hub. Your only problem will be deciding where to stay since there are so many adorable towns and charming hotels.

In Chianti we highly recommend meandering through the countryside, stopping at quaint hamlets, exploring perched villages, and visiting vineyards. Take a detailed map so that if you get lost, you can find your way home, but otherwise just wander the small lanes that twist through the splendid countryside. Enjoy the freedom to discover your own perfect village, your own charming restaurant, and your own favorite wine. Although in your wanderings you are sure to find some very special places that we have missed, we share below some of the towns we find irresistible and vineyards that are especially fun to visit. All of the places mentioned below are in Tuscany and within driving distance of whichever town you choose on Map 8.

SUGGESTED SIGHTSEEING:

Monteriggioni: If you are looking for a town that is truly storybook-perfect, none can surpass the tiny, magical hamlet of Monteriggioni. It is such a gem that it is hard to believe it is real and not a creation by Disney! You can spot it from afar, nestled on the top of a small hill, with 14 towers punctuating the perfectly preserved enclosing walls. No cars are allowed here, so you have to park in the designated area below the walls before walking up to the town, which is composed almost entirely of a main square with small streets radiating from it. On the square you find a Romanesque church, restaurants, boutiques, and shops selling olive oil, cheeses, and wine. It takes only a few minutes to stroll from one end of the town to the other but I assure you, you will be enchanted. As a bonus, Monteriggioni produces its own fine wine, Castello di Monteriggioni.

Monteriggioni

Passignano in Chianti: Passignano in Chianti is rarely on a tourist route, but we can't help mentioning this tiny hamlet that exudes such a tranquil beauty. For sightseeing, there really isn't much to see except the **Badia a Passignano Abbey**, founded by Benedictine monks in the 11th century. The abbey is set in a pocket of lush landscape and dominates the village, which is no more than a cluster of houses and a restaurant. However, as you drive into the valley, approaching from the west, the abbey with its towering ring of cypresses has such an idyllic setting that it is one of our favorites—a photographer's delight. The abbey can be visited on Sundays at 3 pm; tours leave from the church (please check to verify the abbey is open the Sunday you want to visit). Fine wines, produced by the abbey's vineyards, can be purchased at the Osteria, tel: (055) 80 71 278.

Radda: Located in the very heart of the Chianti wine region, Radda makes a good base of operations. However, not only is the town very conveniently located for sightseeing, but it is also extremely quaint and some of its walls are still intact. It was in Radda in 1924 that 33 producers gathered to found a consortium to protect a very special blend of wine that was known as **Chianti Classico**. Only vintners who maintain the standards of the consortium are allowed to proudly display its symbol of the black rooster. In the center of town you can stay in luxury at the charming **Relais Fattoria Vignale**, whose owners produce superb wines that can be tasted in the wine cellars adjacent to the hotel.

San Gimignano: During your exploration of Tuscany, one town you must not miss is San Gimignano. What is so dramatic about San Gimignano is that at one time this walled town was surrounded by 72 towers. During the Middle Ages it was a status symbol for noble families to build personal towers for their protection—the higher the tower, the greater the image of wealth and importance. It is amazing that 14 of the original towers are still standing. They make a striking silhouette, soaring like skyscrapers, and on a clear day you can see them on the horizon from far away. San Gimignano is truly a jewel—plan to spend at least a day here. There are many shops and marvelous restaurants tucked along the maze of streets. On Fridays walking tours with

San Gimignano

English-speaking guides leave from the Porta San Giovanni at 11 am (best check with the tourist office to be sure the time and day haven't changed). If you want to spend the night, we highly recommended the **L'Antico Pozzo**, a charming hotel in the center of town. One of our favorite restaurants in San Gimignano is the delightful **Ristorante**

Dorando, which has great food served in cozy rooms with coved ceilings that create the ambiance of an old wine cellar. Located on Vicolo del Oro 2, a small side street just off Piazza Duomo, tel: (0577) 94 18 62. Another favorite, **Ristorante Il Pino**, offers mouthwatering homemade pastas—some of the best we have ever eaten. Located on Via Collolese, 8–10, just down the street from L'Antico Pozzo, tel: (0577) 94 04 15.

Siena: This is an entrancing walled hilltown that deserves many hours to savor its rich delights—you should allow yourself at least one full day here. The ramparts are perfectly preserved with a series of massive gates guarding a meticulously maintained medieval stronghold. Drive as close as you can to the main square, park your car, and set out to explore on foot. You cannot drive into the center of the city, but there are designated parking areas (marked by "P") near each of the gates. One of the most convenient is the parking at the Porta Romana. Once you leave your car, head for the giant **Piazza del Campo**. This central piazza is immense and, instead of being square, is fan-shaped and slopes downward like a bowl. Eleven streets surrounding the square converge into it like spokes of a massive wheel. Like the Spanish Steps in Rome, the Piazza del Campo is a favorite for tourists who linger here just enjoying the medieval ambiance. It is in this gigantic piazza that the colorful **Palio delle Contrade** (dating back to the 11th century) takes place twice a year, on July 2 and August 16. The horse race is only a part of a colorful spectacle of medieval costumes, impressive banners, and parades, and the festivities extend beyond the actual date of the races. Monopolizing one side of the Piazza del Campo is the 13th-century Gothic **Palazzo Pubblico** (Town Hall) whose graceful arches are embellished with Siena's coat of arms. The Palazzo Pubblico is open as a museum where you can stroll through the governor's living quarters.

Although Siena looks like a large city, it is easily negotiable on foot and most of the museums are in one small area. After visiting the Piazza del Campo, most of the other major places of interest are just a few minutes' walk away, clustered about the Piazza del Duomo. There are excellent signs that will guide you along the maze of narrow streets to all the museums.

You absolutely must not miss Siena's 12th-century **Duomo**, facing the Piazza del Duomo. This is one of Italy's most astounding cathedrals. Not only is its exterior breathtaking, but once you enter, you will be overwhelmed by its dramatic black-and-white, zebra-striped marble columns. Don't miss the intricately carved, 13th-century panels depicting the life of Christ on the octagonal pulpit. Also, be sure to see the **Piccolomini Library**. You need to buy a ticket to enter, but it is well worth it. This relatively small room is totally frescoed with gorgeous murals in still-vibrant colors portraying the life of Pope Pius II. The cathedral also has 59 fabulous inlaid-marble mosaic panels on the floor depicting religious scenes. However, some of the most precious of these are covered to protect them and are on display only from the end of August to the first of October.

After visiting the Duomo, the following museums are just steps away. One of our favorites is the **Ospedale di Santa Maria della Scala**, located across from the entrance to the Duomo. At first glance, it is difficult to truly appreciate its wealth of things to see. The museum goes on and on—it is enormous. Just when you think you have finished, a discreet sign will lead you ever downwards to a lower level and a stunning array of artifacts. The building, dating back to the 800s, was originally constructed as a hospital. Be sure not to miss the former infirmary with its lushly colored frescoes by the master Domenico di Bartolo depicting scenes of patients being treated by their doctors. Another nearby museum is the **Baptistry**, a small museum that, as its name implies, houses the baptismal font for the Duomo. In addition to its beautifully frescoed walls and vaulted ceiling, of prime interest is the 15th-century baptismal font, which is adorned by religious scenes cast in bronze by some of Italy's most famous Renaissance masters, including one panel by Donatello. The **Museo dell'Opera Metropolitana** is worth a visit if for no other reason that to see the sublime *Maestá* by Duccio, painted in 1311. The central scene of the Virgin Mary is truly awesome. For art lovers, the **Museo Civico** must not be missed. Here you will see stunning masterpieces by Ambrogio Lorenzetti, Spinello Aretino, and Simone Martini. It is overwhelming to ponder how Italy could have produced so many geniuses.

NOTE: There is a comprehensive ticket valid for three days that allows you entrance into many of Siena's prime sightseeing attractions—this is a bargain compared to buying individual tickets. When you buy your ticket for the first museum ask about it and which museums it includes.

Volterra: Just a short drive from San Gimignano, Volterra is a delightful, non-touristy town enclosed by still-intact, 12th-century walls. Like so many of the cities founded by the Etruscans, Volterra is built upon the flat top of a steep hill. As you drive toward the city, the landscape becomes increasingly barren, since the soil is not conducive to growing grapes or olive trees. Instead, alabaster is king here and objects made of alabaster are sold in all of the shops. Not to be missed is the alabaster museum called **Museo Etrusco Guaracci**, which has a fabulous collection of works of art, including sculptures and beautiful vases, displayed with great taste in a series of interlinking rooms that show the art to perfection. There is an adjacent shop selling many alabaster items. The whole town is a jewel whose charm is best experienced by strolling through the narrow cobbled streets. Its main square, **Piazza dei Priori**, the heart of the town, is surrounded by fine examples of beautifully preserved medieval buildings and with its towers, splendid town hall (the oldest in Tuscany), and Romanesque church, it is considered by some to be one of the finest squares in Tuscany. Stroll to visit one of the main gates, the **Porta all'Arco**, the origins of which date back to the 7th century B.C. During World War II, the loyal citizens of Volterra buried the stones of the gate to keep the Nazis from blowing it up.

WINERIES

The production of wine plays an enormous role throughout Tuscany, and between Florence and Siena (where **Chianti Classico** is produced) you are constantly reminded of this as you pass through vast rolling hills splendidly adorned with neatly tended vineyards. The Chianti Classico area covers over 172,000 acres, with Siena and Florence being the two "capitals" of the region. Included in the area are the towns of Castellina, Gaiole, Greve, Radda, and some of Barberino Val d'Elsa, Castelnuovo Berardenga,

Poggibonsi, San Casciano Val di Pesa, and Tavarnelle Val di Pesa. Even if you are not a wine connoisseur, it would be a pity not to make at least one winery stop both for the fun of observing the production process and for an understanding of the industry that is so central to the soul and character of Tuscany. Many of the wineries also have gift shops and sell marvelous olive oils and cheeses in addition to wine.

As you meander through the countryside you see signs with Chianti Classico's black rooster symbol and you can buy directly from the producer where you see *Vendita Diretta*. In some cases there are also tours of the winery (these are sometimes free, but sometimes there is a charge). A *Cantina* sign means that the winery has a shop where wine is sold and can usually be sampled. One of the delights of touring the back roads of Tuscany is just to stop on whim. When you spot a *Vendita Diretta*, drive in, introduce yourself, and sample some wines. You might well discover one that will become one of your favorites.

On our Tuscany and Umbria itinerary map, the locations of the wineries described below are indicated.

Castello di Brolio: If you visit only one winery, Castello di Brolio should be it since this is not only one of the oldest wineries the world, but also where Chianti wine was "born." Although the production of wine in Tuscany dates back to Etruscan times, the enormously wealthy Ricasoli family, owners of the Castello di Brolio since 1167, are responsible for the special blending of grapes we now consider "Chianti Classico." At one time the enormously powerful Ricasoli family owned most of the land and castles lying between Florence and Siena. The remote family castle, Castello di Brolio, had largely been abandoned when Bettino Ricasoli decided to move into it (so the story goes) after becoming jealous at a winter ball in Florence when his young bride danced a bit too closely to one of her young admirers. Thinking it best to take his wife away from temptation, he rebuilt the huge, remote, crenellated castle, replanted the vineyards, and experimented with the blending of grapes, coming up with the original formula that forms the basis of what is known today as Chianti Classico. The fortified castle tops a high, forested hill. You leave your car in the designated parking area and climb for about 20 minutes up a path or on the road through a parklike forest to the castle gates. Open daily from 9 am to noon and 3 pm to sunset. The castle is located about 10 kilometers south of Gaiole. Tel: (0577) 74 90 66.

Castello d'Albola, wine tasting

Castello d'Albola: The Castello d'Albola, a spectacular property just a short drive north of Radda on a gentle hill laced with grapes, is owned by the Zonin family, who have restored the entire medieval complex beautifully. This is an intimate, extremely pretty place to taste wines and take a tour. What we particularly like about the Castello d'Albola is that it is in such a beautiful setting and offers delightfully informal, friendly, free tours. Drive up the hill to the castle, leave your car in the parking area, and walk into an inner castle courtyard, off which you find the wine-tasting room and cantina. Before or after wine tasting, your hostess leads you on a short, professional tour showing you how fine wines are produced. The owner has other enormous estates as well as the Castello d'Albola and is one of the largest producers of wine in the world. Tours start at noon, 3 pm, and 5 pm daily. The cantina is open for complimentary wine tasting Monday through Friday from 10:30 am to 6:30 pm. Tel: (0577) 73 80 19, *www.albola.it.*

Castello di Volpaia: The 12th-century Castello di Volpaia, located on a narrow lane about 7 kilometers north of Radda, is one of our favorite places for wine tasting. Plan to spend a day on this outing, with ample time to meander through the countryside en route, tour the winery, taste the superb wines, and enjoy a wonderful lunch at the winery's excellent restaurant, La Bottega. Although the winery is called *Castello* it really isn't located inside a castle at all, but rather in various medieval stone houses in a picture-perfect village wrapped by vineyards where you find a small church, a cluster of houses, La Bottega Ristorante, and the wine-tasting room. You need to preplan this wine tour and also make reservations for lunch since both are very popular and usually booked far in advance. There is a fee for the tour based on the number of people in the group. Tel: (0577) 73 80 66, *www.volpaia.com.*

Castello di Meleto: Another favorite destination for wine tasting is the beautiful Castello di Meleto, which has an idyllic setting in the gentle hills near the town of Gaiole. Just across from the dramatic castle you find a pretty wine-tasting room and gift shop where fine wines and olive oils produced on the estate can be purchased. On request, tastings of olive oil and aromatic vinegars can be arranged. What makes this a very special experience is that there is an added bonus: not only can you sample wines, but you can also visit the beautiful interior of the castle. In addition to splendidly frescoed rooms, the castle has one exceptionally intriguing feature—a whimsical private theater complete with its original stage settings. Call ahead on (0577) 73 80 66 to find out the time and cost of the guided tours of the cellars and castle. *NOTE*: In our companion guide to Italy, *Karen Brown's Italy: Charming Bed & Breakfasts*, we highly recommend bed and breakfast accommodations in the Castello di Meleto.

Castello di Meleto

Romantic Hilltowns of Tuscany & Umbria

Mountain & Lake Adventures

Chiavenna

Cannero
Riviera

Lake
Maggiore

Valsolda

Breuil Cervinia   Stresa   Luino

Champoluc   Belgirate   Argegno   Lake Como   Bellagio

Cogne   Pescatori

Orta   Cernobbio

San Giulio   Bergamo

Milan

Erbusco

Gargnano

Gardone

Sirmione   S. Viglio

Verona

Limone

Riva

Lake
Garda

Trento   Pergine

Bressanone

Merano   Castelrotto   Rasun di Sopra

Bolzano   Fie   Sesto

Tires   San Cassiano

Corvara   Cortina d'Ampezzo

Belluno

Follina   Rivarotta

Maser

Asolo   Treviso

Scorzè   Quarto d'Altino

Mira   Venice

● Overnight stops
○ Sightseeing/orientation
▬ ▬ Itinerary route
✳ Suggested alternate hotels

Rome

83

Mountain & Lake Adventures

Santa Maria Rezzónico, Lake Como

For the traveler who wants to combine the magic of seeing some of the world's most splendid mountains with the joy of visiting Italy's scenic northern lakes, this itinerary is ideal. Contrasts will heighten the impact of visual delights as you meander through lovely mountain passes. Along the way you pass lush green meadows splashed with wildflowers and giant mountains piercing the sky with their jagged granite peaks. Farther on you come to lazy blue lakes whose steep shorelines are decorated with villages wrapped in misty cloaks of siennas and ochres. This itinerary can stand alone. However, it is also perfect for the traveler arriving in or departing from neighboring countries. We show detours for the tourist who will be leaving for or entering from Austria, Switzerland, or France. All too often the tourist thinks he has finished Italy when his tour ends in Venice, and he rushes north into Austria or Switzerland. What a waste—a very picturesque region still remains. Please linger to enjoy the mountains and lakes that truly are some of Italy's greatest natural treasures.

ORIGINATING CITY   VENICE

This itinerary begins in **Venice**, one of the most romantic cities in the world. Her many narrow waterways are criss-crossed by storybook bridges and shadowed by majestic palaces whose soft hues reflect warmly in the shimmering water. Black gondolas quietly glide through the narrow canals as the gondolier in his red-and-white-striped shirt softly serenades his passengers with an operatic selection.

Venice is not a traditional city with streets and automobile traffic, but rather an archipelago of 117 islands glued together by 400 bridges. There is a wealth of things to do here: pick up a guidebook at one of the tourist stalls to give you an idea of what you want to see. On pages 41–44 we give brief sightseeing suggestions.

DESTINATION I   ASOLO

You need not rush your departure this morning. Venice is a city that should be enjoyed slowly and since your journey today is short, you can certainly have the luxury of a last leisurely breakfast before embarking on your countryside adventure.

Since all the "streets" in Venice are canals, you will need to take a boat to your car. It will probably be at the **Piazzale Roma** where most of the car rental companies are located. Also in the Piazzale Roma there are overnight car parks for storing your car if you drive into Venice. The choice of conveyance will depend upon your budget and your inclination. The **vaporetti** are the most reasonable: similar to river buses. They leave regularly from St. Mark's Square for the approximately half-hour ride to the Piazzale Roma. The **motoscafi** are motorboats that duck through the back canals and usually take about 15 minutes to the Piazzale Roma. The motoscafi are like private cabs and are much more expensive than the "bus," but can be very convenient, especially if your hotel has a private motorboat landing. The most deluxe mode of transportation is by private **gondola**: however, these are very expensive and usually take about an hour to reach the Piazzale Roma.

Once you have retrieved your car from the parking garage, head north from Venice toward **Treviso**, about an hour's drive. If time allows, stop here. Stroll through this picturesque city spider-webbed with canals and surrounded by 15th-century ramparts— perhaps have a cup of coffee or a bite of lunch. Treviso is famous for its arcaded streets, churches lavishly decorated with frescoes, and painted houses. You might want to climb the ramparts for a view of the Alps beckoning you on.

From Treviso it is approximately another hour north to Asolo. However, just a few kilometers before you reach Asolo you see signs for the town of **Maser** where the **Villa di Maser** (some of your books might use the name of **Villa Bararo**) is located. This is a splendid villa designed by Palladio and fabulously decorated with frescoes by Paolo Veronese. It also has a very interesting museum of old carriages and antique cars. This elegant villa has erratic days and hours when it is open to the public—usually in late afternoons on Tuesdays, Saturdays, and Sundays. However, it is only about 1½ kilometers out of your way, so it is well worth a detour to investigate.

Your prize tonight is **Asolo**, a gem of a medieval village snuggled on the side of a hill with exquisite views of the countryside. As you drive toward Asolo, the terrain does not seem to hold much promise—just modern towns and industry. Then a side road winds up a lovely hillside and into the intimate little town. Although definitely a tourist destination, Asolo maintains the atmosphere of a *real* town with colorful fruit stands, candy shops, and the neighborhood grocer for those lucky few who live here. In addition, there are boutiques with exquisite merchandise for the tourist. Of course, a castle adorns the hill above the village—mostly in ruins but setting the proper stage. Naturally, there is a wonderful cathedral dominating the square, just as it should. You will find all this plus vineyards and olive trees on the hillsides and the scent of roses in the air.

No wonder Robert Browning fell in love with Asolo and chose it as his home. It might not be possible for everyone to live here, but at least you have the marvelous option of staying at the **Villa Cipriani**, an enchanting villa that was once Browning's home. Here you can dream on the peaceful terrace in the evening and watch the soft lights paint the distant villa-dotted hills in mellow shades of gold. *NOTE:* We also highly recommend two less expensive hotels in Asolo, the **Hotel Duse** and the **Albergo al Sole**.

Villa Cipriani, Asolo

There are a couple of towns that are worth seeing while you are in the Asolo area. If brandy holds a special interest for you, visit **Bassano del Grappa,** an old town famous for its production of grappa (or brandy). The town is also a pottery center. However, it is rather large and, in our estimation, much less interesting than **Marostica**, a tiny town just a few kilometers farther on. If you are in this area in September, check your calendar and consider a stop in Marostica. Here, during the first part of September (in alternate years) the central square is transformed into a giant chess board and local citizens become the human chess pieces. Even if it isn't the year of the chess game, you will enjoy this picturesque little medieval town encircled by ramparts, its pretty central square enclosed by colorful buildings and castle walls. There is also a second castle guarding the town from the top of the hill.

Quite frankly, we think one of the most stunning regions of Italy is the **Dolomites**—truly breathtaking mountains! Look at Map 2 (a and b) in the back of this guide to find the locations of our recommended places to stay—any one of them would make a good base for walking and soaking in the beauty of these soaring, saw-toothed mountain peaks. It is important to have a very detailed map of the region because this is a confusing area for driving. Adding to the confusion of finding your way is the fact that most of the towns have two names: one Italian and one Austrian. Before World War I this section of Italy belonged to the Austrian Empire, and most of the towns have retained their original names along with their new ones. The food is a mixture of Italian and German—strudel is the favorite dessert and ravioli stuffed with meat, vegetables, and cream cheese is called either ravioletti or schulpfkrapfeln.

The Dolomites

There are various routes for driving north into the Dolomites. The major highway heads north through **Feltre** and **Belluno** and then goes on to Cortina d'Ampezzo. However, if the day is nice and your spirit of adventure high, there is really nothing more fun than taking the back roads through the mountains. Journey through tiny hamlets and gorgeous mountain valleys far from the normal tourist path—always keeping a map accessible so that you don't wind up hopelessly lost.

You might want to travel casually and stop in a village that captures your heart as you drive through the picturesque Dolomite valleys. A good base for exploring the region is **Corvara**, a small village ringed by breathtaking mountains. Another excellent choice where we recommend several hotels is **Cortina d'Ampezzo**, a tourist center that is larger due to its excellent skiing facilities. Its location is truly breathtaking—the town spreads across a sunny meadow ringed by gigantic granite peaks. Although the true allure of Cortina is its beauty, there are a few other attractions—the lovely frescoes in the Romanesque **Church of SS Filippo e Giacomo**; the **stadium** where the 1956 Olympic ice-skating competition was held; and the **Museo Ciasa de Ra Regoles** with its geological display and contemporary art exhibition.

This is a mountain lovers' area where the roads are slow and winding. The scenery is beautiful, with green valleys dominated by the stark mountain walls, but the driving is hard, with lots of hairpin bends. Many routes are spectacular. The 48 and 241 from Cortina to Bolzano form the stupendous **Great Dolomite Road** (*Grande Strada delle Dolomiti*). Another lovely route runs through the **Alpe di Siusi**, high Alpine meadowlands beneath towering mountains. (From the Verona-Brennero autostrada exit at Bolzano Nord and follow a route through Völs [Fiè allo Sciliar], Siusi, and Castelrotto.) It continues on into the **Val Gardena** (Grödner Tal) to **Ortisei** (Sankt Ulrich) and up to the **Sella Pass**. We enjoyed a sensational 50-kilometer drive over four mountain passes that ring the **Gruppo Sella** mountain group—from Corvara we took the Gardena Pass, the Sella Pass, the Podoi Pass, and the Campolongo Pass, which returned us to Corvara.

The only relaxing (albeit strenuous) way to truly appreciate the Dolomites is to get out of your car and walk the well-marked trails that feather out into the hills. Cable cars and ski lifts run in summer and are excellent ways to assist the walker to higher altitudes. At gift shops or tourist offices you can purchase detailed hiking maps that show every little path.

DESTINATION III   LAKE GARDA

Moving on, drive to Bolzano where you join the expressway (E7), heading south toward Trento (Trent). **Trent** is best known as the town where the Catholic Council met in the 16th century to establish important articles of faith that emphasized the authority of the Catholic church.

Northern Italian Lake District

Leave the freeway at Trent and head west on 45 toward the small, but lovely, green **Lake Toblino**, which is enhanced by a superb castle on its north shore where you can stop for lunch. From Toblino head south on the pretty country road, lined with fruit trees and vineyards, heading directly south toward Lake Garda, Italy's largest lake. When you come to Arco, the road splits. Take the road to the left and continue south to Lake Garda and then follow the 249 as it curves along the eastern shore of the lake.

Allow several nights in the **Lake Garda** area so that you can enjoy at a leisurely pace romantic boat excursions on the lake plus a side trip to nearby **Verona** (which also has some excellent hotel choices should you wish to spend the night). Take a look at Map 3 to locate towns in the area where we recommend hotels and then read their descriptions to see what most appeals to you.

Happily, around Lake Garda there are fabulous choices for places to stay in every price range, and many adorable villages tucked along the lake. One of the most picturesque towns is **Sirmione**, which is so alluring that you must visit, even if you don't stay overnight. This is a walled medieval village at the south end of Lake Garda, positioned on a miniature peninsula that juts into the lake and is accessed by a bridge. During the summer Sirmione is absolutely bursting with tourists, but you can easily understand why: this is another one of Italy's "stage-set" villages, almost too perfect to be real. If you have the pleasure of spending the night here, you can capture the magic of Sirmione in the evening after the hordes of tourists have departed and again in the morning when the town is blissfully quiet.

Hotel Grifone, Sirmione, Lake Garda

If you take the ferry or hydrofoil to Sirmione, your boat will dock in the center of the town. Stroll by the little boutiques, then have lunch at one of the many restaurants. One of our favorite places to eat is on the terrace of the Grifone Restaurant at the **Hotel Grifone**, which also has 16 small, immaculately clean guestrooms that we highly recommend for those seeking simple accommodations offering excellent value.

Villa Feltrinelli, Gargnano, Lake Garda

If your heart gravitates toward super luxury, splurge on the stunning **Villa Feltrinelli**, one of Lake Garda's most magnificent lake-front mansions, which opened as a hotel in 2001 in the quaint, colorful town of Gargnano. Here you will be pampered as a guest in a private home. From the hotel you can easily walk into the town of Gargnano to hop aboard a ferry to explore the lake.

Lake Garda abounds with romance. Don't rush. Take time to explore the lake by boat. Get off at colorful small hamlets that capture your fancy. Have lunch, then hop back on a later boat to continue along your way. The boat schedules are posted at each dock, and if you ask the attendant, he can usually give you a printed timetable. If time permits, take the ferry to **Riva** on the northern tip of the lake. Although much of the town is of new construction, it has at its medieval core the **Piazza III Novembre** and 13th-century **Tower of Apponale**. A good place to eat lunch is on the terrace of the **Hotel Sole**, located directly across from the boat dock. Another excursion is by car to **Gardone Riviera** to see a nearby museum, the **Vittoriale**, once the home of Gabriele d'Annunzio, the celebrated Italian poet. (For those of us who love stories of romance, **d'Annunzio** is also famous for his love affair with Eleanora Duse.) While there, if you enjoy gourmet dining, try the nearby **Villa Fiordaliso**, which also has a tidbit of historical romance—this was once the hideaway of Mussolini and his mistress, Claretta.

It might be easier to leave the Lake Garda knowing that beautiful Lake Como awaits your arrival.

Bergamo

On your way from Lake Garda to Lake Como, stop at **Bergamo**, about an hour's drive west on the A4. As you approach Bergamo, the congested city doesn't appear to be worth a stop—but it is. The shell of the city is deceiving because it hides a lovely kernel, the **Cita Alta**, or high city. The lower part of Bergamo is modern and a bit dreary, but the old medieval city snuggled on the top of the hill holds such treasures as the **Piazza Vecchia**, the **Colleoni Chapel**, and the **Church of St. Mary Major**. Should you want to time your stop in Bergamo with lunch, there are several excellent restaurants. One suggestion would be the **Agnello d'Oro**, a cozy, charming, l7th-century inn in the Cita Alta.

From Bergamo it is a short drive on to **Bellagio**, a medieval fishing village located at the tip of a peninsula. This peninsula divides the lower section of Lake Como into two lakes, Lake Como on the west and Lake Lecco on the east. Bellagio makes an excellent base for exploring beautiful Lake Como. In the hotel description section we list three hotel suggestions in various price ranges. The **Grand Hotel Villa Serbelioni**, found behind gates opening onto the main square of Bellagio, is a large, imposing, old-world palace. It offers everything you could wish for in a lakeside interlude—tennis, swimming pool, boat excursions, private beach, and more. It is very ornate, still retaining its glory of bygone days with soaring, intricately painted ceilings, heavy chandeliers, and a fabulous sweeping staircase. The setting of the Villa Serbelloni is superb and overshadows what might be perceived as the slightly faded elegance of the hotel's decor. Just outside the gates of the Villa Serbelloni, with a prime location across from the lake, the **Hotel Florence** is also very highly recommended. This moderately priced small hotel is more intimate than the Villa Serbelloni and offers the warmth of welcome found only at family-run hotels.

Bellagio, Lake Como

Bellagio is a delightful town. Not only can you meander through its quaint medieval streets, but you can walk to the pier for one of the boats that will take you to all corners of the lake. **Lake Como** is absolutely beautiful—especially the lower eastern branch of the lake called **Lake Lecco** where cliffs enclose the shorelines like gorgeous walls and give a fjord-like beauty to the area. There are numerous romantic steamers that glide in and out of the picturesque, softly hued little hamlets dotting the lake shore. You can settle onto a steamer equipped with bar and restaurant and from your armchair lazily enjoy the constantly changing but always intriguing shoreline as the boat maneuvers in and out of the colorful little harbors, past elegant private villas, by postcard-pretty villages. From Bellagio you can also step on board one of the swift hydrofoils that will whisk you about the lake or put your car right on the ferry to either **Varenna** on the eastern shore or **Cadenabbia** on the western shore to visit the **Villa Carlotta**, a fairy-tale-like 18th-century palace—worthy of the Prussian Princess Carlotta for whom it was named. You reach the villa, which is encircled by its own gorgeous park of terraced gardens, by a short drive from the ferry landing along the beautiful tree-lined Via del Paradiso.

DESTINATION V   ISOLA DEI PESCATORI

Continuing on toward Lake Maggiore, take advantage of the expressways to make your drive as easy as possible because there is usually heavy traffic in this part of Italy. It is best to head directly south from Bellagio to pick up the freeway in the direction of Milan. Keep on the bypass which skirts the north of Milan and follow the freeway northwest to **Lake Maggiore**. When you reach the lake, continue along the western shore to Stresa. It seems only suitable that for a "mountain and lake adventure" one of your hotels should be located on an island in a lake—so we have chosen for you one of the **Borromean Islands**, **Isola dei Pescatori** (Fisherman's Island), in Lake Maggiore. This is an enchanting little island with twisting, narrow, alley-like streets and colorful fishermen's cottages. As the name implies, this is still an active fishing village. During the tourist season the island teems with people and the streets are lined with souvenir shops, but it is hard to dull the charm of this quaint town.

Isola dei Pescatori can be reached by ferry from Stresa, Baveno, or Pallanza, but the most convenient of these is **Stresa** from where there are frequent scheduled departures to the island. Be sure to take one of the scheduled public ferries—these are very reasonable in contrast to the very expensive private speedboats whose captains will attempt to take you to the island. Your best choice for a place to stay here is the **Hotel Verbano**. This is not a deluxe hotel, but its setting is superb, and over the years (since our first visit) the decor of this most romantic hotel has improved enormously. The bedrooms are pleasantly decorated, but lovely vistas are their most enchanting feature. The view from the terrace,

Isola Bella, Lake Maggiore

where guests enjoy dining while overlooking the lake, is also outstanding. The food is delicious, and the service of the Zacchera family, who own and manage the Verbano, is warm and gracious. How smug you will feel as you settle into your room then sip a drink on the lovely terrace while watching the last of the tourists hustle onto the boat for shore, leaving you to enjoy the sunset.

This tiny archipelago consisting of Isola Bella (Beautiful Island), Isola dei Pescatori, and Isola Madre (Mother Island) is world-famous for its dramatic palaces and spectacular, fragrant gardens. **Isola Bella** is the closest island to dei Pescatori—be sure to allow enough time to visit its sumptuous palace and glorious terraced gardens before returning to the mainland.

NOTE: If your next destination is Switzerland, then it is time to leave Italy by heading north in the direction of **Domodossola**. You used to be able to drive your car onto a train and ride through the Simplon Tunnel. However, the trains no longer carry cars—so you need to drive over the Simplon Pass and on into Brig, Switzerland.

From Isola Bella, take the ferry back to pick up your car and drive south to the main freeway and head west toward Turin. Before reaching Turin watch for the signs and take the branch of the expressway heading toward Aosta. When you come to Verres, leave the highway and take the small road north to Champoluc, an hour's drive. The road follows

Villa Anna Maria, Champoluc

the Evancon River as it cuts its path through the mountains. At first the valley is quite steep and narrow and then opens up into wide meadows lazily stretching out on both sides of the river. In early summer the meadows are truly lovely, blanketed in brilliantly colored wildflowers.

Just before the road leaves **Champoluc**, you see a marker for the Anna Maria. At this sign turn to the right and follow the road for a very short drive up the hill until you see the small chalet-style inn. It is beautifully located amid pine trees and has views in every direction of the spectacular mountains. The **Villa Anna Maria**'s dining room is cozy and inviting with gay red-checked curtains at the windows and rustic Alpine-style carved wooden chairs. The bedrooms, although small, all have private bathrooms and are very appealing with paneled walls and a country look.

When it is time to leave Champoluc, if you want to travel into Switzerland you must drive back to the main expressway and head west. In about half an hour you will come to Aosta, at which point you can leave the expressway for the road leading north to the **Gran San Bernardo Tunnel** and into Switzerland's Rhône Valley. Or, by continuing on the expressway west through the village of Courmayeur, you arrive at the **Mont Blanc Tunnel**, which delivers you briefly into France and then on to Geneva via the main highway.

Of course, by taking the short drive to Milan you can easily tie in with another Italian tour suggested in this guide.

Rome to Milan
via the Italian Riviera

MILAN

Pavia Carthusian
Monastery

Genoa

Chiavari a Leivi

Camogli

Sestri Levante

Portofino

Levanto

Monterosso al Mare

Carrara

Cinque Terre

Pietrasanta

La Spezia

Lucca

Tellaro

Pisa

Livorno

FLORENCE

Finale Ligure

Campiglia Marittima

Grosetto

Scansano

Elba

Orbetello
Peninsula

Orbetello

Farnese

Porto San Stefano

Porto Ercole

Tarquinia

Bracciano

Civitavecchia

Anguillara Sabazia

Ladispoli

Tivoli

ROME

Rome

● Overnight stops

* Suggested alternate hotels

○ Sightseeing

-- Itinerary route

Rome to Milan via the Italian Riviera

Vernazza, Cinque Terre

This itinerary traces the western coast of Italy as far as Genoa before heading north for the final stretch to Milan. To break the journey, the first stop is Orbetello, a picturesque peninsula-like island joined to the coast by three spits of land. The next destination is Cinque Terre—a string of five tiny fishing villages along the coast that have not yet fallen prey to a great influx of tourists. As you follow the highway up the coast, it becomes a masterpiece of engineering—bridging deep ravines and tunneling in and out of the cliffs, which rise steeply from the sea. Along the way you pass picturesque small towns snuggled into small coves. Then it's on to Portofino—one of Italy's most treasured jewels—before the final destination of Milan.

ORIGINATING CITY   ROME

This itinerary begins in **Rome**, a perfect introduction to Italy. The joy of Rome is that every place you walk you are immersed in history. The whole of the city is a virtual museum—buildings over 2,000 years old, ancient fountains designed by the world's greatest masters, the Vatican, Renaissance paintings that have never been surpassed in beauty. On pages 47–52 we give just a few suggestions of places you must not miss, but we only touch on the wealth of sightseeing possibilities. Buy a guidebook at one of the many bookstores or magazine stands to plan what you most want to see and do. Also buy a detailed city map and mark each day's excursion. Most places are within walking distance—if not, consider taking the subway, which stretches to most of the major points of interest.

Rome has a rich selection of places to stay. We suggest that you browse through the hotel section in the back of this guide where we describe hotels we think are especially appealing. Make a reservation in advance because space is very tight—particularly during the busy summer season. Plan to stay in Rome for several days. When you are saturated with the overwhelming number of sights and are ready to continue your journey, ask someone at the hotel desk to mark your map for the best route out of town.

DESTINATION I   ORBETELLO–PORTO ERCOLE

From Rome follow the well-marked signs for the expressway heading west toward the Leonardo da Vinci airport. About 5 kilometers before you arrive at the airport, head north on A12 in the direction of **Civitavecchia**.

About 13 kilometers beyond the Civitavecchia Nord exit, turn right (east) on S1 BIS in the direction of Viterbo. Continue a bit more than 3 kilometers and turn left toward **Tarquinia**, an Etruscan city that historians date back to the 12th century B.C. Even if it is not quite that old, archaeologists have established that people were living here as early as 600 years before Christ. Before you reach Tarquinia, you will see on your right an open-air **museum**—an open field dotted with Etruscan tombs. The site is not well-marked, but your clue will be tour buses lining the road. Park your car, buy a ticket at the gate, and explore the fascinating tombs. There are over a thousand tombs stretching over 5 kilometers, but only a small, select group is open to the public. You can wander at leisure. Each tomb has a sign describing what drawings are found within. You will find a rich treasure trove of paintings depicting the life of the ancient Etruscans, including scenes of hunting, dining, fishing, drinking, and frolicking. All of the burial sites are underground. To access a tomb, you have to climb down a narrow flight of steps and when you reach the bottom, everything is semi-dark. However, when you push a button, the tomb is magically illuminated behind a glass window. Each tomb is individually decorated with paintings that offer a poignant glimpse of life over a thousand years ago. There is no way you can visit all the burial chambers, but one of the most popular is the **Tomb of the Leopards** where there is a well-preserved banquet scene.

After viewing the tombs, ask the attendant at the gate for directions to the **Museo Nazionale Tarquiniese**, which is located in the center of town in the 15th-century **Vitelleschi Palace**. Even if you do not have time to savor all of the beautiful Etruscan vases and handsome carved stone sarcophagi, you must make at least a brief stop to view the astonishing winged horses dramatically displayed in a large room on an upper floor. You will be spellbound by these superb horses on an ornate relief that adorned the altar of the Queen's temple.

After your brush with Etruscan civilization, continue north for approximately 50 kilometers to Scalo/Orbetello where you turn west. The road crosses 6 kilometers of lagoons on a narrow spit of land (going through the town of Orbetello) before reaching the large, bulbous peninsula dominated by Monte Argentario. Turn left when you reach the peninsula (which looks like an island) and continue through the town of **Porto Ercole**, following signs to the exquisite resort of **Il Pellicano**, romantically perched on the cliffs overlooking the sea. If time and pocketbook allow, settle in to relax for a few days in this hideaway of the rich and famous before heading north. Enjoy the romantic setting, the swimming pool, tennis courts, and excellent food. Also explore the small peninsula, admire the many splendid yachts in the harbor at Porto Ercole, then continue on to the picturesque old fishing village of **Porto Santo Stefano**.

NOTE: If the luxurious Il Pellicano exceeds your budget, consider the **Hotel Torre di Cala Piccola**, located across the peninsula from Il Pellicano in Porto Santo Stefano. This is a less expensive hotel with a beautiful clifftop setting overlooking the sea. Or, if you would like to experience the natural, unspoiled beauty of Upper Latium, we highly recommend **Il Voltone**, located near the town of Farnese in an idyllic hamlet that has been converted into a small hotel. It is tucked far up in the hills above the coast next to the Selva del Lamone nature park. Map 10 shows the location of these towns and the hotels are described further on in the book.

DESTINATION II   CINQUE TERRE–LEVANTO

Leaning Tower of Pisa

When it is time to continue, return to S1 and head north on the highway as it follows the coast. Get an early start if you want to stop in Pisa, Lucca, and Carrara along the way.

About 35 kilometers before you come to the large city of Livorno (which you want to avoid at all costs), the road divides. One split goes to Livorno and the other becomes the A12, which heads inland and bypasses the city. The next large town after Livorno is **Pisa**. Exit here and follow signs into the congested center of the old town. There is such a solid mass of tourists during the summer that you can hardly find a place to park close to the Piazza del Duomo, which is dominated by the Pisa's famous tower. The **Leaning Tower** is threatening to topple so it has been strengthened by massive cables that run to counterweights behind the square. Sitting photogenically beside the tower is the **Duomo**, built in marbles of alternating colors.

Even more interesting and not nearly so touristy as Pisa is the extremely picturesque city of **Lucca**, only a few kilometers to the north. Lucca too is an ancient city, even more perfectly preserved than its neighbor, Pisa. Completely surrounding the town is an enormous wall—a wall so wide that it even supports pretty, small parks and a road that runs along the top. Lucca is truly a jewel. Take time to wander through her maze of narrow streets, admiring imposing mansions and colorful squares. *NOTE*: If you want to spend the night right in this fascinating city, we recommend two charming small hotels, the **Palazzo Alexander** and the **Albergo San Martino**.

Leaving Lucca, return to the expressway A12 and head north to Genoa. Along the way you see what appears to be a glacier shimmering white in the mountains that rise in the distance to the right of the highway. This is not snow at all, but rather your introduction to the renowned white Italian marble. Unless it is too late in the day, detour to visit some of the marble quarries. Exit the highway at Carrara and take the winding drive up into the hills to the ancient village of **Colonnata**—famous through the ages for its marvelous white marble. As you wander this tiny town you're following the footsteps of Michelangelo, who used to come to here to choose huge blocks of marble from which to carve his masterpieces.

Take the small road from Carrara west to join the A12 and continue north for an entirely different kind of experience—exploring the lovely, remote coast called **Cinque Terre**. This area is quickly becoming linked with civilization, so do not tarry if you love the thrill of discovering old fishing villages still untouched by time. En route you come to an exit to **La Spezia**, a large seaport and navy town. If you want to take a detour, go to La Spezia and from there take the short drive to the tip of the peninsula south of town to visit the old fishing village of **Portovenere**, which clings to the steep rocks rising from the sea. This was one of Lord Byron's haunts when he lived across the bay at **San Terenzo**. After Portovenere, return to the A12 and continue north.

Along the Cinque Terre there used to be five completely isolated fishing villages dotted along the coast between La Spezia to the south and Levanto to the north. First only a footpath connected these hamlets, then a train was installed, and now civilization is encroaching, with a road under construction which will open them up to greater commercialism. Three of these little villages, (**Riomaggiore**, **Monterosso**, and **Manarola**) are already accessible by road. Still completely cut off from car traffic are the colorful fishing hamlets of **Vernazza** and **Corniglia**.

If you want to spend the night in one of the villages along the Cinque Terre, **Monterosso al Mare** offers the best selection of accommodations and we recommend three places to stay. These are not super deluxe (two are very simple) but all make good bases for exploring the Cinque Terre. Read the descriptions of these hotels in the back of the book to see which one most appeals to you.

To reach Monterosso al Mare, exit the A12 at Carrodano and follow signs to Levanto. From Levanto take the road up the hill at the south end of town, signposted Monterosso al Mare. If you have reservations at either the **Hotel Porto Roca**

Cinque Terre

or the **Hotel Pasquale**, just after the road goes through the tunnel, turn right at the sign to Monterosso Fegina and go down the hill for 5 kilometers to Monterosso where there is a large public car park. If you are staying at the **Hotel Villa Steno**, the driving directions are different because there is parking space for a few cars at the hotel (a rare commodity in this town). In this case, ask Matteo, the owner, to send you detailed instructions on how to drive directly to his hotel. A massive rock formation jutting into the sea divides Monterosso into two distinct sections that are connected by a train tunnel. You can walk between the two parts of town, but you cannot drive. So if you leave your car in the public parking area, which is located in the "north" village, you will need to take a taxi to the hotels we recommend, which are located in the "south" village.

You do not need a car to enjoy the Cinque Terre: this is a region that lures those who love to hike and be out of doors. You can explore the villages by train, boat, or walking: the most fun is to combine all three. If you have the time, plan to spend several days in Monterosso. If the weather is pleasant, hike the trail that traces the rocky coast and links the villages, stopping for lunch along the way (one of our favorite restaurants is the Pensione Cecio in Corniglia). After lunch, hop aboard one of the frequent trains (each of the towns has a train station and the schedules are clearly posted) or take one of the ferries (which only operate in the summer season) to return "home." Let your mood and the weather dictate your explorations. Although this is a remote coast, be prepared that you will not be alone: the path along the Cinque Terre is popular and always busy— filled with the holidaymakers who have come to enjoy the natural beauty.

If you have time to see only one of the scenic towns, Vernazza, which clings perilously to a rocky headland above a tiny harbor, is the most picturesque. This colorful jewel has brightly painted fishermen's houses, quaint restaurants, a harbor with small boats bobbing in the clear, turquoise water, and a maze of twisting narrow steps that lead up to the promontory overlooking the village.

DESTINATION III   PORTOFINO

After Cinque Terre, continue north beside the coast. Stop for lunch along the way in **Sestri Levante**, one of the most picturesque coastal villages en route. Continue along the small coastal road that goes through Chiàvari and on to San Margherita where you take the small road south for the short drive to the picture-book village of **Portofino**. This last section of the road, especially in summer, is jammed with traffic, but the prize at the end is worth the trials endured to reach it. Portofino is by no means undiscovered, but is well deserving of its accolades—it is one of the most picturesque tiny harbors in the world.

Portofino

Before you reach Portofino, watch on your right for the sign for the **Hotel Splendido**. From the main road, a small lane winds up the wooded hillside to the magnificent villa-style hotel. Be prepared: the deluxe Splendido is a super-expensive hotel whose prices include breakfast and dinner. But what a glorious setting! The hotel is perched in the hills above Portofino with breathtaking views of the sea and the harbor. A swimming pool and tennis courts nestle below the hotel and enchanting little paths thread their way through the gardens, offering strategically placed benches for quiet moments to savor the stunning view. It is an easy walk into Portofino if you can bear to leave this haven. In 1998 the Splendido opened a "sister" hotel, the delightful **Splendido Mare**, for guests who want to be in the heart of town. *NOTE:* If you are on a tight budget, the **Hotel Eden** (a basic, 12-room hotel in the heart of town) is at the opposite end of the measure for ambiance and luxury, but has a good location and the warmth and caring of a family-owned small hotel.

Portofino is a national treasure—it truly is a jewel. Its tiny harbor is filled with glamorous yachts, small ferries, and colorful fishing boats. Enveloping the harbor are narrow fishermen's cottages, poetically painted in warm tones of sienna, ochre, and pink and all sporting green shutters. Bright flowerboxes accent the windows and the laundry flaps gaily in the breeze. Vivid reflections of these quaint little houses shimmer in the emerald water. In the center of town is a small square, lined with restaurants, which faces the harbor. Forming a backdrop to the town are steep, heavily forested hills, which complete this idyllic scene.

NOTE: While staying in Portofino, if you appreciate gourmet dining, drive south to one of Italy's finest restaurants, the **Ca'Peo**, located in **Chiavari a Leivi**. You must make prior reservations because Franco and his wife, Melly, only take guests who call ahead since the food is specially prepared depending upon how many will be dining: tel: (0185) 31 90 90. The Ca'Peo, whose origins date back to a very old farmhouse, is located high in the hills overlooking the coast. Be forewarned: the meals are VERY expensive. If you want to spend the night, there are moderately priced suites available.

DESTINATION IV   MILAN

When leaving Portofino, return to the A12 highway and continue west for about 30 kilometers to Genoa. As go through the city, watch for the A7 going north to Milan. An interesting detour on the last leg of your journey is the **Pavia Carthusian Monastery** (*Certosa di Pavia*). Probably the simplest way to find it is to watch for the turnoff to Pavia (96 kilometers north of Genoa): take the road east to Pavia and from there go north about 10 kilometers to the monastery. Lavishly built in the 15th century, this splendid monastery is claimed by some to be one of the finest buildings in Italy. (Check carefully the days and hours open—the monastery is usually closed on Mondays and for several hours midday.) The outside of the building is lavishly designed with colorful marble and intricate designs. Inside, the small cloisters are especially charming with 122 arches framed by beautiful terra-cotta moldings. It also has a baroque fountain and several small gardens. Next to the monastery you find the **Palace of the Dukes of Milan**, which is now a museum. After your tour of the monastery it is approximately 26 kilometers farther north to **Milan**.

The outskirts of Milan are not very inviting—you find frustrating traffic and modern commercial buildings. However, the heart of Milan has much to offer. Take time to see Leonardo da Vinci's famous mural, **The Last Supper**, which is once again on view in the church of **Santa Maria delle Grazie** after more than two decades of controversial restoration. (You must have an advance appointment for this—see page 37.) If you enjoy shopping (and Milan has some of the finest shops in Italy), pay a visit to the splendid **Galleria Vittorio Emanuele**, one of the prettiest shopping arcades in the world. Even if you are not a shopper, you should take time to browse. Located between Milan's other two sightseeing stars, the Duomo and La Scala, the Galleria Vittorio Emanuele is the forerunner of the modern shopping mall, but with much more pizzazz. In this Victorian-era fantasy there are two main, intersecting wings, both completely domed with intricately patterned glass. Along the pedestrian-only arcades you find many boutiques and colorful restaurants with outside tables.

After a stroll through the arcade, you emerge into an imposing square dominated by the truly spectacular **Duomo**, the third-largest cathedral in the world. Not only is the size impressive, but this sensational cathedral has a multi-colored marble façade enhanced by over 100 slender spires piercing the sky. This spectacular cathedral faces onto an enormous square lined with cafés, office buildings, and shops. Stop to have a snack at one of the outdoor restaurants—you could sit for hours just watching the people go by.

Another site not to be missed is Milan's opera house. Every opera buff knows about **La Scala**. Even if you have not been an opera enthusiast in the past, if you are going to be in Milan during the opera season (which usually runs from December to May), write ahead and try to get tickets. The theater is stunning and an experience not to be

La Scala, Milan

missed. When it is not opera season, there is usually some other performance or concert featured. If you haven't purchased seats in advance, you can try to buy them on the day of the performance (the ticket office is located down a flight of stairs to the left of the opera house).

Milan offers a large selection of places to stay. If you want to splurge, the **Four Seasons Hotel Milano** is truly a superstar. Built within the walls of a 15th-century convent, the Four Seasons is just about as luxurious as you can get, offering every possible amenity. More in the tradition of old-world opulence is another gem, the deluxe **Grand Hotel et de Milan**. We also recommend several other hotels in Milan that are very nice and less expensive, such as the **Hotel de la Ville** and the **Antica Locanda dei Mercanti**.

Highlights of
Southern Italy

ROME

Anzio
Nettuno

Abbey of
Monte Cassino

Trani

Monopoli

Bari

Savelletri di
Fasano

Castel del Monte

Naples

Pumpeii

Salerno

Matera

Alberobello

to Corfu-Greece

Sorrento
Capri

Positano
Amalfi
Ravello

Potenza

Taranto

Brindisi

Paestum
Acquafredda

Marina di Pulsano

Santa Maria
di Castellabate

Maratea

Sibari

● Overnight stops

✳ Suggested alternate hotels

○ Sightseeing

▪▪▪ Itinerary route

⋯⋯ Suggested sidetrips

Cittadella del
Capo-Bonifati

Tropea

Messina

PALERMO

Villa San Giovanni

Erice

Trapani

Cefalu

Taormina

Marsala

Gangivecchio

Selinunte

Enna

Catania

Agrigento

Piazza
Armerina

Syracuse

Marina di Ragusa

Rome

Highlights of Southern Italy

Amalfi Coast

Having visited the justifiably famous trio of Rome, Florence, and Venice, many tourists think that they have seen Italy. Memories of childhood history lessons vaguely call forth such names as Pompeii, Herculaneum, and Paestum, yet, all too frequently, the urge to visit these jewels is lost in the misconception that southern Italy is an uninteresting destination. What a mistake! Southern Italy has fascinating archaeological sites, gorgeous coastlines, medieval walled villages, beautiful sand beaches, marvelous hilltowns, and some of the most unusual sights in Italy. Many visitors who venture south from Rome are amazed to discover that the Emerald Grotto on the Amalfi Coast rivals the Blue Grotto of Capri and that the Greek ruins of Paestum outshine many found in Greece, and they are haunted by the mysterious town of Alberobello.

Therefore, for those of you who have already seen the fantastic highlights of northern Italy, we take pleasure in presenting to you the best of southern Italy. This itinerary makes a circle of the south in order to suit the travel needs of a wide selection of tourists. Follow the entire route or select the portion best for you since this itinerary is particularly suitable for the traveler who wants to take only a segment. For instance, the journey from Rome to Brindisi is a favorite one for the lucky tourists on their way to Greece, while the west coast is a popular drive for the tourist who wants to visit Sicily and then return to Rome by air or ferry. Most popular of all is the segment from Rome to the Amalfi Drive. This itinerary allows you to custom-tailor your journey and gives you tantalizing sightseeing along the way.

ORIGINATING CITY ROME

Rome is a most convenient starting point to begin a tour of southern Italy, since its airport is the destination of planes from all over the world. In Rome you can immerse yourself in a wealth of history, art, architecture, museums, and monuments—and build a foundation for the sights that will be encountered on your journey southward. See pages 47–52 for suggestions of what to see and do in Rome.

There is a wide selection of accommodations in Rome in various price categories and locations. Choose the hotel that best suits your personality and budget from the hotel description section in the back of this guide. You will find that Rome has many excellent hotels and, even though the city is large, most of the hotels are still within walking distance of both shopping and sightseeing highlights. If you do not like to walk, ask the concierge at your desk to call you a taxi or direct you to the nearest subway station. Rome's main subway line stretches across the city—conveniently connecting most of the places of interest for the tourist.

When leaving the city by car, bear in mind that Rome always has a monumental traffic problem. Within the city look for strategically placed signs indicating that there is an expressway ahead. It might be quite a distance, but be patient as these signs lead you to the outskirts of Rome to the highway that makes a ring around the city with various spokes going off to different destinations. Follow the ring and take the exit for the A2, the expressway heading south toward Naples. Continue south for approximately 128 kilometers to the exit for **Cassino** where you leave the expressway. Actually, you can spot your destination from several kilometers away—the **Abbey of Monte Cassino** crowns the top of a large mountain to the left of the highway as you drive south. The road that winds up to the summit of the mountain to the Abbey is clearly marked about midway through Cassino. This abbey, founded by St. Benedict in 529 A.D., is extremely interesting both religiously and historically. For war historians it brings back many battle memories—this is where the Germans staunchly held out against the Allied forces for almost a year in World War II. When the mountain was finally conquered in May 1944, it opened the way for the Allies to finally move into Rome. As you read your history books, it seems strange that one fort could hold out for so long, but when you see the abbey you understand: it is an enormous building on the crest of a precipitous mountain. In the siege the abbey was almost destroyed, but it has been rebuilt according to the original plans.

NOTE: For those of you who for sentimental or historical reasons are especially interested in World War II, there is another destination you might well want to visit in this day's journey. **Anzio** is a town on the coast about 56 kilometers south of Rome and could easily be included as a stop before Cassino. It was at Anzio that the British and Americans forces landed in January 1944. The emotional reminder of this terrible battle is a few kilometers south at **Nettuno** where 8,000 white crosses and stars of David range—row after row across the green lawn. There is a circular drive around the beautifully manicured, parklike grounds where you also find a memorial chapel and small war museum. For those who lost family or friends during the invasion, there is an information office to the right as you drive in where you can stop to find out exactly where your loved ones are buried—you will need help because the park is huge.

From Cassino return to the expressway and continue south for about 60 kilometers until you see the sign for **Pompeii**. Unless you have absolutely NO interest in archaeology, you must see the city of your childhood history books. This is where time was frozen in 79 A.D. for the 25,000 people who were smothered by ashes from the eruption of **Mount Vesuvius**. If you are a dedicated student of archaeology, you must also visit the **National Archaeological Museum** in **Naples**, which houses many of the artifacts from Pompeii.

Time slips back 2,000 years and you feel the pulse of how people lived in ancient times as you wander the streets of Pompeii and visit the temples, lovely homes, wine shops, bakeries, and public baths. Many of the private homes have been reconstructed so you can marvel at the pretty inner courtyards, sumptuous dining rooms in Pompeii-red with intricate paintings on the walls, fountains, servants' quarters, bathrooms, and gardens. At the entrance to Pompeii there are souvenir stands where you can purchase a guidebook to the city, or, if you prefer, you can hire a private guide at the entrance. If you have time, visit the nearby ruins of **Herculaneum** which was also buried in the ashes of Vesuvius. See pages 52–53 for additional details about Pompeii.

Leaving Pompeii, head to the coast in the direction of Sorrento where the **Amalfi Drive** begins, tracing one of the most beautiful stretches of shoreline in the world. Be sure to make the journey in daylight because you want to savor every magnificent vista as well as safely negotiate this extremely twisty and precipitous road.

It is hard to recommend our favorite town along the Amalfi Drive since each has its own personality: **Sorrento** is an old fishing town perched on a rocky bluff overlooking the sea. It makes an especially convenient place to stay if you want to make a side trip to Capri by ferry or hydrofoil. **Ravello** is a tiny village tucked high in the hills above the coast with absolutely dazzling views down to the sea. **Positano** is an especially romantic coastal town with a picturesque medley of whitewashed houses terracing down an ever-so-steep embankment to a pebble beach dotted with brightly painted fishing boats. **Amalfi** is a small harbor town nestled in a narrow ravine.

Positano

There are many excellent places to stay along the Amalfi Drive—concentrated in just a few kilometers are some of the most splendid hotels in all of Italy. Study the various choices in Sorrento, Ravello, Amalfi, and Positano in the hotel descriptions section to see what most appeals to you.

From whatever hub you choose as your hotel base, venture out to do some exploring. The traffic during the tourist season is staggering, with buses, trucks, and cars all jockeying for position on the narrow twisting roads. Prepare for much shouting, waving of hands, honking, and general bedlam as long buses inch around the hairpin curves. The best advice is to relax and consider the colorful scene part of the sightseeing. Also, begin your excursions as early in the day as possible to try to avoid the major traffic.

If you are not overnighting in Ravello, you must plan to take the narrow winding road up to this romantic clifftop town. When you arrive, leave your car in one of the designated parking areas, pick up a map at the tourist office, then walk along the well-marked path to the **Villa Rufolo** and the **Villa Cimbrone**—both have beautiful gardens that are open to the public and enchanting views of the Bay of Salerno.

If you are not overnighting in Positano, by all means make this a day's excursion. The town is a photographer's dream—houses painted a dazzling white step down the impossibly steep hillside to a pebble beach lapped by brilliant blue water. To reach the small plaza dominated by a church topped by a colorful mosaic-tiled dome you have to climb one of the town's many staircases. Today Positano attracts artists and tourists from around the world, but in the 16th and 17th centuries it was an important seaport with tall-masted ships bringing in wares from around the world. When steamships came into vogue in the 19th century, Positano's prosperity declined and three-quarters of its population emigrated to the United States.

If you have not been able to include an interlude on **Capri** during your Italian holiday, it is easy to arrange an excursion to this enchanted island as a side trip from the Amalfi Coast. Steamers and hydrofoils depart regularly from Sorrento, Amalfi, and Positano. Ask at the tourist bureau or your hotel for the schedule. *NOTE:* If you have time, you could leave your car in Sorrento and spend several nights on Capri. See pages 54–56 for further information on what to see and do on Capri.

While exploring the Amalfi Coast, visit the **Emerald Grotto**, located between the towns of Amalfi and Positano. After parking, buy a ticket and descend by elevator down the steep cliff to a small rocky terrace. Upon entering the water-filled cave, you're rowed about the grotto in a small boat. Your guide explains how the effect of shimmering green water is created by a secret tunnel allowing sunlight to filter from deep below the surface. The cave is filled with colorful stalactites and stalagmites which further enhance the mysterious mood. There is also a nativity scene below the water which mysteriously appears and then drifts again from view.

DESTINATION II   GULF OF POLICASTRO–MARATEA

When it is time to leave the Amalfi area, take the coastal road south as it twists and turns along the dramatic cliffs toward Salerno. At Salerno, join the expressway A3 for about 19 kilometers until the turnoff for **Paestum**, which is located on a side road about a half-hour drive from the freeway. Magically, when you enter the gates of the ancient city, you enter a peaceful environment of a lovely country meadow dotted with some of the world's best-preserved Greek temples. As you walk along the remains of streets criss-crossing the city, your senses are thrilled by the sound of birds singing and the scent of roses. Before leaving Paestum, stop for a snack at the **Marini Sea Garden**, a former villa set in a garden whose gates open onto the west side of the excavation.

From Paestum return to the A3 and continue south until you come to the Lagonegro Nord-Maratea exit. Do not be tempted by some of the short cuts you see on the map that lead to the coast, but stay on the main road 585. In about 25 kilometers the road comes to the sea where you turn north at Castrocucco, following signs to **Maratea**.

We have three hotel choices in this area, each lovely, each with its special merits. The **Santavenere Hotel** is a superb hotel in a glorious setting overlooking the sea; **La Locanda delle Donne Monache**, housed in an 18th-century convent, is

Maratea, Gulf of Policastro

snuggled in the hills above the quaint town of Maratea; and the **Villa Cheta Elite**, located a short drive north of Maratea in **Acquafredda**, is a moderately priced hotel whose gracious owners welcome guests as friends. If possible, spend several days in Maratea. Not well known to foreigners, this lovely section of coast, known as the **Gulf of Policastro**, is a popular resort area for Italians. The loveliest section of the road is between Maratea and Sapri where the road traces the sea along a high corniche, providing lovely vistas of small coves and rocky promontories. This is not an area for intensive sightseeing, but provides a quiet interlude for several days of relaxation.

DESTINATION III   ALBEROBELLO, MONOPOLI or SAVELLETRI

From the Gulf of Policastro, take road 585 back to the A3 and continue south for about 75 kilometers, turning east at Frascineto/Castrovillari toward the instep of Italy's boot. After about 25 kilometers you near the coast. Here you turn left on 106 to **Taranto**. Stop to see this ancient port, which is connected by a bridge to the modern city. Even if you are not interested in ancient history, it is fun to see the Italian naval ships—giant gray monsters—sitting in the protected harbor.

From Taranto take 172 north and continue on for about 45 kilometers following signs to Alberobello. We suggest three hotels in this area, all conveniently located for sightseeing and relaxing. The first is in Alberobello, which is in the center of the Trulli district. The other two are located near the coast—one in Monopoli and the other close by in Savelletri. If you are staying in **Alberobello**, go into town and follow signs to the **Hotel dei Trulli**. If your chosen destination is **Monopoli** or **Savelletri**, do not go into Alberobello: instead, turn right and follow the ring road around town and continue on for 23 kilometers to Monopoli where you find the **Il Melograno**, a deluxe hotel built within a massive white 17th-century farmhouse. South of Monopoli is Savelletri where, just south of town, you will find **Masseria San Domenico**, a charming, beautifully managed hotel that exudes the character of its heritage, an old farm, built in the Moorish style. All three of the above places to stay are described in the hotel description section.

You are now in the province of **Apulia**, not a well-known destination, but all the more fun to visit because it is off the beaten path. With Monopoli, Alberobello, or Savelletri as your hub, venture out to explore the fascinating sights in the area. Some suggestions are listed below.

Trulli District: Trulli houses (whose origins date back to at least the 13th century) are some of the strangest structures in Italy—circular stone buildings, usually in small clusters, standing crisply white with conical slate roofs and whimsical, twisted chimneys. Outside ladders frequently lead to upper stories. Often several of these houses are joined together to form a larger complex. What a strange and

Trulli Houses, Alberobello

fascinating sight—these beehive-like little houses intertwined with cobbled streets form a jumble of a small village that looks as though it should be inhabited by elves instead of *real* people. The heart of the trulli region is Alberobello where there are so many trulli houses (more than 1,000 along the narrow streets) that the trulli district of town has been declared a national monument.

Trulli houses are not confined just to the town of Alberobello though this is where you find them composing an entire village. In fact, the trulli houses you see outside Alberobello are sometimes more interesting than those in the town itself. As you drive along the small roads, you spot gorgeous villas cleverly converted from trulli houses, which are now obviously the homes of wealthy Italians. Others are now farmhouses with goats munching their lunch in the front yard. Occasionally you spot a charming old trulli home nestled cozily in the center of a vineyard. But most fun of all are the trulli homes of the free spirits: their homes, instead of displaying the typical white exteriors, have been painted a brilliant yellow, pink, or bright green with contrasting shutters.

Grotte di Castellana: As you are exploring the countryside near Alberobello, take the short drive north to see the Castellana Caves—the largest in Italy. In a two-hour tour you see many rooms of richly colored stalagmites and stalactites.

Coastal Villages: Be sure to include in your sightseeing some of the characterful towns along the coast. They look entirely different from the colorful fishing villages in the north of Italy. These are Moorish-looking, with stark-white houses lining narrow, alley-like streets. The Adriatic looks an even deeper blue as it laps against the white buildings, many of which rise from the sea with small windows perched over the water. Besides Monopoli, other coastal towns to see are **Polignano a Mare** and **Trani**.

Castel del Monte: On the same day that you explore the coastal villages, include a visit to the 13th-century Castel del Monte. Built by Emperor Frederick II of Swab, it is somewhat of a mystery, having none of the fortifications usually associated with a medieval castle. Nevertheless, it is dramatic—a huge stone structure crowning the top of a hill with eight circular towers, which stretch 24 meters into the sky. There are stunning views in every direction.

When it is time to leave Apulia, you can breeze back to Rome by an expressway. Or, if your next destination is Greece, it is just a short drive to **Brindisi** where you can board the ferry for Corfu, Igoumenitsa, or Patras. Best of all, if you can extend your holiday in Italy, join the following itinerary, *Exploring the Wonders of Sicily*.

Castel del Monte

Highlights of Southern Italy

Exploring the Wonders of Sicily

- ● Overnight stops
- ✳ Suggested alternate hotels
- ○ Sightseeing
- ▬▬ Itinerary route
- ⋯⋯ Suggested sidetrips
- ▲ Archaeological sites

Exploring the Wonders of Sicily

Greek Theater, Taormina

Sicily, the largest island in the Mediterranean, is a wondrous destination. This triangular hunk of land jutting out from the tip of Italy's toe became the crossroads of the ancient world. Nowhere in your travels can you discover a more diverse archaeological treasure-trove. Stone-Age tools and figures carved in the Grotta di Addaura at Monte Pellegrino indicate people were living in Sicily during the Palaeolithic Age. About 1270 B.C. the island was invaded by a Mediterranean tribe called Siculians, but they were not the only settlers: excavations show the arrival of tribes from Asia. Beginning in the 10th century B.C., pioneering Phoenicians took a fancy to this fertile land, followed later by their descendants, the Carthaginians. However, the true dawn of Sicily's reign of glory began with the colonization by the Greeks whose enormous influence permeates Sicily today.

However, the rich fabric of Sicily's heritage does not end with the Greek influence: later the Romans invaded, then the Normans, then the Spanish, and on and on. This resulting melting pot of cultures makes Sicily an absolute MUST for those who delight in the romance of archaeology. The true magic of Sicily is that most of the ruins are so natural in their setting. Frequently you discover you are alone—the only tourist walking through a field of wildflowers to gaze in awe at an exquisite temple.

As mentioned, the greatest age of glory for Sicily began when the Greeks founded their first colony here about 770 B.C. Apparently these early Greeks left their native country for economic and political reasons, but many were also undoubtedly motivated by pure curiosity—the desire to discover what awaited across the sea. Like the immigrants who came to America, the early settlers wanted a fresh start in a new land and an opportunity to establish a better life for themselves. And they did. Prospering enormously from the richness of the fertile soil, the early Greeks became extremely wealthy. As the *nouveaux riche* tend to do, they flaunted their success, building great cities, elaborate houses, theaters, spas, and stadiums—all bigger and better than those they left at home. Syracuse, the mightiest city in Sicily, eventually became more powerful than Athens. The temples they built surpassed in size and splendor those left in their native land. Not losing their passion for sports, every four years the new colonialists sent their finest athletes back to Greece where they dominated the Olympic games.

ORIGINATING CITY   TAORMINA

Exploring the Wonders of Sicily makes a natural extension from the previous driving tour, *Highlights of Southern Italy*. After ending that itinerary, drive to the tip of Italy's toe and take one of the ferries that cross the narrow channel twice an hour from **Villa San Giovanni** to **Messina**, Sicily. After buying your ticket, go to the indicated lane and wait with all the trucks, campers, and other cars for the signal to drive onto the boat. When on board, you may leave your car and go upstairs to the lounge area where you can buy snacks while traversing the short channel. In 35 minutes the large ferry draws up to the pier in Messina and you drive off to begin your adventures.

If you prefer to fly to Sicily, just reverse this itinerary. Start in Palermo and finish in Taormina. Alternatively, you can take a ferry from Naples to Palermo (a ten-hour journey).

Taormina makes an ideal starting point for your introduction to Sicily. Whereas good hotels are scarce in most of Sicily, there are many to choose from in Taormina. In the heart of town, we recommend the luxury-category, superb **Grand Hotel Timeo & Villa Flora**. If you prefer to isolate yourself a bit from the bustle of tourists and yet be just a quick cable car ride away, the **Villa Sant'Andrea**, nestled just below the village on a beautiful little cove, is outstanding. If you are looking for a more moderately priced hotel, book into the **Hotel Belvedere**, which combines the charm of a family-run hotel with a stunning location overlooking the sea.

Picture-perfect Taormina, with the dramatic peak of **Mont Etna** as a backdrop, hugs the crest of a small peninsula that juts out to the sea. Steep cliffs drop to the unbelievably blue sea. Quaint streets wind through the colorful town where you can browse in the many smart boutiques, sip a cappuccino at a small café, or simply enjoy the incredible view. The scent of oranges is in the air and brilliantly colored bougainvilleas lace the medieval buildings.

However, it is not just the natural beauty of its spectacular setting that makes Taormina so popular. As in all of Sicily, your leisure pleasure is enhanced with fabulous sights to see. The prime archaeological target for your sightseeing is the **Greek Theater**. From the center of town an easy walk up Via Teatro Greco takes you to a magnificent theater dug into the sloping hillside above the town. Built by the Greeks in the 3rd century B.C., the open-air amphitheater has only a token few of its original columns remaining, making the effect even more romantic. As you gaze beyond the rows of seats to the stage below and out to the vivid blue sea beyond, you will think there is no prettier picture in all of Italy.

After visiting the Greek Theater, most of the remainder of your sightseeing can be done informally while strolling through town. First pick up a map and general information at the tourist office in the **Palazzo Corvaia**, a 15th-century palace located on the Piazza Vittorio Emanuele. From the Palazzo Corvaia, continue through town and stop at the 17th-century **St. Giuseppe Church** in Piazza Nove Aprile. As you walk on, be sure to step inside the 13th-century **Cathedral** in the Piazza del Duomo to enjoy the paintings. Farther on you come to the 12th-century **Torre dell'Orologio**, the portal that leads into the oldest and most colorful part of Taormina, **Borgo Medieval**.

DESTINATION I AGRIGENTO

When it is time to leave Taormina, follow the A18 south toward Catania. When you reach Catania, take the A19 west in the direction of Palermo, then when the highway splits (not long after passing Enna), instead of continuing north to Palermo, head southwest in the direction of Caltanissetta and Agrigento. After Caltanissetta, the expressway ends and you are on a two-lane road for the final leg of your journey to Agrigento.

Along the route from Taormina to Agrigento, we recommend two side excursions. It would make your day too long to include them both, but if you get an early start, you will have enough time to squeeze in one of them.

Suggested Side Excursion I: If you are a Greek history buff, take this 128-kilometer detour to see one of the wealthiest, most powerful cities of the ancient Greek Empire (rivaling only Athens in importance). When you reach Catania, don't turn west toward Palermo, but continue south, following signs to **Syracuse**, founded in 734 B.C. by the Corinthians. In the **Archaeological Park** at the edge of town are two theaters—a 6th-century B.C. **Greek Theater** (one of the most magnificently preserved in the world) and the ruins of a 2nd-century A.D. **Roman Amphitheater** (one of the largest arenas the Romans ever built). From the Archaeological Park, skip the sprawling modern city and cross the Ponte Nuovo that spans Syracuse's harbor to **Ortygia**, the island where the

Greeks first founded Syracuse. Visit the two main squares, the beautiful **Piazza del Duomo** where the cathedral (built upon the ancient temple of Minerva) is located and the **Piazza Archimede** enhanced by a baroque fountain. After sightseeing in Syracuse, return to Catania and take A19 west in the direction of Palermo.

Suggested Side Excursion II: If you are a Roman history buff, take this 74-kilometer round-trip excursion to visit the Villa of Casale. En route from Taormina to Agrigento on the A19, turn south at Enna to **Piazza Armerina**. Continue southwest beyond Piazza Armerina for 5 kilometers to your sightseeing target, the **Villa of Casale**, rivaling in splendor the home built by Tiberius on the island of Capri. The foundations of this sumptuous Roman villa were hidden under a blanket of mud for 700 years—not discovered by archaeologists until 1950. The fact that this ostentatious villa was built when the Roman Empire was on the verge of financial ruin is all the more fascinating. You cannot help wondering if the obviously vast expense of its construction was indicative of the flamboyant spending style that led to the collapse of the Roman Empire. Built in the 3rd century A.D., this mansion surely must have belonged to someone of enormous importance—perhaps Emperor Maximilian. The ruins are beautifully displayed in a covered museum with walkways guiding you from one opulent room to the next, each overlooking courtyards. But don't start until you have studied a mockup as you enter showing an artist's rendering of what the huge villa looked like in its prime—a look at this will increase your appreciation of the incredible grandeur of what you will be seeing. In all, the home covers an area almost three times the size of a football field. The outstanding feature is the 3,500 square meters of mosaics that decorated the floors of this splendid villa. Following the home's foundations are 40 mosaic floors of extraordinary quality. These beautifully preserved ancient Roman mosaics are considered the finest in the world. Slip back almost 1,700 years and imagine what life must have been like: the scenes show hunting expeditions, wild animals, mythical sea creatures, chariot races, cupids fishing, slaves working, girls cavorting. Once you have visited this Roman showplace, return north to Enna, then turn west following the route to Agrigento.

The hotels we suggest are not in the center of **Agrigento**, which is a congested, not very pretty city. Instead, follow the signs for the **Valle dei Templi**. This is the archaeological zone where both your sightseeing and our hotel recommendations are located. The name is misleading: the archeological site is actually on a plateau to the west of town—not in a valley at all. If you are lucky enough to get a reservation, go directly to the **Villa Athena** and get settled. The Villa Athena has a somewhat commercial ambiance since, because of

its superb location, it is a favorite luncheon stop for small tour groups. But it is a very pretty villa, has a friendly staff, and a truly incomparable setting—in Agrigento, the Villa Athena is definitely THE place to stay for location. Ask for a room with a view of the archeological zone—these cost a bit more, but are worth it. To wake up in the morning and look across at the sun rising on the Temple of Concordia is certainly the way to begin your day of sightseeing. Just a short drive away from the ruins we also recommend the **Foresteria Baglio della Luna**, another lovely place to stay with prettily decorated rooms, a delightful terrace, and a view of the Valle dei Templi in the distance.

Plan to spend two nights in Agrigento so that you can spend one entire day leisurely seeing the ruins. From the gardens of the Villa Athena, walk down a footpath directly to the area where the temples are located. A wide pedestrian road connects the temples—start at one end and savor the haunting beauty of each. Most of these Doric temples are in ruins, with only enough columns remaining to give you an idea of what they used to be in their glory. The best preserved is the **Temple of Concordia**, which dates back to 440 B.C. See them all: the **Temple of Juno**, the **Temple of Hercules**, the **Temple of Dioscuri**, the **Temple of Jupiter**, and the **Temple of Castor and Pollux**. The setting is beautiful with the sea in the distance and wildflowers in the surrounding fields. It is a thrill to stroll from one temple to the other, marveling at their grandeur and trying to envision what these incredible structures dedicated to Greek gods looked like 2,000 years ago.

To complement your sightseeing at the temples, walk to the **Archaeological Museum** (take the same path as to the temples, but go in the opposite direction). The museum has a mock-up of the Temple of Jupiter, plus many vases and artifacts from the site.

DESTINATION II   ERICE

From Agrigento, continue west on 115 toward Castelvetrano. About 10 kilometers before you arrive in Castelvetrano, turn left on the 115dir toward the coast, signposted to Selinunte. For such major ruins, there is little commercialism. You might well miss the main east entrance on the 115dir—as you drive toward the coast, look for a parking area to the right of the road (if you go under the railroad tracks, you have gone too far).

Park your car in the designated area, buy your ticket, and walk through the tunnel into the enormous field where the remains of the temples of Selinunte lie scattered amongst the wildflowers. In its prime, **Selinunte** was one of the finest cities in Sicily. It met disaster in 407 B.C. when the Carthaginians (it is thought under the command of Hannibal) razed the city, slaughtered 16,000 people, and took thousands into slavery. The giant temples, however, were probably destroyed by earthquake, not by the sword. Here, spread along a huge plateau overlooking the ocean, are the impressive remains of some of the most gigantic temples built by the Greeks. It is staggering to imagine how more than 2,500 years ago they had the skill and technology to lift and piece together these huge blocks of stone weighing over 100 tons each (slaves undoubtedly helped). Of the original seven temples, only one has been reconstructed, but the massive columns lying on the ground indicate the scope and grandeur of what used to be.

From Selinunte, return to the 115, taking the coastal route to Erice. En route, stop for lunch at one of the restaurants along the seafront promenade in **Mazara del Vallo**, an ancient city that was at one time a colony of Selinunte. Browse through the historic center of town to see the beautiful **Piazza della Repubblica** and the **Cathedral**.

The next large town after Mazara del Vallo is **Marsala**, a large city well known throughout the world for its excellent wine. Ironically, it was not an Italian, but an Englishman, named John Woodhouse, who experimented by lacing the native wine with an extra bit of alcohol. Based on Woodhouse's formula, Marsala quickly became one of the staples of the British Navy and a special favorite of Lord Nelson. Along the road between Selinunte and Marsala are various wineries that are open to the public. One of the most popular is the **Florio Winery**—one of the three original companies to produce Marsala.

From Marsala, the road heads north to Trapani. Bypass Trapani and head northeast to **Erice**. Positioned over 750 meters above the coast (about 10 kilometers from Trapani), Erice is a delightful medieval walled town, cooled by breezes from the sea. Park your car and walk through the **Porta Trapani** and up the cobbled street. A few blocks on your right is the **Moderno**, a friendly, well-run small hotel. The Moderno is simple, but very pleasant, and well located in the heart of town, close to restaurants and shopping. There are no deluxe hotels in Erice.

Erice is best discovered by exploring on foot. Narrow cobbled streets and steep stairways form a maze throughout the town, which is so small that you cannot get lost for long. Just wander, discovering tiny churches, picturesque squares, characterful stone houses, arcaded passageways, and shops selling the locally produced handmade carpets with colorful geometric designs. Walk to the **Castello Normanno**, built upon the ruins of the Temple of Venus. From the tower you have a splendid view looking over the town of Trapani and out to the sea.

Erice, Sicily

If you like to get off the beaten path, from Erice drive down to Trapani and take a hydrofoil to the **Egadi Isles**, all less than an hour away. Just a short distance off shore, **Favignana**, the largest of the three islands, was once a great center for tuna. The major cannery was owned by Ignazio Florio (the same Florio who founded the Florio Winery). **Levanzo**, the smallest of the islands, has a very small population due to its lack of fresh water. The island farthest from Trapani, **Maréttimo**, is basically a fishermen's island.

Erice also makes a convenient base for an excursion to **Segesta**. Wind down the hill from Erice and turn left on the A29 going east in the direction of Palermo. Thirty kilometers after getting on the freeway, take the Segesta exit and follow signs for the Segesta archaeological site, located close the highway. Although you have seen many ruins by this stage of your holiday in Sicily, don't miss this one—it is special.

First drive to the designated parking area and walk up the hillside to visit what most experts believe to be the world's finest example of a **Doric temple**. The temple with 36 columns looks much as it must have in 400 B.C. There is no roof—there never was because this isolated temple to some unknown god was never completed. One of the most superb aspects of this temple is its setting—there is nothing to jar the senses. The temple stands alone in a field of wildflowers with great natural beauty all around. Enjoy the romance of this gem at your leisure, then drive down the hill and park your car by the information center where there is a nice restaurant. Eat lunch here and then walk the marked path to see the **Greek Theater**. It is about a kilometer away, but a lovely walk through untouched fields. There are so few signs, you'll wonder if you are going the right way and be tempted to verify your destination with a fellow tourist you pass en route. Again, the location is what makes this theater so special. What an eye the Greeks had for beauty: the stage is set in such a way that the spectators look out across the mountains to the sea. The theater is mostly in ruins, but sit on one of the ancient benches, enjoy the beautiful surroundings, and imagine dramas that took place over 2,000 years ago.

DESTINATION III   PALERMO

From Erice return to the A29 and head east to Palermo. Palermo is a commercial, traffic-congested city, but there are some very interesting places to see both within the city and on its outskirts. Happily, Palermo has a couple of very good places to stay. The deluxe **Villa Igiea Grand Hotel**, located on the edge of the sea on the west edge of town, is expensive, but a welcome oasis of peace and quiet. It has a swimming pool on the bluffs above the sea and even has its own small ancient temple in the garden. If you want to be in the heart of Palermo, within walking distance of all the main sightseeing, the **Centrale Palace Hotel** is a superb choice. *NOTE:* If you want to skip overnighting in Palermo, the following sightseeing suggestions could also be accomplished from Erice.

The most dramatic sightseeing excursion (just 8 kilometers south of Palermo) is to visit **Monreale**, an awesome cathedral built by William II in 1174. It seems that William II was visited in a dream by an angel who told him of a secret treasure, and with his new-found wealth he built Monreale, one of the world's greatest medieval monuments. From the outside, the cathedral doesn't look special, but just wait: the interior is stunning. When you step inside you find 130 panels of shimmering mosaic, illustrating stories from both the Old and the New Testaments. The bronze doors of the cathedral are spectacular, designed by Bonanno Pisano in the 12th century. This is a cathedral not to be missed.

Another sight near Palermo is **Monte Pellegrino**, a 600-meter mountain rising on the west edge of the city. There are several caves in the mountain. The **Grotta di Addaura** is a three-chamber cave with carvings dating to the Palaeolithic Age. Another cave has been transformed into a chapel, the **Sanctuary of Santa Rosalia**, commemorating Santa Rosalia, the niece of King William II, who became a hermit—living and dying in this cave. You need to obtain permission from the National Archaeological Museum in Palermo if you want to visit these caves.

Another recommended side trip from Palermo is to visit the ancient fishing village of **Cefalù**, built on a rocky peninsula about an hour's drive east from Palermo. Not only is this a very colorful fishing village, complete with brightly-hued boats and twisting narrow streets, but there is also a splendid Norman **Cathedral** built by King Roger II in the 12th century in fulfillment of a promise he made to God for sparing his life during a storm at sea.

When you are ready to leave Palermo, there are several choices. You can take one of the many flights from Palermo to Rome, board a ferry to Naples, or complete your circle of Sicily by driving to Messina for the short ferry ride back to the mainland.

Hotel Descriptions

The attractive Palazzo Finati is located right in the heart of medieval Alba, capital of the Langhe area, famous for its production of white truffles and top-notch wines. Charming shops and award-winning restaurants line the cobblestone streets of this well-preserved town, an excellent base for exploring the scenic surrounding countryside and villages. Romano and Nadia have completely restored the early-19th-century palazzo to create a refined, intimate hotel with every possible comfort and amenity. Nadia is most obviously the perfectionist in her acute attention to detail and passion for decorating. World travelers themselves, the couple's desire is to offer guests high standards combined with warm and personalized hospitality and their "hands-on" approach of running the operation personally gives them total control of this objective. Guests walk right into the luminous living room with white sofas and plump armchairs and proceed by elevator up to the bedrooms, all tastefully and classically appointed with the finest fabrics and linens, exquisite bathrooms, parquet floors, Oriental carpets, and occasional contemporary artwork. Some rooms have additional features such as painted decorative ceilings and private terraces facing out to the back. Breakfast or occasional meals and wine tastings are offered in the cellar with its vaulted brick ceiling. Truly delightful. *Directions:* Via Vernazza is around the corner from the main piazza.

PALAZZO FINATI   New
Owners: Romano & Nadia Ferrero
Via Vernazza, 8
Alba (CN) 12051, Italy
Tel: (0173) 36 63 84, Fax: (0173) 44 39 96
6 rooms, Double: €140
Open: all year, Credit cards: all major
In the center of historic Alba, 62 km SE of Torino
Region: Piedmont, Michelin Map: 428
www.karenbrown.com/italyinns/finati.html

There is a fascinating area in southeastern Italy with a collection of strange round white buildings with gray-stone conical-shaped roofs. These ancient houses, which seem to be left over from some Moorish tribe that must have inhabited this part of Italy long ago, are called trulli and are usually seen in groups of two or three throughout the countryside. In the town of Alberobello you will discover a whole village of these whimsical little houses whose jumble of domed roofs, whitewashed walls, and crooked little chimneys creates a most unusual sight. Be sure to stroll through the pedestrian zone of Aberobello, which oozes charm. Fortunately there is a good hotel in the area that is located within walking distance of the center of the trulli village. Not only is its location excellent, but the hotel captures the mood of the area since it is constructed within some of the trulli houses. Small bungalows are scattered around a large parklike area connected by winding pathways under the pine trees. Each bungalow is a suite with a living room with fireplace, one or more bedrooms, and a private patio. The suites are spacious and have attractively tiled bathrooms. The dining rooms and the reception area each occupy their own trulli. Within the grounds are a pool and children's play yard. If you are on your way to Greece, you will find the Hotel dei Trulli a convenient choice: very close to Brindisi and Bari, the two major ferry ports.

HOTEL DEI TRULLI
Manager: Musella Salvatore
Via Cadore, 28
Alberobello (BA) 70011, Italy
Tel: (080) 43 23 555, Fax: (080) 43 23 560
28 rooms, Double: €196–€220*
*Includes breakfast & dinner
Open: all year, Credit cards: all major
68 km NW of Brindisi, 55 km SW of Bari
Region: Apulia, Michelin Map: 431
www.karenbrown.com/italyinns/trulli.html

The choice place to stay in Amalfi is the deluxe Hotel Santa Caterina. It is not in the town center, but since Amalfi has the main highway separating it from the sea, the hotel has a far superior setting—just to the north of town on a cliff rising above the blue Mediterranean. Although larger than most hotels in our guide, the Santa Caterina has the intimacy and warmth of a small hotel. Since 1880 the property has belonged to the Gambardella family who have imbued in their excellent staff the art of making each guest feel special and with over 100 staff members for 62 rooms, you can understand how everyone is properly pampered. The hotel terraces down the hill from the highway to the sea where you find a large saltwater swimming pool. Guestrooms, all individual in decor, are charming, with whitewashed walls, antique furniture accents, and colorful, local, handmade tiles on the floors and in the bathrooms. Many rooms have a balcony with a view to the sea. The main dining room is cheerful, with coved ceiling and sunlight streaming in through walls of glass. However, most guests choose to dine outside on the bougainvillea-bedecked terrace. On a terrace above the pool is a second outdoor restaurant where lunch is served. Almost all of the fruits and vegetables used in the restaurant are freshly gathered from the hotel's own gardens. If you want to splurge, there are several cottages tucked in amongst the lemon orchards.

❄ ⚓ ☕ 🛵 💳 ☎ ♿ 🏋 🍸 P 🍴 🏊 🖼 ⚒ 🐶 🍇

HOTEL SANTA CATERINA
Owner: Gambardella family
S.S. Amalfitana, 9
Amalfi (SA) 84011, Italy
Tel: (089) 87 10 12, Fax: (089) 87 13 51
62 rooms, Double: €330–€990
Open: all year, Credit cards: all major
69 km S of Naples, 24 km N of Salern
Region: Campania, Michelin Map: 431
www.karenbrown.com/italyinns/santacaterina.html

I Due Laghi, named for its position between the two Roman lakes of Bracciano and Martignano, was born 13 years ago with all the characteristics of an agritourism farm—and has remained the only one around Lake Bracciano. It has developed over time into more of a country hotel with all the service and upgraded amenities of a four-star establishment, yet conserves the informal, rustic flavor of a ranch. On 375 acres of cultivated fields and woods, horses and cattle graze and sports activities take center stage, from riding (even drag hunts) and biking to swimming in the pool. In addition, you can enjoy two nearby golf courses, tennis courts, and lake sailing. Its close proximity to Rome and surrounding Etruscan towns makes it a relaxing and peaceful haven for travelers. The equestrian theme prevails in the bar and lounge area and there is a large restaurant, La Posta de'Cavalieri, which has received a Veronelli rating. Matteo and his staff are very attentive to guests' needs and are thorough believers in the beauty that the area offers the more adventurous guest. Bedrooms, rather standard in decor, are all off one wing of the main house with suites that have separate garden entrances. The hotel is an easy 40-minute train ride from Rome. *Directions:* From Rome leave the GRA ring road at exit 5-Cassia Bis and follow it to the Bracciano-Anguillara exit left. Turn left again at the lake and follow signs to I Due Laghi. 49 km from the airport.

COUNTRY RELAIS I DUE LAGHI
Owner: Matteo Marzano
Anguillara Sabazia (RM) 00061, Italy
Tel: (06) 99 60 70 59, Fax: (06) 99 60 70 68
32 rooms, Double: €150–€253
Open: all year, Credit cards: all major
39 km NW of Rome
Region: Lazio, Michelin Map: 430
www.karenbrown.com/italyinns/iduelaghi.html

For those yearning to take a closer look at the architectural marvels of 14th-century master Andrea Palladio, among other treasures of the Veneto region, the Villa Michelangelo could not be a more idyllic base. Scenically positioned in the Berici Hills surrounding historic Vicenza, this very appealing countryside retreat allows easy access to the 23 Palladian palazzos within the city plus 16 country villas scattered about the province. Formerly an 18th-century private residence, the extensive L-shaped main building includes two dining rooms with outdoor porticos serving excellent regional specialties. The very comfortable bedrooms and suites, with many amenities, are classically appointed in soft-peach or celestial-blue hues. Some have beamed ceilings and others have delightfully soothing views over an expansive manicured lawn bordered by a stone wall and balustrade and up to the wooded hillsides. A cleverly designed indoor/outdoor pool, tucked below the lawn level, looks out over this same stunning panorama. Impeccably kept grounds add much to the overall peaceful and romantic ambiance. Attractions abound, including golf, concerts and local festivals, wine estates, jewelry and silversmith artisans, and medieval villages to explore. *Directions:* Exit the A4 at Vicenza Ovest and at the rotonda turn right. At the stop sign head for Arcugnano and continue up through the town. Turn right at the hotel sign onto a narrow road.

VILLA MICHELANGELO   New
Manager: Sebastiano Leder
Via Sacco, 19
Arcugnano (VI) 36057, Italy
Tel: (0444) 55 03 00, Fax: (0444) 55 04 90
52 rooms, Double: €158–€191
Open: all year, Credit cards: all major
4 km S of Vicenza, 60 km W of Venice
Region: Veneto, Michelin Map: 429
www.karenbrown.com/italyinns/michelangelo.html

As the road twists and turns ever further into the wooded hills above Assisi, one can't help wondering what treasure awaits at the trail's end, or if anyone could possibly have found this romantic hideaway before you. What a surprise then to finally turn off the graveled road and discover the parking lot filled with luxury cars. In this glorious hillside setting with its sweeping panorama of wooded hills, worldly cares quickly melt away. Although the hotel is built into a cluster of 10th-century stone houses, all the modern-day luxuries are present including a beautiful swimming pool on the right as you enter and, on a lower terrace, tennis courts. Behind the main building is a separate stone house where you find a most appealing lounge with deep-green sofas and chairs grouped around a giant fireplace. Doors from the lounge lead into an intimate little bar and beyond to a dining room with honey-colored stone walls, beamed ceiling, and terra-cotta floors with tables dressed in the finest of linens. Marvelous meals are served, prepared almost totally from ingredients from the hotel's own farm, which is part of the property. The individually decorated bedrooms sport a rustic, yet elegant, ambiance. *Directions:* From Assisi follow signs toward Gualdo-Tadino and immediately as you leave the town walls of Assisi, watch for and take the road to the right signposted Armenzano. From Armenzano, the hotel is well marked.

ROMANTIK HOTEL "LE SILVE DI ARMENZANO"
Innkeeper: Daniela Taddia family
Localita: Armenzano
Armenzano–Assisi (PG) 06081, Italy
Tel: (075) 80 19 000, Fax: (075) 80 19 005
15 rooms, Double: €166–€199
Open: Mar to mid-Nov, Credit cards: all major
10 km E of Assisi
Region: Umbria, Michelin Map: 430
www.karenbrown.com/italyinns/lesilvediarmenzano.html

Asolo, a jewel of a village tucked into hills northwest of Venice, is one of Italy's best-kept secrets. While once again exploring this magical town, we looked up from the main square and saw the pretty mustard-yellow Albergo al Sole nestled on the hill above us. What a great addition to Asolo! The hotel, which had lain derelict for almost a quarter of a century, was brought to new life after three years of extensive renovation by the De Checchi family. With excellent quality and pretty furnishings throughout, the Albergo al Sole is a terrific value. The guestrooms are spacious and decorated appealingly. The bathrooms too are exceptionally large and prettily tiled. All the rooms have satellite TV and mini bar. If you are on a budget, even the least expensive rooms are very lovely, although they do not have the same view as the more expensive rooms which look out over the village. If you are looking for a truly special room, you need not splurge on a suite, but rather ask for a deluxe double. Our favorite, the Eleonora Duse, is a very pretty corner room decorated with antiques and with large windows overlooking Asolo. The entire hotel follows a basic color scheme that combines the cheerful colors of pretty blues and yellows. As an added bonus the hotel has a fitness center and massage room.

ALBERGO AL SOLE
Manager: Silvia De Checchi
Asolo (TV) 31011, Italy
Tel: (0423) 52 81 11, Fax: (0423) 52 83 99
23 rooms, Double: €198–€248
Open: all year, Credit cards: AX, VS
65 km NW of Venice, 14 km E of Bassano
Region: Veneto, Michelin Map: 429
www.karenbrown.com/italyinns/albergoalsole.html

Asolo is a beautiful medieval town in the low-lying hills northwest of Venice, dominated by castle ruins on the hillside above and filled with charming streets, Gothic arcades, and frescoed façades. Here in this magical town one of our favorite hotels in Italy, the Villa Cipriani, is secreted in a garden just a short stroll from the center of the village. However, since the price tag at the Cipriani does not fit everyone's budget, for those who do not want to splurge on accommodations, a good alternative choice is the Hotel Duse. Its location is superb—right in the very heart of Asolo, surrounded by quaint streets lined with elegant shops. There is a tiny reception lobby leading up to freshly renovated guestrooms. Although small, each room is attractively decorated with a cozy provincial charm. The decor is similar throughout, with nicely framed prints over the beds, a pretty ribbon tied in a bow accenting the frame. The fabric matches the shades on the reading lamps. The cozy mood prevails in each room—only the color scheme varies. Although the rooms are very reasonably priced, they all offer air conditioning, television, direct-dial phone, mini bar, and a spotlessly clean bathroom. The hotel has changed hands since our last visit.

HOTEL DUSE
Manager: Alessandro Zavattiero
Via Browning, 190
Asolo (TV) 31011, Italy
Tel: (0423) 55 241, Fax: (0423) 95 04 04
14 rooms, Double: €95–€130
Open: all year, Credit cards: AX, VS
65 km NW of Venice, 14 km E of Bassano
Region: Veneto, Michelin Map: 429
www.karenbrown.com/italyinns/hotelduse.html

The Villa Cipriani is just as I had envisioned in every dream of Italy: an old villa snuggled on a hill, her softly faded exterior emphasized by dark-green shutters, masses of roses creeping over trellises, columns adorned with vines, lazy views over rolling green hills, faded ocher-colored walls half-hidden by tall cypress trees dotting nearby hilltops, birds singing in the garden, the sentimental rhythmical peal of church bells, a pianist on the terrace playing old love songs, the fragrance of flowers drifting through the air like the finest perfume—perfection. My impression of a romantic paradise must not have been a unique experience for in the garden was a wedding party. A beautiful bride, a handsome groom, they had fallen in love at the Cipriani and had returned with family and friends from the United States for their marriage. The Villa Cipriani is located in Asolo, a charming, small, medieval walled hilltown less than two hours northwest of Venice which has an atmosphere so delightful that Robert Browning chose it as a residence. And the home he chose? The Cipriani. Luckily, his home is now a hotel and you, too, can live for a while in Asolo. Although the Villa Cipriani is a sophisticated, polished hotel, the warmth of reception is as gracious as in a small, family-run inn: all the guests are properly pampered.

VILLA CIPRIANI
Manager: Giulio Polegato
Via Canova, 298
Asolo (TV) 31011, Italy
Tel: (0423) 52 34 11, Fax: (0423) 95 20 95
31 rooms, Double: €300–€455
Open: all year, Credit cards: all major
65 km NW of Venice, 14 km E of Bassano
Region: Veneto, Michelin Map: 429
www.karenbrown.com/italyinns/villacipriani.html

A reader highly recommended La Fortezza, saying that it was a wonderful bargain and that he enjoyed the best meal of his entire trip there. We too were immediately captivated by this simple, charming place to stay in the center of Assisi. The restaurant seems to be the star attraction, with Guglielmo Chiocchetti in the kitchen cooking while his wife, Tina, takes care of the many dinner guests. Their two wonderful sons, Luca and Lorenzo, are also totally involved in this family operation, helping out wherever needed, assisted by Luca's pretty wife who was serving the day we stopped by. Without a doubt, it is the gentle, caring Chiocchetti family with their exceptional warmth that makes La Fortezza so special. Their restaurant's superior food features many Umbrian dishes, served in a cozy dining room with vaulted stone ceiling and wooden chairs painted a cheerful red. The guestrooms, which are an outstanding value, are located on two floors above the restaurant. Although not large, each is spotlessly clean and very tastefully decorated in a simple, country style. The choice bedroom even has its own little terrace. The hotel is hidden up a lane of stone steps at the northeast corner of the Piazza del Comune. There are lots of steps getting to the hotel, but then this is true throughout Assisi, which seems pasted to the side of the hillside. Just remember, bring a small suitcase. Closest parking: Piazza Matteotti.

LA FORTEZZA
Owner: Chiocchetti family
Above NE corner of Piazza del Comune
Assisi (PG) 06081, Italy
Tel: (075) 81 24 18, Fax: (075) 81 98 035
7 rooms, Double: €52–€55*
*Breakfast not included: €7
Closed: Feb, Credit cards: all major
177 km N of Rome, 26 km E of Perugia
Region: Umbria, Michelin Map: 430
www.karenbrown.com/italyinns/lafortezza.html

Il Palazzo, a three-star hotel in the heart of Assisi, offers surprisingly attractive accommodations for a modest price. Built in the 1500s as a palace for the prosperous Bindangoli-Bartocci family, its foundations date back even further. Amazingly, the hotel is still owned by Bartocci descendants. Indications of the palace's rich heritage can still be seen in the many important oil paintings and 18th-century tempera mythical scenes. As you enter off the street there is a simple reception area. Beyond is a large, beamed-ceilinged living room with comfortable sitting areas. The right wing of the palace has been turned into a restaurant serving local dishes. A buffet breakfast is served on the second floor. To reach the bedrooms, you walk out into a central courtyard and then up an exterior steel staircase. I assure you the climb is worthwhile because once you throw open the shutters of your bedroom, you are treated to a stunning panorama of the Umbrian countryside. Definitely splurge—request one of the superior bedrooms, all very spacious and attractively furnished with appealing antiques. One of my favorites, 204, has twin beds with pretty, painted iron headboards. Room 203, a corner room, is also a real winner with a canopy bed—it would be my first choice except that the bathroom is not very large. As with all the hotels in Assisi, take just a small overnight suitcase. Closest parking: Piazza San Francesco.

IL PALAZZO
Manager: Arianna Bartocci Fontana
Via San Francesco, 8
Assisi (PG) 06081, Italy
Tel: (075) 81 68 41 2, Fax: (075) 81 23 70
12 rooms, Double: €100–€120
Dinner by prior request
Closed: mid-Jan to mid-Mar, Credit cards: all major
177 km N of Rome, 26 km E of Perugia
Region: Umbria, Michelin Map: 430
www.karenbrown.com/italyinns/palazzo.html

Assisi is one of our favorite places to stay and our guide can never recommend enough hotels here, so we were delighted to find the Residenza d'Epoca San Crispino, a fabulous, enchanting new hotel. Dating back to the 14th century when it was a religious site for the order of San Crispino, the hotel has been tenderly restored to maintain its rich heritage while adding every comfort for the 21st century. Almost all of the furnishings are beautiful antiques previously used in a nunnery. Throughout this tiny inn you find simple, uncluttered, tasteful decor with white walls, stone floors, crisp white embroidered curtains, bouquets of fresh flowers, and handsome antiques. The mood is set as you enter through very old double doors into a courtyard, bound on one side by the small, 5th-century church of San Biagio. From the courtyard, steps lead up to the foyer where the reception desk is an antique confessional. Accommodations are all suites, varying in size from a studio to a two-bedroom, two-bath apartment. Every room has an armoire, which conceals a small refrigerator, espresso machine, hot plate, dishes, and utensils for preparing light snacks. Fresh rolls are left each day so that guests can prepare breakfast at their leisure. Each room is a dream, but my very favorite is The Moon and The Stars, which not only has a lovely view, but also its own huge private garden. This small hotel is really special and a marvelous value.

RESIDENZA D'EPOCA SAN CRISPINO
Manager: Isabella Fischi
Via San Agnese, 11
Assisi (PG) 06081, Italy
Tel: (075) 81 55 124, Fax: (075) 81 55 124 (9 am to 6 pm)
7 suites, Double: €104- €181*
*Breakfast not included
Open: all year, Credit cards: all major
177 km N of Rome, 26 km E of Perugia
Region: Umbria, Michelin Map: 430
www.karenbrown.com/italyinns/sancrispino.html

For a moderately priced place to stay in the heart of Assisi, the Hotel Umbra is an unbeatable choice. The hotel is located just a few steps down a narrow little alley that leads off the Piazza del Comune, one of the central plazas in town. The entrance is through wrought-iron gates that open to a tiny patio where you are treated to an idyllic oasis with tables set under a trellis covered by vines creating a lacy pattern of shadows. There is a lovely view from this intimate terrace. After passing through the patio, you enter into a lounge/reception area with doors opening into the dining room where very good meals are served. The public rooms have accents of antiques, but have a homey rather than grand ambiance. Steps lead to the simple bedrooms, which are individually decorated and very pleasant. Splurge and ask for a room (such as 34) with a panoramic vista of the Umbrian valley. However, do not be disappointed if one is not available—the rooms (such as 35) overlooking the jumble of tiled roofs are also very nice. If you like small, family-run hotels that are not decorator-perfect in every detail, but offer great heart and hospitality, the Hotel Umbra is an excellent choice. The delightful Alberto Laudenzi family oversees every detail of this small inn and makes guests feel at home. The staff too is extremely gracious and accommodating. The location is absolutely perfect.

HOTEL UMBRA
Owner: Alberto Laudenzi family
Via degli Archi, 6-Piazza del Comune
Assisi (PG) 06081, Italy
Tel: (075) 81 22 40, Fax: (075) 81 36 53
26 rooms, Double: €93–€116
Closed: mid-Jan to mid-Mar, Credit cards: all major
177 km N of Rome, 26 km E of Perugia
Region: Umbria, Michelin Map: 430
www.karenbrown.com/italyinns/hotelumbra.html

If you are flying into or out of Milan, the Locanda dei Mai Intees, a charming, family-run hotel with wonderful, traditional Italian cooking, about half an hour's drive north of Malpensa Airport, makes a delightful choice for a place to spend the night. This small inn is managed by your charming host, Paolo Crosta, whose gracious mother, Carla, oversees the kitchen. Azzate, a town near Lake Varese, seems characterless from the outskirts, but at its historic heart you find a cluster of medieval buildings, including the Locanda dei Mai Intees. The hotel used to be several separate buildings and what was once the village square is now the hotel's courtyard where meals are served in warm weather. On chilly evenings, dinner is served in one of several cozy dining rooms warmed by a roaring fire, where tables are beautifully set with fine linens. The original stone staircase leads up to guestrooms decorated with personal photographs, paintings, and antique furnishings. My favorite, Carla, a larger corner room, has windows on two sides, while Juliet has a cute carved wooden balcony. No matter what room you choose, you will be charmed by the warmth of the Crosta family, who welcome guests as friends. *Directions:* From Malpensa Airport, head north on A7 toward Varese. Exit at Azzate. Do not turn at the Azzate sign, but continue for 3 km and go left at the roundabout. Go 300 meters, turn left at the roundabout, and continue for 200 meters to the hotel.

LOCANDA DEI MAI INTEES   *New*
Manager: Paolo Crosta
Via Nobile Claudio Riva, 2
Azzate (VA) 21022, Italy
Tel: (0332) 45 72 23, Fax: (0332) 45 93 39
13 rooms, Double: €182–€208
Open: all year, Credit cards: all major
54 km NW of Milan, 30 km W of Como
Region: Lombardy, Michelin Map: 428
www.karenbrown.com/italyinns/maiintees.html

If you want to feel like a guest of royalty, shamelessly pampered and enveloped in the lap of luxury, make a reservation at the Villa Dal Pozzo d'Annone. Nestled on a hillside across the road from Lake Maggiore, this splendid mansion offers incredible, sweeping lake and mountain views. Here you will be warmly welcomed as a guest, for this is the private home of the Marchesi Dal Pozzo d'Annone, a member of one of Italy's oldest, most prestigious families, and while many gorgeous properties have been made into deluxe hotels, here you will find that nothing feels contrived. Everything is absolutely authentic, with exquisite antique furniture (some dating back to the 15th century) placed as it has been for generations, museum-quality portraits adorning the walls, and family treasures displayed on desks and tables. There are six large, elegantly furnished guestrooms in the villa, each with satellite TV, mini bar, luxurious bathroom, and direct-dial telephones. Everything is of the finest quality, including the linens, the towels, and the thick bathrobes. The 12-acre estate is like a splendid natural park with woodlands, ponds, gardens, waterfalls, streams, Roman statues, rare trees, and a swimming pool. Since our last visit, 14 new lake-view suites in a charming house in the garden have been added. There is also a new bistro for hotel guests, a private gym, and sauna with Turkish bath. *Directions:* Drive south from Stresa 3 km and the villa is on the right.

VILLA DAL POZZO D'ANNONE
Owner: Marchesi Dal Pozzo d'Annone
S. Strada del Sempione, 5
Belgirate–Lake Maggiore (VB) 28832, Italy
Tel: (0322) 72 55, Fax: (0322) 77 20 21
20 rooms, Double: €260–€620
Open: May to Oct, Credit cards: all major
74 km NW of Milan, 3 km S of Stresa
Region: Piedmont, Michelin Map: 428
www.karenbrown.com/italyinns/villadalpozzo.html

The Hotel Florence offers moderately priced accommodations in the charming ancient port of Bellagio. The location is prime—facing the lake in the heart of the old part of town. Across the road from the hotel, next to the lake, is a romantic, wisteria-covered terrace where meals are served when the weather is balmy. If you are lucky enough to snare a front room with a balcony, you can step out through your French doors and be treated to a splendid view of Lake Como. The lounge, which is just off the reception area, is the oldest part of the building, dating back to the 18th century. Here you find a beamed ceiling and a large fireplace. There is also a bar where jazz sessions are held every Sunday during the summer. A staircase leads to the upper floor where the guest dining room is located—it has no view of the lake, but does have a fireplace to warm the room on chilly days. There is also a gourmet restaurant open to the public. All of the individually decorated guestrooms have antique furnishings, satellite TVs, safety boxes, and hairdryers. Splurge and ask for the corner room with French doors opening onto a large terrace with lounge chairs invitingly set for viewing the lake. The hotel is owned by the Ketzlar family, who are real pros—the inn has been in their family for over 150 years. It is now managed by Freidl Ketzlar, her son, Ronald, and her daughter, Roberta. The family tradition lives on.

HOTEL FLORENCE
Owner: Ketzlar family
Piazza Mazzini, 46
Bellagio–Lake Como (CO) 22021, Italy
Tel: (031) 95 03 42, Fax: (031) 95 17 22
32 rooms, Double: €135–€250
Open: Apr to Oct, Credit cards: all major
Lakefront, 80 km N of Milan, 31 km NE of Como
Region: Lombardy, Michelin Map: 428
www.karenbrown.com/italyinns/hotelflorence.html

The Grand Hotel Villa Serbelloni is certainly appropriately named—it is definitely "grand." Indeed, the public rooms will take your breath away with their intricately frescoed ceilings, gold mirrors, ornate columns, Oriental carpets, gilded chairs, massive chandeliers, and a sweeping marble staircase. The bedrooms too are lovely and the quality throughout is superb: fine percale sheets, soft down pillows, and large towels. The service excels, with a friendly staff eager to please. The parklike grounds, enhanced by colorful beds of well-tended flowers, stretch to the very edge of the lake where a large swimming pool holds center stage. There are two more indoor pools (one for adults and one for children) opening to the garden. In addition, there are two tennis courts, a fitness/beauty center, and a squash court. The hotel has two restaurants, one terrace restaurant and the gourmet Mistral. For sightseeing and shopping, the quaint port of Bellagio is adjacent to the hotel. If you want to explore some of the other charming lakeside villages, the ferry is just steps away, or the concierge can arrange a private boat to pick you up at the hotel's pier. For opulent surroundings and palatial splendor, the Grand Hotel Villa Serbelloni can't be beat. The hotel also has 13 apartments with cooking facilities available, one-week minimum. *Directions:* In the center of Bellagio.

GRAND HOTEL VILLA SERBELLONI
Manager: Giuseppe Spinelli
Bellagio–Lake Como (CO) 22021, Italy
Tel: (031) 95 02 16, Fax: (031) 95 15 29
83 rooms, Double: €296–€738
Open: Mar 27 to Nov 17, Credit cards: all major
80 km N of Milan, 31 km NE of Como
Region: Lombardy, Michelin Map: 428
www.karenbrown.com/italyinns/villaserbelloni.html

I fell instantly in love with La Pergola, a charming hotel nestled in a quaint hamlet just a short walk over the hill from Bellagio. Although it officially rates only one star, in my estimation this romantic hotel deserves far more. Originally a 15th-century convent, it came into Marilena Mazzoni's family in 1732 and has been passed down from generation to generation ever since. The pretty, creamy-yellow building with dark-green shutters snuggles right by the lake and features an enchanting terrace-restaurant at the edge of the water. The charm of the hotel continues within where a fresh, uncluttered, old-world ambiance is displayed throughout. The dining room is most attractive, with fresh white walls accented by copper pots, wooden chairs and tables, and a vaulted ceiling. The spacious guestrooms vary in size but each is decorated with excellent taste using some antique furnishings; all have modern, tiled bathrooms. I was captivated by La Pergola, but Signora Mazzoni was reluctant to have her property in our guide for fear that it would attract the wrong kind of guests—those looking for more amenities than her simple hotel provides. I assured her our readers are different, valuing charm and comfort rather than luxurious amenities. Please convince her that I am telling the truth! *Directions:* Take the road from Como to Bellagio. Just before Bellagio, turn right toward Lecco, then left toward Pescallo. The hotel is in the town plaza.

LA PERGOLA
Owners: Marilena Mazzoni/Livio & Lara Gatti
Piazza del Porto, 4, Pescallo
Bellagio (Pescallo)–Lake Como (CO) 22021, Italy
Tel: (031) 95 02 63, Fax: (031) 95 02 53
11 rooms, Double: €90–€110
Open: all year
80 km N of Milan, 31 km NE of Como
Region: Lombardy, Michelin Map: 428
www.karenbrown.com/italyinns/lapergola.html

L'Orto degli Angeli is a rare jewel. Located in the historic center of Bevagna (a small, picture-perfect walled village of Roman origin), this intimate inn exudes the genuine warmth of a private home, yet offers the comfort and sophistication of a fine hotel. The handsome stone house has been in the family of your gracious host, Francesco Antonini, since 1788. He and his sweet wife, Tiziana, welcome guests with such a gentle kindness that you will be immediately captivated by their charm. On the first floor is a pretty breakfast room for guests and an outstanding restaurant (built upon the ruins of a Roman temple), which is as cozy as can be with deep-yellow walls, beamed ceiling, soft lighting, and cheerful blue chairs. An impressive staircase leads up to the guest lounge, which has a stunning frescoed ceiling and comfortable sofa and chairs grouped around an immense stone fireplace. All of the individually decorated guestrooms have pretty, tiled bathrooms, some antique furnishings, and color-coordinating fabrics on the bedspreads and curtains. Many of the rooms overlook a central garden, built upon an old Roman theater. Bevagna is rich in historical importance—don't miss the stunning little 19th-century opera house, the well-preserved mosaics in the Roman baths, and the many picturesque churches. *Directions:* From Perugia take 75 to Assisi-Foligno. Exit to the 316 to Bevagna and look for L'Orto degli Angeli signs.

❄ ☕ ♨ CREDIT ☎ 🐕 🧍 🚶 🏇 ▼ 🍴 🚭 🍇

L'ORTO DEGLI ANGELI
Owners: Tiziana & Francesco Antonini
Via Dante Alighieri, 1
Bevagna (PG) 06031, Italy
Tel: (0742) 36 01 30, Fax: (0742) 36 17 56
9 rooms, Double: €130–€230
Closed: Jan to Apr, Credit cards: all major
25 km S of Assisi
Region: Umbria, Michelin Map: 430
www.karenbrown.com/italyinns/lortodegliangeli.html

Although surrounded by a sprawling, uninteresting concrete metropolis, the center of Bologna shelters a fascinating maze of ancient twisting streets, arcaded passageways, marvelous shopping under porticoed walkways, and some of the best food in all of Italy. The Corona d'Oro, ideally located in the heart of the medieval quarter, is a small, well-managed hotel whose elegantly designed construction conserves architectural elements of various periods. In the inner courtyard (covered over with a skylight that rolls back to allow the room to return to its original open-air status) you can admire a portico that dates back to the 14th century. The hall and stairwell, exquisitely done in the Liberty style of the early 1900s, lead up to the bedrooms, which are individually decorated, mostly with modern furnishings, but with a touch of the traditional in the sedate color schemes and prints nicely displayed on the walls. Some of the rooms have recessed block-panel ceilings with paintings of coats of arms and landscapes dating back to the 15th and 16th centuries. The hotel does not charge a premium for the few rooms that have small balconies or terraces. *Directions:* Located on a small side street just a few blocks from the large, central plaza. The hotel is very difficult to drive to because of one-way streets. The best bet is to arrive by train and take a cab. If driving, ask the hotel for detailed directions. Good luck.

※ ☛ ▭ ☎ 🐕 👫 Y P 👤

HOTEL CORONA D'ORO 1890
Manager: Mauro Orsi
Via Oberdan, 12
Bologna 40126, Italy
Tel: (051) 23 64 56, Fax: (051) 26 26 79
35 rooms, Double: €238–€298
Closed: Aug, Credit cards: all major
In the heart of Bologna
Region: Emilia-Romagna, Michelin Maps: 429, 430
www.karenbrown.com/italyinns/coronadoro.html

The Villa Clementina is a gem of a small hotel, romantically secreted behind high walls. It is not until the green gates swing slowly open that the stunning gardens and charming inn come magically into view. This gorgeous property was once the home of a famous artist, Lorenzo Vespignani, and your enchanting young host, Dimitri Bonnetti, is also a well-known painter and studied under Vespignani. Today Dimitri uses the same light-filled studio that was once his mentor's. However, one of his greatest masterpieces isn't on canvas—it is the Villa Clementina. The property is truly a work of art: each room has hand-painted frescoed walls, lamps and beds made by Dimitri, furniture placed in perfect positions, handsome fabrics, and quality in every detail. My favorite guestroom, Romana, is a particularly spacious room with a fireplace and replicas of ancient Roman frescoes enhancing the walls. The inn is built within several houses nestled on terraces that step down a gentle hill. The grounds are like a beautiful park, with many exotic trees and perfectly manicured gardens filled with the fragrance of jasmine and the sweet song of birds. On one of the terraces there is a charming restaurant, on another a large swimming pool, and on the lowest level, a clay tennis court. The Villa Clementina's location is superb: it is within an easy drive of the Rome airport and about a half-hour train ride into the heart of Rome.

HOTEL VILLA CLEMENTINA
Owner: Dimitri Bonetti
Via Traversa Quarto del Lago, 12
Bracciano (RM) 00062, Italy
Tel: (06) 99 86 268, Fax: (06) 99 86 268
7 rooms, Double: €130–€260
Dinner by request
Open: Apr to Nov (or by request), Credit cards: all major
30 km NW of Rome
Region: Lazio, Michelin Map: 430
www.karenbrown.com/italyinns/villaclementina.html

In 1550, King John of Portugal decided to give a "little" gift to the Emperor Ferdinand of Austria, so he purchased an elephant in India, shipped it to Genoa, then planned to walk it to Austria. This giant beast grew weary about the time it reached Bressanone and was stabled for two weeks at the Am Hohen Feld Inn. Young and old came from far and wide to see this impromptu circus. The proprietor of the Am Hohen Feld was obviously a master at marketing: to maintain the fame of his establishment, he promptly renamed his hotel—you guessed it—the Elephant. A picture of our friend the elephant was painted on the front of the building to commemorate the sensational event. But even without an elephant story this hotel is a winner with its old-fashioned charm. The sitting room, hallways, and dining rooms (three cozy rooms) incorporate antiques, museum-quality paintings, and magnificent paneling. The Elephant is also well known for its good food— fresh fruits come from the adjacent walled garden where you also find the swimming pool and an old home that has been converted into very nice bedrooms. I particularly liked our room 12 for its spaciousness, room 11 for its corner location, and room 29 for its comfortable decor and balcony. *Directions:* Leave the autostrada at Bressanone and follow the main road through town. The hotel is well signposted in the quiet pedestrian zone.

HOTEL ELEPHANT
Manager: Elisabeth Heiss
Director: Heinrich Radmüller
Via Rio Bianco, 4
Bressanone (Brixen) (BZ) 39042, Italy
Tel: (0472) 83 27 50, Fax: (0472) 83 65 79
44 rooms, Double: €192–€275
Open: Mar to Nov & Christmas, Credit cards: all major
40 km NE of Bolzano, near Brenner Pass
Region: Trentino-Alto Adige, Michelin Map: 429
www.karenbrown.com/italyinns/elephant.html

Hotel Hermitage is our recommendation for the best accommodations in Breuil Cervinia, well known throughout the world for its fine skiing. Its mighty mountains back right up to the Matterhorn and skiers can ski into Switzerland and have lunch in Zermatt. Summer is also a glorious time of year here, with fabulous hiking trails. Most of the hotels in town are high-rise buildings without much style or charm but happily this is not the case with the Hermitage. The setting is excellent: the hotel is snuggled on the side of the mountain, looking over the village below to incredible mountain peaks across the narrow valley. Although not an old building, it is constructed in the traditional chalet style seen throughout the region. The sturdy stone-and-wood façade, enhanced in summer with balconies laden with colorful geraniums, presents an appealing first impression. Inside, the decor is filled with old-world charm. The walls are paneled with blond wood that came from a 17th-century mountain chalet. There are many antiques and bouquets of fresh flowers throughout to further enhance the cozy mountain ambiance. The guestrooms, too, are charming and each has a balcony capturing a view of the mountains. The final touch of perfection for the Hotel Hermitage is that it is owned and managed by the gracious Neyroz family. *Directions:* From the A5, exit at Chatillon and follow signs to Breuil Cervinia. The hotel is signposted in the village.

HOTEL HERMITAGE
Owner: Corrado Neyroz
Breuil Cervinia (AO) 11021, Italy
Tel: (0166) 94 89 98, Fax: (0166) 94 90 32
40 rooms, Double: €300–€1200
Closed: May to Jul & Sep to Dec, Credit cards: all major
55 km NE of Aosta, 187 km NW of Milan
Region: Valle d'Aosta, Michelin Map: 428
Relais & Châteaux
www.karenbrown.com/italyinns/hotelhermitage.html

If you are captivated by nature at its finest, then you must detour to the tiny Relais Torre Pratesi. Stop for a few days to refresh your soul, become acquainted with the gentle kindness of Letty and Nerio Raccagni, dine memorably on food from the farm, and sleep in lovely, peaceful surroundings. The Relais Torre Pratesi, a picturesque, salmon-colored farmhouse with a typical tiled roof, brown shutters, and a sturdy, 16th-century stone watchtower, sits serenely in the center of a meadow high on a hilltop. The sweeping views in every direction are breathtaking—gently rolling hills with terraced fields of grapes, pine forests, groves of olive trees, and square patches of manicured fields stretch to the distant mountains. The accomodations are fantastic. The lovingly decorated bedrooms are very large (most are suites) and offer every comfort. The most romantic room is tucked at the top of the tower where small windows on all four walls frame views in every direction like miniature oil paintings. Meals, featuring produce fresh from the farm, are served in a charmingly rustic dining room. The owners, Letty and Nerio Raccagni, speak no English, but their radiantly warm welcome overcomes all language barriers. *Directions:* From A14 take the Faenza exit, following Firenze and Brisighella signs around Faenza. Go through Brisighella to Fognano. At the end of the village, turn right toward Zattaglia and follow signs to Relais Torre Pratesi.

❄ ☕ ☕ 💳 ☎ 🏠 ♿ 🏋 🚶 🚶‍♂️ 🐎 🍷 P 🍽 🏊 🖼 ♿ 🍇

RELAIS TORRE PRATESI
Owners: Letty & Nerio Raccagni
Via Cavina, 11
Brisighella–Cavina (RA) 48013, Italy
Tel: (0546) 845 45, Fax: (0546) 845 58
9 rooms, Double: €150–€180
Open: all year, Credit cards: all major
75 km SE of Bologna
Region: Emilia-Romagna, Michelin Map: 430
www.karenbrown.com/italyinns/torrepratesi.html

The Cenobio dei Dogi was formerly the summer home of the Genoese doges, so it is no wonder that it has such an idyllic location nestled on a small hill that forms one end of Camogli's miniature half-moon bay. From the hotel terrace there is an enchanting view of the tiny cove lined with marvelous narrow old fishermen's cottages painted in all shades of ochres and siennas. The hotel has a very nice swimming pool, as well as a private (though pebbly) beach. Many of the bedrooms have balconies boasting romantic views of this storybook scene. There is a tennis court for tennis buffs, although I cannot imagine anyone wanting to play tennis with all the beautiful walking trails, which make enticing spider-web designs on the peninsula. The Cenobio dei Dogi is a larger hotel than most that appear in this guide, but the hotel possesses a solid, comfortable, no-nonsense kind of charm. Both public and guest rooms have been completely renovated, and they have done a beautiful job. It is not chic in the jet-set style of hotels frequently found on the Riviera, but has a lovely, fresh appeal. If you are enticed by pretty flower gardens and exceptional views, you will certainly like the Cenobio dei Dogi. *Directions:* To reach the hotel, exit the A12 at Recco and follow signs to Camogli. The hotel is located at the east end of town.

HOTEL CENOBIO DEI DOGI
Manager: Mauro Siri
Via Nicolo Cuneo, 34
Camogli (GE) 16032, Italy
Tel: (0185) 72 41, Fax: (0185) 77 27 96
107 rooms, Double: €150–€336
Open: all year, Credit cards: all major
Near Portofino-Italian Riviera, 20 km SE of Genoa
Region: Liguria, Michelin Map: 428
www.karenbrown.com/italyinns/cenobiodeidogi.html

Just when we thought we had seen almost every castle in Italy, another pops up offering hospitality in a private, historic home, enabling the fortunate traveler to personally experience an entirely new dimension of Italian culture and history. The Castello di Magona in Maremma, a lesser-known part of Tuscany opposite Elba, is truly a dream—sumptuous accommodation within the walls of a gray-stone castle dating to the days of Leopoldo II, Grand Duke of Tuscany. Situated atop a hill below the charming village of Campiglia Marittima, the restored home with its turreted tower peeking above the surrounding trees offers six luxurious suites, four double rooms, and the Grand Duke's spacious bedroom. The luminous bedrooms are decorated with exquisite antiques, with every modern amenity including Internet access. Rooms look out onto a lovely garden with access to a shaded swimming pool whose surrounding trees hide the view of a rather drab modern town below. Guests can gaze at 16th-century paintings while relaxing in one of several formal sitting rooms before an enormous fireplace and enjoy a buffet breakfast in the stately dining room. Although containing museum-quality furnishings, the impeccable castle with its earth-tone colors exudes warmth and comfort. *Directions:* Coming from Rome, leave the Aurelia route 1 at Venturina/Campiglia and follow signs through Venturina to Campiglia. The castle is 2 km from Venturina, before Campiglia.

CASTELLO DI MAGONA
Owner: Cesare Merciai
Via Venturina, 27
Campiglia Marittima (LI) 57021, Italy
Tel: (0565) 85 12 35, Fax: (0565) 85 51 27
11 rooms, Double: €284–€625
Meals for hotel guests only
Open: Mar to Nov, Credit cards: all major
252 km NW of Rome, 68 km S of Livorno
Region: Tuscany, Michelin Map: 430
www.karenbrown.com/italyinns/castellodimagona.html

Relais Il Canalicchio is snuggled within a medieval village on a hilltop overlooking a breathtaking vista of vineyards, olive groves, tiny villages, and forested hills that melt into the horizon. Because the hotel occupies almost the entire romantic village, it has secret little terraces and enchanting nooks to explore. The castle dates back to the 13th century and in its excellent restoration, great care was taken to preserve its original architectural features such as terra-cotta floor tiles, beamed ceilings, thick stone walls, massive fireplaces, and arched brick doorways. The ancient Roman fortified walls of the village are incorporated into one side of the hotel and allow for a romantic lush garden that stretches to the edge of the wall and, on a lower terrace, a splendid swimming pool and a panoramic restaurant. Giant terra-cotta pots filled with brilliant red geraniums add color to the immaculately tended grounds. Inside, everything is decorator-perfect with a homelike, comfortable ambiance created by the use of fine antiques and lovely fabrics. The spacious bedrooms have the feel of an English country manor, with pretty floral fabrics, coordinating wallpapers, and accents of antiques. A footbridge takes you to an adjacent building with 16 new deluxe suites, all with private entrances. *Directions:* From Perugia go south on E45 in the direction of Roma/Terni, exit at Ripabianca-Foligno, and follow signs to the hotel.

RELAIS IL CANALICCHIO
Manager: Orfeo Vassallo
Via della Piazza, 4
Canalicchio di Collazone (PG) 06050, Italy
Tel: (075) 87 07 325, Fax: (075) 87 07 296
53 rooms, Double: €155–€279
Open: all year, Credit cards: all major
39 km SW of Assisi, 20 km N of Todi
Region: Umbria, Michelin Map: 430
www.karenbrown.com/italyinns/relaiscanalicchio.html

In 2002 the Gallinotto family had presided over this little lakeside resort just south of the Swiss border for a century. With Maria Carla Gallinotto's presence, and her four children (Felice, Samuele, Annalisa, and Alfredo) working alongside her, you can be certain that you will meet caring family members during your stay. The family is always improving the hotel—one of the wonderful things about returning here on a regular basis is that you can personally check out the most recent changes. Ferries that visit all the delightful resorts and islands of Lake Maggiore leave from the dock in front of the hotel. However, do not confine your explorations to the lake, for the valleys and mountains to the west offer spectacular scenery. On the other hand, the hotel is so delightful that you may wish to limit your excursions to the pool and strolls along the lakeside pedestrian promenade. Lake-facing bedrooms are found on four floors—all are charming. Additional guestrooms look out to the swimming pool, as do ten self-catering apartments that can accommodate from two to four persons (breakfast only, €106). Dinner is served in the lovely lakefront restaurant. *Directions:* Arriving at the lake, drive north along the pedestrian promenade to the hotel. If space is not available next to the hotel, you will be directed to the hotel's parking lot in the village.

CANNERO LAKESIDE HOTEL
Owner: Gallinotto family
Cannero Riviera–Lake Maggiore (VB) 28821, Italy
Tel: (0323) 78 80 46, Fax: (0323) 78 80 48
55 rooms, Double: €126–€238*
*Includes breakfast & dinner
Open: Mar 12 to Nov 3, Credit cards: all major
12 km N of Verbania, 20 km S of Locarno
Region: Piedmont, Michelin Map: 428
www.karenbrown.com/italyinns/cannerolakeside.html

The Morganos are superb hoteliers, maintaining a family tradition that traces back for three generations in Capri, and when I first visited the Casa Morgano, Nicolino Morgano's pretty, young daughter was helping behind the desk, a welcome hint that the hotel business will continue into yet another generation. The brothers currently own the Grand Hotel Quisisana, La Scalinatella, and the Casa Morgano, all fine hotels that feature proudly in our guide. From the Via Tragara, one of Capri's prettiest walkways, a flagstone path, fragrant with honeysuckle, leads you to the entrance of the Casa Morgano. The essence of Capri is captured in the spacious, airy reception hall with its whitewashed walls, bright-yellow sofas, gorgeous blue-and-white-tiled floor, Oriental carpets, and walls of windows. Doors lead out to a terrace where an incredible view is enhance by towering pines. The guestrooms are nestled on various levels of the hotel as it terraces down the hillside. Each is beautifully furnished in color-coordinating drapes and bedspreads. Best of all, each guestroom looks out to the sea and has a balcony or terrace so that you can enjoy the vista to its fullest. Although there is no formal restaurant as such, next to the pool is a bar where refreshing drinks and light lunches are served. Although deluxe, this hotel exudes the character of a small, intimate, family-run establishment.

CASA MORGANO
Owner: Nicolino Morgano
Via Tragara, 6
Capri (NA) 80073, Italy
Tel: (081) 83 70 158, Fax: (081) 83 70 681
28 rooms, Double: €230–€430
Poolside bar for light lunch
Open: mid-Mar to Nov, Credit cards: all major
Island of Capri, ferry from Sorrento or Naples
Region: Campania, Michelin Map: 431
www.karenbrown.com/italyinns/morgano.html

The Grand Quisisana, a stately, elegant hotel, has a superb setting, right in the heart of Capri. You can't miss this handsome building, which is painted a creamy yellow with white trim and has jaunty flags decorating the entrance. It conjures the image of a hideaway for the rich and famous. The women, adorned in jewels and the latest swimming ensembles, lounge in the sun and gossip about current scandals while their husbands (or boyfriends?) sit pool-side drinking Scotch and playing the game of grown boys—discussing their latest business ventures. But it is all great fun and quite in the mood of Capri, which has been a playground for the wealthy since the time of the early Romans. The Grand Quisisana is an imposing hotel with a gorgeous oval pool overlooking the blue Mediterranean. The air of formal elegance appears as soon as you enter the lobby with its marble floors, sumptuous furnishings, Oriental carpets, ornate statues, crystal chandeliers, and beautiful paintings. All the bedrooms are well appointed and the deluxe rooms even have separate his-and-hers half-baths. Room rates include breakfast and lunch or dinner and you can choose from almost anything on the menu. The opulent Grand Hotel Quisisana most definitely provides a setting and atmosphere to reflect the image of, and cater to, their jet-set clientele.

❄ ⌁ ☕ 💳 ☎ ♿ 🍴 @ 🍴 ≈ 🎿 🖼 ⚓

GRAND HOTEL QUISISANA
Manager: Gianfranco Morgano
Via Camerelle, 2
Capri (NA) 80073, Italy
Tel: (081) 83 70 788, Fax: (081) 83 76 080
150 rooms, Double: €260–€760*
*Includes breakfast & lunch or dinner
Open: mid-Mar to Nov, Credit cards: all major
Island of Capri, ferry from Sorrento or Naples
Region: Campania, Michelin Map: 431
www.karenbrown.com/italyinns/quisisana.html

The Hotel Luna savors one of the most beautiful, tranquil locations on the island of Capri. It is just a short walk from the village yet, in atmosphere, it seems a world away from the bustle and noise. The overall mood at the hotel is set by its delightful approach, a covered trellis pathway which in summer is completely shaded by brilliant bougainvillea and grapevines and bordered by flowers: a wonderful introduction to the Hotel Luna and to a restful interlude by the sea. To the left of the path as you approach the hotel, you see the Luna's large swimming pool surrounded by flowers and a view to the sea. The hotel is perched on the cliffs overlooking a spectacular coastline of green hills dropping straight into the sea, from which emerge giant rock formations. On two sides of the hotel there is a terrace with comfortable chairs where guests may enjoy this spectacular view. Just below the terrace is an open-air bar set on a balcony that hangs out over the cliffs with an unsurpassed panorama of the sea. The reception area and the lounges are attractively decorated using a pleasing, fresh color scheme of white, blue, and yellow. The bar is especially appealing with slipcovered chairs that pick up the rich colors in the tiled floors. There are a few antiques around to add charm. The guestrooms are also attractive. If you want to splurge, ask for one of the guestrooms facing the sea—the vista is memorable.

HOTEL LUNA
Manager: Luisa Vuotto
Viale Giacomo Matteotti, 3
Capri (NA) 80073, Italy
Tel: (081) 83 70 433, Fax: (081) 83 77 459
50 rooms, Double: €225–€435
Open: Apr to Oct, Credit cards: all major
Island of Capri, ferry from Sorrento or Naples
Region: Campania, Michelin Map: 431
www.karenbrown.com/italyinns/capriluna.html

Hugging a hillside with a ship's prow position overlooking the sea, the Hotel Punta Tragara is definitely one of Capri's landmarks. Whereas most of the island's villas and hotels have white façades that sparkle in the sunlight, the Hotel Punta Tragara is painted a deep sandy beige, accented by wrought-iron grills, dark-green shutters, and, of course, the profusion of flowers and greenery that make Capri so special. The hotel is reached by a pleasant 15-minute walk from the center of town—a path that dead-ends at the point where the hillside drops steeply down to the sea. Here the picturesque Faraglioni Islands thrust their jagged peaks just below the hotel, affording fabulous views. Perhaps this spectacular setting is what made Eisenhower and Churchill choose the Punta Tragara for accommodation when they visited Capri. There is a certain formality to this small hotel—the staff seems professionally accommodating, but there is not the warmth often found in a small, family-run establishment. Sea chests, paintings of old sailing vessels, aged-bronze divers' helmets, ships' bells, and antique maps create a pleasing, nautical theme. It is not the decor, but rather the setting that makes Hotel Punta Tragara special. Request a deluxe room with a view. However, even if your room is not one of the deluxe category, you can settle by one of the two swimming pools and soak up the sun.

❄ ☕ 💳 ☎ ♿ 🏋 Ψ 🍽 ≈ 🖼

HOTEL PUNTA TRAGARA
Manager: Ceglia Goffredo
Via Tragara, 57
Capri (NA) 80073, Italy
Tel: (081) 83 70 844, Fax: (081) 83 77 790
50 rooms, Double: €352–€434
Open: Easter to Oct, Credit cards: all major
Island of Capri, ferry from Sorrento or Naples
Region: Campania, Michelin Map: 431
www.karenbrown.com/italyinns/tragara.html

La Scalinatella, although with far fewer rooms than its beautiful "big sister", the Grand Hotel Quisisana, radiates the same opulent luxury. A courtyard in front, dotted with small tables and chairs, leads to an imposing glass doorway majestically flanked by two stone lions. There is a slightly Moorish feel to the sparkling white building embellished by a crenellated roof that lends a whimsical, castle-like character. Inside, colorful tiled floors, handsomely framed portraits, and ornate furnishings create the mood of a formal, grand, private home. Snuggled next to the hotel is one of its most outstanding features: an absolutely stunning terrace where, shaded by trees and enhanced by gardens, you find a splendid swimming pool. On this terrace, the heart of the hotel, guests relax on comfortable lounge chairs strategically placed to capture the breathtaking view. You have no need to leave this oasis, for next to the pool is a bar serving drinks and delicious light lunches. La Scalinatella terraces down the hillside, and the guestrooms are staggered on various levels that offer beautiful vistas. All of the attractive bedrooms are tastefully furnished and offer every deluxe amenity. If you are looking for a luxurious, ornate ambiance and yet prefer the intimacy of a small hotel, La Scalinatella might be for you. It is owned by Enrico Morgano, one of the three Morgano brothers whose small deluxe hotels are all stars in Capri.

❄ ⚓ ☕ 📷 ♨ ❢ ⅋ ≈ 🏃 🖼 🍇

LA SCALINATELLA
Owner: Enrico Morgano
Via Tragara, 10
Capri (NA) 80073, Italy
Tel: (081) 83 70 633, Fax: (081) 83 78 291
30 rooms, Double: €380–€530
Poolside bar for light lunch
Open: mid-Mar to Nov
Island of Capri, ferry from Sorrento or Naples
Region: Campania, Michelin Map: 431
www.karenbrown.com/italyinns/scalinatella.html

The Villa Brunella is a tiny jewel located on the picturesque Via Tragara, only a ten-minute walk to the center of town. This romantic hotel, overlooking the Marina Piccola, squeezes the greatest advantage from its narrow, deep lot. It is built on terraces starting at street level where its superb restaurant with a view balcony is located, and steps down the steep hillside to the blue swimming pool. The hotel is run more like a private home than a commercial hotel. The charming owner, Vincenzo Ruggiero (whose father was a fisherman) was born on Capri. He built the villa and named it after his lovely wife Brunella. This is truly a family operation: Vincenzo and Brunella are now ably assisted by their three handsome sons (Massimo Salvatore, and Luigi) and charming daughter (Antonella). The whole family seems to take genuine pleasure in entertaining guests and making them feel welcome. The 20 bedrooms, each with private bath, telephone, mini bar, and air conditioning, are tastefully put together with pretty pink or powder-blue floral bedspreads and matching curtains. The cool ceramic-tiled floors, creamy-white walls, and potted plants add to the charm. Splurge and ask for one of the deluxe-category rooms—these offer dramatic views of the sea and islands from their own private terraces. Simply heavenly. *NOTE:* The setting is spectacular but because the rooms are on a steep hillside, be aware there are many steps.

❄ ⚓ ☎ 🧹 CREDIT ☎ 👥 🍸 🍴 🏊 🖼 🚣

VILLA BRUNELLA
Owners: Brunella & Vincenzo Ruggiero
Via Tragara, 24
Capri (NA) 80073, Italy
Tel: (081) 83 70 122, Fax: (081) 83 70 430
20 rooms, Double: €230–€340
Open: Mar 19 to Nov 6, Credit cards: all major
Island of Capri, ferry from Sorrento or Naples
Region: Campania, Michelin Map: 431
www.karenbrown.com/italyinns/villabrunella.html

If you are approaching Florence from the west, perhaps on your way from Milan, we highly recommend stopping just before you reach Florence at the Paggeria Medicea. The hotel's address is Artimino, but the town is so small that I doubt you will find it on any map. Mark Carmignano on your map instead and when you arrive there, you will find signs to Artimino, only a few minutes' drive farther on. The hotel is cleverly incorporated into what were once the pages' quarters for the adjoining 16th-century Medicea Villa La Ferdinanda. The long, narrow structure has been cleverly restored, preserving the many original chimneys that adorn the heavy, red-tiled roof. An open corridor whose heavily beamed ceiling is supported by a stately row of columns forms a walkway in front of the rooms. All of the guestrooms are simple, but very inviting, with tiled floors, pretty prints on the white walls, hand-loomed-looking white drapes hanging from wooden rods above the windows, and attractive antiques or copies of antiques as accents in each room. There is a snack bar in the same wing as the hotel, but the main restaurant, Biagio Pignatta (which serves simple but delicious Italian cooking), is located in a nearby building which at one time housed the butler for the villa. There is also a small Etruscan museum situated in the vaults of the Medicea Villa La Ferdinanda.

PAGGERIA MEDICEA
Manager: Alessandro Gualtieri
Viale Papa Giovanni XXIII
Carmignano–Artimino (FI) 59015, Italy
Tel: (055) 87 51 41, Fax: (055) 87 51 470
37 rooms, Double: €125–€180
Open: all year, Credit cards: AX, VS
20 km SW of Florence, 15 km S of Prato
Region: Tuscany, Michelin Map: 430
www.karenbrown.com/italyinns/paggeriamedicea.html

The Solarola, a sunny yellow villa, as its name implies, in the flat countryside around Bologna is, in a word, "perfect." Gracious hosts Antonella and Valentino (a renowned architect) took over the vast family property, transforming one of its two turn-of-the-last-century villas into a private home and the other into a guesthouse with five double rooms, a restaurant, living room, billiard room, outdoor gazebo, and beautiful swimming pool. Additional rooms with air conditioning and all amenities were opened after that in the former barn directly in front with downstairs living room and library. Antonella decorated the guest villas to be romantic and refined, yet warm and inviting. Each room is named after a flower and everything—wallpaper, botanical prints, fluffy comforters, motifs on lampshades and bed frames, bouquets, and even room fragrance—conforms to the floral theme. Victoriana abounds in details such as antiques filled with china, lace curtains and doilies, dried-flower bouquets, old family photos, and Tiffany lamps. The real treat at Solarola is the inventive cuisine created by owner-chef Antonella Scardovi who has earned one Michelin star. *Directions:* Exit from autostrada A14 at Castel S. Pietro and turn right towards Medicina for 5 km. Turn right at Via S. Paolo, follow the road to the end then turn right on Via S. Croce to the Solarola.

LOCANDA SOLAROLA
Owners: Antonella Scardovi & Valentino Parmiani
Via San Croce, 5
Castel Guelfo (BO) 40023, Italy
Tel: (0542) 67 01 02, Fax: (0542) 67 02 22
13 rooms, Double: €186–€350
Open: all year, Credit cards: all major
28 km E of Bologna
Region: Emilia-Romagna, Michelin Maps: 429, 430
www.karenbrown.com/italyinns/locandasolarola.html

If your dream is to discover a small luxury hotel in Tuscany that is truly "off the beaten path" look no further—the romantic Locanda Le Piazze is about as remote as you will find. Tucked in the heart of Tuscany's richest wine-growing region, the hotel crowns a gentle hill. In every direction there is nothing but a breathtaking patchwork of vineyards sweeping like the open sea across undulating hills, dotted with enchanting old farmhouses. After three years in which the buildings were totally renovated and a beautiful pool added, the hotel opened to guests in the summer of 1995. It is no wonder the design and decor are in absolutely faultless taste: the owner, Maureen Bonini, has for over 40 years been a design consultant in Florence. All of the hotel's rooms exude sophisticated country elegance. Huge bouquets of fresh flowers highlight white walls, terra-cotta floors, and beamed ceilings. Each of the guestrooms has its own personality, but all exude a similar comfortable, homelike ambiance. The fabrics used throughout are all from Maureen's good friend, Ralph Lauren. The stunning swimming pool, tucked in amongst the vineyards, is reached by a path through fragrant beds of lavender. *Directions:* From Castellina take the road toward Poggibonsi. As you leave Castellina, turn left at the first road, marked to Gagliole, Castellare, and Castagnoli and follow signs to the hotel—a 15-minute drive on a gravel road (ask for directions).

LOCANDA LE PIAZZE
Owner: Maureen Bonini
Manager: Nicoletta Anne Bonini
Le Piazze
Castellina in Chianti (SI) 53011, Italy
Tel: (0577) 74 31 90, Fax: (0577) 74 31 91
20 rooms, Double: €155–€250
Open: Apr to Nov, Credit cards: all major
Midway between Castellina & Poggibonsi
Region: Tuscany, Michelin Map: 430
www.karenbrown.com/italyinns/locandalepiazze.html

The Tenuta di Ricavo is unique—not a hotel at all in the usual connotation, but rather a tiny, very old, Tuscan hamlet with peasants' cottages that have been transformed into delightful guestrooms. The stables are now the dining room and the barn is now the office. Unlike many of the over-renovated hotels in Tuscany where most of what you see is actually new construction, Ricavo is all real. The guestrooms have been lovingly restored to enhance their original rustic charm and are attractively furnished with country antiques. You enter the large property following a lane through a vast pine forest that leads to the cluster of weathered stone cottages, romantically embellished by climbing roses. Flowers are everywhere and in one of the gardens are two swimming pools. Before it became a hotel, the village was the summer-holiday retreat of a Swiss family who, after World War II, transformed their home into a unique, village-style hotel. However, the Tenuta di Ricavo is not for everyone. It is quiet. It is remote. But it is a haven for the traveler for whom a good book, a walk through the forest, and a delicious dinner are fulfillment. Excellent English is spoken—especially by the gracious owner, Christina Lobrano, whose charming husband, Alessandro, is the talented chef. *NOTE:* There is a seven-night minimum during high season. *Directions:* From Castellina, take the road to San Donato. A long way out of town, the hotel is on your right.

❄ ☕ 🆔 ☎ 🏋 🚶 👫 🐎 🍸 P 🍴 🏊 🖼 🍇

ROMANTIK HOTEL TENUTA DI RICAVO
Owners: Christina & Alessandro Lobrano
Castellina in Chianti (SI) 53011, Italy
Tel: (0577) 74 02 21, Fax: (0577) 74 10 14
23 rooms, Double: €200–€370
Open: mid-Mar to mid-Nov, Credit cards: MC, VS
21 km N of Siena on road 22
Region: Tuscany, Michelin Map: 430
www.karenbrown.com/italyinns/tenutadiricavo.html

The Hotel Relais Borgo San Felice, located in the heart of Tuscany, is built within a feudal hamlet consisting of a cluster of stone, ivy-laced buildings linked by quaint cobbled lanes. The various buildings, including a small chapel, have been cleverly converted into reception area, guestrooms, dining rooms, lounges, conference room, and bar. The tiny village is not entirely consecrated to the hotel: local farmers still live in some of the buildings and olive oil and wine are produced. The San Felice wines, produced from grapes grown on the 2,400 surrounding acres, are some of Italy's finest. Although the hotel is secluded deep in the countryside, there is no need for guests to sacrifice any creature comforts. The Borgo San Felice, a member of the prestigious Relais & Châteaux group, is a sophisticated property offering all the amenities and services of a deluxe hotel. Although the façade is rustic, the interior exudes a gracious charm and the guestrooms, which are decorated with soft, pleasing colors, floral fabrics, and many antiques, offer every amenity. When not exploring the wealth of fascinating towns and historic sites round about, guests can relax by a large swimming pool with a view terrace, enjoy a game of tennis, or be pampered at the beauty center. *Directions:* From Florence take S2 south, exiting at Siena north. Follow signs toward Arezzo-Monteaperti to San Felice, which is between the towns of Pianella and Villa a Sesta.

HOTEL RELAIS BORGO SAN FELICE   *New*
Manager: Birgit Fleig
Localita San Felice
Castelnuovo Berardenga (SI) 53019, Italy
Tel: (0577) 39 64, Fax: (0577) 35 90 89
43 rooms, Double: €270–€516
Closed: Nov to Apr, Credit cards: all major
19 km E Siena
Region: Tuscany, Michelin Map: 430
Relais & Châteaux
www.karenbrown.com/italyinns/sanfelice.html

Castelrotto is the loveliest of medieval towns in the western Dolomites. Surrounded by high mountain meadows dotted with chalets and backed by towering mountains, it's a sight to behold. Snuggled in the heart of town, the 14th-century Cavallino d'Oro has a deep-mustard-color façade highlighted by dark-green shutters and flowerboxes overflowing with geraniums. There is an old-world atmosphere throughout this small inn. The guestrooms, some with balconies and mountain views, are individual in decor, and delightfully furnished in a typical Tyrolean style—three rooms with light-pine, four-poster beds are especially pretty. From its beginning the Cavallino has offered accommodations, originally being a coaching station providing food and rooms for weary travelers. This hospitality is certainly ongoing—Susanne and Stefan (both of whom speak excellent English) have now taken over as the third generation of the Urthaler family to run the hotel. Not only do they exude boundless enthusiasm and gracious warmth of welcome, they are also constantly improving their small hotel by incorporating more antiques into the decor and continuously renovating and upgrading. The restaurant has an excellent reputation, with the chef specializing in regional dishes. *Directions:* Exit at Bolzano Nord from the Verona-Brennero autostrada and follow signs for Siusi and Castelrotto. The hotel faces the market square.

HOTEL CAVALLINO D'ORO
Owners: Susanne & Stefan Urthaler
Castelrotto (Kastelruth) (BZ) 39040, Italy
Tel: (0471) 70 63 37, Fax: (0471) 70 71 72
24 rooms, Double: €75–€145
Open: all year, Credit cards: all major
140 km S of Innsbruck, 24 km NE of Bolzano
Region: Trentino-Alto Adige, Michelin Map: 429
www.karenbrown.com/italyinns/hotelcavallinodoro.html

The family-run Relais San Pietro is an absolute dream. It offers the finest quality throughout, gorgeous views, excellent location, spectacular swimming pool, and outstanding cuisine, all at remarkably reasonable prices. This gem of a little hotel has the added benefit of superb hospitality: Luigi Protti, your host, radiates a gentle, old-fashioned, welcoming kindness. Upon retirement he and his wife, Antonietta, decided to move back to the peaceful Tuscan countryside, along with their son, Franco, and his wife, Franca, and open a hotel. They bought a long-neglected farmhouse only a few kilometers from the town where Signora Protti had been born and after two years of restoration, opened it in 1998 as a small, intimate hotel. The interior of the hotel has a refreshing light, uncluttered appeal. All of the original architectural features such as beamed ceilings and beautiful brick archways have been meticulously preserved. Bedrooms feature beautiful wrought-iron headboards, white bedspreads, excellent lighting, doors painted with regional designs, and superb bathrooms. The romantic dining rooms occupy what were formerly the stables. Signora Protti and her daughter-in-law preside over the kitchen and the food is fabulous. *Directions:* From Cortona, go north on 71 toward Arezzo. At Castiglion Fiorentino, turn right toward Città di Castello. After 6 km, turn left at a sign to Polvano. Go up the hill. Relais San Pietro is on the left.

RELAIS SAN PIETRO
Owner: Luigi Protti
Castiglion Fiorentino–Polvano (AR) 52043, Italy
Tel: (0575) 65 01 00, Fax: (0575) 65 02 55
12 rooms, Double: €145–€310
Meals for hotel guests
Closed: Nov 5 to Mar 15, Credit cards: all major
14 km N of Cortona
Region: Tuscany, Michelin Map: 430
www.karenbrown.com/italyinns/relaissanpietro.html

A book on the most charming hotels in Italy would not be complete without including one of the world's premier hotels, the Villa d'Este. Originally the hotel was a private villa built in 1568 by Cardinal Tolomeo Gallio. He obviously had elegant taste, for the Villa d'Este is truly a fantasy come true. From the moment you step into the vast lobby with its sweeping staircase, huge Venetian-glass chandeliers, marble columns, statues, and soaring ceiling, you will feel you are entering a dream. The bedrooms are all elegantly furnished—no two are alike, but all are beautiful with color-coordinated carpets, wall-coverings, and bedspreads. Some of the bedrooms have prime locations with enchanting views out over the lake. Although the interior is outstanding, it is the outside where the fun really begins. The hotel opens onto a large terrace where guests relax with refreshing drinks. Just a short distance beyond the terrace is the lake where there is a dock for boats and a very large swimming pool that extends out over the water, plus an indoor pool and a very popular state-of-the-art spa. Tucked away in the park there are eight tennis courts, and in the area, seven golf courses. However, the most stunning feature of the Villa d'Este is the park: it surrounds the hotel with lovely pathways winding between the trees, statues, and even a formal garden with dramatic mosaic colonnade. *Directions:* Well-signposted in the center of Cernobbio.

VILLA D'ESTE
Manager: Claudio Ceccherelli
Cernobbio–Lake Como (CO) 22010, Italy
Tel: (031) 34 81, Fax: (031) 34 88 44
162 rooms, Double: €360–€645
Open: Mar to Nov, Credit cards: all major
53 km N of Milan, 5 km N of Como (town)
Region: Lombardy, Michelin Map: 428
www.karenbrown.com/italyinns/villadeste.html

La Frateria di Padre Eligio, a very special, enchanting hotel, makes an outstanding base for exploring the beauties of Tuscany and Umbria. The guestrooms of this 13th-century convent (founded by St. Francis) are the original guest quarters where the friars lodged passing pilgrims. They are simply, yet tastefully, furnished with antiques. There is nothing to interrupt the enchantment—bathrooms and telephones are the only concessions to the modern era. The silence is sweetened by the song of birds and the air by the fragrance of flowers. A centuries-old forest surrounds the hotel with beckoning paths where you can stroll in perfect stillness. The restoration of this masterpiece of history is superb, but the miracle is how it was accomplished. La Frateria di Padre, in addition to housing a deluxe hotel, is home to a commune of once-troubled young people who toiled for 12 years to restore the Convento San Francesco to its former beauty. Today these remarkable young men and women awaken at dawn to begin long days of labor. They meticulously groom the gardens, tend the vegetable garden, run the hotel, bake the fresh breads, prepare the meals (exclusively using produce from the farm), and serve in the restaurant. *Directions:* Exit the A1 at Chiusi Chianciano and follow signs to Cetona. Go through town towards Sarteano. Just after leaving Cetona, turn left at a sign "Mondo X—La Frateria di P. Eligio." Go about 700 meters to the hotel.

LA FRATERIA DI PADRE ELIGIO
Manager: Maria Grazia Daolio
Convento San Francesco
Cetona (SI) 53040, Italy
Tel: (0578) 23 80 15, Fax: (0578) 23 92 20
6 rooms, Double: €200–€260
Closed: Nov, Credit cards: MC, VS
89 km SE of Siena, 62 km NW of Orvieto
Region: Tuscany, Michelin Map: 430
www.karenbrown.com/italyinns/padreeligio.html

The Villa Anna Maria is located in Champoluc, a small town at the end of the beautiful Ayas Valley, which stretches north into the Alps almost to the Swiss border. The glaciers of the Monte Rosa (one of the 4,000-meter peaks of the Alps) provide a glorious backdrop as you drive up the valley. Champoluc is a well-known ski center in winter as well as a favorite mountain summer resort. The Villa Anna Maria is not a luxury hotel, but rather a simple, charming mountain chalet with great warmth of welcome from Miki Origone and his gracious son, Jean Noël. Together they run the villa with meticulous care for every comfort of their guests. Inside there is a delightful dining room that exudes a romantic coziness with its wooden Alpine-style country chairs, wooden tables, and gay red-checked curtains—just the place to return to for a good lunch or dinner after walking in the mountains (organized walks can be arranged). Upstairs, the bedrooms are spotlessly clean and very comfortable, with wooden paneling on the walls and a rustic ambiance. The atmosphere is homey—wonderful for those seeking a friendly, family-oriented country inn in a mountain village. *Directions:* Exit the A5 at Verres and follow the valley up to Champoluc. Drive through Champoluc and you see a small sign for the hotel on the right side of the road just before you leave town. Turn right on this little lane, which winds up the hill, and the Anna Maria is on your right.

VILLA ANNA MARIA
Owners: Miki & Jean Noël Origone
Via Croues, 5
Champoluc (AO) 11020, Italy
Tel: (0125) 30 71 28, Fax: (0125) 30 79 84
20 rooms, Double: €72–€93
Open: all year, Credit cards: MC, VS
Region: Valle d'Aosta, Michelin Map: 428
www.karenbrown.com/italyinns/villaannamaria.html

The Ca'Peo, a well-known restaurant serving some of the finest food in Italy, is located high in the coastal hills south of Genoa. You might think you will never arrive as the road winds ever upward from the coast through groves of olive and chestnut trees, but the way is well signposted, and just about the time you might be ready to despair, you will find a wonderful old farmhouse, owned by the charming Franco Solari, who is host and in charge of the wines, and his talented wife, Melly, who is the chef. Their enchanting daughter, Nicoletta, who will immediately win your heart, helps out wherever needed. The intimate dining room, which has only nine tables, is enclosed on three sides by large arched windows to take advantage of a sweeping view to the sea. Be aware that the meals are expensive, but if you appreciate fine food and wines, superb. Dining is definitely the main feature; however, in a modern annex there are five rooms (most are suites) available for guests who want to spend the night. The decor here is simple, but after lingering over a wonderful meal accompanied by delicious wines, how nice to walk just a few steps to your bed. The Ca'Peo is only about half-an-hour's drive from the popular resort of Portofino, so you might want to stay here instead or treat yourself to a memorable meal—but reservations are necessary. *Directions:* Exit the A12 at Chiavari. Follow signs to Leivi, then pick up and follow signs to Ca'Peo.

CA'PEO
Owners: Melly & Franco Solari
Via dei Caduti, 80
Chiavari a Leivi (GE) 16040, Italy
Tel: (0185) 31 96 96, Fax: (0185) 31 96 71
5 rooms, Double: €88*
*Breakfast not included: €8
Closed: Nov, Credit cards: all major
44 km SE of Genoa, 22 km NE of Portofino
Region: Liguria, Michelin Map: 428
www.karenbrown.com/italyinns/capeo.html

The 16th-century Locanda del Sant'Uffizio, originally a Benedictine monastery, then a farm, has been converted over the years into a delightful resort offering 33 guestrooms and an exquisite restaurant serving the finest of Piedmontese cuisine. All furnishings are antique and every detail of the decor has been rigorously overseen, with the result being a very tasteful, elegant, yet relaxed hotel with its own swimming pool and tennis courts cozily nestled amongst vineyards. Our favorite bedrooms are the cloister rooms looking towards the swimming pool with either terrace or balcony. An ambiance of warmth and hospitality radiates throughout the hotel. The food is outstanding, but be aware that the meals, the wines, and the before-dinner aperitifs are expensive, as would be expected in a one-Michelin-star restaurant. (A complimentary aperitif is offered to all hotel guests when ordered from the restaurant; a charge applies when ordering from the garden.)
Directions: Exit the A21 at Asti Est, turn right, then next right on the 457 towards Casale Monferrato. After passing through Calliano go 1 km and turn right for Cioccaro then follow signs to the Locanda.

LOCANDA DEL SANT'UFFIZIO
Manager: Vito Andresini
Cioccaro di Penango (AT) 14030, Italy
Tel: (0141) 91 62 92, Fax: (0141) 91 60 68
33 rooms, Double: €161–€380
Open: all year, Credit cards: all major
5 km SE of Moncalvo, 60 km E of Turin
Region: Piedmont, Michelin Map: 428
www.karenbrown.com/italyinns/santuffizio.html

Just on the border between Umbria and Tuscany and conveniently close to the walled town of Citta della Pieve, the Relais dei Magi, which opened in 2001, adds another excellent choice for accommodations in this enchanting part of Italy. A quiet, tree-lined lane leads up to the handsome 18th-century yellow villa with symmetrical windows accented by green shutters and roof adorned by rustic tile. The setting is utterly tranquil, with idyllic views in every direction—over 160 acres of woodlands, olive groves, and meadows stretch out as far as the eye can see. To the right of the villa, perfectly positioned to capture the view, is a stunning swimming pool romantically nestled on a grassy terrace amongst beds of flowers and towering cypresses. In the villa there are five deluxe suites, two with stunning view terraces and all with fireplaces and Jacuzzi tubs. Also in the villa are comfortable lounges and a beautiful dining room where a set-menu dinner is offered. A homelike ambiance prevails, with comfortable yet decorator-perfect furnishings throughout. Additional suites are found in a wing of rooms near the pool, while for longer stays or for families/friends there are apartments for two to six persons with kitchens complete with dishwashers and every modern amenity. Spa facilities include a fitness center, sauna, Turkish bath, and small heated pool. *Directions:* From Citta della Pieve take N220 toward Perugia. The hotel is on the left side of the road.

RELAIS DEI MAGI   **New**
Owner: Paolo De Marchis
Localita Le Selve Nuove, 45
Città delle Pieve (PG) 06062, Italy
Tel: (0578) 29 81 33, Fax: (0578) 29 88 58
8 rooms, Double: €165–€310
Closed: Jan & Feb, Credit cards: all major
43 km N of Orvieto, 79 km S of Arezzo
Region: Umbria, Michelin Map: 430
www.karenbrown.com/italyinns/relaismagi.html

The Palazzo del Capo is a handsome, pastel-yellow hotel accented by white trim, with an imposing location on a bluff overlooking the sea. You will find this hotel on the west coast, a bit off the beaten path, as you head south toward Italy's "tip of the toe." It is no wonder the setting is so special since this property (dating back to the 11th century) was originally a palace belonging to the dukes of De Aloe. Now a polished, sophisticated hotel has been created within the renovated shell of this once-grand old palace. As you approach, you see in front of the property a large swimming pool surrounded by a beautifully tended lush lawn. As you enter, the reception is on your left, while to the right is a charming small, private chapel. Continuing on, you come to an inviting inner courtyard, enclosed on three sides, one of which is an ancient tower that houses several romantic suites. This pleasant courtyard is dotted with tall palm trees and faces onto a handsome, three-tiered, arcaded grand entry where the majestic marble staircase is open to the air. The public rooms are all pleasantly furnished and exude a traditional, formal ambiance. The bedrooms too are very attractive and many have a view of the sea. A spacious terrace wraps around the back of the hotel and overlooks a pebbly beach and crystal-clear water. For guests who would rather swim in the sea than in the pool, there is a staircase descending to the beach.

❄ ⬔ 🍵 💳 🖂 ☎ 🛗 🏃 🏇 Ⓨ P 🍴 ≋ 🏃 🖼 🔥 🐾

PALAZZO DEL CAPO
Manager: Antonio Goffredi
Via C. Colombo, 5
Cittadella del Capo–Bonifati (CS) 87020, Italy
Tel & fax: (0982) 95 674
16 rooms, Double: €273–€340
Open: all year, Credit cards: all major
150 km N of Reggio-Calabria, 75 km N of Cosenza
Region: Calabria, Michelin Map: 431
www.karenbrown.com/italyinns/capo.html

The setting of the Hotel Bellevue is stunning—it's nestled on a gorgeous meadow enclosed by Italy's highest mountains. Paths from the hotel lead across the lush meadow to the Grand Paradis National Park, a heavenly place to enjoy nature. From the outside, this hotel looks like many others that you encounter in mountain resorts—an attractive, well-maintained building with balconies and windowboxes. However, from the moment you step inside, it becomes instantly apparent that this is a very, very special inn. It absolutely oozes charm and although the façade is not old, the interior certainly is. Parts of centuries-old farmhouses and regional artifacts have been cleverly incorporated into the enchanting interior, including mellow paneling, intricate beamed ceilings, carved doors, lovely fireplaces, planked-wood floors, antique light fixtures, and wrought-iron ornaments. All of the furnishings are either family heirlooms or 15th- to 17th-century antiques that came from farmhouses in the Valle d'Aosta. Every room is absolutely picture-perfect. Every tiny detail throughout shows love, and the quality is superb. Boundless amenities include fine dining, an indoor pool, saunas, Turkish baths, and hay baths. The Jeantet-Roullet family's genuine warmth and tender care of guests adds the final touch of perfection. *Directions:* Exit the A5 at Aosta west and follow signs to Cogne. The hotel is on the main road on your right as you leave town.

HOTEL BELLEVUE
Owner: Jeantet-Roullet family
Rue Grand Paradis, 22
Cogne (AO) 11012, Italy
Tel: (0165) 74 825, Fax: (0165) 74 91 92
35 rooms, Double: €229–€349
Closed: Oct to mid-Dec, Credit cards: all major
27 km S of Aosta, 110 km N of Turin
Region: Valle d'Aosta, Michelin Map: 428
Relais & Châteaux
www.karenbrown.com/italyinns/hotelbellevue.html

The Hotel Petit Dahu, a rustic, 18th-century stone farmhouse with heavy slate roof, sits in a garden of colorful flowers and is further enhanced by a profusion of pots of brilliant red geraniums. The location is stunning. If you love the mountains, you will be overwhelmed by the setting of this very simple, very inexpensive small hotel. Located in a beautiful national park, the hotel nestles amongst a cluster of other very old, extremely picturesque farmhouses that lie at the tip of the finger of the Cogne Valley—at this point the road can go no farther as it is blocked by the Gran Paradiso. From this point on, only trails beckon you onward into the mountains. Be forewarned: nothing is deluxe or fancy at the Hotel Petit Dahu. This is a place for those who love the out of doors and do not care if the guestrooms are simple and amenities few. Although small, the bedrooms are as tidy as can be and reflect the same ambiance of rustic simplicity as the rest of the house. The light-pine walls are enhanced by bouquets of dried flowers, prettily displayed in baskets with a ruffle of hand-made lace. Also on the walls are figures fashioned of dough, dressed in the regional costumes of the area. Your hosts are Cecilia and Luciano Fraschetto. Luciano is also the chef and most of the produce comes from Cecilia's garden. *Directions:* Exit the A5 at Sarre and follow the road up and through Cogne to Valnontey—the hotel is on your left.

HOTEL PETIT DAHU
Owners: Cecilia & Luciano Fraschetto
Valnontey 27
Cogne–Valnontey (AO) 11012, Italy
Tel: (0165) 74 146, Fax: (0165) 74 95 64
8 rooms, Double: €53–€80*
*Includes breakfast & dinner, closed Mon to Wed
Open: Dec to Oct, Credit cards: MC, VS
3 km S of Cogne, 30 km S of Aosta
Region: Valle d'Aosta, Michelin Map: 428
www.karenbrown.com/italyinns/petitdahu.html

Leaving behind the road from Perugia with its developing industries, a country gravel road takes you up to the splendid 17th-century Villa di Montesolare overlooking in all directions its hilly estate of olive groves and vineyards. A wide, gray-stone staircase leads up to an elegant salon with marble fireplace and crystal chandelier off which are eight lovely guestrooms and two suites on two floors. They are individually appointed with authentic period antiques, which harmonize perfectly with the original features of the villa left intact. Seven newer suites and five bedrooms are located within two 350-year-old farmhouses just down the road, offering magnificent views and utter tranquillity. A separate breakfast room is inside one of these two houses. Back at the main house, guests enjoy a drink at the bar before dinner served in one of the two intimate, frescoed dining rooms where varied Tuscan cuisine is presented along with a selection of 200 Umbrian wines. Summer concerts are held in a chapel in the formal Italian garden. Other activities include swimming in one of the two hillside pools, tennis, or horseback riding. Gracious and warm hosts Filippo and Rosemarie do an absolutely superb job of making guests feel totally pampered at their romantic retreat. *Directions:* From Perugia take S.S. 220 toward Citta di Pieve. After Fontignano (3 km), turn right at Colle Sao Paolo to the villa (4 km).

❄ ☕ 🎿 ♨ 📺 ☎ 🐕 🍽 🚶 🏇 🍷 P ≈ 🚶 🖼 🔔 🍇 🌿

ROMANTIK HOTEL VILLA DI MONTESOLARE
Owners: Rosemarie & Filippo Strunk Iannarone
Colle San Paolo–Panicale (PG) 06064, Italy
Tel: (075) 83 23 76, Fax: (075) 83 55 462
24 rooms, Double: €176–€216
Meals for hotel guests
Closed: mid-Dec to mid-Jan, Credit cards: all major
25 km SW of Perugia
Region: Umbria, Michelin Map: 430
www.karenbrown.com/italyinns/villadimontesolare.html

The Hotel Menardi, over 200 years old, was originally a farmhouse, but as Cortina's popularity as a fabulous ski center has spread, so has the town, and now the farm is located on the outskirts of town. The Menardi farm just naturally evolved into a hotel. At first it gave shelter to the men carting loads over the Cimabanche Pass who needed a place to sleep. Today the inn is a simple but wonderful small hotel whose special ingredient is the old-fashioned warmth and hospitality of the gracious Menardi family— Franca Menardi assisted by her three sons Antonio, Alberto, and Andrea. The hotel maintains a country flavor with old prints on the walls, old clocks, giant dowry chests, Oriental carpets, and beautiful hanging cupboards all set off by the warmth and gaiety of flowers everywhere. The dining room is most appealing and serves an excellent dinner— be sure to request the half-pension rate. The individually decorated bedrooms are all attractive, several have balconies and all have double-glazing to guard against road noise. Several delightful rooms are located across the garden, with three lovely rooms sacrificing a mountain view for a private terrace. *Directions:* Arriving in Cortina, follow the one-way system around town and signposts for Dobbiaco. You find the hotel on your right on the outskirts of town.

HOTEL MENARDI
Owner: Menardi family
112 Via Majon
Cortina d'Ampezzo (BL) 32043, Italy
Tel: (0436) 24 00, Fax: (0436) 86 21 83
51 rooms, Double: €110–€200
Open: Jun 6 to Sep 21 & Dec 20 to Apr 10
Credit cards: all major
133 km E of Bolzano, 71 km N of Belluno
Region: Veneto, Michelin Map: 429
www.karenbrown.com/italyinns/menardi.html

As Cortina has grown from a mountain outpost to a chic resort, so the Hôtel de la Poste has grown from a simple mail coach stop to a resort hotel, the last big expansion being made to accommodate visitors to the 1956 Olympics. The Manaigo family has been at the helm for the last century and the current generation—Marisa, her nephew Gottardo, and her daughter Michela—continues to keep the hotel in tip-top condition while offering guests the warmest of welcomes. Add to family involvement a long-term staff and you have a winning combination. Bedrooms vary from a sumptuous suite in the oldest, thick-walled building to a snug single room with small shower room in the new wing. You can choose from mountain views to town views and decor that varies from traditional to modern. Breakfast is taken in the snug breakfast room or outside on the patio in sunny weather. Dinner is enjoyed in the grand dining room with its soaring ceiling and ornate plasterwork. In winter skiing is de rigueur, while in summer walking in the mountains, shopping in the sophisticated stores, and simply just enjoying stunning views of the Dolomites are the order of the day. *Directions:* When you arrive in Cortina keep on the one-way system round town until you come to the Hôtel de la Poste garage. Park here to unload. You can leave your car here (€15 per day) or at a free car park in town.

HOTEL DE LA POSTE
Owner: Manaigo family
Cortina d'Ampezzo (BL) 32043, Italy
Tel: (0436) 42 71, Fax: (0436) 86 84 35
80 rooms, Double: €183–€334*
*Includes breakfast & dinner
Closed: Apr to Jun & Oct to Dec 23
Credit cards: all major
133 km E of Bolzano, 71 km N of Belluno
Region: Veneto, Michelin Map: 429
www.karenbrown.com/italyinns/laposte.html

If you want to find the perfect little hotel to use as a base to explore the wonders of Tuscany and Umbria, look no farther than Il Falconiere—a jewel snuggled in the countryside just a few kilometers outside Cortona. From this convenient location you can venture out each day to such beauties as Siena, Florence, Assisi, San Gimignano, Orvieto, and Pienza, all easily accessible by car. The joy is that you can return each evening to relax by the gorgeous swimming pool, enjoy some of the best food in Italy, then sleep peacefully in the hushed tranquility of the countryside. And what a value! You can stay here for much less than you would pay for a deluxe room in Florence or Rome. Il Falconiere is owned by Silvia and Riccardo Baracchi, a charming, talented young couple who have achieved amazing results from their labor of love and long years of hard work. Riccardo, who inherited the property from his grandmother, was born in the small pretty villa that now houses several of the guestrooms. His wife, Silvia, was born nearby and is the incredibly talented chef whose superb meals lure Italians from far and near to dine here. The guestrooms are individually decorated with great flair. Many antiques are used throughout, creating a comfortable, quietly sophisticated elegance. Il Falconiere is truly a very special place offering superb quality, charm, and genuine hospitality. *Directions:* Just north of Cortona, signposted off the road to Arezzo.

❄ ☕ 💳 ☎ ♿ P ⑪ ≈ 🖼 ♿

IL FALCONIERE RELAIS E RISTORANTE
Owners: Silvia & Riccardo Baracchi
Localita: San Martino, 43
Cortona (AR) 52044, Italy
Tel: (0575) 61 26 79, Fax: (0575) 61 29 27
19 rooms, Double: €240–€550
Open: all year, Credit cards: all major
3 km N of Cortona
Region: Tuscany, Michelin Map: 430
Relais & Châteaux
www.karenbrown.com/italyinns/ilfalconiere.html

If you are looking for a place to stay in the heart of the charming walled hilltown of Cortona, the Hotel San Michele is a real winner. Originally a magnificent palazzo, it still maintains its fine architectural details. The mood is set as you enter: look up and you will see a marvelous vaulted stone ceiling. As you walk the halls, notice the arched doorways, frescoed walls, massive stone fireplaces, and intricate beamed ceilings. The guestrooms are tucked along a maze of hallways connected by a series of stone staircases—finding your room is like a treasure hunt. All of the guestrooms are different, but similar in ambiance with tiled floors, off-white walls, prettily framed antique prints, wrought-iron headboards, and antique armoires. The suites cost only a little bit more than the standard doubles. The honeymoon suite is really special, having a small sitting room with windows on three sides capturing a memorable view of the Val d'Chiana. However, you must be young and nimble to stay in this suite because a wooden ladderlike stairway leads very steeply up to the sleeping alcove and the bathroom is tiny, with an open shower. For the older romantics, suite 441 is spacious and has a beautifully designed beamed ceiling that slopes almost to the floor. *Directions:* Follow signs to the center of Cortona. On the lower edge of town, park close to the main gate, Porta San Agostino, go through the gate, and follow Via Guelfa to the hotel.

❄ ⛱ ☕ 💳 ☎ 🛗 🎋 🚶 🐎 ♈ P 🚭 🖼 ⛵ 🔔 🍇

HOTEL SAN MICHELE
Owner: Paolo Alunno
Via Guelfa, 15
Cortona (AR) 52044, Italy
Tel: (0575) 60 43 48, Fax: (0575) 63 01 47
55 rooms, Double: €134–€200
Open: Mar to Jan, Credit cards: all major
51 km NW of Perugia
Region: Tuscany, Michelin Map: 430
www.karenbrown.com/italyinns/sanmichele.html

Cortona, a picturesque walled city in Tuscany, is a favorite with tourists. On the main road that wraps around the east side of the city, the Villa Marsili has the advantages of parking facilities and of being easy to find, and is within walking distance of the center of town. The ground the hotel stands on has an interesting history: at the beginning of the 14th century a church, with connections to the Etruscan era and containing remarkable works of art, was built here, being replaced in 1730 by a larger church. This was in turn demolished in 1786 when an elegant mansion was built in its place. A gated entrance leads into the front courtyard of this handsome yellow villa accented by dark-green shutters and beds of colorful flowers. Inside, the villa has been totally remodeled into a deluxe hotel with every modern amenity. The staff is exceptionally cordial, so even though there is a commercial air, the welcome by the well-trained staff is warm and gracious. The bedrooms are all tastefully decorated and have all the comforts and appointments of a first-class hotel. Throughout the hotel a quiet, refined ambiance prevails, with soft colors enhanced by antique furniture and ceilings adorned by frescoes. There is no restaurant—breakfast is the only meal served—but there is a rich selection of restaurants within walking distance. *Directions:* Located on the east side of Cortona on the road to Arezzo.

VILLA MARSILI   *New*
Owner: Valter Petrucci
Viale C. Battisti, 13
Cortona (AR) 52044, Italy
Tel: (0575) 60 51 99, Fax: (0575) 60 56 18
27 rooms, Double: €165–€310
Closed: Feb, Credit cards: all major
51 km NW of Perugia
Region: Tuscany, Michelin Map: 430
www.karenbrown.com/italyinns/villamarsili.html

Corvara is a lovely Alpine village sitting high in the Dolomites and ringed by towering peaks. Fortunately, it's one of those places that combines an exquisite setting with a superb hotel run by the most welcoming of families, the Costas. You will doubtless meet Ernesto, Anny, sons Michil, Maxi, and Mathias, and daughter-in-law Petra during your stay. From the exterior the hotel looks like a typical Alpine hotel but once inside you realize that this is very different—all five lovely dining rooms are rooms from very old local houses that have been re-built here. The conservatory breakfast room offers the largest breakfast selection I have ever seen, from fresh-squeezed juices to eggs cooked any way you want them. The indoor swimming pool with its whirlpool features is a swimming adventure, though if you prefer swimming outdoors, there is also a large garden pool. Bedrooms are absolutely delightful, ranging from romantic rooms with balconies offering stunning mountain views to two exquisite junior suites decked out in white pine accented by blue-and-white fabric. In winter this is a paradise for skiers and in summer for walkers. It's a wonderful base for exploring the Dolomites and if you do not want to explore alone, you can join in the hotel's activities of picnics and walks. *Directions:* Corvara is 50 km west of Cortina d' Ampezzo. Arriving in the town, you find the hotel on the hill next to the church.

ROMANTIK HOTEL LA PERLA
Owner: Costa family
Corvara (BZ) 39033, Italy
Tel: (0471) 83 10 00, Fax: (0471) 83 65 68
52 rooms, Double: €210–€430
Open: Jun to Sep & Dec to Easter
Credit cards: all major
65 km E of Bolzano, 47 km W of Cortina
Region: Trentino-Alto Adige, Michelin Map: 429
www.karenbrown.com/italyinns/hotellaperla.html

For many years the Locanda San Vigilio, tucked on a small peninsula on Lake Garda, has been featured in our guides. In 2002 the owners opened the Locanda San Verolo, a romantic small inn—once a farmhouse—nestled in the rolling hills of the tranquil countryside about a 15-minute drive away. Beyond the outer stone wall you find a courtyard where tables are set for open-air dining in balmy weather. The restaurant, reception area, and some of the guestrooms are in the largest of the ochre-colored houses facing the courtyard, while the other guestrooms are in three other buildings. My favorite accommodations are on the top floor of the main house because of the beautiful views, but all the spacious, individually furnished guestrooms are decorator-perfect and exceptionally appealing, with a simple elegance appropriate for a farmhouse. Gorgeous fabrics, fine antiques, original art, rich colors, hand-painted wooden headboards, fine linens, and splendid large bathrooms are featured in all. Obviously no expense was spared to make this a luxurious yet rustic hideaway. A path leads up a gentle slope to a large swimming pool terraced on the hillside with a beautiful view of the countryside and to the bell tower of a tiny church peeking out of the trees just below the hotel. *Directions:* From Garda take the road to Caprino. At Costermano, turn left toward Castion and Zeno. In a few minutes you will see a sign on the right for the hotel.

※ ⚓ ☕ 🛉 CREDIT ☎ 🐕 🚶 👫 🏇 ♈ P 🍴 ≈ 🖼 ⛵ 🍇

LOCANDA SAN VEROLO   New
Owners: Agostino & Guarienti Di Brenzone
Localita San Verolo
Costermano (VR) 37010, Italy
Tel: (045) 72 00 930, Fax: (045) 62 01 116
13 rooms, Double: €280–€330
Open: all year, Credit cards: all major
78 km S of Trento, 68 km E of Brescia
Region: Veneto, Michelin Map: 429
www.karenbrown.com/italyinns/sanverolo.html

Elba is a beautiful small island, easily accessible in one hour by car ferry from Piombino. After exploring Tuscany, or while en route along the coast heading north from Rome, you will find that Elba makes a delightful stopover where you can happily spend several days relaxing and exploring the island's many pretty inlets and picturesque fishing villages. The Hotel Villa Ottone is idyllically nestled in a tranquil park and has its own private beach (there is also a swimming pool). The original part of the hotel is a romantic villa (which belonged to Signor Di Mario's grandfather) facing directly onto the sea. If you want to splurge, ask for a deluxe room in the villa. Some of the guestrooms are located in an attractive building that also houses the reception area and the dining room, while more guestrooms are found in a separate wing nestled amongst the trees. The furnishings throughout are tasteful and everything is immaculately maintained. Be sure to visit the bar, which has a stunning ceiling of intricate plasterwork and lovely frescoes. In high season you need to take the modified American plan (MAP), which includes breakfast and either lunch or dinner and there is a three-night minimum. However, this is no problem as the food is very good and beautifully served. Villa Ottone is a hotel with great personality, overseen with meticulous attention to detail by the gracious Signor Di Mario.

HOTEL VILLA OTTONE
Owner: Di Mario family
Localita: Ottone
Elba (Isola di)–Ottone (LI) 57037, Italy
Tel: (0565) 93 30 42, Fax: (0565) 93 32 57
75 rooms, Double: €160–€410*
*Includes breakfast & dinner
Open: May to Oct, Credit cards: all major
11 km SE of Portoferraio
Region: Tuscany, Michelin Map: 430
www.karenbrown.com/italyinns/villaottone.html

To the west of famous Lake Garda lies the smaller, lesser known but equally lovely Lake Iseo. Here, tucked into the gentle Franciacorta hills, you find L'Albereta, a deluxe property with the heart and intimacy of a small family hotel whose warmth and friendliness is undoubtedly due to its caring, hands-on owner, Carmen Moretti de Rosa. You feel a happy ambiance as soon as you walk into the sunny reception area with light streaming in through walls of glass. To the right is a charming, intimate sitting area with comfortable chairs set off by checkerboard-pattern walls. From the foyer steps lead down to a swimming pool with windows that slide open to the pretty garden. Carmen Moretti de Rosa decorated the bedrooms herself, and although each has its own personality, there is a subdued elegance and excellent taste throughout. The walls in the bedrooms and hallways are whimsically painted with individual designs that tie in with the color and decor. The most dramatic rooms are the suites in the tower, one of which was occupied by the actress Sophia Loren. The restaurant has a coveted two-star Michelin rating and the dining room is also very special: serenely furnished in muted tones of green, it has a wall of windows that look out over the wooded hills, capturing a splendid view of Lake Iseo in the distance. *Directions:* From the A4, take the Rovato exit and follow signs to Samico. After 3 km, turn right at the sign for the hotel.

L'ALBERETA
Owner: Carmen Moretti de Rosa
Via Vittorio Emanuele, 11
Erbusco–Lake Iseo (BS) 25030, Italy
Tel: (03077) 605 50, Fax: (03077) 605 73
44 rooms, Double: €290–€800, Breakfast not included: €24
Closed: mid-Jan to Mar, Credit cards: all major
60 km W of Verona, 65 km E of Milan
Region: Lombardy, Michelin Map: 428
Relais & Châteaux
www.karenbrown.com/italyinns/lalbereta.html

For many generations the 15th-century hamlet of Il Voltone (along with the surrounding 1,000 acres) has belonged to the Parenti family. When the last farmers and their families moved out of Il Voltone in 1960, the tiny community fell into ruin but, happily for the traveler, the charming Parenti sisters, Daniela and Donatella, have meticulously restored the small cluster of abandoned buildings into a delightful small hotel. You enter through an open archway into a courtyard framed by connecting houses and a tiny church—all painted in pastel hues of pinks and creams. The guestrooms are spacious and prettily decorated with color-coordinating fabrics and nice pieces of furniture. The restaurant serves delicious meals accompanied by wine produced on the property. But what makes this hotel truly special is its setting: Il Voltone crowns a gentle hill and in every direction there is a sweeping view of forests, vineyards, lush pastures, and hilltop towns. Guests can enjoy this view from teak deck chairs placed under the chestnut trees or by the swimming pool. Another plus—Il Voltone is in the center of rich archaeological sites, great Etruscan ruins, and fascinating hilltop towns. Daniela and Donatella have prepared a series of day tours to help you explore the countryside. *Directions:* It is an adventure to find Il Voltone—have a detailed map and ask for directions when making reservations.

IL VOLTONE
Owners: Daniela & Donatella Parenti
Localita: Voltone
Farnese–Voltone (VT) 01010, Italy
Tel & fax: (0761) 42 25 40
30 rooms, Double: €114–€166
Open: Mar 28 to Nov 4, Credit cards: MC, VS
12 km N of Farnese, 45 km N of Tarquinia
Region: Lazio, Michelin Map: 430
www.karenbrown.com/italyinns/ilvoltone.html

Located in the historic heart of Ferrara, the five-star Duchessa Isabella Hotel is absolute perfection. You are totally immersed in breathtaking opulence from the moment you step into the stunning reception hall with its soaring, ornately decorated ceiling and handsome marble staircase sweeping up to a second foyer enhanced by Greek columns, Persian carpets, two huge gilt candelabra, fine paintings, soft lighting, and ornate antique furniture. Sometimes such spectacular palaces reflect a faded elegance, but not this one: it is so well maintained that it looks as beautiful as when the palace was built in the 16th century. This world of refinement is orchestrated by Evelina Bonzagni, an attractive, hard-working woman who reflects the image of the gracious hostess, warmly greeting returning clients as friends and watching every detail of the management with a keen eye. All the guestrooms are splendidly decorated with antiques, as are the dining rooms. Dinner at the Duchessa Isabella is an exquisite affair. Not only is the food superb, but also the dining rooms are absolutely gorgeous. There is not one large restaurant, but rather a series of lovely, intimate dining rooms, with beautiful painted wooden ceilings bordered in gold, authentic doors dating back to the 16th century, chairs richly upholstered in fine fabrics, and incredible frescoes. *Directions:* The Via Palestro is a main street that runs into the piazza where the cathedral is.

❄ ☕ 💳 ☎ 🛗 🧍 P 🍴 🖼

DUCHESSA ISABELLA HOTEL
Owner: Evelina Bonzagni
Via Palestro, 70
Ferrara (FE) 44100, Italy
Tel: (0532) 20 21 21, Fax: (0532) 20 26 38
28 rooms, Double: €300
Closed: Aug, Credit cards: all major
51 km NE of Bologna, 110 km SW of Venice
Region: Emilia-Romagna, Michelin Map: 429
Relais & Châteaux
www.karenbrown.com/italyinns/duchessaisabella.html

Opened for guests in 2000, the Locanda della Duchessina is the latest of Evelina Bonzagni's artistic creations. Each of her hotels in Ferrara has its own personality and is outstanding in its own way. The Locanda della Duchessina is the most intimate, giving guests the feeling of staying in a private home. Painted a soft pastel pink with windows enhanced by shutters and boxes of geraniums, the building is instantly appealing. Evelina Bonzagni's decor in her other two hotels ranges from opulent splendor to sedate grandeur, whereas the Locanda della Duchessina's rooms are decorated in gentle pastel colors with walls enhanced by lovely papers. It is not surprising that the charmingly decorated bedrooms have a feminine flair since each of the five bedrooms is named for the daughter of one of Ferrara's wealthy noble families. Wallpapers in pink check, pastel plaids, miniature florals, or pretty blue designs set the decor in each with coordinating bedspreads and draperies, lacy white curtains, and pillows with matching fabrics. The guestrooms are not large, but each is perfect and has a beautiful bathroom where the tiles pick up the room's decor. In the rear of the hotel is a romantic little garden, gently shaded by trees and enhanced by flowers. The locanda offers incredible value with beautifully decorated rooms and superb quality. *Directions:* Located on a tiny street off Via Palestro, just steps from the Hotel Duchessa Isabella.

LOCANDA DELLA DUCHESSINA
Owner: Evelina Bonzagni
Vicolo del Voltino, 11
Ferrara (FE) 44100, Italy
Tel: (0532) 20 69 81, Fax: (0532) 20 26 38
5 rooms, Double: €114–€166
Open: all year, Credit cards: all major
51 km NE of Bologna, 110 km SW of Venice
Region: Emilia-Romagna, Michelin Map: 429
www.karenbrown.com/italyinns/duchessina.html

If you don't need the ultimate in luxury provided by Ferrara's opulent Duchessa Isabella Hotel, her "sister" hotel just around the corner, the Principessa Leonora, which is also owned by Evelina Bonzagni, is equally outstanding in its own way. The mood here is one of subdued, quiet elegance. Here Evelina Bonzagni again shows her impeccable taste, but the style is more sedate—less gilt and fewer ornate antiques. This 16th-century residence was once the home of Leonardo Mascheraio, whose fame for making masks was so great that the street was named for him, and the hotel's beautiful suites are named in honor of the many illustrious guests who visited the mansion. The standard bedrooms are designated by their past use, such as the stable, the wine cellar, the oil press, olive store, etc. Guestrooms offer every latest modern amenity such as Internet access with modem, satellite TV, safety deposit box, and mini bar. Behind the hotel is a charming garden where guests can relax after a day of sightseeing and, for the more active, there is also a fitness room. The hotel is exceptionally attractive with terra-cotta floors, marble columns, many fireplaces, beamed ceilings, centuries-old arched doorways, thick walls, Oriental carpets on polished floors, walls enhanced with a fabulous collection of French tapestries, and fine antiques throughout. *Directions:* Via Mascheraio runs from the Via Palestro where the Duchessa Isabella Hotel is located.

HOTEL PRINCIPESSA LEONORA
Owner: Evelina Bonzagni
Viu Mascheraio, 39
Ferrara (FE) 44100, Italy
Tel: (0532) 20 60 20, Fax: (0532) 24 27 07
22 rooms, Double: €166
Open: all year, Credit cards: all major
51 km NE of Bologna, 110 km SW of Venice
Region: Emilia-Romagna, Michelin Map: 429
www.karenbrown.com/italyinns/leonora.html

Sitting high above the valley, the delightful village of Völs nestles beneath the Schlern Mountain—hence you see local signposts for Völs am Schlern. At the heart of the village the Romantik Hotel Turm dates back to the 13th century when it functioned as a castle. Today it is certainly not a castle of drafty corridors and sparse rooms but a delightful hotel that displays its castle origins in its barrel-vaulted rooms and thick stone walls. Instead of a gloomy dungeon you have an indoor swimming pool (as well as an outdoor one set on a grassy garden terrace). Karl Pramstrahler's art collection lines every available inch of wall space and includes everything from old oil paintings to contemporary art. His son Stefan, who is responsible for the delicious food, assists Karl in the running of the hotel. Bedrooms come in all shapes and sizes, from lovely rooms set beneath the eaves to a turret suite with a four-poster bed and a little house (Wagenhaus) with a sitting room and child's bedroom downstairs, and a master bedroom upstairs. Amenities include a full spa with swimming pool, whirlpool, sauna, wine bath, solarium, and massage services. The hotel was remodeled in 2002 and we look forward to seeing the changes. *Directions:* Exit at Bolzano Nord from the Verona-Brennero autostrada. Follow signs for Siusi and Fiè (also called Völs), at the main intersection in the village turn left, following the road to the hotel, next to the church.

ROMANTIK HOTEL TURM
Owners: Karl & Stefan Pramstrahler
Kirchplatz, 9
Fiè (Völs) (BZ) 39050, Italy
Tel: (0471) 72 50 14, Fax: (0471) 72 54 74
24 rooms, Double: €152–€248
Closed: Nov 5 to Jun 16, Credit cards: MC, VS
16 km E of Bolzano, 7 km S of Siusi (Seis)
Region: Trentino-Alto Adige, Michelin Map: 429
www.karenbrown.com/italyinns/romantikhotelturm.html

The Punta Est is a delightful villa perched on a hilltop overlooking the sea. When the home was converted to a hotel, an annex was added to provide more bedrooms, but it still radiates the friendly ambiance of a private home. This warmth of reception and attention to detail are the result of the management of the gracious Podestà family who own and personally manage the inn. They seem dedicated to making your stay as enjoyable as possible—even their German Shepherd wags his tail in welcome. This small hotel is constantly being maintained with loving care. Every time we visit the property has been upgraded, the latest addition being two beautiful new suites. There are little terraces with lovely views snuggled at various levels among the trees and on one of these terraces is a swimming pool. There is also access to the public beach (where the hotel has its own area with lounge chairs), which can easily be reached by walking down the path to the main highway and following the tunnel beneath the highway to the beach. The rooms in the main villa are smaller and more old-fashioned than those in the newer annex, which are more reminiscent of an American motel. There is a small dining room for breakfast, which is especially inviting with its blue-and-white English bone-china service. The hotel is located east of Finale Ligure, just before the tunnel.

HOTEL PUNTA EST
Owner: Podestà family
Via Aurelia N.1
Finale Ligure (SV) 17024, Italy
Tel & fax: (019) 60 06 11
40 rooms, Double: €180–€400
Open: May to Oct, Credit cards: all major
72 km SW of Genoa
Region: Liguria, Michelin Map: 428
www.karenbrown.com/italyinns/puntaest.html

It is often difficult to secure a room in Florence, a justifiably popular tourist destination, so we were delighted to receive a letter from Donatella Bruscoli in 2001, just as we were leaving for Italy, saying that she had recently opened the Hotel Curtatone. Its entrance, which is hard to spot, is shared with other business establishments and is rather drab, but do not let this put you off. Once the elevator whisks you up a floor, you open the doors into a fresh and pretty, sweet little reception area where you will be warmly welcomed. Along one wall is a table with a computer with Internet access—an indication of the attention to small details the hotel provides for guests. A hallway leads to a charmingly decorated room that combines a cute bar and cozy lounge, which is also where a buffet breakfast is served each morning. A gentle elegance prevails, with prettily slipcovered chairs and sofas, lovely fabrics, fresh flowers, and nicely framed prints. The guestrooms are fairly small but very attractive and continue the same high degree of good taste, with beautiful fabrics, antique-style furnishings, and pretty pictures on the walls. Every room has air conditioning and a new, modern bathroom. This hotel obviously has an owner with a flair for decorating and who really cares about the comfort of her guests. The hotel, a 15-minute walk along the river to the heart of Florence, offers great value and pretty accommodations.

HOTEL CURTATONE
Owners: Donatella Bruscoli & Regina Da Cruz
Via Curtatone, 12
Florence 50123, Italy
Tel: (055) 26 45 171, Fax: (055) 26 48 875
13 rooms, Double: €110–€210
Open: all year, Credit cards: all major
15-minute walk to heart of Florence
Region: Tuscany, Michelin Map: 430
www.karenbrown.com/italyinns/curtatone.html

The Grand Hotel Villa Cora is a mansion, originally built during the 19th century by the Baron Oppenheim as a gift for his beautiful young bride. Among the many romantic tales of the Villa Cora is the one about Oppenheim's wife who, so the story goes, became enamored of one of her many admirers. The jealous baron was so enraged that he threatened to burn the entire mansion, but, luckily for you and me, he was stopped in time from this mad endeavor by his friends, and today this magnificent villa is a stunning hotel. Although only about a five-minute taxi ride from the center of Florence (or a twenty-minute walk), the Grand Hotel Villa Cora is eons away in atmosphere—you feel more like a guest on a country estate rather than in a city hotel. The interior of the hotel is rather ornate and sumptuous. The villa is set in intricate gardens and even has a pool. You can almost hear the sounds of laughter and music drifting through the gardens, and indeed the mansion has always been famous for its dramatic parties: at one time the villa was the residence of Napoleon's wife, Empress Eugenia, whose gay entertaining was the talk of Florence. Now this grand, palace-like home can be yours for days of dreams and romance. Another excellent bonus is free limousine service to/from the heart of Florence.

GRAND HOTEL VILLA CORA
Manager: Luigi Zaccardi
Viale Machiavelli, 18/20
Florence 50125, Italy
Tel: (055) 22 98 451, Fax: (055) 22 90 86
48 rooms, Double: €270–€830
Open: all year, Credit cards: all major
20-minute walk from the heart of Florence
Region: Tuscany, Michelin Map: 430
www.karenbrown.com/italyinns/hotelvillacora.html

In our estimation, the Hotel Helvetia and Bristol is one of the finest luxury hotels in the center of Florence. Nothing has been spared to make this showplace a true beauty—the decor is outstanding. The lounges, exquisitely decorated with an elegant, yet extremely comfortable, homelike ambiance, exude quality without flamboyance. Each of the guestrooms is also superbly decorated, and, as in a private home, no two are alike. Abundant use of exquisite padded-fabric wall coverings, with color-coordinated draperies, upholstered chairs, and bedspreads along with lovely antiques make each one special. I fell in love with each of the rooms, but my very favorites were the mini suites: room 257 in gorgeous shades of muted green and room 363 in lovely golds, creams, and dusty pinks, with a sumptuous marble bathroom with Jacuzzi tub, heated towel racks, plus the added bonus of a tiny terrace. The dining room, cozy yet elegant with dark walls and soft lighting, features Tuscan cuisine. For light refreshments, a cool drink, or just relaxing, the Giardino d'Inverno (Winter Garden) is a marvelous retreat—light and airy with a domed, old-fashioned skylight, potted plants, and nostalgic wicker furniture. The Helvetia and Bristol is expensive, but no more so than the other luxury hotels in Florence, and for those who appreciate quality and refinement, it is unsurpassed.

❄ ⚓ ☕ 🖌 CREDIT ☎ 🐕 ♿ 🚶 🚶‍♂️ 🐎 ⅄ P 🍴 🚭 🖼 💧 👞 ♿ 🍇

HOTEL HELVETIA AND BRISTOL
Manager: Pietro Panelli
Via dei Pescioni, 2
Florence 50123, Italy
Tel: (055) 26 651, Fax: (055) 28 83 53
67 rooms, Double: €374–€1210
Open: all year, Credit cards: all major
In the heart of Florence
Region: Tuscany, Michelin Map: 430
www.karenbrown.com/italyinns/helvetiaandbristol.html

Moderately priced accommodations are rare in Florence, so we were happy to discover the Hotel Il Guelfo Bianco, which combines reasonable rates with a choice location in the heart of Florence, just steps to all the prime tourist spots. Most importantly, this small hotel has an owner, Alessandro Bargiacchi, whose presence is seen and felt. He speaks only a little English, but his smile and genuine warmth of welcome make guests feel right at home. Everyone who assists him is exceptionally friendly and all converse in several languages, including the gracious manager, Antonella Rocchini, and two charming ladies, Sonia and Gaia. When it first opened, the Il Guelfo Bianco had only 29 rooms, but it has added an annex, the adjacent Hotel Cristallo, bringing the total to 43. The unpretentious but inviting lobby sets the tone of the hotel. The intimate reception area ends in a cozy bar, and from there a hall leads to the breakfast room (in pleasant weather, breakfast is served outside in the pretty central courtyard). The bedrooms vary in size and shape, as one would expect in an historical 14th-century building. All are nicely decorated and some even have beautiful paintings on the ceilings. One of my favorite rooms, number 11, has an especially pretty outlook over a back garden. The Hotel Il Guelfo Bianco is not a deluxe hotel, nor does it pretend to be, but it makes an excellent choice for a friendly, pleasant place to stay in the heart of Florence.

HOTEL IL GUELFO BIANCO
Owner: Alessandro Bargiacchi
Via Cavour, 29
Florence 50129, Italy
Tel: (055) 28 83 30, Fax: (055) 29 52 03
43 rooms, Double: €180–€235
Open: all year, Credit cards: all major
In the heart of Florence
Region: Tuscany, Michelin Map: 430
www.karenbrown.com/italyinns/hotelilguelfobianco.html

The Hotel Lungarno, one of our favorite hotels, is superbly located directly on the River Arno, a few minutes' walk from the Ponte Vecchio. Although it is basically of new construction, the architect cleverly incorporated into the hotel an ancient stone tower, which houses several romantic suites. The hotel changed hands in 1997 and the new owners have renovated the entire hotel and made it even more perfect. The new decor is superb, with fine-quality furnishings accented by an appealing color scheme of pretty blues and creamy whites. In addition to the redecoration of all the rooms, a restaurant was opened in 1999. Also added were six splendid two-bedroom, two-bath apartments, which are an exceptional value if you are traveling with friends or family. Throughout the hotel a gracious ambiance of understated elegance prevails, enhanced by admirable management and a warm reception. Bountiful bouquets of fresh flowers and an outstanding collection of original art add the final touch of perfection. When making a reservation, request a bedroom overlooking the Arno—one might not be available, but you can always try. If you plan far in advance, you might even be lucky enough to snare a room with a large terrace overlooking the river—these are very special and well worth the extra cost. What a treat to sit on your own terrace in the evening and watch the Arno fade into gold in the setting sun.

HOTEL LUNGARNO
Manager: Martin Elsner
Borgo San Jacopo, 14
Florence 50125, Italy
Tel: (055) 27 261, Fax: (055) 26 84 37
73 rooms, Double: €390–€960
Open: all year, Credit cards: all major
On the Arno near Ponte Vecchio
Region: Tuscany, Michelin Map: 430
www.karenbrown.com/italyinns/lungarno.html

The hills immediately surrounding Florence, dotted with stately villas and country homes dating back to the Renaissance, offered Florentine aristocrats cool respite in summer from the higher temperatures in the city below. The gracious Bulleri family chose this alternative to the city some 30 years ago, and after a successful career in the fashion industry, Claudio and Paola transformed their splendid wooded property into a top-notch inn for discerning guests. Nine very comfortable, immaculate rooms, personally decorated by Paola, have been created in a house across from the family's villa. This includes an elegant main living and dining room with fireplace and large windows looking out over the garden. Classic-style bedrooms have parquet floors, matching fabrics for beds and drapes, and spacious sparkling-white bathrooms. Amenities include satellite TV, mini bar, safe, air conditioning, and a selection from the wine cellar. A full country breakfast is served out in the gazebo in warmer months. The swimming pool, on a level below the home, has gorgeous hillside views over olive groves. The Bulleris share their personal lifestyle: charming son Lorenzo assists guests with local itineraries and Paola conducts cooking lessons, while Claudio accompanies guests to his nearby golf club.

MARIGNOLLE RELAIS & CHARME   ***New***
Owner: Claudio Bulleri family
Florence 50124, Italy
Tel: (055) 22 86 910, Fax: (055) 20 47 396
9 rooms, Double: €195–€255
Open: all year, Credit cards: all major
3.5 km from heart of Florence
Region: Tuscany, Michelin Map: 430
www.karenbrown.com/italyinns/marignolle.html

Mario's came highly recommended to us by several readers, and when we saw the hotel for ourselves, we agreed that it is a delightful small hotel, moderately priced for Florence. It is conveniently located two blocks from the train station, and within easy walking distance of the city's major sightseeing. From the street, the appeal of the hotel is not readily evident as it is housed in a rather nondescript building. But after ascending the stairs to the second floor and stepping into the cozy, beamed-ceilinged lobby, you know you've arrived at a well-tended small hotel with an old Florentine ambiance. Facing the reception desk is a sitting area with sofas arranged under a wall of pictures, Oriental carpets enhancing the dark tile floors, and artfully arranged pictures and plants setting off the cream-colored walls. All of the guestrooms have a country-fresh feeling with antique armoires, wrought-iron headboards, rustic wooden desks and chairs, and pretty bedspreads. The rooms are not large, but are very pleasing and immaculately tidy. A copious breakfast is served buffet-style in the charming breakfast room. Guests choose from a wonderful selection of breads, cheese, salami, ham, yogurt, coffee, tea, and chocolate. The nicest aspect of this hotel is the fact that it is small enough to be very personalized. Mario sees that every guest feels special, and will even (upon prior arrangement) give driving tours around Tuscany.

MARIO'S
Owner: Mario Noce
Via Faenza, 89
Florence 50123, Italy
Tel: (055) 21 68 01, Fax: (055) 21 20 39
16 rooms, Double: €90–€165
Open: all year, Credit cards: all major
2 blocks from the Florence train station
Region: Tuscany, Michelin Map: 430
www.karenbrown.com/italyinns/marios.html

The stunning Palazzo Magnani Feroni, an ancient private residence of the Gianotti family, dating back to the 1500s, is on the "left bank"of the River Arno four blocks away from the Ponte Vecchio. The sensation of being in a true palace is captured immediately upon entering the grand foyer with vaulted ceilings, marble busts, statues, and precious period paintings, many from the couple's world travels. This is a unique upscale accommodation in that the owners have purposefully avoided adding any obvious signs of its being a hotel (a small reception room sits off the main entrance) in order to retain the aura of living in an elegant historical residence. Sumptuous bedrooms with soaring ceilings, mostly enormous suites, have retained their original architectural features and have been appointed with antique and reproduction pieces, gilded framed mirrors, Oriental carpets, brocaded gold fabrics on sofas, and tapestries. Rooms on the ground floor look out onto an inner courtyard and one has two walls entirely covered with a fresco depicting a bucolic countryside scene. Breakfast is served in the suites or in the long upstairs dining room with its showcase displaying antique silk fabrics left over from the days when the palazzo was also an antique gallery. Other highlights include a rooftop terrace with superb views over the city, an antique kitchen set up for aperitifs, and a small exercise room for guests' use.

❄ ☕ ⚒ ♨ 🖳 ☎ 🛗 👤 ♂ 👟 🐴 ♈ P ⊘ 🖼 🏊 🍇

PALAZZO MAGNANI FERONI   **New**
Owners: Dr. Alberto Gianotti & Claudia J. Jerger
Borgo San Frediano, 5
Florence 50124, Italy
Tel: (055) 23 99 544, Fax: (055) 26 08 908
11 suites, Double: €260–€590
Open: all year, Credit cards: all major
Center of Florence
Region: Tuscany, Michelin Map: 430
www.karenbrown.com/italyinns/feroni.html

The Regency, facing out to a park in the most exclusive residential area, is one of Florence's finest luxury hotels and a welcome haven in the overcrowded tourist scene. Gracious hospitality comes naturally to owner Amedeo Ottaviani (also of the Lord Byron in Rome) and his philosophy that every guest should be treated with the best possible personal attention goes hand in hand with the intimate ambiance of the hotel, a former private home. Upon arrival guests are warmly greeted by manager Monica and invited into one of the cozy English-style sitting rooms richly appointed with fine antiques and paintings, floral-patterned carpeting, and exquisite fabrics in warm red tones. Beyond are two intimate, formal dining rooms, where the house chef is praised for his innovative creations based on Tuscan specialities incorporating the region's top-quality ingredients. The larger glassed-in dining area looks out over the exceptionally lush courtyard garden where romantic candlelit dinners are served in the summer months. Comfortable bedrooms and suites are spread among the top floors and a separate building connected to the main villa. They are uniquely appointed with white furnishings reproduced from original Tuscan antiques, patterned carpeting, and contrasting wall fabrics. Each has its own marble bathroom, with only a handful left to be refurbished. The concierge is on hand to organize museum and concert reservations, private visits, and guides.

❄ ☕ 💳 ☎ 🏠 ⬆ 🚶 ⚘ 🐎 ♈ P 🍴 🚭 🖼 🔔 🍇

HOTEL REGENCY
Owner: Amedeo Ottaviani
Piazza Massimo d'Azeglio, 3
Florence 50121, Italy
Tel: (055) 24 52 47, Fax: (055) 23 46 735
34 rooms, Double: €250–€800
Open: all year, Credit cards: all major
10-minute walk to the city center
Region: Tuscany, Michelin Map: 430
www.karenbrown.com/italyinns/hotelregency.html

If you are looking for a hotel in Florence that offers both a fabulous location and reasonably priced, pleasant rooms, the simple Relais Uffizi is for you. The double wood doors into the hotel are located on the Chiasso del Buco, a cute little walking lane accessed through an ancient arch from the Chiasso de' Baroncelli, off the Piazza della Signoria. Upstairs in the main reception lounge, either the gracious owner, Elisabetta Matucci, or one of her friendly assistants will be at the desk to give you a warm welcome. Because there are so few rooms and the hotel is family-managed, guests are known by name and made to feel like friends. Nothing is contrived or overly sophisticated: instead there is a homey, comfortable ambiance. The heart of the hotel is the lounge where large windows look down upon the Piazza della Signoria. From your perch, you can relax in quiet comfort and enjoy all the drama and activity of Florence unfolding just below you. Although this is a simple hotel with remarkably low rates, no deluxe hotel in Florence can surpass this view of Florence. A maze of hallways leads to the individually decorated guestrooms. They vary in shape and size (number 3 with a canopy bed is especially spacious), but all are attractive in decor and have some antique furnishings. Best of all, they are immaculately clean and offer such amenities as air conditioning, direct-dial phone, mini bar, hairdryer, and television.

RELAIS UFFIZI
Owner: Elisabetta Matucci
Chiasso de' Baroncelli/Chiasso del Buco, 16
Florence 50122, Italy
Tel: (055) 26 76 239, Fax: (055) 26 57 909
13 rooms, Double: €170–€220
Open: all year, Credit cards: all major
Overlooking Piazza della Signoria
Region: Tuscany, Michelin Map: 430
www.karenbrown.com/italyinns/relaisuffizi.html

The Torre di Bellosguardo is a romantic villa nestled on the shelf of a hill with an unsurpassed view of Florence. Below the hotel, the tiled rooftops, steeples, towers, and domes of the city seem like a fairyland at your fingertips. It is not surprising that the setting of the Torre di Bellosguardo is so breathtaking: it was chosen by a nobleman, Guido Cavalcanti (a friend of Dante's), as the most beautiful site in Florence. The villa is owned today by Amerigo Franchetti who inherited the fabulous property from his grandmother, a baroness. Amerigo takes great pride in his stunning home and, with a passion for perfection, is restoring the villa to its original glory. The guestrooms are decorated in antiques and vary in size as they would in a private home. The most splendid features of the hotel are its incredible setting and meticulously groomed garden, which highlights a swimming pool nestled on a terrace overlooking Florence. What happiness to relax after a day of sightseeing and watch the superb buildings below you melt in the twilight, to reappear as a panorama of twinkling lights. In summer lunch is served by the swimming pool, otherwise breakfast is the only meal available. For dinner, you must wind down a narrow twisting road to go to a restaurant. If you want to walk into Florence, ask about the "secret" path—a short cut down the hill to the city.

TORRE DI BELLOSGUARDO
Owner: Amerigo Franchetti
Via Roti Michelozzi, 2
Florence 50124, Italy
Tel: (055) 22 98 145, Fax: (055) 22 90 08
16 rooms, Double: €280–€380*
*Breakfast not included: €20, Poolside lunch in summer
Open: all year, Credit cards: all major
5-minute drive to city center
Region: Tuscany, Michelin Map: 430
www.karenbrown.com/italyinns/bellosguardo.html

The Villa Montartino, which opened as a deluxe small hotel in 1999, is located on the outskirts of Florence with the advantage of being easy to find and providing convenient parking. In the future a shuttle service to and from the city is planned, and in the meantime taxis are readily available. In the 11th century Montartino was built as a watchtower to ensure safe transit for goods coming into Florence. As you enter the gates and wind up to the enchanting small villa crowning the hilltop, you can quickly see why this site was chosen for protection since the Ema Valley stretches below as far as the eye can see. You feel like a guest in a secluded country estate, yet Florence is only 3 kilometers away. The house has been lovingly restored, with great care taken to retain its original architectural features, and terra-cotta floors, whitewashed walls, beamed ceilings, handsome wooden furniture, and many beautiful antiques create the ambiance of a noble home. The guestrooms are all spacious and the decor luxurious without being pretentious. All of the rooms are air-conditioned, have satellite TV, safe, mini bar, direct-dial phone, and a computer line. Added bonuses are a large, heated swimming pool, Jacuzzi, and steam bath. *Directions:* From A1 take the Florence Certosa exit. At the second stoplight turn right on Via Gherardo Silvani for 1.3 km. When the road splits, keep to the right. The hotel is on the left, behind a gated entrance.

VILLA MONTARTINO
Director: Dr. Gianluca Fontana
Via Gherardo Silvani, 151
Florence 50125, Italy
Tel: (055) 22 35 20, Fax: (055) 22 34 95
7 rooms, Double: €248–€300
Meals by prior arrangement
Open: all year, Credit cards: all major
3 km S of Ponte Vecchio
Region: Tuscany, Michelin Map: 430
www.karenbrown.com/italyinns/villamontartino.html

If you want to see Florence, yet be blissfully removed from its swarm of tourists and traffic congestion, the Villa La Massa makes a fabulous choice for a place to stay. Here you can enjoy the best of all worlds—the tranquil beauty of the countryside combined with the convenience of a courtesy bus to take you to and from the heart of the city (15 minutes away). This gorgeous Renaissance villa originally belonged to the rich and powerful Giraldi family—inscribed tombstones, underground tunnels, and a chapel still remain from this period of the villa's history. What makes Villa La Massa so stunning is not only the appeal of the hotel, but also its setting. This idyllic property sits on a gentle bluff that hugs the edge of the River Arno as it loops its way east from Florence. During the day guests relax by a lovely swimming pool in the central garden courtyard. The restaurant is very special, with tables set on a terrace right above the Arno, making dinner truly romantic. In 1998 Villa La Massa was bought by the owners of the Villa d'Este and totally renovated, with the hotel emerging as a shining new gem in the Florence scene. The grounds are now meticulously groomed, the gardens are splendid, and the interior lovely, reflecting the same standard of excellence as the Villa d'Este. *Directions:* Exit A1 at Firenze Sud and follow signs to Bagno a Ripoli and Candeli. At Candeli, watch for a sign on the left to the hotel.

HOTEL VILLA LA MASSA
Manager: Giampaolo Ottazzi
Florence–Candeli (FI) 50012, Italy
Tel: (055) 62 611, Fax: (055) 63 31 02
37 rooms, Double: €480–€1100
Open: Mar to Nov, Credit cards: all major
On the River Arno, 7 km E of Florence
Region: Tuscany, Michelin Map: 430
Relais & Châteaux
www.karenbrown.com/italyinns/villalamassa.html

The Bencista is a real find for the traveler looking for a congenial, unpretentious, family-run hotel near Florence that has charm and yet is reasonably priced. The villa, romantically nestled in the foothills with a bird's-eye view of Florence, is owned and managed by the Simoni family who are always about, personally seeing to every need of their guests. Simone Simoni speaks excellent English, and on the day of my arrival he was patiently engrossed in conversation with one of the guests, giving him tips for sightseeing. Downstairs there is a jumble of sitting rooms, bars, and parlors, each decorated with dark Victorian furniture. Upstairs are the bedrooms, which vary in size, location, and furnishings. Some are far superior to others, but they are all divided into only two price categories: with or without private bathroom. Many people return year after year to their own favorite room. During the season, reservations are usually given only to guests who plan to spend several days at the hotel—this is an easy requirement because the hotel is beautifully located for sightseeing in both Florence and Tuscany. (If you do not have a car, you can take the bus that runs regularly into Florence from the top of the road.) Two meals (breakfast and a choice of lunch or dinner) are included in the price. One of the outstanding features of the pensione is its splendid terrace where guests can enjoy a sweeping panorama of Florence.

PENSIONE BENCISTA
Owner: Simone Simoni
Florence–Fiesole (FI) 50014, Italy
Tel & fax: (055) 59 163
45 rooms, Double: €180*
*Includes breakfast & dinner, Meals for hotel guests only
Open: all year, Credit cards: MC, VS
8 km NE of Florence
Region: Tuscany, Michelin Map: 430
www.karenbrown.com/italyinns/pensionebencista.html

Fiesole, a small town tucked in the green wooded hills above Florence, has long been a favorite of ours. Staying here gives you the best of both worlds—you can enjoy the peacefulness of the countryside while being just a short ride away from Florence. If you are looking for ultimate luxury, nothing can compete with the Villa San Michele, but the Hotel Villa Fiesole offers a delightful alternative for those on a more conservative budget. You can easily spot the Villa Fiesole, set just above the road as it loops up the wooded hillside. Originally a private mansion, the Villa Fiesole was converted into a delightful small hotel in 1995, being equipped with all the finest modern amenities but keeping the overall ambiance of an exquisite home. In this part of the hotel, the rooms vary somewhat in size because of the nature of the building. A new wing has been added and the construction, although obviously recent, was done in excellent taste so that it blends in beautifully with the original villa. Here the rooms are almost identical in size and furnishings. Each is especially spacious and decorated in a most appealing way, using tones of rich blue and whites, giving an overall ambiance of refined good taste. The hotel does not have a formal restaurant but, in addition to breakfast, a light lunch, dinner, and simple buffet supper are available for guests. The Florence bus #7 stops in front of the villa every 20 minutes until 6 pm.

HOTEL VILLA FIESOLE
Director: Simone Taddeifront
Via Beato Angelico, 35
Florence–Fiesole (FI) 50014, Italy
Tel: (055) 59 72 52, Fax: (055) 59 91 33
28 rooms, Double: €200–€350
Meals for hotel guests only
Open: all year, Credit cards: all major
8 km NE of Florence
Region: Tuscany, Michelin Map: 430
www.karenbrown.com/italyinns/hotelvillafiesole.html

It would be difficult to find another hotel with as many attributes as the Villa San Michele—in fact, almost impossible. How could you surpass a wooded hillside setting overlooking Florence, a stunning view, gorgeous antiques, impeccable management, gourmet dining, and, as if this were not enough, a building designed by Michelangelo. The Villa San Michele was originally a monastery dating back to the 15th century and occupied by Franciscan friars until Napoleon turned it into his headquarters. The adaptation of its rooms and public areas to today's standards has been made without affecting the ambiance of serenity and history. Most of the rooms are in the historical building and have been recently renovated and redecorated with taste and somber elegance. Eleven suites are located in the Italian garden and two in the Limonaia, once the greenhouse for storing lemon plants during the winter. All have stunning views of Florence and the Arno Valley. The lounges, dining rooms, terraces, and gardens are also exquisite. Meals can be enjoyed either in a beautiful dining room or on a lovely veranda that stretches along the entire length of the building. A beautiful swimming pool has been built on a secluded terrace above the hotel. The pool is perfectly situated to capture the view and is surrounded by fragrant gardens.

VILLA SAN MICHELE
Manager: Maurizio Saccani
Via Doccia, 4
Florence–Fiesole (FI) 50014, Italy
Tel: (055) 56 78 200, Fax: (055) 56 78 250
45 rooms, Double: €910–€1046*
*Includes breakfast & dinner
Open: Mar to Nov, Credit cards: all major
7 km NE of Florence
Region: Tuscany, Michelin Map: 430
www.karenbrown.com/italyinns/michele.html

Nestled in a small village in the foothills of the Alps, you'll find one of our favorite hotels, the very special Villa Abbazia, situated across from a picturesque 12th-century abbey. When you enter into the 17th-century palazzo—which is graced by fine antiques, Oriental carpets, lovely fabrics, and bouquets of fresh flowers—the Zanon family welcomes you as if you were a friend in their own home. All of the palazzo's bedrooms and suites are stunning. Each guestroom has been splendidly decorated and exudes the ambiance of an English country manor. Meticulous care and tender love has gone into every tiny detail, including the fresh flowers and individual breakfast china, which reflects the color scheme of each room. In addition to the bedrooms in the Palazzo, there are four beautiful suites in the magnificently restored 19th-century, Liberty-style villa across the garden. The Abbazia is surrounded by excellent places to dine, including its own restaurant, La Corte, where one can find delicious foods typical of the region in a pleasant and intimate environment. The Villa Abbazia is located in a region rich in medieval villages and Palladian villas, most appealing for lovers of art and architecture. The historic towns of Asolo and Vittorio Veneto are nearby.

VILLA ABBAZIA
Owner: Zanon family
Via Martiri della Liberta
Follina (TV) 31051, Italy
Tel: (0438) 97 12 77, Fax: (0438) 97 00 01
18 rooms, Double: €207–€450
Open: all year, Credit cards: all major
90 km S of Cortina, 60 km NW of Venice
Region: Veneto, Michelin Map: 429
Relais & Châteaux
www.karenbrown.com/italyinns/villaabbazia.html

Staying in the Albani hills just south of Rome is an excellent alternative to the higher-priced accommodations in the city—the area offers easy public transportation, proximity to both airports, and picturesque towns, lakes, and gardens. Frascati is best known for its wine and many restaurants, which Romans invade on weekends. The Hotel Flora stands out among the choice of smaller hotels. Formerly a private residence, the turn-of-the-last-century gray-and-white pristine villa has a courtyard and surrounding garden where breakfast is served in the summer months. The best rooms, a variety of doubles, junior suites, and suites, are spacious, with terraces and high ceilings. These are on the upper floors, while the rest are in a newer building next door. The polished decor throughout is neoclassical, with black-and-white marble floors and bathrooms, and antique furnishings, and the guestrooms include many amenities as well as air conditioning. Top-floor rooms have balconies with nice views. To the right of the reception area guests enjoy a comfortable lounge and bar. Sightseeing in the vicinity includes lakes Nemi and Albano, the gardens of Ninfa and Villa Aldobrandini, and Rocca di Papa. A shuttle service is available for transfers to and from airports and the metro station (€58 for two). *Directions:* Exit from Rome's GRA ring road at Via Tuscolana and continue straight to Frascati. Hotel signs are posted in the town.

HOTEL FLORA
Owner: Giannandrea Barbante
Viale Vittorio Veneto, 8
Frascati (RM) 00044, Italy
Tel: (06) 94 16 110, Fax: (06) 94 16 546
32 rooms, Double: €135–€220
Open: all year, Credit cards: all major
19 km south of Rome
Region: Lazio, Michelin Map: 430
www.karenbrown.com/italyinns/flora.html

The Castello di Spaltenna is a charming hotel nestled within a feudal hamlet in the heart of Tuscany's glorious Chianti wine region. From the castle with its fortified monastery and adjacent church adorned by an 11th-century bell tower, you can look out in every direction to a blissful scene of rolling hills, valleys, and woodlands dotted with castles and medieval villages. Although deluxe in every detail, the hotel reflects its heritage with beamed ceilings, thick walls, stone floors, and watchtowers. The decor too pays tribute to the past, with old oil paintings, tapestries, Persian carpets, handmade wrought-iron beds, and splendid antique furniture. The heart of the hotel is the internal courtyard, which becomes a fairytale setting each night for fine dining when tables, softly illuminated by candles, are set with lovely linens and fresh flowers, with a harp playing in the background. On a terrace below the castle guests enjoy a large swimming pool and there is also an indoor pool, which is part of a deluxe spa facility. Scheduled to open in 2003 is an incredible new addition for those who want ultimate privacy and supreme accommodations: a tower in the adorable village of Vertine has been converted into a suite, complete with a helicopter pad for discreet arrivals, servants' quarters, and even a private pool on the top commanding fantastic views (breakfast not included with the Tower Suite). *Directions:* From Gaiole in Chianti, follow signs to the castle.

❄ ☕ 🏊 💳 ☎ 🛗 🏋 🍷 P 🍴 🏊 🏃 🖼 🍇

*CASTELLO DI SPALTENNA   **New***
Manager: Guido Conti
Gaiole in Chianti (SI) 53013, Italy
Tel: (0577) 74 94 83, Fax: (0577) 74 92 69
38 rooms, Double: €212–€490
Closed: Feb & Mar, Credit cards: all major
50 km S of Florence, 30 km N of Siena
Region: Tuscany, Michelin Map: 430
www.karenbrown.com/italyinns/spaltenna.html

When dreaming of Tuscany, one usually envisions sweeping fields of vineyards and gentle hills dotted with olive trees. L'Ultimo Mulino has a totally different type of setting, in a heavily wooded nook by a small stream. This small hotel was originally a medieval olive mill and the antique millstone in the lounge stands testament to the hotel's colorful past, as do many architectural features, including 13 dramatic brick arches, which form a vaulted ceiling in the lounge. The primary color scheme throughout is white and blue—seen in the sofas and also in the dining room in the cushions and the table linens and china. The guestrooms all have a rustic ambiance, appropriate to the old mill, with wrought-iron headboards used throughout. The price of the rooms depends upon the size and the amenities. The least expensive rooms are fairly small but those in the upper category are large, and several have their own private terrace. The bathrooms are especially nice, and many have the added luxury of Jacuzzi tubs. All the rooms have air conditioning, direct-dial phones, mini bars, good lighting by the beds, and satellite televisions. One of the most pleasant features of the hotel is a 20-meter swimming pool built into a terrace above the hotel. *Directions:* From Radda in Chianti, take the road for Gaiole and Siena. About 5 km from Radda, turn left at the sign to L'Ultimo Mulino. The hotel is about midway between Radda and Gaiole.

❄ ☕ 🍴 🍲 CREDIT 🛍 ☎ 🏠 🐕 👫 🏇 ♈ P ≋ 🖼 🐾 ♿ 🍇

L'ULTIMO MULINO
Manager: Lorenza Padoan
Localita: La Ripresa di Vistarenni
Gaiole in Chianti (SI) 53013, Italy
Tel: (0577) 73 85 20, Fax: (0577) 73 86 59
13 rooms, Double: €245–€300
Meals for hotel guests (Tues-Sun)
Closed: mid-Nov to mid-Mar, Credit cards: all major
50 km S of Florence, 30 km N of Siena
Region: Tuscany, Michelin Map: 430
www.karenbrown.com/italyinns/lultimo.html

I was enchanted with the Villa Fiordaliso (a fetching pink and white villa superbly located on the shore of Lake Garda) when I spent the night in one of its antique-filled bedrooms overlooking the lake many years ago. At that time, I wrote a glowing description of this beautiful little hotel, only to learn the villa was closing to the public. Nevertheless, when researching for a later edition, I went by the Villa Fiordaliso for old times' sake and, to my delight, found it open again as a small hotel. Although the emphasis now is definitely on dining (the meals are expensive, but excellent), there are seven bedrooms—each unique in decor, yet each with every modern comfort. The rooms facing the lake have a lovely view and are quieter since they are away from the noise of the street. Throughout the interior there is a blend of antique and stylish modern furniture, nicely set off by ornate parquetry floors, cool marble pillars, and magnificent gilded and painted ceilings. For history buffs, the hotel offers a bit of romance—the Villa Fiordaliso was a gift from Mussolini to his mistress, Claretta Petacci. In fact, Claretta's bedroom is one of the rooms available and is a real winner, with an enormous marble bathroom. The Villa Fiordaliso is owned and managed by the Tossetti family whose warmth of welcome mellows the sophisticated ambiance of this small hotel.

VILLA FIORDALISO
Owner: Giuseppe Tossetti
Via Zanardelli, 132
Gardone Riviera–Lake Garda (BS) 25083, Italy
Tel: (0365) 20 15 8, Fax: (0365) 29 00 11
7 rooms, Double: €200–€540
Open: Feb to Nov, Credit cards: all major
66 km W of Verona
Region: Lombardy, Michelin Maps: 428, 429
Relais & Châteaux
www.karenbrown.com/italyinns/fiordaliso.html

La Foresteria Serego Alighieri is on a working farm producing wine and olive oil. Only a discreet brass sign on the gate hints at any commercialism, yet it is indeed a fabulous place to stay. Each reasonably priced guestroom is a one- or two-bedroom apartment with a well-equipped kitchen, charming living room, and a large bathroom tiled in local marble. The decor throughout reflects tasteful, elegant simplicity—whitewashed walls set off country antiques, and comfortable sofas are upholstered in Venetian pure-cotton fabrics in green and cream stripes. Soft green is repeated in the pretty cotton drapes and bedspreads. It is not surprising that La Foresteria has been developed with such love and meticulous care to maintain the estate's authentic charm—the present owner, the gracious Count di Serego Alighieri, is the 20th generation to own the property! Family records indicate the first ancestor to own the land was the poet Dante's son, who purchased the estate in 1353. This vast farm was almost doomed at the end of World War II when the retreating armies had orders to destroy it. As a forestalling tactic, the present count's father invited the commanding officers to a magnificent party. Perhaps it was the abundance of the excellent wines served, but happily the officers forgot their orders. To celebrate this miracle of the saving of the town, every April the local townspeople make a pilgrimage to the estate to celebrate mass—followed, of course, by a little wine.

LA FORESTERIA SEREGO ALIGHIERI
Owner: Count Pieralvise di Serègo Alighieri
Manager: R. Corradi
Via Stazione, 2
Gurgagnago (VR) 37020, Italy
Tel: (045) 77 03 622, Fax: (045) 77 03 523
8 rooms, Double: €125–€307
Closed: Jan, Credit cards: all major
18 km NW of Verona
Region: Veneto, Michelin Maps: 428, 429
www.karenbrown.com/italyinns/laforesteriaserego.html

The Grand Hotel a Villa Feltrinelli, snuggled on the shore of romantic Lake Garda just steps from the tiny, picturesque village of Gargnano, is an incredible property. This fairy-tale villa—painted in muted cream and peach-colored stripes accented by a jaunty tower and turreted roof—is so appealing it makes you smile from first glance. It was built as a private home for the Feltrinelli family, who made their fortune in lumber. The building had been long neglected when Bob Burns became captivated by its romantic charm and for three years poured unrestricted love and money into meticulously returning the mansion to its original glory. Talented artisans worked around the clock restoring gorgeous murals, stained-glass windows, handsome paneling, massive chandeliers, and splendid floors. Although this is a super-luxurious, exquisite jewel of a hotel, the ambiance exudes the warmth and friendliness of a private home. There is hardly a hint of commercialism: guests are warmly welcomed at the door; registration is discreetly accomplished in the guestroom; the mini bar is stocked with complimentary drinks; suitcases are unpacked (if the guest so desires) and whisked away to storage; laundry and dry cleaning are complimentary; drinks in the bar can be signed for on the honor system. For quality and sumptuous accommodations, the Villa Feltrinelli is an incredible value. *Directions:* Located at the north end of Gargnano.

GRAND HOTEL A VILLA FELTRINELLI
Manager: Marcus Odermatt
Gargnano–Lake Garda (BS) 25084, Italy
Tel: (0365) 79 80 00, Fax: (0365) 79 80 01
20 rooms, Double: €475–€1400
Closed: Jan, Credit cards: all major
140 km E of Milan, 78 km W of Verona
Region: Lombardy, Michelin Maps: 428, 429
www.karenbrown.com/italyinns/villafeltrinelli.html

The Hotel Villa Giulia is an outstanding small hotel just on the edge of the quaint, colorful, medieval village of Gargnano. It has a prime location: not only lakefront, but also surrounded by large, parklike grounds. The main house, reminiscent of a quaint Victorian villa, sits center stage with a tree-studded lawn stretching down to a terrace overlooking the lake. In the garden is a wonderful swimming pool tucked in under the frame that in days gone by was used to protect the precious lemon trees that are so famous in this part of Italy. Some of the guestrooms are located in the main villa, others in two separate renovated buildings on the property, but they all share the facilities in the main house. Here you find a parlor with an old-fashioned appeal and a spacious dining room with super views of the lake. The guestrooms in this original villa are my favorites, especially rooms such as 7 or 17, which have stunning views. In addition to its attractive rooms, great Italian cooking, and outstanding location, the Hotel Villa Giulia has another ingredient that makes it even more special—it is run by your sweet and charming hostess Barbara (ably assisted by her husband Giovani), who took over the management of the hotel a few years ago from her aunt. The hotel has been lovingly redecorated and is a wonderful choice for accommodations along the ever-so-romantic Lake Garda. *Directions:* Located on the north edge of Gargnano.

HOTEL VILLA GIULIA
Owner: Bombardelli family
Viale Rimembranza, 20
Gargnano–Lake Garda (BS) 25084, Italy
Tel: (0365) 71 022, Fax: (0365) 72 774
24 rooms, Double: €200–€250
Open: Easter to Oct, Credit cards: all major
140 km E of Milan, 78 km W of Verona
Region: Lombardy, Michelin Maps: 428, 429
www.karenbrown.com/italyinns/villagiulia.html

The entrance to Baia d'Oro is off the narrow cobbled street that runs through the quaint lakeside town of Gargnano-Villa. Inside, you find a small lounge, bar, and dining room. To truly appreciate the attributes that make this small inn special, you must step outside to the terrace stretching out over the water. In the daytime this sun-drenched oasis is a favorite with the luncheon crowd, then in the evening as the sun sets, fresh flowers and candles are placed on small tables dressed with fresh linens. Although open only in high season, the restaurant lives up to all expectations: the pasta is homemade in the kitchen, the fish is fresh from the lake. As you eat, there is a constant parade of beautiful yachts pulling up to the dock, unloading their cargo of chicly dressed, obviously well-to-do Italians who have come to dine. After dinner, you go up a narrow staircase to the basic bedrooms, which are ideal for the young of heart who are not expecting decorator-perfect furnishings. Room 9, which overlooks the lake, is my favorite. Although very simple, the rooms are tidy and very clean. The hotel does not have parking and parking is a problem. The best bet is to drive through town, take any space your find and walk to the hotel. English isn't spoken, but you can communicate in sign language and a smile. The Baia d'Oro is owned by the Terzi family. Gianbattista Terzi is an artist and his paintings decorate the walls.

BAIA D'ORO
Manager: Gabriele Terzi
Via Gamberera, 13
Gargnano-Villa–Lake Garda (BS) 25084, Italy
Tel: (0365) 71 17 1, Fax: (0365) 72 56 8
13 rooms, Double: €110
Open: mid-Mar to mid-Nov
140 km E of Milan, 78 km W of Verona
Region: Lombardy, Michelin Maps: 428, 429
www.karenbrown.com/italyinns/baiadoro.html

Hotel du Lac, an intimate, family-managed hotel in the colorful, tiny village of Villa di Gargnano, is very special. If you want an elegant hotel decorated with opulent fabrics and ornate furnishings, this would not be your cup of tea. But for genuine hospitality, superb lakefront setting, and spotlessly clean, attractive rooms at very reasonable prices, the Hotel du Lac is a real winner. From the moment we walked in and met the charming young owner, Valerio Arosio, I knew this would be a special hotel. The reception and sitting areas as you enter are simply decorated with modern, nondescript furnishings. In contrast, the bedrooms are unexpectedly attractive for such moderately priced accommodations. Each has a lovely antique headboard and a sweet, simple charm. There is satellite TV in all the rooms and the bathrooms are modern and even have hairdryers. Splurge and ask for one of the bedrooms with a terrace and view of the lake. When the weather is warm, most meals are served outside. However, there is an attractive dining room with windows on three sides capturing views of the lake. Guests at the Hotel du Lac can park their cars at Hotel Gardenia al Lago, Valerio's brother's property just down the street. This is a tremendous bonus since parking is nearly impossible along the narrow medieval lanes of Villa di Gargnano. *Directions:* Villa di Gargnano is located just south of Gargnano. The hotel is in the center of town.

HOTEL DU LAC
Owner: Valerio Arosio
Via Colletta, 21
Gargnano-Villa–Lake Garda (BS) 25084, Italy
Tel: (0365) 71 107, Fax: (0365) 71 055
12 rooms, Double: €77–€113
Open: Mar to Dec, Credit cards: MC, VS
140 km E of Milan, 78 km W of Verona
Region: Lombardy, Michelin Maps: 428, 429
www.karenbrown.com/italyinns/hoteldulac.html

The Frascati hillside wine area just south of Rome is an alternative to staying in the city. Before opening its doors in 1997, the 16th-century Villa Grazioli undertook ten years of tedious restoration work—it was imperative to conserve the architecture, grounds, and the many important frescoed ceilings by G.P. Pannini. After the restoration it was transformed into a splendid hotel under the strict regulations of the Ministry of Historical Buildings. The spacious reception area and four inviting frescoed sitting rooms on the first floor remind us that this was once a private residence. Ten spacious double rooms and two suites are offered right in the villa off the impressive galleria—a head-spinning vaulted hall completely frescoed from floor to ceiling, overlooking the front garden. The remaining more standard rooms are located across the garden in what was originally the lemon-tree greenhouse, all decorated conservatively with antiques and rich fabrics and offering all the modern amenities. An underground tunnel connects the two buildings. The four formal, high-ceilinged dining rooms have an enormous terrace taking in the surrounding park, Italian gardens, and a panoramic view over Rome. The hotel has a shuttle service to Frascati, Rome, or the local train station. *Directions:* From the GRA (the circle road around Rome) exit onto the N21/22. Go south to Grottaferrata. At the end of town, a sign to the left marks the way to the hotel.

PARK HOTEL VILLA GRAZIOLI
Director: Rolf Rampf
Via Umberto Pavoni, 19
Grottaferrata (RM) 00046, Italy
Tel: (06) 94 54 00, Fax: (06) 94 13 506
58 rooms, Double: €240–€450
Open: all year, Credit cards: all major
20 km south of Rome
Region: Lazio, Michelin Map: 430
Relais & Châteaux
www.karenbrown.com/italyinns/hotelvillagrazioli.html

Gubbio is one of Umbria's many jewels: a small, wonderfully intact medieval town that presses against the wooded hillside. A not-to-be-missed sight in Gubbio is the Piazza Grande, considered to be one of the boldest examples of medieval town planning, and facing onto this awesome masterpiece is the Relais Ducale. Gazing from the square, you would hardly know that a hotel is secreted within the building, but you will notice a large, open, stone passageway. Enter here and climb up the stairs through a tunnel-like corridor where you will emerge into a little lane. Continue on until you come to a hotel sign by the gate on a stone wall. Ring the bell for entrance and suddenly the hotel reveals itself with a charming inner garden courtyard off which you find the discreet reception office. The hotel, once the guest quarters for the Ducale Palace, has been sleekly renovated, but impressive features of its past are seen throughout with massive thick walls, high vaulted ceilings, and stone archways. On the fourth level of the hotel there is a romantic garden with one side enclosed by a carved stone balustrade, where you can gaze out to a beautiful panoramic view. Fine antique furniture is used for accent, handsome oil paints adorn the walls, and Oriental carpets brighten the floors. The pretty guestrooms have a sedate, refined decor, showing an effort to preserve the aristocratic aura of the hotel's heritage.

RELAIS DUCALE
Owner: Rodolfo Mencarelli
Via Ducale, 2
Gubbio (PG) 06024, Italy
Tel: (075) 92 20 157, Fax: (075) 92 20 159
32 rooms, Double: €130–€227
Open: all year, Credit cards: all major
54 km NW of Assisi, 92 km E of Arezzo
Region: Umbria, Michelin Map: 430
www.karenbrown.com/italyinns/relaisducale.html

La Posta Vecchia, a spectacular villa nestled on the edge of the ocean just north of Rome's airport, was the home of the late John Paul Getty. There are 19 bedrooms (mostly suites) tucked into a stunning mansion secluded by manicured gardens artfully designed to emphasize the ruins of the Pompeii-like villa. The magic starts from the moment you ring the bell at the gated entrance—the gate swings open, you drive through a vast park, and suddenly, the storybook villa comes into view. Within the mansion, priceless antique furniture, statues, and fine fabrics richly adorn the rooms, creating an opulent, tasteful splendor in the lounges and the guestrooms. The dining room is exquisite, but even more romantic is to dine on balmy evenings on the terrace perched above the ocean. When Getty was installing the magnificent pool in the northern wing, he discovered the foundations of a Roman villa—thought perhaps to be the weekend retreat of Julius Caesar. Getty, who was profoundly interested in archaeology, spared no expense to preserve this antiquity. These Roman ruins are now encompassed by the lower level of the home and guests can view the splendid mosaic floors, walls, and pottery—displayed as if in a living museum. La Posta Vecchia is expensive, but a once-in-a-lifetime experience. *Directions:* Exit the A12 at Ladispoli and follow signs to town. La Posta Vecchia is in Palo Laziale, 2.2 km south of Ladispoli.

LA POSTA VECCHIA
Manager: Franco Ottaviani
Ladispoli–Palo Laziale (RM) 00055, Italy
Tel: (06) 99 49 501, Fax: (06) 99 49 507
19 rooms, Double: €348–€512
Open: mid-Mar to early Nov, Credit cards: all major
25 km N of Rome airport
Region: Lazio, Michelin Map: 430
Relais & Châteaux
www.karenbrown.com/italyinns/lapostavecchia.html

Cinque Terre is the name given to five villages (Monterosso, Riomaggiore, Vernazza, Manarola, and Corniglia) that are built into the mountainous coast of Liguria. Several of these picturesque villages are accessible only by foot or train. There are several choices of places from which you can explore these tiny fishing hamlets, one of these being the modest, rather dated resort of Levanto. The Hotel Stella Maris is a simple, two-star hotel, but it exudes warmth and caring, and is recommended to the traveler who is looking for a reasonably priced place to stay and who values hospitality rather than decorator-perfect accommodation. Not that the hotel is lacking in character: it is located on the second floor of a 17th-century palazzo and remnants of its past grandeur remain. Many of the bedrooms feature high, elaborately frescoed ceilings and handsome antique beds. I think my favorite is number 4, an especially inviting room with a romantic wooden, French-style headboard. The dining room also has a frescoed ceiling and a fancy mural depicting a maharajah and his elephant train. Breakfast and dinner are included in the room rate. Although only a little English is spoken, Renza and Sandro exude a merry warmth that is sure to touch your heart.

HOTEL STELLA MARIS
Owners: Renza & Alexandro Italiani
Via Marconi, 4
Levanto (SP) 19015, Italy
Tel: (0187) 80 82 58, Fax: (0187) 80 73 51
14 rooms, Double: €200*
*Includes breakfast & dinner
Closed: Nov, Credit cards: all major
83 km SE of Genoa, 36 km NW of La Spezia
Region: Liguria, Michelin Map: 428
www.karenbrown.com/italyinns/stellamaris.html

Limone sul Garda is a small town tucked into a pocket of a hillside at the edge of Lake Garda. This very old town of pastel-colored houses adorned with bougainvillea and twisting cobbled streets attracts so many visitors that in high season it is wall-to-wall tourists. Nevertheless, the town is very quaint, and especially appealing off season when you can avoid some of the crowds. The Hotel Le Palme (in a building dating back to the 17th century) is in the heart of town, directly on the lake. Whereas many of our suggestions in the Lake Garda area are intimate, family-operated inns, Le Palme is a hotel with a more commercial ambiance. You enter into the lobby and go down a few steps to a small bar and an especially attractive dining room with handsome wooden, antique-style, high-back chairs and beautifully set tables. From the dining room, French doors open onto an appealing outside dining area on a balcony overlooking the lake. Along the side of the hotel is another, more casual, place to eat in a garden terrace overlooking the lake where white wrought-iron tables and chairs are set under the centuries-old palm trees among many plants and colorful flowers. The rooms, all with satellite TV and air conditioning, are pleasant and a few have some antique pieces of furniture. Prime rooms overlook the lake. The Risatti brothers who own Le Palme own several hotels in town and guests can use the pool at another of their hotels, La Pergola.

❄ ⚓ ☕ 💳 ☎ 🛗 🏇 P ⚍ 🏊 🖼 🏄 🍇

HOTEL LE PALME
Owner: Risatti family
Via Porto, 36
Limone sul Garda–Lake Garda 25010, Italy
Tel: (0365) 95 46 81, Fax: (0365) 95 41 20
28 rooms, Double: €66–€138
Open: Easter to Oct, Credit cards: MC, VS
160 km NE of Milan, 97 km NW of Verona
Region: Lombardy, Michelin Maps: 428, 429
www.karenbrown.com/italyinns/hotellepalme.html

For a simple, sweet, friendly little hotel, the Albergo San Martino offers excellent quality at a reasonable price. This cheerful inn looked so inviting we had to go in to see if it was as cute inside as out. The building had also caught the eye of the owners, the young, very friendly Andrea Martinelli and his partners who, being in the tourism business in Lucca, knew of its lack of good hotels. We usually hear stories of years of delays from when a property is bought until it reopens after refurbishments, but Andrea and his associates must be miracle workers because they purchased the property in February 1999 and opened the hotel in November 1999. Named for San Martino Cathedral, which is just steps away, the hotel is painted a soft yellow, which is accented by pretty white shutters. In front, an appealing little garden area with white umbrellas shading tables and chairs is prettily defined by potted trees and plants. You enter into a fresh and tidy lobby with a reception desk to your left and a sitting area and intimate bar to your right. Every evening Andrea or one of his partners sits here with his guests to share his knowledge of what to do and see in the area. On the walls are art exhibits that change every two months. The simply furnished guestrooms offer air conditioning, satellite TVs, direct-dial phones, and mini bars. *Directions:* Lucca is a maze of tiny streets, so it is best to ask for detailed instructions.

ALBERGO SAN MARTINO
Director: Andrea Martinelli
Via della Dogana, 9
Lucca 55100, Italy
Tel: (0583) 46 91 81, Fax: (0583) 99 19 40
8 rooms, Double: €106–€155
Open: all year, Credit cards: all major
70 km W of Florence, in historic center
Region: Tuscany, Michelin Map: 430
www.karenbrown.com/italyinns/albergosanmartino.html

Lucca is an outstanding walled town—truly one of Italy's jewels—but it is rather lacking in deluxe hotels. However, just a ten-minute drive away sits the sumptuous Locanda L'Elisa, a pretty, deep-lavender villa with white trim peeking out from a frame of trees. The hotel has the appearance of a private home and, happily, this intimate, homelike quality remains even after you step inside where you are warmly greeted. As you look around, it is obvious that this was previously the residence of a wealthy family. Fine antiques, splendid paintings, and luxurious fabrics combine to create a mood of refined elegance. All of the guestrooms are individually decorated, but exude a similar old-world ambiance created with dark woods and opulent materials. The walls are richly covered in damask fabrics that color-coordinate with the draperies and bedspreads. However, the mood changes dramatically in the appealing dining room, found in a glass-enclosed conservatory. During the day, sunlight streams in through the windows and guests can enjoy both excellent cuisine and a view of the trees, green lawn, and colorful, well-tended beds of flowers. In this same garden you find a refreshing swimming pool. The Locanda L'Elisa is small and very special—a real luxury hideaway with a gracious warmth of welcome. *Directions:* Take the A11 to Lucca then take N12r (not 12) toward Pisa. Soon after leaving Lucca, watch for a sign on the left for Locanda L'Elisa.

LOCANDA L'ELISA
Owner: Alessandro Del Grande
Via Nuova per Pisa, 1952 (S.S. 12B1S), Massa Pisana
Lucca 55050, Italy
Tel: (0583) 37 97 37, Fax: (0583) 37 90 19
8 rooms, Double: €284–€450, Breakfast not included: €16
Open: Feb 11 to Nov 26, Credit cards: all major
4.5 km S of Lucca on N12r, 65 km W of Florence
Region: Tuscany, Michelin Map: 430
Relais & Châteaux
www.karenbrown.com/italyinns/locandalelisa.html

It was welcome news to hear that a small deluxe hotel had opened in the historical center of Lucca, one of our favorite medieval walled cities. After years of meticulous restoration, the 12th-century Palazzo Alexander first opened for guests in 2000. Your gracious host and creator of this small inn is Mario Maraviglia, who welcomes guests as friends with hardly a hint of commercialism—there isn't even a hotel sign in front—and his team shares his philosophy. To the left of the marble-floored reception foyer is an ornate, intimate breakfast room and bar, set with small tables and fancy, gold-embellished chairs. Two huge chandeliers enhance the dark, handsome, beamed ceiling. As well as the elevator, a wonderful, very old stone staircase, illuminated by a stained-glass skylight, leads up to the guestrooms, each named after a famous Italian opera. The bedrooms are furnished with antique reproduction furniture in an ornate Venetian style. All the rooms have mini-bars, hairdryers, TVs, direct-dial phones, and elegant marble bathrooms. If you want to splurge, ask for "Tosca" which has a romantic little terrace tucked in amongst the rooftops. At the moment there are only a few rooms, but the building next door has been purchased and soon there will be ten additional suites. *Directions:* The hotel has a parking lot nearby and you can drive through the pedestrian zone to the hotel. Ask for a diagram on how to reach the hotel.

PALAZZO ALEXANDER
Owner: Mario Maraviglia
Via Santa Giustina, 48
Lucca (FI) 55100, Italy
Tel: (0583) 58 35 71, Fax: (0583) 58 36 10
13 rooms, Double: €120–€255
Open: all year, Credit cards: all major
70 km W of Florence, in historic center
Region: Tuscany, Michelin Map: 430
www.karenbrown.com/italyinns/palazzoalexander.html

The Luz family bought and restored this lovely turn-of-the-last-century villa across from the lake more than 30 years ago. It retains its Liberty-style decor (1920s) throughout the several sitting and dining rooms with high, frescoed ceilings, stained-glass and lead windows, and ornate chandeliers. The reception area has an old-fashioned wooden bar with leather stools, velvet sofas and armchairs, Oriental carpets, and an enormous stone fireplace. Bedrooms upstairs vary in size (single, double, or suite) and are in keeping with the general decor of the accommodation. Many amenities are offered such as air conditioning and hydrojet baths in suites. A garden surrounds the villa where in the summer months tables and umbrellas are set up for dinner or buffet breakfast. Gracious Signora Renate runs the show, assisting her guests with various itineraries around the lake area. Guests have access as well to the family's other lakefront hotel, with its alternative restaurant, park, and swimming. This place exudes old-world charm. *Directions:* Luino is halfway up the eastern side of the lake and the hotel is easily found right in town.

CAMIN HOTEL LUINO
Owner: Luz family
Viale Dante, 35
Luino–Lake Maggiore (VA) 21016, Italy
Tel: (0332) 53 01 18, Fax: (0332) 53 72 26
14 rooms, Double: €150–€250
Open: Feb to Dec 20, Credit cards: all major
100 km NW of Milan, 20 km S of Lugano
Region: Lombardy, Michelin Map: 428
www.karenbrown.com/italyinns/hotelluino.html

The enchanting Villa delle Rose, idyllically nestled on the bank of the Lecco branch of Lake Como, exudes a tranquil, unpretentious charm. A lush lawn accented with towering firs and lacy shade trees stretches out to a stone balustrade at the water's edge. The romantic two-story, white stucco building was originally a private home before being sold and opened in 1999 as an intimate, family-managed hotel. Your exceptionally gracious hosts, Maria Cristina and Armando Masarin, previously owned a hotel on the island of Zanzibar off the coast of Tanzania. When the political situation in Africa became difficult, they returned home and bought the villa, where Armando planted hundreds of fragrant old-fashioned roses. The decor throughout has many rose motifs plus a subtle accent of Africa. The ground floor of the hotel is mostly dedicated to its excellent restaurant—if you enjoy gourmet dining, splurge on one of the superb meals, which always include fresh lake fish. When the weather is balmy, the favorite place to dine is outside where tables with white awnings are set on a terrace with a splendid view of the lake. A curving staircase leads up to the breakfast room and the individually decorated guestrooms. Request the Rosa Silver or the Rosa Elina, as these have the best lake views. *Directions:* From Lecco, go north on S36 and exit at Abbadia. Continue to Mandello del Lario, following signs to Villa delle Rose on the north edge of town.

RELAIS VILLA DELLE ROSE   *New*
Owners: Maria Cristina & Armando Masarin
Via Statale, 125/127
Mandello del Lario (LC) 23826, Italy
Tel & fax: (0341) 73 13 04
6 rooms, Double: €130
Open: all year, Credit cards: all major
67 km N of Milan, 40 km NE of Como
Region: Lombardy, Michelin Map: 428
www.karenbrown.com/italyinns/villadellerose.html

If you have never been to Mantova, go—and plan to stay for several days. It is a jewel of a medieval walled town, wrapped on three sides by lakes, with one picturesque plaza melting into another, each with its own special charm. Luckily, there is a very nice hotel right in the heart of this historic town—the Albergo San Lorenzo. From the moment you enter the intimate small reception area, a mood of sedate, old-world elegance is set by three awesome antique mirrors, ornately adorned with gold frames. A staircase leads up to an appealing, homelike lounge with pretty chairs and comfy slipcovered couches. Here you also find a small bar and an attractive breakfast room. There is no restaurant, but the town abounds with marvelous restaurants, so finding a good place to dine becomes an adventure. Splurge and request one of the junior suites with a terrace and a view overlooking the town. These are really special and worth the additional cost. Not only are the antiques in the rooms lovely, but from your spacious terrace you can relax while soaking in the romantic ambiance of this stunning medieval town. If you don't opt for a junior suite, you can relax in the sunshine on a large terrace tucked in the rooftops and enjoy a fabulous view of Mantova. The hotel is managed by twin brothers Ottorino and Giuseppe Tosi, who ensure that guests are given excellent service and treated with great courtesy. *Directions:* Located in the center of Mantova.

ALBERGO SAN LORENZO
Owners: Ottorino & Giuseppe Tosi
Piazza Concordia, 14
Mantova (MN) 46100, Italy
Tel: (0376) 22 05 00, Fax: (0376) 32 71 94
32 rooms, Double: €187–€220
Open: all year, Credit cards: all major
42 km S of Verona, 89 km NW of Ferrara
Region: Emilia-Romagna, Michelin Map: 429
www.karenbrown.com/italyinns/lorenzo.html

Clinging to the steep hillside above the beautiful coast of Basilicata, Maratea is a charming village of very old colorful houses and narrow cobbled streets. As the road loops ever-upward through the town, you soon come to the Locanda delle Donne Monache, carved into the rocky slope next to the tiny parish church of St. Maria. Originally a nunnery dating back to the early 1700s, the convent has been transformed into a deluxe small hotel. The exterior—salmon-colored stuccoed walls with white trim and rustic heavy-tiled roof—blends well with other houses in the village. Inside, the color scheme continues with sky-blue added for accent. The bedrooms are tucked throughout the hotel, each taking advantage of its special vista. The largest guestrooms are designated as suites. Number 9 is especially interesting, with a dramatic bathtub carved into the rocks and a pretty view out over the tiled rooftops. The most outstanding feature of the hotel is its garden where, located on the upper terrace next to the small church, a swimming pool seems to float in the air, romantically suspended above the jumble of village rooftops. Overlooking the garden, on balmy summer evenings, guests enjoy superb meals outside under the stars. The quiet serenity must have appealed to the nuns so long ago. *Directions:* Follow the road up to Maratea following signs for Centro Storico. In the main square you will see signs pointing to the hotel.

LA LOCANDA DELLE DONNE MONACHE
Owner: Mondo Maratea
Via Carlo Mazzei, 4
Maratea (PZ) 85046, Italy
Tel: (0973) 87 74 87, Fax: (0973) 87 76 87
30 rooms, Double: €120–€250
Open: all year, Credit cards: all major
220 km S of Naples, 5 km W of Maratea
Region: Basilicata, Michelin Map: 431
www.karenbrown.com/italyinns/donnemonache.html

One of our favorite recommendations along the southern coast of Italy is the Santavenere Hotel, an ideal stopping point if you are driving south to Sicily. However, don't just consider it as a place to spend the night en route—the Santavenere is so special you will want to linger and use it as a base to explore this lovely niche of Italy. The hotel, built in 1956, is perfectly positioned on a promontory above the sea, affording unsurpassed views of the gorgeous, sparkling, turquoise water. Although the hotel is of contemporary construction, its interior radiates an old-world charm combined with a nautical flair. The living room is elegant, but not stuffy—comfortable slipcovered chairs and sofas form cozy conversation nooks, while fine antiques and beautiful ship models lend further charm. The guestrooms too are extremely attractive in their decor and, best of all, each has its own terrace or balcony with a view of the sea or the park. The property is very large and in the meticulously groomed gardens there are gorgeous displays of flowers and lush lawns. Here you find a beautiful swimming pool from which a path leads to the edge of the cliff and then loops down through a fragrant pine forest to the sea where guests can swim in the crystal-clear water. *Directions:* Take the coastal highway N18 to Maratea. Do not go into the town, but instead follow signs for the porto and Fiumicello, then for the hotel.

SANTAVENERE HOTEL
Manager: Francesca Romano
Maratea (PZ) 85040, Italy
Tel: (0973) 87 69 10, Fax: (0973) 87 76 54
44 rooms, Double: €260–€761
Open: Apr to Oct, Credit cards: all major
220 km S of Naples, adjacent to Maratea Porto
Region: Basilicata, Michelin Map: 431
www.karenbrown.com/italyinns/santavenere.html

The sienna-and-cream-colored, Liberty-style Villa Cheta Elite is located on the main coastal road just south of Acquafredda. A steep path winds up through the garden to the hotel, which has a series of tall French doors opening onto a shaded terrace where glimpses of the sea can be seen through the flowers and the trees. The hotel retains the genuine warmth and charm of a private home, without any hint of the formal commercialism of a hotel. Throughout there is a comfortable lived-in, old-fashioned elegance. Stefanie, the exceptionally gracious owner, personally supervises every detail in the operation of her small hotel and welcomes one and all as personal guests. Each bedroom is individually decorated using homey family antiques. When the weather is balmy guests eat dinner on the terrace whose white wrought-iron tables are prettily set with fresh linens and bouquets of flowers from the garden. The home-cooked meals are outstanding. If you prefer small, family-owned hotels to the sophisticated glamour of expensive resort-style hotels along this magical coast of southern Italy, the Villa Cheta Elite will definitely win your heart.

ROMANTIK HOTEL VILLA CHETA ELITE
Owner: Stefanie Aquadro
Via Timpone, 46
Maratea–Acquafredda (PZ) 85041, Italy
Tel: (0973) 87 81 34, Fax: (0973) 87 81 35
18 rooms, Double: €115–€150
Open: all year, Credit cards: all major
1 km S of Acquafredda, 210 km S of Naples
Region: Basilicata, Michelin Map: 431
www.karenbrown.com/italyinns/villachetaelite.html

If you are intrigued with the idea of really getting off the beaten path, look no further than the Tenuta del Barco, a vast farming estate of over 100 hectares that sweeps right down to the sand dunes of the Ionian Sea. The extraordinary warmth and charm of your hosts, Maria Cristina and Nick Donadio, combined with their good taste and professionalism, make the Tenuta del Barco a special place to stay. Both Maria and Nick went to school in the United States and speak fluent English—a great bonus since they can advise you how to explore this enchanting niche of southern Italy. If you are traveling with children, the Tenuta del Barco is ideal since there is a playground on the property, a pool, an excellent beach just a few minutes away, and each room has a kitchenette. The farm has been in Nick's family for over 250 years and almost everything served in the restaurant comes from the estate. You enter through a gate into a large, square courtyard bound by pure-white, Moorish-style buildings that reflect the brilliant sun. To the left are the reception and the restaurant, built into the old stables. When the weather is warm, dining is outside on the terrace. The buildings date back to the 16th century and great care has been taken to preserve their superb architectural features, including incredible soaring, cathedral-like stone ceilings. The decor is refreshingly simple and in perfect harmony with the architecture.

TENUTA DEL BARCO
Owners: Maria Cristina & Nick Donadio
Marina di Pulsano (TA) 74026, Italy
Tel & fax: (099) 53 33 051
7 rooms, Double: €95–€160
Minimum nights required: 7 (Jul & Aug)
Open: all year, Credit cards: all major
22 km SE of Taranto, 5 km SE of Pulsano
Region: Apulia, Michelin Map: 431
www.karenbrown.com/italyinns/tenutadelbarco.html

Castello Labers (also called Schloss Labers) is a lovely old castle which, while dating back to the 11th century, has more of a feel of a grand Victorian home than a fortification. It has a picturesque setting on a hillside surrounded by vineyards and overlooking the beautiful Merano Valley, which is framed by dramatic mountains. Although not luxurious, this castle has character and charm. Signor Neubert told me that his great-grandfather came from Copenhagen in 1885 and bought the castle, which became so popular with his visiting friends that it soon became a prosperous hotel. The lounges and dining rooms are not fancy, but have a lived-in, comfortable atmosphere. Many fresh foods are included in the menu and both red and white wines, produced from the inn's own vineyards, are served with meals. The central staircase leads dramatically upstairs where many of the bedrooms have lovely mountain views (I loved our room 14b). After a day of sightseeing you can swim in the pool or the more energetic can enjoy a game of tennis. There is also a restored 16th-century chapel on the grounds that offers a holy mass every Saturday at 6 pm. For guests staying three nights or more the hotel offers half board (breakfast and dinner) for €80–€150 extra per day. *Directions:* Take the Merano Sud exit from the new Bolzano-Merano road. Follow signs for Hafling for 4.5 km, then turn right towards Labers and the castle is soon visible on your left.

HOTEL CASTELLO LABERS
Owner: Stapf-Neubert family
Via Labers, 25
Merano (BZ) 39012, Italy
Tel: (0473) 23 44 84, Fax: (0473) 23 41 46
36 rooms, Double: €136–€300
Minimum nights required: 3
Open: Apr to Nov, Credit cards: MC, VS
28 km NW of Bolzano, 150 km N of Verona
Region: Trentino-Alto Adige, Michelin Map: 429
www.karenbrown.com/italyinns/labers.html

Alexander Ortner's grandfather bought this shooting lodge in 1954 and over the years the family has expanded it to become the smallest four-star hotel in Merano. It really deserves accolades, for it is a simply delightful hotel, hospitably run by the Ortners, with the most spectacular views across the vineyards of the Merano Valley. This gorgeous view is the focus of the vine-covered terrace and in warm months guests are assigned a table both here and in the dining room so that they always have a choice of where to dine. The set dinner menu ranges from five to seven courses (with a choice of main course), depending on the season and what is fresh and available (the executive chef has received numerous awards). Select one of the estate's wines to accompany the meal. Relax by the pool in the shade of the old apple trees or sunbathe au naturel on the secluded deck. If you want the most private of rooms, choose the doll-like chalet tucked away in the woods with its terrace offering splendid valley views. The hotel was renovated in 2001: a new wellness and beauty spa was added and now most rooms are two-room suites with balconies and splendid views, large enough for a family of four. I was very struck by the variety of nationalities among the guests. *Directions:* Take the Merano Sud exit from the new Bolzano-Merano road, follow signs for Hafling for 4 km, then turn right towards Labers. Follow this road for 5 km to the hotel.

HOTEL CASTLE FRAGSBURG
Owner: Ortner family
Via Fragsburger Strasse, 3
Merano (BZ) 39012, Italy
Tel: (0473) 24 40 71, Fax: (0473) 24 44 93
16 rooms, Double: €190–€280*
*Includes breakfast & dinner
Closed: Nov 5 to Apr 10, Credit cards: MC, VS
28 km NW of Bolzano, 150 km N of Verona
Region: Trentino-Alto Adige, Michelin Map: 429
www.karenbrown.com/italyinns/hotelfragsburg.html

If you are looking for a hotel that is well-priced in the expensive city of Milan, the Antica Locanda dei Mercanti is a good choice. Not that it has all the trappings of a deluxe city hotel—you could walk right by without knowing the hotel was there because there is no sign at all, just its name on one of the many buzzers on a brass panel beside a large green door. Inside, there is no elaborate lounge, no noisy bar, no fancy restaurant, no expensive boutiques. Instead, there is an intimate counter with a receptionist who offers a warm welcome and shows you to your room. For the price, you would expect minimum accommodations but, instead, all of the guestrooms are quite attractive. Although no two are alike, they are tastefully decorated and each room has fresh flowers. The least expensive rooms are fairly small but the rooms in the next category up are more spacious. Request a room either on the second or third floors. At the top of the list are four air-conditioned rooms with private rooftop garden terraces. The location is excellent—just a five-minute walk to the Duomo, a five-minute walk to the Castello, and a few blocks to La Scala. *Directions:* The hotel is a bit complicated to find. Ask for detailed instructions when making reservations.

ANTICA LOCANDA DEI MERCANTI
Manager: Paola Ora
Via San Tomaso, 6
Milan 20121, Italy
Tel: (02) 80 54 080, Fax: (02) 80 54 090
16 rooms, Double: €130–€250*
*Breakfast not included
Open: all year, Credit cards: all major
Heart of Milan, between the Duomo & the Castello
Region: Lombardy, Michelin Map: 428
www.karenbrown.com/italyinns/anticalocanda.html

The Four Seasons opened its doors in 1993 to well-deserved rave reviews and instant success. The hotel (whose origins date back to a 15th-century convent) is superbly set in Milan's fantasy shopping area whose rich selection of chic designer boutiques is unrivaled anywhere in the world. For sightseeing, just a comfortable stroll through quaint cobbled streets brings you to La Scala Theatre, the Galleria, and the stunning Duomo. The hotel is an oasis of refined, understated elegance and restful tranquillity. You enter into what was originally the chapel, now a spacious, refreshingly uncluttered room decorated in muted tones of beiges and creamy whites. Fresh flowers abound, enhancing vaulted ceilings, fine contemporary furnishings, fragments of stunning frescoes (uncovered during renovation and meticulously restored), and accents of museum-quality antiques. Unfortunately, there is not enough space on this page to go into greater detail about the hotel. In essence, the two restaurants are superb, the inner courtyard garden lovely, the guestrooms have every conceivable convenience, the linens are the finest. No expense was spared to pamper the guest—as an example, the marble walls, floors, and even mirrors in the bathrooms are heated so that no fog will collect. The icing on the cake is the caring staff who pamper you shamelessly.

FOUR SEASONS HOTEL MILANO
Manager: Vincenzo Finizzola
Via Gesù, 8
Milan 20121, Italy
Tel: (02) 77 088, Fax: (02) 77 08 50 04
118 rooms, Double: €560–€4,100*
*Breakfast not included: €35
Open: all year, Credit cards: all major
Heart of Milan, close to shopping & sightseeing
Region: Lombardy, Michelin Map: 428
www.karenbrown.com/italyinns/fourseasonmilan.html

In the first edition of our guide to Italy, the Grand Hotel et de Milan was featured as our favorite hotel in Milan. Soon after the book was in print, the hotel closed for renovation but now has reopened its doors and is more beautiful than ever. There is no hotel in Milan more richly imbued with tradition. Dating back to 1863, it is located only two blocks from La Scala Theatre and has been "home" for many of the world's most famous artists, including Giuseppe Verdi who composed some of his operas while living here. From first glance you are immediately enveloped in a romantic mood of the past. The heart of the hotel is the spacious lounge, gently illuminated by a large domed skylight, with cream-colored wood paneling, marble floor accented by Oriental carpets, comfortable sofas and chairs, potted palms, and a marble fireplace completing the elegant scene. Beyond the lounge there is a nostalgic, old-fashioned bar whose mirrored walls and elegant drapes form the perfect backdrop for afternoon tea or a post-theater drink. The hotel's Don Carlos restaurant (named after one of Verdi's operas) continues the romantic theme with dark-green fabric walls almost covered with pictures of famous artists who have performed at La Scala. As you would expect, the guestrooms too are superbly decorated with fine furniture, lovely fabrics, and many antiques.

GRAND HOTEL ET DE MILAN
Manager: Antonio Cailotto
Via Manzoni, 29
Milan 20121, Italy
Tel: (02) 72 31 41, Fax: (02) 86 46 08 61
95 rooms, Double: €448–€2600*
*Breakfast not included: €35
Open: all year, Credit cards: all major
Heart of Milan, 2 blocks from La Scala
Region: Lombardy, Michelin Map: 428
www.karenbrown.com/italyinns/etdemilan.html

The Hotel de la Ville is a gem of a hotel. The location just couldn't be more perfect—a few minutes' walk takes you to La Scala, the spectacular Duomo, or to the Galleria, Milan's romantic glass-domed shopping arcade. The exterior, a modern glass-and-stone façade, doesn't prepare you for the interior, which exudes a cozy, old-world charm. You enter into a lovely reception area, softly illuminated from a domed skylight. Just off the reception is a cozy lounge in a color scheme of rich green and gold where comfortable upholstered sofas and chairs are arranged in small groupings. An intimate cherry-paneled bar is tucked in one corner, discreetly available for afternoon tea or an aperitif. The ambiance is one of genteel, old-world elegance. The individually decorated guestrooms all boast of the same quality: the walls are covered with elegant Italian silk fabric that color-coordinates with the fabric on the beds and draperies. All rooms have completely modernized bathrooms, beautifully tiled in marble in tones of beige, cream, or green. The hotel's L'Opera Restaurant is well known for its regional cuisine and vintage wine cellar. The son and daughter of the founder, the late Count Bocca, continue his tradition of excellence and the finest hospitality. *Directions:* From the central ring road take the Corso Venezia to Piazza S. Babila, the Corso Matteotti to the Piazza Meda, and the Via Hoepli to the hotel.

HOTEL DE LA VILLE
Manager: Giuliano Nardiotti
Via Hoepli, 6
Milan 20121, Italy
Tel: (02) 87 97 311, Fax: (02) 86 66 09
109 rooms, Double: €280–€318
Open: all year, Credit cards: all major
Heart of Milan, between the Duomo & La Scala
Region: Lombardy, Michelin Map: 428
www.karenbrown.com/italyinns/delaville.html

Hotel Villa Malpensa is less than a five-minute drive from the Milan Malpensa airport. This stately, four-story formal mansion was once the home of the counts of Caproni (one of the wealthiest families of northern Italy). This is more of a commercial hotel than a charming small inn and lacks the personal touch of an owner-managed property, but if you are nervous about catching an early morning flight, its location can't be beat. You enter into a formal hallway painted a soft-cream color, with a soaring ceiling, walls enhanced by ornate plaster sculpturing, marble floors, and Oriental carpets. Throughout the original core of the hotel, the past magnificence of this 1931 villa lives on through ornate architectural features. However, throughout the rest of the hotel there is no great flair to the décor. The furnishings are contemporary, but you cannot fault the amenities. All of the guestrooms have built-in headboards with proper reading lights, comfortable mattresses, satellite televisions, mini bars, direct-dial telephones, hairdryers, and air conditioning. The standard rooms are not large, but the superior rooms are more spacious and some have balconies where you can watch the planes taking off and landing. *Directions:* From Milan, follow signs to the Malpensa airport. Exit at Terminal One, turn right immediately, then go straight. The hotel is on your right, about a two-minute drive.

HOTEL VILLA MALPENSA
Owner: Fausto Bonini
Manager: Patrizio Strino
Via Don Andrea Sacconago, 1
Milan–Vizzola Ticino (VA) 21010, Italy
Tel: (0331) 23 09 44, Fax: (0331) 23 09 50
65 rooms, Double: €170–€260
Open: all year, Credit cards: all major
1 km SW of Malpensa Airport
Region: Lombardy, Michelin Map: 428
www.karenbrown.com/italyinns/villamalpensa.html

During the 17th and 18th centuries it was fashionable for wealthy Venetian nobles to build palatial retreats along the cool banks of the River Brenta, and so the waterway became lined with sensational villas all the way from Venice to Padua. Today villages and commerce have built up in the area, but many of the mansions still survive, filled with statues, frescos, and Murano glasswork, attesting to the opulent lifestyle of days gone by. Some mansions are now open as museums but for those who really want to experience living the noble life, there is the lovely 17th-century Villa Margherita, an elegant small hotel. It is situated across the highway from the canal, just a short stroll from one of the villa museums and a short drive from the others. Many converted villas in Italy are beautiful but faded, reflecting genteel neglect: not so with the Villa Margherita where all is beautifully maintained and every detail is perfect. From the lounges with their elegant antiques to the guestrooms with color-coordinated fabrics, each detail shows the care and involvement of the owners, Valeria and Remigio dal Corso. Far from the hubbub of Venice, yet only a 20-minute drive away, the Villa Margherita is an excellent hotel choice for those who prefer to avoid the hustle and bustle of the city. If you go into Venice, it's easiest to take the bus, thus avoiding the congestion of traffic and high cost of parking.

ROMANTIK HOTEL VILLA MARGHERITA
Owners: Valeria & Remigio dal Corso
Manager: Stefano Maggiolini
Via Nazionale, 416
Mira (VE) 30030, Italy
Tel: (041) 42 65 800, Fax: (041) 42 65 838
19 rooms, Double: €145–€248
Open: all year, Credit cards: all major
On canal 2 km W of Mira, 16 km W of Venice
Region: Veneto, Michelin Map: 429
www.karenbrown.com/italyinns/villamargherita.html

The Villa Beccaris is just the sort of charming inn we search for and is especially welcome in a region where there are surprisingly few of its breed. The Langhe wine country southeast of industrial Turin is characterized by gently rolling hillsides covered with endless rows of vineyards and dotted with enchanting ancient villages and fortified castles. Monforte is one such village and the 18th-century Villa Beccaris is found just outside its ancient walls. The individually decorated bedrooms are spread about the main villa, two attached wings forming the inner courtyard, and a separate adjacent guesthouse. The owners of the inn are all local industrialists and wine producers who have striven to retain a distinct aura of romance and elegance. A private-home ambiance is created with precious antiques throughout bedrooms, with Oriental carpets, parquet floors, stenciled walls and ceilings, fine linens, portrait paintings, and elegant chandeliers. The golden breakfast room with antique bar and original wood floors leads out to the flower-laden courtyard to one side and to the surrounding park with enormous oak trees to the other. The garden reveals a curved swimming pool and picturesque views over the ancient village. Downstairs is the original vaulted wine cellar, which serves as a lounge area for guests in the evenings. *Directions:* From the main square follow signs for Roddino, taking the first left up the Via Fracchia to the inn.

VILLA BECCARIS   New
Manager: Federica Giachino
Via Bava Beccaris, 1
Monforte d'Alba (CN) 12065, Italy
Tel: (0173) 78 158, Fax: (0173) 78 190
23 rooms, Double: €200
Open: all year, Credit cards: all major
60 km SE of Turin
Region: Piedmont, Michelin Map: 428
www.karenbrown.com/italyinns/beccaris.html

Il Melograno is a rarity: a small, luxury hotel that is truly managed by the family, creating a warmth and cordiality seldom found in a hotel of this sophistication. Camillo Guerra oversees every detail of his hotel, ably assisted by his children. White walls enclose the large property whose core is a stunning, white, 16th-century fortified farmhouse, which for many years was the holiday retreat of the Guerra family. In 1985, Signor Guerra (an antique and fine-art dealer from Bari) decided to expand his home-away-from-home into a hotel. Taking meticulous care to preserve the hundreds of ancient olive trees, he built a series of superbly furnished guestrooms clustered in white Moorish-style buildings facing intimate patios. The original farmhouse now houses the reception, romantic bar, beautiful dining room, and various intimate lounges. Throughout, everything is exquisitely decorated in antiques. Cheerful floral slipcovered chairs and Oriental carpets accent stark white walls and floors. One of the inner patios is a fragrant small orange grove, watered by an ancient stone irrigation system. Breakfast is served on the poolside terrace overlooking the pomegranate and fig trees. Il Melograno makes an excellent, luxurious base for exploring the fascinating Apulia region of southern Italy. *Directions:* Located just west of Monopoli on the road to Alberobello. As you head toward Alerobello, there is a sign to the hotel on the right.

IL MELOGRANO
Owner: Guerra family
Contrada Torricella, 345
Monopoli (BA) 70043, Italy
Tel: (080) 69 09 030, Fax: (080) 74 79 08
37 rooms, Double: €290–€800
Open: mid-Mar to mid-Jan, Credit cards: all major
On the heel of Italy, 70 km NW of Brindisi
Region: Apulia, Michelin Map: 431
Relais & Châteaux
www.karenbrown.com/italyinns/ilmelograno.html

Montagnana is an exceptionally picturesque medieval village with walls that are still intact, punctuated by 24 towers. However, it is not only the appeal of this cute town that attracts visitors. People also come from afar to dine at the Ristorante Aldo Moro, drawn by its fabulous food and beautiful dining rooms where tables are set with fine linens and bouquets of fresh flowers. Happily, the Ristorante Aldo Moro also has guestrooms, so you do not need to worry about driving "home" after a splendid meal with fabulous wines. The guestrooms are all attractively decorated and offer all the modern amenities such as air conditioning, mini bars, and satellite TVs. Bedrooms are all similar in decor, with traditional-style furnishings. Suites are larger, but the standard rooms are quite spacious enough, so no need to splurge. The public lounges are also most appealing, with antique furnishings that lend a lovely, old-world, sedate elegance. Behind the hotel there is a small garden where guests are welcome to sit and relax. It is no wonder that this is such a superior hotel—it is a family-run operation, with the Moro family always present, overseeing both the restaurant and the hotel with great care for quality. *Directions:* Exit the A13 at Monselice and take the N10 west to Montagnana. Via Marconi is a small street off the piazza.

HOTEL RISTORANTE ALDO MORO
Owner: Moro family
Via Marconi, 27
Montagnana (PD) 35044, Italy
Tel: (0429) 81 351, Fax: (0429) 82 842
34 rooms, Double: €90–€105*
*Breakfast not included: €8
Closed: mid-Jul to mid-Aug, Credit cards: all major
85 km SW of Venice, 57 km S of Padova
Region: Veneto, Michelin Map: 429
www.karenbrown.com/italyinns/aldomoro.html

The Castelletto di Montebenichi is an enchanting small castle in a tiny, storybook-perfect, medieval village perched on a hilltop in Tuscany, romantically facing a miniature plaza enclosed by a circle of homes built into the old tower walls. This is a sturdy, stone building with a crenellated roof, arched windows, and a row of colorful coats of armor stretching across the top. Inside, it seems as if you are truly stepping back into the past—the renovation has been so carefully accomplished that you don't realize any changes have been made at all (until you see the modern bathrooms). All the fabulous murals have been restored and the floors and beamed ceilings reflect the rich patina of age. The furnishings, too, reflect another era, with rich fabrics, beautiful light fixtures, lovely oil paintings, and many fine antiques. Your exceptionally personable hosts, Marco Gasparini and Arnaldo Soriani, want their guests to feel like friends. Everything possible is done to create this ambiance, including an open bar where guests can fix themselves refreshment whenever they want. Breakfast is served in a charming, sunny room with arched windows on three sides. There are also various cozy lounges, a stunning library, a swimming pool, and a sauna. This is a non-smoking hotel. No children under 14. *Directions:* Midway between Siena and Arezzo. From the A1, exit at Valdarno and follow signs for Montevarchi, Bucine, Ambra, and then Montebenichi.

CASTELLETTO DI MONTEBENICHI
Owners: Marco Gasparini & Arnaldo Soriani
Montebenichi (AR) 52020, Italy
Tel: (055) 99 10 110, Fax: (055) 99 10 113
9 rooms, Double: €227–€276
Open: Apr to Nov, Credit cards: all major
26 km NE of Siena
Region: Tuscany, Michelin Map: 430
www.karenbrown.com/italyinns/dimontebenichi.html

For those who wish for accommodations with all the trimmings, yet still want to feel like a pampered guest in a private home, Villa Pambuffetti is an ideal choice. Situated in Umbria in the well-preserved hilltop town of Montefalco with its 13th-century Francescano frescoes, this splendid villa was once a private home. Although the hotel is managed with professional skill, the gracious Pambuffetti family has a magic touch that makes each guest feel very special. The decision to transform their country house into a 15-room inn seemed a natural choice when Signora Pambuffetti's daughter, Alessandra, and her husband, Mauro, returned from the United States with a wealth of experience in the hotel and restaurant business. Alessandra demonstrates her culinary skills preparing Umbrian specialties for guests. Her delicious cakes, tarts, and homemade jams are part of the full breakfast served in the elegant cream-and-dusty-rose-colored dining room. Here guests are treated to the same spectacular panoramic view taking in Assisi, Perugia, Spoleto, and Spello as described by the Nobel-prize-winning author Herman Hesse in 1907. The villa itself, with its manicured gardens and centuries-old cypress trees, is also mentioned. Every small detail is tended to in the individually decorated rooms with their travertine marble bathrooms. The room in the tower, the Torre dell'Amore, with its 360-degree vista, is a favorite.

VILLA PAMBUFFETTI
Owner: Pambuffetti family
Via della Vittoria, 20
Montefalco (PG) 06036, Italy
Tel: (0742) 37 94 17, Fax: (0742) 37 92 45
15 rooms, Double: €163–€242
Open: all year, Credit cards: all major
30 km S of Assisi, 80 km NE of Orvieto
Region: Umbria, Michelin Map: 430
www.karenbrown.com/italyinns/villapambuffetti.html

Il Borghetto Country Inn is an absolute dream, an idyllic hideaway in one of the most enchanting areas of Tuscany. It is owned by the Cavallini family who originally bought a farmhouse in the heart of the exquisite Chianti district to use as a family weekend retreat. When the adjacent farmhouse came on the market, they bought it too, restored it to perfection, and opened a tiny hotel. Now they have added a third farmhouse and have converted it into three deluxe apartments. What makes this small inn so special is that it is a family operation. The father, Roberto Cavallini, watches over the operation from Milan, his son, Antonio, is the on-site manager, and the charming daughter, Hilaria, ably helps out. Guests have their own intimate, beautifully decorated lounge, which also serves as the breakfast room (in warm weather breakfast is served outside on the lovely terrace). Rosi Cavallini did all the decorating and every detail is of superb quality with beautiful fabrics, original paintings, abundant displays of fresh flowers, Oriental carpets, and fine antiques. But the best I've saved for last—the view. It is incredible: a sweeping vista of vineyards and olive groves stretching as far as the eye can see. *Directions:* Leave the Florence-Siena expressway at Bargino. As you exit, turn right and then almost immediately turn up the hill toward Montefiridolfi. 2.6 km after leaving the highway, Il Borghetto is on your right.

IL BORGHETTO COUNTRY INN
Owner: Cavallini family
Via Collina S. Angelo, 23
Montefiridolfi (FI) 50020, Italy
Tel: (055) 82 44 442, Fax: (055) 82 44 247
9 rooms, Double: €180–€300
Lunch & dinner by special request
Open: Mar to Nov, Credit cards: AX, VS
17 km S of Florence
Region: Tuscany, Michelin Map: 430
www.karenbrown.com/italyinns/ilborghetto.html

La Chiusa, nestled in the hills of Tuscany southeast of Siena, is an old stone farmhouse whose restaurant is so well known that guests come from far and wide to enjoy the meals where everything is fresh, homemade, and delicious. Dania and Umberto Lucherini are the gracious owners and Dania is the talented chef. Almost all the vegetables, olive oil, meats, wines, and cheeses come either from the inn's own farm or from those nearby. The original wood-burning oven still stands in the courtyard in front of the inn, emitting delicious aromas of freshly baking bread. The dining room is large and airy, with an uncluttered simple elegance enhanced by windows overlooking rolling hills. When the weather is balmy, meals are also served on the back terrace, which is ideally positioned to capture a sweeping view. The emphasis here is definitely on the exquisite meals, but there are also bedrooms for guests who want to spend the night. Like the dining room, the guestrooms are perfectly in keeping with the ambiance of the old farmhouse, lovely in their rustic simplicity yet with every modern convenience. In addition to the standard guestrooms, there are some deluxe suites—one even has an olive press in the bathroom!

LA CHIUSA
Owner: Lucherini family
Manager: Franco Sodi
Via della Madonnina, 88
Montefollonico (SI) 53040, Italy
Tel: (0577) 66 96 68, Fax: (0577) 66 95 93
15 rooms, Double: €200–€400
Open: Mar 20 to Nov 25, Credit cards: all major
60 km S of Siena, 10 km NW of Montepulciano
Region: Tuscany, Michelin Map: 430
www.karenbrown.com/italyinns/chiusa.html

The tiny medieval village of Montegridolfo, nestling on the crown of a gentle hill, seems too perfect to be real—everything looks fresh and new and all the buildings homogeneous. At first it is a bit confusing because every picture-perfect little restaurant, shop, and boutique has the same buff-colored brick façade, the same pretty red geraniums out front, and the same white embroidered curtains peeking behind brown-shuttered windows. Yes, the village is real, but was totally reconstructed at one time as one development. The Albergo Palazzo Viviani, a part of this development, is a hotel converted from a noble palace and still retains the charm of a private home. The living room with its honey-colored walls, oil paintings, opulent drapes, open fireplace, and handsome antique furnishings is extremely attractive. Upstairs are eight elegant, luxurious guestrooms. The most dramatic is the Affreschi suite, with gorgeous frescoes on the walls, ornately painted ceiling, and, best of all, windows on three sides letting light stream into the room. In a separate building in the garden there are more rooms, each named for a flower. These guestrooms are less expensive, but although smaller than those in the Palazzo, are beautifully decorated. There are also five suites in various buildings around the town. *Directions:* From A14 take the Pesaro-Urbino exit. Follow signs to Montecchio then turn right following signs to Montegridolfo.

ALBERGO PALAZZO VIVIANI
Director: Danilo Di Pasquale
Montegridolfo (RN) 47837, Italy
Tel: (0541) 85 53 50, Fax: (0541) 85 53 40
24 rooms, Double: €129–€258
Open: all year, Credit cards: all major
35 km NW of Rimini
Region: Emilia-Romagna, Michelin Map: 430
www.karenbrown.com/italyinns/viviani.html

La Dionora is a delightful hotel just outside the walled town of Montepulciano, one of Tuscany's jewels. This appealing small inn, made of tan stone and accented by brown shutters, has a stunning location, crowning a gentle hill with a 360-degree view, with absolutely nothing to mar the beauty and solitude of the setting. As far as the eye can see there are rolling hills covered with forests, fields of sunflowers, olive groves, and, in the distance, the sweet walled village of Pienza. As you approach, it is obvious that this is a well-cared-for, beautifully managed property. Everything is absolutely meticulous, from the perfectly tended flowerbeds to the lovingly decorated bedrooms. Three of the guestrooms are located upstairs in the farmhouse with windows that capture the splendid view. The other rooms, each with a private terrace, are in a similar one-story stone building just steps away. All have Tuscan-style antiques enhanced by Ferragamo fabrics. Breakfast is served in the garden in a most attractive stone "winter garden" with arched glass walls on four sides through which the sunlight streams in. Also in the garden is a beautiful swimming pool. Mario Angelini, the friendly owner, is ably assisted by Giulo D'Antonio and they are perfect hosts who are very familiar with Tuscany and offer assistance with planning your day. *Directions:* Take N146 from Montepulciano toward Pienza. After 3 km, turn left at the sign for La Dionora.

LA DIONORA
Owner: Dr. Mario Angelini
Via Vicinale di Poggiano
Montepulciano (SI) 53040, Italy
Tel: (0578) 71 74 96, Fax: (0578) 71 74 98
6 rooms, Double: €250–€350
Closed: Jan 7 to mid-Feb, Credit cards: all major
65 km S of Siena, 4 km W of Montepulciano
Region: Tuscany, Michelin Map: 430
www.karenbrown.com/italyinns/ladionara.html

Montorio is a gem offering everything your heart could possibly desire when dreaming of a perfect holiday in Tuscany: spacious, beautifully decorated guestrooms; a rich selection of restaurants within walking distance; convenient location for exploring Tuscany and Umbria; a glorious setting; spectacular views; cooking facilities in every room; large modern bathrooms; excellent prices; and best of all, Stefania Savini, your charming, beautiful young hostess. This characterful, 15th-century golden-stone farmhouse is perfectly located on a hill surrounded by olive groves, vineyards, and cypress trees. The views are awesome, with nothing to disturb the mood of absolute serenity except perhaps for the song of birds and the ringing of church bells. The inn is within walking distance of the marvelous walled city of Montepulciano and through towering cypress trees you can see below the fabulous Renaissance church of San Biagio. In another direction, the adorable walled town of Pienza nestles on a hilltop. Each of the suites has a kitchen or kitchenette and is tastefully decorated with simple Tuscan-style, antique furniture. The terrace is embellished by centuries-old trees and flowers cascading from terra-cotta pots. Montorio is no longer limited to weekly stays, but even a week would not be enough at this jewel. *Directions:* Just on the north edge of Montepulciano, on the road to Pienza.

MONTORIO
Owner: Stefania Savini
Strada per Pienza, 2
Montepulciano (SI) 53045, Italy
Tel: (0578) 71 74 42, Fax: (0578) 71 54 56
5 rooms, Double: €135–€233
Open: Mar to mid-Nov, Credit cards: all major
65 km S of Siena
Region: Tuscany, Michelin Map: 430
www.karenbrown.com/italyinns/montorio.html

If you are looking for a budget hotel and want to be in the center of the charming walled city of Montepulciano, the Mueblé Il Riccio makes a good choice. Remember, this is not a deluxe hotel so don't expect large rooms and plush accommodations, but for the price and location it has a lot to offer. It is only a few steps away from the Piazza Grande, on the upper floor of a handsome 13th-century palazzo. You enter into a courtyard and go upstairs to a pretty galleried walkway with travertine columns and pots of colorful geraniums. You step first into a large, multi-purpose room with soaring ceiling accented by large chandeliers. This is a family-owned and -managed hotel so the gracious owner, Giorgio Caroti, or his wife, Ivana, will probably be at the desk to welcome you. At one end of the room is a sitting area with pretty sofas and chairs grouped around a stone fireplace and at the other end is a cluster of cozy round tables for breakfast. The most dramatic feature of the room is a splendid wood antique bar that doubles as the reception desk. The guestrooms are small and quite simple in their decor, but quite amazingly, they all have direct-dial phones, safes, and satellite TV. Breakfast is not included in the room rate, but is available each morning. The fact that no other meals are included is absolutely no problem since Montepulciano offers a rich selection of wonderful places to dine in all price ranges. *Directions:* Half a block from the Piazza Grande.

MUEBLE IL RICCIO   New
Owners: Ivana & Giorgio Caroti
Via Talosa, 21
Montepulciano (SI) 53045, Italy
Tel & fax: (0578) 75 77 13
6 rooms, Double: €80–€85*
*Breakfast not included: €8
Open: all year, Credit cards: all major
65 km S of Siena
Region: Tuscany, Michelin Map: 430
www.karenbrown.com/italyinns/ilriccio.html

The romantic, ochre-colored, 17th-century Villa Poggiano is truly a gem. The Savini family bought the abandoned mansion, which nestles on a wooded hillside near the charming walled city of Montepulciano, and have tenderly restored it to its original splendor. An intimate, cozy parlor with comfortable chairs grouped around an open fireplace, a sweet breakfast room, and two enormous suites are on the ground floor. A wide staircase leads to four more beautiful rooms. There are also four delightful suites in a separate brick building facing a sweeping panorama of the countryside. The tasteful decor creates a warm, homelike ambiance. Throughout the villa, everything is on a grand scale with handsome fireplaces, sumptuous bathrooms, gorgeous antique furniture, exceptionally spacious rooms, and ornate chandeliers. The villa faces an idyllic Tuscan countryside with olive trees dotting the gentle hillside. Behind the villa is a thick forest with romantic paths meandering through the woodlands. There is also an enormous travertine swimming pool with a granite wall on one side embellished with a large sculpture, while on the other side, lounge chairs are set on a wide terrace outlined by very old cypress trees. The warmth of welcome by Stefania and her charming mother is so genuine you will never want to leave. *Directions:* Take the N146 from Montepulciano toward Pienza and after about 2 km, turn left at the sign for Villa Poggiano.

VILLA POGGIANO
Owner: Stefania Savini
Via di Poggiano, 7
Montepulciano (SI) 53045, Italy
Tel: (0578) 75 82 92, Fax: (0578) 71 54 56
3 rooms, 7 suites, Double: €181–€285
Open: all year, Credit cards: all major
65 km S of Siena, 4 km W of Montepulciano
Region: Tuscany, Michelin Map: 430
www.karenbrown.com/italyinns/villapoggiano.html

Tucked in the gentle Tuscan hills, Monteriggioni is a stunning sight. You will be captivated from afar at your first glimpse the romantic town crowning the hilltop with its circular stone wall, punctuated by tall towers, still intact. If you have come just to sightsee, you must park your car below the town, but if you are one of the lucky ones who have a reservation at the Hotel Monteriggioni, drive through the portal in the wall to the hotel, which is located at the far end of the little square. It is hard to believe that this lovely small hotel, now so beautiful, used to be a stable. It took three years for the present owners to achieve the miracle you see today. Michela Cagnazzo, the owner, is responsible for the decoration and her taste is faultless. White walls, handsome antique furniture, white slipcovered sofas, and bouquets of fresh flowers create a fresh, appealing country ambiance. The guestrooms are also charming, with the same style of decor as the public rooms. Behind the hotel there is a terrace where breakfast is served, weather permitting. Just beyond is a small swimming pool tucked in the garden with a serene backdrop of the old moat, now filled with olive trees, and the stone walls of the town. The hotel has no restaurant but there is one just next door, plus others close by. It is a delightful small hotel that does credit to a charming village. *Directions:* From the S2 at Monteriggioni, follow signs to the town.

HOTEL MONTERIGGIONI
Owner: Michela Gozzi Cagnazzo
Monteriggioni (SI) 53035, Italy
Tel: (0577) 30 50 09, Fax: (0577) 30 50 11
12 rooms, Double: €210
Closed: Jan 7 to end Feb, Credit cards: all major
15 km NW of Siena, 55 km S of Florence
Region: Tuscany, Michelin Map: 430
www.karenbrown.com/italyinns/monteriggioni.html

The Hotel Pasquale was named after Marco Pasini's maternal grandfather, Pasquale, who was born in the Lake Como area. During World War II he was stationed in Monterosso al Mare where he fell in love and married a charming young girl, Fortunata, and never returned to northern Italy. Instead, after the war, they opened a tiny restaurant and later added guestrooms, a simple enterprise which has grown so that now the family owns two hotels. Marco Pasini and his mother Felicita manage the Hotel Pasquale and his brother, Matteo, manages the Villa Steno. Both hotels offer clean, simple, appealing rooms, great service, and loving attention to guests. There is no private parking at the Hotel Pasquale and the bedrooms are slightly smaller than those at the Villa Steno, but every bedroom has a great bonus—a view of the sea. Also, each of the bedrooms has a nice bathroom with an enclosed shower. Like so many hotels that we most highly recommend, the Hotel Pasquale is a family operation run with great heart, with grandmother Fortunata still working wherever she's needed and Marco's hard-working mother, Felicita, often on duty at the front desk. Marco's father is also an integral part of the operation and guests eagerly look forward to the excellent pastries he bakes fresh each morning. *Directions:* Ask Marco to send you detailed instructions to the public parking area. From there you can take a taxi or walk through the tunnel to the hotel.

HOTEL PASQUALE
Owners: Felicita & Marco Pasini
Via Fegina, 4
Monterosso al Mare–Cinque Terre (SP) 19016, Italy
Tel: (0187) 81 75 50, Fax: (0187) 81 70 56
15 rooms, Double: €130
Open: all year, Credit cards: all major
30 km N of La Spezia, 94 km SE of Genoa
Region: Liguria, Michelin Map: 428
www.karenbrown.com/italyinns/pasquale.html

If you are looking for deluxe accommodations along the popular Cinque Terre, the Hotel Porto Roca comes closest to filling the bill. A narrow lane leads up the wooded hillside from Monterosso al Mare to the hotel, which is splendidly located on a cliff overlooking the sea. Only taxis are allowed up this road but the hotel will pay the fare from and back to the public car park. The lobby is one very large, all-purpose room with the reception desk as you enter, the guest lounge in the middle, and a bar at the far end. The room has almost a medieval look with dark furniture, large oil paintings, one wall of stone, ornately upholstered sofas and chairs, and, to top it all off, two regal knights standing in suits of armor. The dining room is one level up and has a wall of windows overlooking the sea. However, when the weather is warm, meals are served outside where white wrought-iron tables are set on a delightful terrace overlooking Monterosso al Mare and the sea. Throughout the spacious property there are many secluded nooks where guests can relax, but the most popular place is a terrace perched above the cliffs where lounge chairs are arranged to capture the view. *Directions:* From the A12, exit at Carrodano and follow signs to Levanto. From Levanto follow signs up the hill toward Monterosso al Mare. After the tunnel, turn right at the sign to Monterosso Fegina and go down the hill to Monterosso where there is a large public car park.

HOTEL PORTO ROCA
Manager: Guerrina Arpe
Via Corone, 1
Monterosso al Mare–Cinque Terre (SP) 19016, Italy
Tel: (0187) 81 75 02, Fax: (0187) 81 76 92
43 rooms, Double: €165–€430
Open: mid-Mar to Nov, Credit cards: all major
30 km N of La Spezia, 94 km SE of Genoa
Region: Liguria, Michelin Map: 428
www.karenbrown.com/italyinns/roca.html

Constantly in search of places to stay in the increasingly popular Cinque Terre, we were pleased to receive a letter from one of our readers highly praising the Hotel Villa Steno and its gracious owners, Matteo and Carla. We are pleased to confirm her impressions of the Villa Steno, a simple yet most appealing small, family-run hotel with a tranquil location just above Monterosso. The hotel, an attractive, mustard-yellow villa accented by green shutters, offers guests a warm welcome. Usually Matteo or his sweet wife, Carla, is at the reception desk to greet you (you might also see their adorable daughter, Chiara). The heart of the hotel is the breakfast room where there is also a small guest sitting area. Here modern furnishings made of blond wood and sunlight streaming in through large windows create a pleasing mood. A hearty buffet breakfast includes fantastic pastries baked fresh each morning by Matteo's father. The guestrooms are simply furnished, but fresh and impeccably clean. Each of the bedrooms has a private bathroom, almost all of them with a shower enclosed by a wraparound curtain. Except for two, all of the guestrooms have either a balcony or a private terrace. Matteo's brother, Marco, owns another hotel, the Pasquale, located in the center of the village. Both hotels were started by their enterprising grandfather, Pasquale, and his wife, Fortunata. *Directions:* Ask Matteo to send you his excellent instructions.

❄ ⚓ ☕ 🏌 CREDIT ☎ 🚶 P 🖼 ⛵ 🍇

HOTEL VILLA STENO
Owners: Carla & Matteo Pasini
Via Roma, 109
Monterosso al Mare–Cinque Terre (SP) 19016, Italy
Tel: (0187) 81 70 28, Fax: (0187) 81 73 54
16 rooms, Double: €130
Open: Mar to Nov, Credit cards: all major
30 km N of La Spezia, 94 km SE of Genoa
Region: Liguria, Michelin Map: 428
www.karenbrown.com/italyinns/villasteno.html

La Locanda del Capitano is a tiny inn romantically tucked in the historic center of a medieval, picture-perfect walled village perched on a hilltop overlooking a serene Umbrian landscape of gently rolling hills. The hotel is at heart a restaurant, which has quickly gained well-deserved publicity for the outstanding quality of the kitchen but, luckily for guests, there are also a few bedrooms. The guestrooms are small, but sweetly decorated in an appropriately simple, country style. All have pretty wrought-iron headboards with floral paintings hand-done by a local woman. The choice guestrooms are the two with a small terrace tucked up amongst the ancient tiled rooftops. At the time of our visit, there were eight guestrooms, but plans were under way to add two more suites in the adjacent stone house. La Locanda is the creation of your charming hosts, Carmen and Giancarlo Polito, who decided at the tender ages of 26 and 27 to begin their life together in the countryside and discovered in a newspaper ad the perfect site for their inn, a centuries-old stone house in the idyllic town of Montone. As soon as they saw the house, their hearts were won. Carmen and Giancarlo are wonderful with their guests, and even organize tours for a minimum of seven people into the countryside for truffle hunting during the season. *Directions:* Heading north from Perugia on the E45, take the Montone exit. The hotel is just a block from the town square.

LA LOCANDA DEL CAPITANO   *New*
Owners: Carmen & Giancarlo Polito
Via Roma, 7
Montone (PG) 06014, Italy
Tel: (075) 93 06 521, Fax: (075) 93 06 455
8 rooms, Double: €93
Closed: Jan & Feb, Credit cards: all major
39 km N of Perugia
Region: Umbria, Michelin Map: 430
www.karenbrown.com/italyinns/capitano.html

The promontory of Argentario, facing the islands of Giglio and Giannutri, has always been a favorite seaside haven for Romans. Hotels tend to be rather basic in the area so it was a surprise to come across the San Biagio right in the quaint town of Orbetello, a narrow strip of land between two lakes connecting Argentario to the mainland. The Magnosi family from Rome recently bought and restored the palazzo, originally a private residence dating back to 1851. They have recreated the feeling of a nobleman's home, not only in the rich furnishings, but also with the many original architectural features of the palazzo itself. Some of these wonderful features include the arched entrance hall that leads to a small courtyard where breakfast is served, the high-ceilinged rooms with ornate moldings and frescoed borders, and the central staircase leading up to the thirteen double rooms and four suites. The family's antique pieces collected throughout Europe adorn both the downstairs and upstairs sitting rooms as well as the bedrooms. Very comfortable bedrooms are richly appointed and have luxurious marble travertine bathrooms (the suite has two bathrooms). Although the San Biagio offers no views in a seaside location, it offers top-level accommodation at exceptional comparative rates. *Directions:* From the N1, take the exit to Orbetello and go to the old part of town. Facing the church (Duomo), Via Dante is the street the runs to its left side.

SAN BIAGIO
Owner: Gianfranco Magnosi family
Via Dante, 34
Orbetello (GR) 58015, Italy
Tel: (0564) 86 05 43, Fax: (0564) 86 77 87
17 rooms, Double: €150–€250
Open: all year, Credit cards: MC, VS
Center of Orbetello, 160 km N of Rome
Region: Tuscany, Michelin Map: 430
www.karenbrown.com/italyinns/sanbiagio.html

Orta San Giulio is unbelievably picturesque and one of the most romantic places to dine here is the Albergo Ristorante Leon d'Oro, whose owners, the Ronchetti family, have another small, reasonably priced hotel, La Contrada dei Monti, in the middle of the village. This 16th-century building has been lovingly renovated, with great care taken to preserve the original architectural features such as arches, wood beams, exposed stone walls, and wrought-iron fixtures, but adding all the modern comforts such as tiled bathrooms, telephones, and satellite TVs. The intimate reception area has a charming sitting area with splendid arched ceiling embellished with fresco paintings, a fireplace flanked by prettily upholstered chairs, and a handsome tiled floor highlighted by the family coat of arms. The overall ambiance is one of exceptional quality and charming, refined elegance. The core of the hotel is a central courtyard where breakfast is served on warm days. When it is chilly, guests use a sweet breakfast room with a beamed ceiling. The guestrooms are also attractive, with lovely fabrics that color-coordinate with the bedspreads and draperies. Bedrooms are all very similar in decor, but the color scheme varies with each floor. Dinner, included in the room rate, is served at the Ristorante Leon d'Oro. *Directions:* Leave your car in the public parking area and walk into town. Turn left at Via Contrada dei Monti to the hotel on your right.

LA CONTRADA DEI MONTI
Owner: Ronchetti family
Via Contrada dei Monti, 10
Orta San Giulio–Lake Orta (NO) 28016, Italy
Tel: (0322) 90 51 14, Fax: (0322) 90 58 63
17 rooms, Double: €96–€155*
*Includes breakfast & dinner
Open: all year, Credit cards: all major
84 km NW of Milan Malpensa airport
Region: Piedmont, Michelin Map: 428
www.karenbrown.com/italyinns/contradadeimonti.html

From the moment you see the Villa Crespi, perched on a hillside overlooking Lake Orta, you can't help chuckling at this elaborate, gingerbread castle that looks straight out of the Arabian Nights. And see it you will, for its minaret with an onion dome ending in a pointed needle stretches up above the trees and is visible from far away. The mansion is quite incredible: the façade is embellished with colorful tiles in fancy designs and further enhanced by elaborately carved stonework and Moorish-style arched windows. Inside, the mood continues with an entry hall that soars many stories high and walls lavishly covered with carved stone. This ambiance of opulence is maintained throughout the mansion with gorgeous inlaid wood floors, walls covered with brocade fabric, crystal chandeliers, and ceilings richly adorned by fancy plaster designs. This fairy-tale castle, dating back to 1800s, is the creation of Benigno Crespi, a very wealthy cotton producer who, during his travels to Persia, became fascinated with the romantic palaces he visited. Over the years, poets, kings, and princesses have graced its halls, but now the villa is a deluxe small hotel welcoming paying guests who come to enjoy the wonderful food, sleep in elegant bedrooms, and enjoy the splendid parklike grounds behind the hotel. The hotel also has a full fitness center. *Directions:* Coming from the north, you will see the hotel on your right as you approach town.

VILLA CRESPI
Manager: Cinzia Primatesta
Via G. Fava, 8/10
Orta San Giulio–Lake Orta (NO) 28016, Italy
Tel: (0322) 91 19 02, Fax: (0322) 91 19 19
22 rooms, Double: €165–€480
Closed: Jan to mid-Feb, Credit cards: all major
84 km NW of Milan, 1 km E of Orta San Giulio
Region: Piedmont, Michelin Map: 428
www.karenbrown.com/italyinns/villacrespi.html

The town of Orvieto, just off the main expressway between Rome and Florence, is one of the most picturesque of all the Umbrian hilltowns. This small city is perched on the top of a hill—an intriguing sight that can be viewed from many kilometers away. Less than a ten-minute drive south of Orvieto is a 12th-century Gothic abbey that has been converted into a hotel where you can stay surrounded by the romantic ruins of yesteryear. Although there is a commercial air to La Badia, the reception is caring. The manager, Ettore Pelletti, has been with the hotel for over 20 years, as has the chef, so, as you can see, there is a real continuity of management. Although this is not a cozy, small hotel, you are bound to enjoy the setting, the pool, the old-world ambiance, and the food. The dining room is one of the most attractive rooms in the hotel. It has an enormous, high-vaulted stone ceiling, wrought-iron fixtures, heavy wooden beams, eye-catching copper accents, and, at one end, a cavernous fireplace complete with a roasting spit. The standard bedrooms, although not large or with inspired decor, are comfortable and many have a stunning view up to the town of Orvieto. If you want to splurge, ask for one of the romantic suites, which have much prettier furnishings. In the meadows behind the monastery there is a lovely pool. *Directions:* From Orvieto, follow signs for Viterro. The hotel is 4 km south of Orvieto.

LA BADIA
Owner: Contessa Luisa Fiumi
Manager: Ettore Pelletti
Orvieto (TR) 05019, Italy
Tel: (0763) 30 19 59, Fax: (0763) 30 53 96
28 rooms, Double: €182–€338
Closed: Jan & Feb, Credit cards: all major
4 km S of Orvieto, 115 km N of Rome
Region: Umbria, Michelin Map: 430
www.karenbrown.com/italyinns/badia.html

With a rich history dating back to the 16th century, the Hotel Palazzo Piccolomini in the historic center of Orvieto, an incredible, walled city perched atop a high hill, was once home to the wealthy Piccolomini family. At the end of the 1980s the palace was rescued from neglect and after many years of restoration, opened in 1999 as a hotel. In the entrance some of the original architectural features remain, accented by a few pieces of antique furniture, but overall the mood is contemporary. From the reception hall, a flight of steps leads up to a large lounge where the frescoed ceiling again attests to the hotel's glamorous past. However, the room that most portrays the age of the building is the breakfast room in the cellar. It has a giant stone pillar supporting a coved ceiling, an ancient well tucked in a corner, and a carefully preserved medieval stone staircase leading to secret places far below. The standard bedrooms are moderate in size and well equipped in the style of a modern hotel with good lighting, writing desks, satellite TVs, mini bars, air conditioning, and hairdryers. The hotel sits on a corner facing the small Piazza Ranieri and from here it is a delightful stroll through picturesque little squares to Orvieto's crown jewel, the stunning, not-to-be-missed cathedral. *Directions:* From the A1, exit at Orvieto and follow signs to the center. When the road splits, take the road to the right. Follow signs to the hotel.

HOTEL PALAZZO PICCOLOMINI
Manager: Roberto Mazzolai
Piazza Ranieri, 36
Orvieto (TR) 05018, Italy
Tel: (0763) 34 17 43, Fax: (0763) 39 10 46
29 rooms, Double: €138–€227
Open: all year, Credit cards: all major
4 km S of Orvieto, 115 km N of Rome
Region: Umbria, Michelin Map: 430
www.karenbrown.com/italyinns/piccolomini.html

The Villa Le Barone was once the home of the famous Tuscan family, Della Robbia, whose beautiful terra cottas are still seen throughout Italy. Most of the estate has now been converted into a deluxe small hotel, but the present owner, Duchessa Franca Viviani Della Robbia, still maintains a charming vine-covered cottage for her own use. Although she is now in her 90s, the Duchessa comes frequently to the villa to ensure that her impeccable standards and taste prevail. Staying at the Villa Le Barone is very much like being the guest in a private, elegant home set in the gorgeous Tuscan hills. The lounges are especially inviting, beautifully furnished with charming, family antiques. There are 30 guestrooms, all of which vary in size and are individually decorated with a somewhat dated charm. In addition, there is a lovely swimming pool, romantically set on a terrace looking over the vineyards and out to the mellow hills beyond. Wonderful little hideaways are found secluded in the parklike setting where guests can find a quiet nook to read or just to sit and soak in the beauty. Dinner is served in the restaurant, which formerly housed the stables. *Directions:* From the center of Panzano, follow signs to the hotel.

VILLA LE BARONE
Owner: Duchessa Franca Viviani Della Robbia
Via San Leolino, 19
Panzano in Chianti (FI) 50020, Italy
Tel: (055) 85 26 21, Fax: (055) 85 22 77
30 rooms, Double: €210–€270*
*Includes breakfast & dinner, Meals for hotel guests only
Open: Apr to Nov, Credit cards: all major
31 km S of Florence, 6 km S of Greve
Region: Tuscany, Michelin Map: 430
www.karenbrown.com/italyinns/villalebarone.html

Relax in the countryside just 6 kilometers from the bustling city of Verona at the exquisite Villa del Quar where you can enjoy excellent accommodations, gourmet dining (a Michelin star), and the warmth and charm of a family-managed hotel. The gracious owner, Leopoldo Montresor, is a talented architect who spared no expense to assure that his renovations resulted in an estate exuding charm and taste. The Montresors live in one wing of the villa, conveniently close for Evelina Acampora-Montresor, who manages the hotel. The property has been in the Montresor family for many generations—ever since Leopoldo's great-great-great-grandfather won the land in a game of cards at the casino in Venice in the early 1800s. Your heart will be captivated from the moment you pass the family chapel and enter the reception lounge, elegantly decorated with finely upholstered sofas in warm shades of pinks and mellow yellows. Sunlight floods the room through a wall of windows, which open onto an inviting side terrace where guests dine in warm weather. There is also a superb 16th-century wine cellar and a most attractive beamed-ceilinged wine-tasting room where meals are served elegantly on tables set with fine linens. The guestrooms are equally appealing and furnished in antiques. A large swimming pool is set enchantingly in a meadow with vineyards stretching almost to the edge of the pool.

HOTEL VILLA DEL QUAR
Owners: Leopoldo Montresor
Via Quar N12
Pedemonte (VR) 37020, Italy
Tel: (045) 68 00 681, Fax: (045) 68 00 604
18 rooms, Double: €235–€390
Open: mid-Mar to Jan, Credit cards: all major
6 km N of Verona, 22 km E of Lake Garda
Region: Veneto, Michelin Map: 429
Relais & Châteaux
www.karenbrown.com/italyinns/hotelvilladelquar.html

The Castel Pergine is a storybook castle delightfully transformed into a small hotel, perfect for the budget-minded tourist. No need to forfeit romance and glamour, for even though the Castel Pergine is good value for money, it has a fabulous location dominating a hilltop above the town of Pergine. The Castel Pergine is more famous as a restaurant than a hotel—the dining room has an engaging medieval decor, gorgeous views, and good food. When Verena and Theo Schneider-Neff came from Switzerland and took over the hotel, they made many improvements, including installing a state-of-the-art kitchen. They also upgraded the bedrooms to add snug shower rooms, something they continue to do so that eventually all the rooms will have private shower rooms. The guestrooms range from rather simple to comfortably charming, the more expensive having en-suite showers, handsome wooden paneling, and country-style furnishings. Room 27, a corner room, is especially pretty, but the beds are shorter and narrower than in the other superior rooms. The Castel Pergine is a real bargain and its secluded hilltop setting is definitely a winner. *Directions:* Exit the autostrada at Trento Nord and follow signs for Padova to Pergine (10 km beyond Trento). Exit for centro and at the first roundabout take the first exit and at the second the second exit. After 1 km turn left at the chapel. Do not go into the center of Pergine.

CASTEL PERGINE
Managers: Verena & Theo Schneider-Neff
Pergine (TN) 38057, Italy
Tel: (0461) 53 11 58, Fax: (0461) 53 13 29
21 rooms, Double: €88–€130*
*Includes breakfast & dinner
Open: Easter to Nov, Credit cards: all major
10 km E of Trento, 2.5 km E of Pergine
Region: Trentino-Alto Adige, Michelin Map: 429
www.karenbrown.com/italyinns/castelpergine.html

I am such a romantic that, as the boat chugged across Lake Maggiore from Stresa to the medieval fishing village of Isola dei Pescatori (Fisherman's Island) and I saw the Hotel Verbano with its reddish-brown walls, dark-green shutters, and tables set on the terrace overlooking the lake, my heart was won—completely. To accommodate the many people who clamber off the excursion boats each day to visit this picturesque island, the hotel has a large dining room with arched windows overlooking the lake. However, when the weather is warm, the favorite place to dine is outside on the idyllic terrace overlooking nearby Isola Bella (Beautiful Island). In the evening, when most of the tourists have departed, the terrace becomes even more romantic—particularly with a full moon reflecting on the rippling water. The food is excellent, featuring fish fresh from the lake. The 12 bedrooms, all with a lake view, are delightful, with high ceilings, wooden floors, and modern bathrooms. Several have balconies and three share a large terrace. *Directions:* Exit the A26 at Stresa and follow signposts for the waterfront where you take the public ferry to Isola dei Pescatori (the ferry is much cheaper than the private water taxis).

HOTEL VERBANO
Owners: Alberto & Roberto Zacchera, Ermano Gafforini
Via Ugo Ara, 2
Pescatori (Isola dei)–Lake Maggiore (VB) 28838, Italy
Tel: (0323) 30 408, Fax: (0323) 33 129
12 rooms, Double: €135
Open: all year, Credit cards: all major
80 km NW of Milan, ferry from Stresa
Region: Piedmont, Michelin Map: 428
www.karenbrown.com/italyinns/hotelverbano.html

When it comes to dining in Cortona, you find the most inventive array of Tuscan-based recipes at the famed Tonino's restaurant with its terrace overlooking the entire valley. The food is so exceptional that the chef was invited to prepare Christmas dinner for the Pope. Following a long tradition in hospitality, the Spiganti family bought and completely restructured a group of five 16th-century brick farmhouses as an elegantly rustic country lodging. This gem of a small hotel is run by their charming daughter, Ilaria, one of the most endearing, gracious hostesses you will ever meet. No two bedrooms are alike and each has been individually decorated with fine brocade fabrics and antiques that set off beautifully the country simplicity of beams and brick floors. The delightful bathrooms have been personalized by a local artist whose whimsical designs reflect the various room names. A bountiful breakfast with a table brimming with fresh-baked goods from grandmother's kitchen is served in its own house facing the bedrooms. A passion for flowers is evident in the surrounding garden, which leads to a large swimming pool. Bordering Umbria and Tuscany, the Alla Corte del Sole is the perfect spot from which to easily explore both regions. *Directions:* Exit the A1 at Valchiana and follow signs for Perugia. Take the second Cortona exit towards Montepulciano and drive 7 km to the turnoff for Petrignano-Pozzolo. The hotel is after Petrignano.

RELAIS ALLA CORTE DEL SOLE
Owner: Ilaria Spiganti
Localita: I Giorgi
Petrignano (PG) 06061, Italy
Tel: (075) 96 89 008, Fax: (075) 96 89 070
18 rooms, Double: €185–€413
Open: all year, Credit cards: MC, VS
16 km S of Cortona
Region: Tuscany, Michelin Map: 430
www.karenbrown.com/italyinns/allacortedelsole.html

The Relais Il Chiostro is idyllically snuggled inside the stone walls of Pienza, a medieval hilltop village that is one of Tuscany's most perfect jewels. The hotel is built within a stunning 15th-century monastery; a heritage immediately apparent when you step through the massive arched wood doors into an exceptionally beautiful small cloister. The hushed courtyard is framed by a colonnade of marble columns linked by stone arches. The restaurant and the various lounges and sitting rooms occupy the ground floor. Upstairs there are 37 attractive, individually decorated guestrooms with splendid frescoed ceilings featured in some of the suites. The choice rooms overlook the beautiful Tuscan countryside, but views from the other rooms are also delightful—overlooking either the garden cloister or the ancient tiled rooftops of Pienza. One of the most outstanding features of the hotel is its spectacular location. Perched above the valley, the hotel takes full advantage of its position with a terrace garden (where meals are served when the weather is warm) which stretches to the edge of the wall where guests can enjoy an incredible panoramic view of Tuscany at its finest. On a terrace below, a large swimming pool nestles in another garden. *Directions:* Located one block from the main square, Piazza Pio II.

HOTEL RELAIS IL CHIOSTRO DI PIENZA   **New**
Manager: Loriana Codogno
Corso Rossellino, 26
Pienza (SI) 53026, Italy
Tel: (0578) 74 84 00, Fax: (0578) 74 84 40
37 rooms, Double: €180–€220
Closed: Jan 7 to Mar 15, Credit cards: all major
52 km SE of Siena
Region: Tuscany, Michelin Map: 430
www.karenbrown.com/italyinns/ilchiostro.html

Nestled in the tranquil Tuscan countryside between two enchanting hilltop villages (Pienza and Monticchiello) is another jewel, L'Olmo. You cannot help instantly losing your heart to this very special little hotel. It has the warmth and intimacy of a bed and breakfast, yet the service and amenities rival those of the finest deluxe hotel. This bit of paradise is owned by the Lindo family. A few years ago they left the bustling city of Turin and bought a beautiful 16th-century stone house, which they lovingly restored to perfection, down to the smallest detail, preserving original terra-cotta floors and wood-beamed ceilings. With superb taste and guests' comfort in mind, five suites were created and appointed with antique chests, locally made wrought-iron beds, and pretty floral fabrics for color. Each has its own travertine marble bathroom and two have a fireplace. The two suites on the ground floor have their own garden and whirlpool bathtubs. Francesca and her mother Loredana, your exceptionally charming hostesses, tend to guests in a warm and highly professional manner. Downstairs are two cozy sitting rooms leading out to the stone courtyard with tables and flower pots. A full buffet breakfast or gourmet candlelit dinner—upon request—is served in the luminous dining room. *Directions:* From Pienza drive south and after 6 km turn left for Monticchiello. Follow signs for L'Olmo on your right before you come to Monticchiello.

L'OLMO
Owners: Francesca & Loredana Lindo
Pienza–Monticchiello (SI) 53020, Italy
Tel: (0578) 75 51 33, Fax: (0578) 75 51 24
5 rooms, Double: €160–€270, 1 apartment
Dinner upon request
Open: Mar 28 to Nov 18, Credit cards: all major
6 km S of Pienza
Region: Tuscany, Michelin Map: 430
www.karenbrown.com/italyinns/lolmo.html

In a small city near the coast, nor far from the charming town of Lucca and the popular town of Pisa, you will find the Albergo Pietrasanta. Although "albergo" suggests a simple hotel, this small, deluxe property does not fit that definition. Located in the center of Pietrasanta, the building dates back to the 17th century when it was the home of the prestigious and wealthy Barsanti Bonetti family. There is a sophisticated, understated elegance throughout the hotel and a mood of luxury is set as you enter the lobby and register at a lovely antique desk. To the right of the spacious foyer are two splendid lounges which exude the ambiance of a private home, with pastel walls, soft lighting, comfortable chairs grouped around a handsome fireplace, polished terrazzo floors, beautiful paintings, and bouquets of fresh flowers. The far end of the lounge opens through arched doors into one of the hotel's most special features, a romantic garden courtyard, part of which is enclosed in glass to create a "winter garden" where a bountiful breakfast is served each morning. Forming one wall of the courtyard is a separate building, formerly the stables, which has been renovated to house additional deluxe accommodations. As would be expected, guestrooms reflect the same subdued, sophisticated good taste as the public rooms. *Directions:* From the A12, exit at Versilia-Forte dei Marmi and follow signs to Pietrasanta. In town follow signs to the hotel.

ALBERGO PIETRASANTA
Manager: Marisa Giuliano
Via Garibaldi, 35
Pietrasanta (LU) 55045, Italy
Tel: (0584) 79 37 26, Fax: (0584) 79 37 28
19 rooms, Double: €210–€440*
*Breakfast not included
Closed: Jan 6 to Mar 1, Credit cards: all major
35 km NW of Lucca, 105 km NW of Florence
Region: Tuscany, Michelin Map: 430
www.karenbrown.com/italyinns/albergopietrasanta.html

It is difficult to find a hotel in Rome with windows thick enough to keep out the ever-present buzz of traffic. Less than an hour's drive from the city, the Borgo Paraelios offers the perfect solution: a luxurious country villa immersed in the lovely Tuscan-like hills of Sabina. In this splendid villa, filled to the brim with elegant antiques, rich, warm-colored tapestries, and period paintings, it is impossible to find a detail overlooked. It is a masterpiece of harmonizing old and new, with antique terra-cotta tile floors, stone fireplaces, beamed ceilings, and antique doors from castles and villas brought here and cleverly incorporated into the building. The very inviting bedrooms, each with its own character and color scheme, look out over the lush garden where guests can breakfast among flower-laden terra-cotta pots. Meandering through the gracious living room, two libraries, and billiard and bridge rooms, one has the sense of having been invited to the country home of nobility for a weekend of absolute peace and tranquillity. For a charge, transportation is available to and from Rome. When you return from the bustle of the city, exquisite meals are served in the frescoed formal dining room. *Directions:* Go north from Rome on the A1, exit at Soratte/Ponzano Romano and proceed to Stimigliano. Cross the railway and turn right to Poggio Mirteto along the S.S.657 Sabina to Km 0. Turn left to Terni on S.S.313 and the hotel is on your left.

❄ ☕ ✂ [CREDIT] ☎ 🐕 ♿ 🏋 🚶 🐎 P 🍴 🚭 ≈ 🏃 🖼 ✍

HOTEL BORGO PARAELIOS
Owner: Adolfo Salabé, Manager: Andrea Salabé
Localita: Valle Collicchia
Poggio Mirteto (RI) 02040, Italy
Tel: (0765) 26 267, Fax: (0765) 26 268
18 rooms, Double: €270–€340
Open: all year, Credit cards: all major
45 km NE of Rome, 2 km N of Poggio Mirteto
Region: Lazio, Michelin Map: 430
Relais & Châteaux
www.karenbrown.com/italyinns/borgoparaelios.html

Gennarino a Mare is primarily a restaurant—one of the best known in Ponza both for its seafood specialties and its prime location right on the waterfront. It even has a large deck that stretches out over the water, built upon wooden pilings. Gennarino a Mare is a favorite place to dine, especially in summer when boats of all shapes and sizes dock at the adjacent pier and the merry yacht set comes to eat and drink. The restaurant has hosted many of the world's rich and famous, so there's no telling who might be sitting at the next table. It is no wonder the restaurant is so popular: as you enjoy dinner, you can watch the reflection of the fishing boats shimmering in the water and, behind them, the gaily painted houses of Ponza stepping up the hill like brightly painted blocks. Owner Francesco Silvestri was born in the same house where the restaurant now stands. The 12 simple bedrooms, located on the floors above the restaurant, are all decorated similarly with colorful matching drapes and bedspreads setting off white walls. Although small, each room has its own little step-out balcony with a romantic view. Remember, Gennarino a Mare is basically a restaurant, but a real winner for a simple, reasonably priced place to stay in Ponza. *Directions:* Take either the ferry or hydrofoil from Anzio to Ponza. The hotel is on the opposite side of the port, so it is best to take a taxi.

GENNARINO A MARE
Hosts: Tilla & Francesco Silvestri
Via Dante, 64
Ponza, Isola di (LT) 04027, Italy
Tel: (0771) 80071, Fax: (0771) 80140
12 rooms, Double: €114–€216
Open: all year, Credit cards: all major
Island of Ponza, ferry from Anzio
Region: Lazio, Michelin Map: 430
www.karenbrown.com/italy/gennarino.html

The Il Pellicano (one of Italy's most idyllic hotels) has been beautifully designed in the traditional villa style and, although not old, looks as though it has snuggled on its prime hillside position overlooking the Mediterranean for many years. The façade is of stucco, painted a typical Italian russet and set off by a heavily tiled roof. Vines enwrap the building, further enhancing its appealing look. You enter into a spacious, attractive lobby where the sun streams through the windows enhancing the white walls, terra-cotta floors, and wood-beamed ceilings. The cheerful ambiance continues with pretty sofas, antique accents, and enormous displays of fresh flowers enlivening every conceivable nook and cranny. The overall impression is one of light and color—and impeccable taste. Beyond the reception area is a spacious terrace where sometimes the chef prepares elaborate buffets, served out of doors overlooking the exquisite bay (the food at Il Pellicano is expensive, but exceptional). From the terrace, a lawn dotted with pine trees extends down the hillside to a beautiful pool romantically perched at the cliff's edge. From the bluff, both steps and an elevator access a pier at the water's edge. Off the stairs, small individual terraces with lounge chairs and mats for sunning have been built into the rocks. The hotel also has a spa, tennis courts, and beauty salon. *Directions:* At the south end of the peninsula. Take the Orbetello exit from Highway 1.

IL PELLICANO
Manager: Signora Cinzia Fanciulli
Porto Ercole (GR) 58018, Italy
Tel: (0564) 85 81 11, Fax: (0564) 83 34 18
50 rooms, Double: €609–€1368
Open: Apr to Oct, Credit cards: all major
160 km N of Rome, 4.5 km S of Porto Ercole
Region: Tuscany, Michelin Map: 430
Relais & Châteaux
www.karenbrown.com/italyinns/ilpellicano.html

Standing proudly on the cliffs overlooking one of Italy's most spectacular coastlines are the remains of a 13th-century Spanish watchtower. The tower has been cleverly incorporated into, and stands as the dramatic symbol for, the Hotel Torre di Cala Piccola, which shares a beautiful small promontory (called Cala Piccola) with luxurious private villas discreetly hidden behind high walls. The hotel looks as though it too might be a private home. The first part of the hotel you see (which houses the reception area, lounge, and bar) is a sienna-toned building with red-tiled roof and green shutters, snuggled amongst silvery olive trees and flowering oleanders. The moderately sized, nicely decorated guestrooms are not in the main building, but instead share romantic stone cottages. Some of the accommodations are designated as one-room apartments with a divider creating a separate sitting area. However, these are a bit cut up and I much preferred the regular doubles. The cottages are strategically placed amongst the trees on the property to capture the view. And what a view! High cliffs drop precipitously down to the sea, forming a series of coves where the rich blue water of the Mediterranean dances in the sunlight. Also capturing this absolutely stunning vista are a lush lawn where, during the summer, dinner is served and, on a lower terrace, a dramatic swimming pool, which seems to almost float high above the sea.

※ ⚓ ☕ CREDIT ☎ Y P ⑪ ≋ 🖼 🛥 🐾 🍇

HOTEL TORRE DI CALA PICCOLA
Managers: Luca Santini & Stefania Marconi
Cala Piccola
Porto Santo Stefano (GR) 58019, Italy
Tel: (0564) 82 51 11, Fax: (0564) 82 52 35
50 rooms, Double: €270–€382
Open: mid-Mar to Nov, Credit cards: all major
On the coast, 10 km SW of Porto Santo Stefano
Region: Tuscany, Michelin Map: 430
www.karenbrown.com/italyinns/torredicalapiccola.html

If money doesn't matter, when in picture-perfect Portofino settle in for a long stay at the incomparable Hotel Splendido, or her sister hotel, the Splendido Mare. But since not everyone's travel budget can stretch to such luxury, the Hotel Eden is a welcome alternative. Although the price at the Eden might seem high for the accommodation offered, just remember that Portofino is the target of the wealthy from around the world, and rates in restaurants and places to stay reflect this popularity. If you are prepared for simplicity and not disturbed by a bit of delayed maintenance, you will be happy to discover the Eden, tucked right in the heart of Portofino, not facing the harbor, but down a little lane, just two minutes' walk away. Wrought-iron gates open to steps leading to the front garden, a peaceful oasis of flowers and green lawn. Facing the garden is a side terrace where meals are served outside when the weather is warm. The hotel is a pastel, mustard-colored villa with green shutters. As you enter, to the right is a porch-like dining room. Farther on you find the registration desk where your host, Signor Osta, will probably be waiting to check you in. The guestrooms we saw, all with air conditioning, were simply decorated. The best rooms are on the second floor—these are larger and have better facilities.

❄ ⚓ ☕ 💳 🧍 🚶 🍴 🏄

HOTEL EDEN
Owner: Ferruccio Osta
Via Dritto, 18
Portofino (GE) 16034, Italy
Tel: (0185) 26 90 91, Fax: (0185) 26 90 47
12 rooms, Double: €190–€270
Open: all year, Credit cards: all major
5 km S of Santa Margherita Ligure, 35 km E of Genoa
Region: Liguria, Michelin Map: 428
www.karenbrown.com/italyinns/hoteleden.html

Located up a winding, wooded road high above the town of Portofino, the super-deluxe Hotel Splendido sits majestically above the beautiful blue Mediterranean, overlooking the boats moored in Portofino's lovely harbor. Stretching across the front of the hotel is a magnificent terrace—a favorite choice of guests who enjoy dining outside with an incredible vista of the sea. As would be expected in such a world-class hotel, the food is outstanding and beautifully served. Leading from the hotel are romantic little pathways where you can stroll through the wooded grounds and stop along the way at strategically placed benches to enjoy incomparable views. For those who would like more serious exercise, on a terrace below the hotel is an enormous swimming pool, while located in the gardens to the left of the hotel are tennis courts. The public rooms are charming, with comfortable chairs covered with floral prints and fresh flowers galore. Every detail is perfect and in excellent taste. The bedrooms too are lovely and decorator-perfect, many with balconies affording a splendid view of Portofino. The Splendido is expensive, but without a doubt one of the most special resorts in Italy.

❄ ⛱ ☕ 💳 ⇅ 🏋 🕴 🚶 ❓ P 🍴 ≈ 🚶 🖼 🏄

HOTEL SPLENDIDO
Manager: Maurizio Saccani
Portofino (GE) 16034, Italy
Tel: (0185) 26 78 01, Fax: (0185) 26 78 06
68 rooms, Double: €831–€1038*
*Includes breakfast & dinner
Open: Mar 25 to Nov 10, Credit cards: all major
5 km S of Santa Margherita Ligure, 35 km E of Genoa
Region: Liguria, Michelin Map: 428
www.karenbrown.com/italyinns/splendido.html

Ask any experienced traveler to name one of the most picturesque harbors in the world, and tiny Portofino, with its cluster of colorful houses reflecting in the turquoise sea, is always right on top of the list. However, this adorable town has only a few places to stay, so it was with great excitement that we learned that one of our very favorite inns, Hotel Splendido (a dazzling jewel on the hillside overlooking Portofino), was opening an extension in the center of town. As would be expected, this new facility rates only superlatives. Everything is done in excellent taste and the quality in every detail is supreme. The ambiance and beautiful decor is much like its "sister" hotel on the hill, with a similar elegantly serene color scheme. There is a pretty, fresh quality throughout, with gleaming hardwood floors, light-colored wood furnishings, and beautiful fabrics. Nothing is heavy or formal—a refined yet happy, cheerful ambiance prevails. The food also is of the same superb standards as the Splendido, with meals served either in a charming dining room or else outside on the terrace overlooking the harbor. If you want to be at the heart of the action of picturesque Portofino, especially if you enjoy watching the glamorous yachts pull into the harbor, the Splendido Mare makes an excellent choice. An added bonus: you can use all of the facilities at the Splendido, which is just a pleasant walk away.

SPLENDIDO MARE
Manager: Maurizio Saccani
Portofino (GE) 16034, Italy
Tel: (0185) 26 78 02, Fax: (0185) 26 78 07
16 rooms, Double: €586–€761
Open: all year, Credit cards: all major
35 km E of Genoa
Region: Liguria, Michelin Map: 428
www.karenbrown.com/italyinns/splendidomare.html

For those travelers wishing to explore the lesser-known Marches region, or about to embark on a ferry to Greece, the unique Fortino Napoleonico hotel offers comfortable and relaxing accommodations. Five kilometers along the coast from the city of Ancona, the hotel boasts a beachfront location. Originally a fortress, the vantage point it affords must have been considered strategic by Napoleon in 1811, when he ordered it constructed. Twelve guestrooms, three suites, and a restaurant are housed within the low white, stone structure while the rest of the bedrooms are in a new building nearby. The restaurant specializes in fresh seafood dishes and looks so directly out to sea that it gives you the impression of being on a ship. At the heart of the fort is a courtyard, complete with cannons, where breakfast is served, and a separate building contains a bar and a spacious living room with fireplace, decorated in neoclassic style. Rich period antiques appoint the three lovely suites, while simpler wicker furniture is found in the double rooms. Just two steps away is the beach, and up on the roof of the one-story fort is a deck with a spectacular coastal view. A swimming pool is also available for guests. *Directions:* From Ancona, follow signs for Camerano. Take a left at Portonovo, heading down to the sea. Watch for signs indicating the hotel's entrance.

FORTINO NAPOLEONICO   **New**
Manager: Amleto Roscioni family
Via Poggio
Portonovo (AN) 60020, Italy
Tel: (071) 80 14 50, Fax: (071) 80 14 54
27 rooms, Double: €140–€233
Closed: Jan, Credit cards: all major
5 km S of Ancona
Region: Marches, Michelin Map: 430
www.karenbrown.com/italyinns/napoleonico.html

The Albergo Casa Albertina is a prime example of what a difference management can make. There is a wide choice of hotels in the picturesque little fishing village of Positano—many, like the Casa Albertina, with spectacular views, pleasant decor, and good meals. However, they don't have Michele Cinque, who is an outstanding hotelier: gracious and warmhearted—willing to do whatever is required to make each guest feel very special. It is not surprising that Michele is such a pro: he had been in the hotel business for many years, having been the manager of one of Positano's most deluxe hotels (Le Sirenuse) before deciding to help his wife and late mother-in-law manage the Casa Albertina full-time. Although Michele has partially retired, his two sons extend the same warmth of welcome as their father and son Lorenzo has officially taken over the management of the hotel. All of the bedrooms have a view and are nicely decorated. Ask for one of the largest rooms—these cost only a bit more. The hotel (which is built into a 12th-century house) clings to the hillside above Positano, a position that affords superlative views, but also means a strenuous walk into town. There are also 70 steps from the parking area to the hotel. *Directions:* As you drive down the hill into Positano, there is a sign on the left pointing to the winding, walking-alleyway to the hotel.

ALBERGO CASA ALBERTINA
Owner: Cinque family
Via della Tavolozza, 3, Positano (SA) 84017, Italy
Tel: (089) 87 51 43, Fax: (089) 81 15 40
20 rooms, Double: €217–€237*
*Includes breakfast & dinner
Meals for hotel guests only
Open: all year, Credit cards: all major
Amalfi Coast, 55 km S of Naples, 17 km S of Sorrento
Region: Campania, Michelin Map: 431
www.karenbrown.com/italyinns/casaalbertina.html

The intimate Buca di Bacco won our hearts immediately—not that it is super-elegant or grandly deluxe, but it possesses all the ingredients that make a hotel very, very special. It has an unbeatable location directly on the beach in the center of Positano, charming decor, excellent food, and spectacular views and—most important of all—radiates a graciously warm welcome. It is no wonder that the hospitality is so genuine: the Rispoli family has been catering to guests for three generations. Grandfather Rispoli emigrated to the United States years ago but his heart longed for his beautiful Positano, so when he saved enough money he returned and bought a property right on the beach where he opened a restaurant with guestrooms. From the moment you enter, you will be impressed by the tasteful decor. The lobby has a tiled floor in a beautiful green, yellow, and white design. The greens and yellow are picked up in the various fabrics used throughout. Salvatore Rispoli is often at the front desk, but the entire family is busy behind the scenes. Salvatore's sister is responsible for the glorious flower arrangements, while Carla and Nicodemo Rispoli are often in the kitchen overseeing the excellent meals. Almost all of the rooms have either a balcony or a terrace with a view. If you really want to splurge, ask for the most deluxe room, number 10, an exceptional corner room with an enormous terrace and the best view in Positano.

BUCA DI BACCO
Owner: Rispoli family
Via Rampa Teglia, 4
Positano (SA) 84017, Italy
Tel: (089) 87 56 99, Fax: (089) 87 57 31
47 rooms, Double: €190–€345
Closed: Nov to Mar, Credit cards: all major
Amalfi Coast, 55 km S of Naples, 17 km S of Sorrento
Region: Campania, Michelin Map: 431
www.karenbrown.com/italyinns/bucadibacco.html

The spectacular, family-run Il San Pietro di Positano is claimed to be one of the most beautiful, deluxe hotels in the world. It is—there is no question about it. From the moment you approach the hotel, class is evident: no large signs; no gaudy advertising; just an ancient chapel along the road indicates to the knowledgeable that an oasis is hidden below the hill. After parking in the designated area near the road, you take an elevator, which whisks you down to the lounge and lobby. You walk out of the elevator to a dream world—an open, spacious oasis of sparkling white walls, tiled floors, colorful lounge chairs, Oriental rugs, antique chests, flowers absolutely everywhere, and arches of glass through which vistas of greenery and sea appear. To the right is a bar and to the left is a marvelous dining room—again with windows of glass opening to the view, but with the outdoors appearing to come in, with the walls and ceilings laced with plants and vines. The bedrooms too seem to be almost a Hollywood creation—more walls of glass, bathrooms with views to the sea, and balconies on which to sit and dream. If you can tear yourself away from your oasis of a bedroom, an elevator will whisk you down the cliff to the small terrace at the water's edge. If all this sounds ostentatious, it isn't. It is perfect. *Directions:* Follow the coastal highway south from Positano. Soon after town a chapel on your right marks the entrance to the hotel.

IL SAN PIETRO DI POSITANO
Owners: Virginia Attanasio Cinque & sons, Vito and Carlo
Positano (SA) 84017, Italy
Tel: (089) 87 54 55, Fax: (089) 81 14 49
61 rooms, Double: €400–€900
Closed: Nov to Apr, Credit cards: all major
2 km S of Positano on Amalfi Drive, 62 km S of Naples
Region: Campania, Michelin Map: 431
Relais & Châteaux
www.karenbrown.com/italyinns/ilsanpietro.html

For those who want to stay in the heart of the colorful fishing village of Positano, the Palazzo Murat, a charming, family-run hotel, makes an excellent choice. It is superbly located—surrounded by shops and only steps down to the beach. The hotel consists of two parts: the original building (a 200-year-old palace) plus an attached new wing that stretches to the side. The palace has a faded-pink patina whose charm is accented by wonderful arched alcoves, intricately designed windows, and magenta bougainvillea clinging to the walls and cascading from the wrought-iron balconies. The entrance to the hotel is through a sun-drenched patio, a favorite gathering spot for guests. In the evening, tables are beautifully set on the patio where guest can dine under the stars with the scent of jasmine perfuming the air. Within, the old-world feeling is maintained with tiled floors, white walls, and formal settings of antique sofas and chairs. My favorite bedrooms are the five upstairs in the palace section: especially appealing are those with shuttered French doors opening onto small balconies that capture a view of the bay. All the rooms are comfortable and have television, radio, and mini bar. The hotel has its own boat that takes guests for excursions along the coast five times a week. *Directions:* Follow signs from the center of the village (located in the pedestrian area).

HOTEL PALAZZO MURAT
Owner: Attanasio family
Via dei Mulini, 23
Positano (SA) 84017, Italy
Tel: (089) 87 51 77, Fax: (089) 81 14 19
30 rooms, Double: €230–€400
Open: Mar to Nov, Credit cards: all major
Amalfi Coast, 55 km S of Naples, 17 km S of Sorrento
Region: Campania, Michelin Map: 431
www.karenbrown.com/italyinns/murat.html

The Hotel Poseidon, owned and lovingly managed by the Aonzo family, is not in the center of town, but perched above the main road as it winds down from the highway. However, it is just a few minutes' easy walk when you want to browse through Positano's maze of romantic cobbled alleyways, shop in the attractive boutiques, or walk along the beach where the colorful fishing boats are moored. As you walk into the hotel there is a reception desk on the first level, but the main part of the hotel is reached up a flight of stairs. Here you find a series of intimate, small rooms that open up one after another through a series of arched doorways. It looks like a private home with many potted plants, Oriental carpets enhancing tiled floors, whitewashed walls, and cozy sitting niches with comfortable, white-slipcovered chairs. There is even a grand piano next to the bar. However, the nicest feature of the hotel is the terrace that sweeps across the front, perched above the street with a lovely view of the town. This terrace is truly the heart of the hotel, for being outside is the essence of Positano. Here, surrounded by cascades of colorful bougainvillea and many plants, guests take most of their meals and also enjoy a large swimming pool. For those who like to truly pamper themselves on vacation, the hotel has the Laura Elos Beauty Center where guests can enjoy various beauty treatments or maintain fitness in the gym.

❄ ⚓ ☕ 🛶 CREDIT ☎ 🐕 ♿ 🏋 🚶 ♈ P 🍴 ≈ 🏖 ⛴ 🐾 🍇

HOTEL POSEIDON
Owner: Aonzo family
Via Pasitea, 148
Positano (SA) 84017, Italy
Tel: (089) 81 11 11, Fax: (089) 87 58 33
50 rooms, Double: €243–€460
Open: Easter to Jan 6, Credit cards: all major
Amalfi Coast, 55 km S of Naples, 17 km S of Sorrento
Region: Campania, Michelin Map: 431
www.karenbrown.com/italyinns/hotelposeidon.html

A wonderful newcomer on the Amalfi Coast is the super-serviced and romantic Punta Regina hotel, located on Positano's main road, which snakes its way down and out of town. The current owners, the Russo family, had the four-story white palazzo totally refurbished, incorporating many amenities. It is obvious that they had two specific goals foremost in mind: guests' comfort and accessibility to the fabulous coastal views on every possible occasion. The 13 generously proportioned bedrooms are primarily junior suites and suites, some having gorgeous terraces larger than the room itself, with Jacuzzis hidden among lush Mediterranean vegetation. Elegantly appointed bedrooms in soft-peach or olive tones have antique furnishings, rich fabrics, and luxurious marble and tiled bathrooms, all using the best-quality local materials and craftsmen available. The top terrace with head-spinning views in every direction has a gazebo where breakfast is served if not in the guestrooms (on terraces, of course!). Although the hotel is right on the main road where traffic can be noisy, the terraces and views make it difficult to leave this romantic spot. It is an easy walk to shops, restaurants, and the beach where the ferry for Capri departs. *Directions:* From the main coastal road, take Via Pasitea down into Positano. The hotel is on the left-hand side at the beginning in the first residential section of town.

❄ ⚓ ☕ 🛷 CREDIT ☎ 🐕 🛗 🚶 🐎 🍸 P 🍽 ⛷ ♿

PUNTA REGINA　　　　*New*
Owner: Salvatore Russo
Via Pasitea, 224
Positano (SA) 84017, Italy
Tel: (089) 81 20 20, Fax: (089) 81 23 161
13 rooms, Double: €170–€365
Closed: Nov to Mar, Credit cards: all major
Amalfi Coast, 55 km S of Naples, 17 km S of Sorrento
Region: Campania, Michelin Map: 431
www.karenbrown.com/italyinns/puntaregina.html

Le Sirenuse is a superb luxury hotel tucked in the picturesque ancient fishing village of Positano. It is no wonder that so many writers and artists have been attracted to this colorful town of brightly hued houses clinging to the precipitous hillside as it drops down to its own small bay. And it is also no wonder that so many of these famous people have found their way to the oasis of Le Sirenuse, a favorite hideaway for discerning travelers seeking discreet, understated elegance. From the moment you enter the hotel lobby the mood is set with fresh white walls, tiled floors, oil paintings on the walls, accents of antiques, and an abundance of colorful flowers everywhere. The hotel is built on terraces cut into the hillside and so almost all the rooms capture a wonderful view out over the quaint rooftops and the tiled domed cathedral to the shimmering blue waters of the bay. It is only a short walk through the perpendicular streets until you are on the beach. The dining room has walls of glass that allow the maximum enjoyment of the vista below, but most diners prefer the splendor of eating outdoors on the terrace, surrounded by flowers and views of the sea. On another level of the hotel there is a swimming pool. The hotel also has a spa and its own parking area (rare for Positano). *Directions:* Located near the center of town, on the right side of the road as you drive up the hill.

LE SIRENUSE HOTEL
Manager: Antonio Sersale
Via C. Colombo, 30
Positano (SA) 84017, Italy
Tel: (089) 87 50 66, Fax: (089) 81 17 98
60 rooms, Double: €250–€1650
Open: all year, Credit cards: all major
Amalfi coast, 55 km S of Naples, 17 km S of Sorrento
Region: Campania, Michelin Map: 431
www.karenbrown.com/italyinns/lesirenuse.html

The Villa Franca, with a commanding position overlooking the sea, is one of Positano's classic villas transformed into a well-priced hotel. The management is extremely friendly and there is an immediate warmth and charm as soon as you walk into the redesigned and redecorated villa. The Russo family wanted to create an attractive full-service hotel combined with the friendliness and service of a small inn, and it is just that. The fresh Mediterranean decor is most appealing, with royal-blue slipcovered armchairs, a profusion of plants, lacquered terra-cotta vases, white-tiled floors and walls, and arched windows everywhere, so that you don't miss the mesmerizing views of the sea for a second. The elegant glassed-in restaurant with floral-tapestry chairs and blue tablecloths specializes in fresh local seafood. The food is exceptional: Mario Russo himself is a talented chef and personally oversees both the food and impeccable service. In the winter, the hotel sponsors a cooking school where Diana Folonari teaches the art of Italian-Mediterranean specialties. The bedrooms follow the same cheerful theme with colorful ceramic-tiled floors, cream bedspreads with green-and-yellow-striped trim and exquisite views. On the rooftop is a swimming pool with a 360-degree view over the world's most beautiful coastline. Guests also enjoy a sauna, massage room, and solarium. *Directions:* Follow the road into Positano and the hotel is on the left.

HOTEL VILLA FRANCA
Owner: Mario Russo
Viale Pasitea, 318
Positano (SA) 84017, Italy
Tel: (089) 87 56 55, Fax: (089) 87 57 35
28 rooms, Double: €190–€310
Open: Apr to Oct, Credit cards: all major
Amalfi Coast, 55 km S of Naples, 17 km S of Sorrento
Region: Campania, Michelin Map: 431
www.karenbrown.com/italyinns/hotelvillafranca.html

The Hotel Villa Odino makes an excellent option for hotel accommodation when visiting Venice—especially if you prefer to return to the tranquillity of the countryside in the evening. The hotel is about a kilometer from the train station where a 20-minute journey brings you into the heart of the city. However, it isn't just its convenience to Venice that makes the Villa Odino such an excellent choice—this jewel of a little hotel would be a winner anyway. The handsome mansion, built in the gentle countryside on the banks of the River Sile, dates back to 1563 when it was a residence for emissaries of the Bishop of Torcello. The mansion has been meticulously restored by the charming Pasini family (including three lovely daughters) who personally manage the hotel, showering attention on their guests. One daughter, beautiful Enrica, showed us around the attractively decorated home. Every detail exudes loving attention, with fresh flowers everywhere and each room individually decorated in an appealing, homelike way. All of the guestrooms are spacious and have large modern bathrooms. My favorite rooms are those in a separate wing facing the pool, each of which has French doors opening onto a private terrace. *Directions:* Take A4 north from Venice and exit at Quarto d'Altino. After leaving the motorway, turn left. At the first intersection, turn right, follow the river to the hotel.

HOTEL VILLA ODINO
Owner: Pasini famly
Manager: Enrica Pasini
Via Roma, 146
Quarto d'Altino (VE) 30020, Italy
Tel: (0422) 82 31 17, Fax: (0422) 82 32 35
30 rooms, Double: €181–€439
Closed: Dec 23 to Jan 6, Credit cards: all major
25 km NE of Venice, 15 km SE of Treviso
Region: Veneto, Michelin Map: 429
www.karenbrown.com/italyinns/villaodino.html

The Relais Fattoria Vignale is a superb small hotel idyllically located in the heart of the Chianti wine region. It enjoys the enviable honor of having the best of both worlds—it feels as if you are secluded in the countryside, yet is right in Radda, one of Tuscany's most picturesque towns. The hotel was the manor house of a large Chianti estate, which still produces fine wines. The hotel sits on the main street, but magically, the back of the hotel opens onto a gorgeous, pristine view of rolling hills laced with vineyards and dotted with olive trees. Some of the guestrooms are in the main manor while others, which also have lovely views, are just across the street. The guestrooms and cozy lounges are tastefully decorated with antiques. Care has been taken in the restoration to preserve many of the enticing architectural features of the manor such as heavy beams, arched hallways, decorative fireplaces, and painted ceilings. Behind the hotel, meticulously kept gardens lead down the hillside to a romantic wisteria- and jasmine-covered terrace where guests enjoy breakfast, or dinner under the stars, with an incredible view. Another bonus of this fine hotel is the swimming pool, overlooking the vineyards. The original wine cellars have been transformed into a tavern with wine tasting and a rustic-style restaurant serving simple meals. Only 300 meters from the hotel is the Ristorante Vignale, which is owned by the hotel.

❋ ☕ ✄ 💳 ☎ 🏃 👫 🏇 ♈ P 🍴 ≋ 🖼 🍇

RELAIS FATTORIA VIGNALE
Manager: Silvia Kummer
Via Pianigiani, 15
Radda in Chianti (SI) 53017, Italy
Tel: (0577) 73 83 00, Fax: (0577) 73 85 92
34 rooms, Double: €160–€340
Open: Mar 15 to Dec 9, Credit cards: all major
In the heart of Chianti, 52 km S of Florence
Region: Tuscany, Michelin Map: 430
www.karenbrown.com/italyinns/fattoriavignale.html

The Ansitz Heufler Hotel, built in 1578 by Count Heufler, is actually a castle, but not one of the large, foreboding castles sometimes found high on mountain peaks. This is a little, friendly castle, located in a sunny mountain valley in northeastern Italy within a short drive of dramatic Dolomite vistas. Inside its thick walls are some absolutely delightful rooms. The smoke-blackened bar where drinks are enjoyed is the place where meat was once smoked. The charming dining rooms with their old paneled walls, planked wooden floors, and tables set with crisp linens are popular places to dine. The broad staircase leads up to a wide hallway off which you find a cozy television room (no TVs in rooms) and a magnificent pine-paneled room with intricate inlaid designs. It is also here that you find the chalet-style bedrooms. Some have sitting nooks set in the towers and several have accent pieces that were made for the castle in the 16th century. Half of the first floor (second in the U.S.) is a lovely suite that can accommodate a family of four. In winter there is skiing nearby and in summer walking trails beckon in every direction. *Directions:* Leave the 49 (Bressanone to Lienz road) at Rasun di Sotto and go through the village to the adjacent village of Rasun di Sopra where you find the castle.

ANSITZ HEUFLER HOTEL
Owner: Steiner family
Valle di Anterselva
Rasun di Sopra (BZ) 39030, Italy
Tel: (0474) 49 85 82, Fax: (0474) 49 80 46
9 rooms, Double: €104–€204
Closed: Apr & Nov, Credit cards: VS
90 km NE of Bolzano, 12 km E of Brunico
Region: Trentino-Alto Adige, Michelin Map: 429
www.karenbrown.com/italyinns/ansitzheufler.html

The Palazzo Sasso, a stunning hotel that opened in 1997, is located in the spectacular village of Ravello with its spellbinding views of the sea. It is built within the Sasso family's private 12th-century villa, which was a favorite romantic hideaway of Ingrid Bergman and Roberto Rossellini. Richard Wagner too loved the Villa Sasso and in 1880 wrote part of "Parsifal" while a guest here. The villa had lain empty for many years before being converted by Richard Branson (creative entrepreneur of Virgin Airlines, music, and hotels) into an opulent, world-class, luxury hotel. Many architectural features—such as vaulted ceilings, marble patterned floors, and Moorish-shaped windows—are enhanced by the predominantly white and gold surroundings, and accented by priceless antique pieces. Most of the white-tiled bedrooms, appointed with neo-classical furnishings, offer the famed sea views through large windows and have compact bathrooms with every amenity imaginable. Rosellini's is the elegant restaurant that looks out onto a flower-laden terrace where breakfast is served. Here top-rated chef, Giuseppe Lavarra, insists on the freshest of local seafood and produce for his innovative creations. The latest enhancement is a beautiful swimming pool with an underwater window positioned on a terrace below the hotel. *Directions:* The Palazzo Sasso is discreet, only a tiny brass plaque designates its location (close to Hotel Palumbo).

PALAZZO SASSO
Manager: Attilio Marro
Via San Giovanni del Toro, 28
Ravello (SA) 84010, Italy
Tel: (089) 81 81 81, Fax: (089) 85 89 00
43 rooms, Double: €310–€1300
Closed: Nov to Feb, Credit cards: all major
66 km S of Naples, 6 km N of Amalfi
Region: Campania, Michelin Map: 431
www.karenbrown.com/italyinns/palazzosasso.html

The Hotel Palumbo is a 12th-century palace, owned since 1875 by the Vuilleumier family. The location is perfect—high in the clouds overlooking terraced vineyards and beyond to the brilliant blue Mediterranean, which dances in and out of the jagged rocky coast. The romance begins when you enter the richly hued, ceramic-tiled lobby with its ancient atrium of arched colonnades, green plants flowing from every nook, masses of fresh flowers, and gorgeous antiques. Each small corner is an oasis of tranquillity, from the intimate bar to the cozy antique-filled tiny lounges. There is a lovely dining room with a crystal chandelier, bentwood chairs, and a fireplace, but usually meals are served on the terrace, which perches like a bird's nest in the sky. Wherever you dine, the food is excellent. There is a stunning garden in the rear featuring a vine-covered terrace overlooking the Amalfi coast. Another tiny patio capturing both the sun and the view is tucked onto the roof of the villa. There are only 21 bedrooms—the size varies since this was an old villa, but all are individually decorated and have their own charming personality. A few guestrooms are located in an annex. The Hotel Palumbo exudes a romantic ambiance and a wealth of old-world character. *Directions:* Located on the upper edge of town. Ask for directions to the hotel garage.

HOTEL PALUMBO
Owner: Vuilleumier family
Manager: Marco Vuilleumier
Via S. Giovanni del Toro, 16
Ravello (SA) 84010, Italy
Tel: (089) 85 72 44, Fax: (089) 85 81 33
21 rooms, Double: €511–€861, Includes breakfast & dinner
Open: all year, Credit cards: all major
66 km S of Naples, 6 km N of Amalfi
Region: Campania, Michelin Map: 431
www.karenbrown.com/italyinns/hotelpalumbo.html

The Villa Cimbrone is not only a hotel: its gardens are one of Ravello's most famous attractions. The tourist office proclaims, "The Villa Cimbrone—essence of all the enchantment of Ravello—hangs like a swallow's nest on the cliffs." The villa is reached by a delightful ten-minute walk from Ravello's main square (the signs are well marked to this favorite sightseeing prize); then, once you pass through the gates, the villa and its magnificent gardens open up like magic. The gardens are truly superb—if you have ever received a postcard from Ravello, chances are it showed the view from the terrace of the Cimbrone. Most dramatic of all is the belvedere with its stately Roman statues accenting the dazzling view. Luckily, this outstanding villa is also a small hotel. The rooms are of museum quality with furniture fit for a king. We toured through the marvelous old building, which is not open to the public, only to guests. This fabulous villa was once the prized possession of an English lord. Later it was sold to the present owner, Marco Vuilleumier, who told us the following romantic tale: Toward the end of World War II, the English nobleman who owned Villa Cimbrone landed with the Allied troops in Salerno. Somehow he was able to find a jeep, and wound up the twisting road to see his beloved villa once again. *Directions:* Because its gardens are open to the public, the hotel is signposted from the center of town. (Pedestrian-only area.)

VILLA CIMBRONE
Owner: Vuilleumier family
Manager: Giorgio Vuilleumier
Ravello 84010, Italy
Tel: (089) 85 74 59, Fax: (089) 85 77 77
20 rooms, Double: €223–€375
Open: Apr to Nov, Credit cards: all major
66 km S of Naples, 6 km N of Amalfi
Region: Campania, Michelin Map: 431
www.karenbrown.com/italyinns/villacimbrone.html

The northeastern corner of Italy, south of Venice, offers such splendid cities as Ferrara, Mantova, Rovigo, and Ravenna. Ravenna has gained worldwide recognition for its stunning gold and brightly-colored mosaics preserved from Byzantine times and shown off in eight of the city's churches and basilicas. Since the city is surrounded by flat marshland, most people get around by bike, which makes its historical center a pleasant place to walk. Accommodation is limited, so it was a great discovery to come across the Albergo Cappello, a truly unique hotel. After the death of one of Italy's foremost industrialists who had spent great sums of money on restoring the 14th-century palazzo, it was taken over by young and enthusiastic entrepreneurs Francesca and Filippo. In order to give the exquisite property back to the citizens of Ravenna, they came up with the concept of a cultural center/art gallery/restaurant/hotel. The three double rooms and four suites are located on the upper floors off a frescoed hall where artwork is displayed. The guestrooms are purposely decorated in minimalist style, using contemporary lighting and soft hues so as not to distract from the original architectural features. Light lunches are served in the cantina, while dinners are served out in the courtyard. This is not a hotel in the standard sense—keys are given to the front door in the evening and breakfast is eaten at the café across the street.

ALBERGO CAPPELLO
Owners: Francesca Fronzoni & Filippo Donati
Via IV Novembre, 41
Ravenna 48100, Italy
Tel: (0544) 21 98 13, Fax: (0544) 21 98 14
7 rooms, Double: €120–€250
Open: all year, Credit cards: all major
In the heart of Ravenna, 74 km E of Bologna
Region: Emilia-Romagna, Michelin Maps: 429, 430
www.karenbrown.com/italyinns/cappello.html

The Villa Rigacci, once a private residence, now an inviting small inn, is only about a half-hour's drive from Florence, easily accessible from the A1 to Rome. This 15th-century building is a picture-perfect example of a Tuscan villa with its creamy-white stucco façade, thick walls, heavy, weathered, red-tile roof, green-shuttered windows, and parklike gardens. Federico Pierazzi and his sister, Fiorenza, take great care to see that all guests receive personal attention and are made to feel "at home." In summer, after a day of sightseeing, guests relax in the back garden where a large pool, surrounded by lounge chairs and umbrellas, stretches out on a terraced lawn. Inside, handsome antiques adorn the sitting rooms and library. The dining room is especially appealing and, according to the guests staying at the inn, the chef is excellent. In summer guests usually choose to have their meals outside on the terrace. Each bedroom is individually decorated with very attractive country-style antiques and lovely fabrics creating rooms that blend beautifully with the old-world ambiance of the villa. Although I personally prefer the area of Tuscany that stretches directly south of Florence where the villages seem more secluded, the conveniently located Villa Rigacci offers easy access to the expressway and accommodation with charm, hospitality, and warmth. *NOTE:* Vaggio is a small town southwest of Reggello.

VILLA RIGACCI
Owners: Fiorenza & Federico Pierazzi
Reggello–Vaggio (FI) 50066, Italy
Tel: (055) 86 56 718, Fax: (055) 86 56 537
25 rooms, Double: €135–€165
Open: all year, Credit cards: all major
30 km SE of Florence, 5 km SW of Reggello
Region: Tuscany, Michelin Map: 430
www.karenbrown.com/italyinns/rigacci.html

The Villa Luppis property, with its rich historical past, was originally an 11th-century monastery restored in 1500 after a devastating war and bought by the Luppis family in 1800. In order to be able to maintain the vast estate, Stefania and Giorgio Ricci Luppis opened its doors as a hotel in 1993. Their intention was to maintain the flavor of their original home by keeping the family's period antiques and precious paintings intact. The effect is true old-world charm that surrounds you within the beamed dining room with enormous fireplace, various frescoed sitting rooms, and arched front hall overlooking the garden. Bedrooms and suites within two wings of the villa are in theme with matching bedspreads and draperies, antique pieces, gilded mirrors, and stenciled bordered or beamed ceilings. On-site activities include a swimming pool and tennis courts, and bikes for touring the surrounding park are offered. The excellent restaurant, where Chef Franco de Bin works wonders with fresh seafood, organizes a three- to five-day cooking school and wine lessons with wine expert Moreno Romano—the classes even include visits to local cantinas and cheese producers. A variety of fascinating local itineraries are suggested to the Villas of Palladio on the Brenta canal, or to the Pordenone, Udine, and Gorizia castles. A shuttle is available daily to/from Venice (40 minutes). Transportation to/from Marco Polo airport is available on request.

VILLA LUPPIS
Owners: Stefania & Giorgio Ricci Luppis
Via S. Martino, 34
Rivarotta (PN) 33080, Italy
Tel: (0434) 62 69 69, Fax: (0434) 62 62 28
28 rooms, Double: €181–€285
Open: all year, Credit cards: all major
15 km SW of Pordenone, 50 km NE of Venice
Region: Friuli-Venezia Giulia, Michelin Map: 429
www.karenbrown.com/italyinns/villaluppis.html

The Hotel Barocco is one of Rome's finest small hotels in the moderate price range. The location is excellent—although the address is shown as being on the busy Piazza Barberini, just a tantalizing narrow portion of the pretty hotel peeks onto the square. The entrance, marked by a row of potted shrubbery, is discreetly tucked around the corner. You enter into an intimate lobby where there is no frenzy of activity, just a reception counter tended by a gracious staff happy to assist you, whether it is with reservations for dinner or transportation to the airport. Beyond the reception area is a lounge which opens onto a cute little bar. The decor features a series of handsome murals depicting scenes of Rome, below which the walls are covered with a rich cherry wood. There is a fresh, uncluttered look, with nothing flamboyant or fussy. The breakfast room (where—except on Sundays—sandwiches, salads, and even pasta are available for guests) has the same decor with scenes of Rome on the wall. The guestrooms (all similar in decor, but different in shape) continue the same smart tailored look, featuring an abundant use of cherry wood in the built-in headboards, wainscoting, desks, chairs, and bedside tables. Deep-blue drapes accent the beautiful wood, giving a sophisticated, refreshing, almost nautical look. The rooms are good-sized, but seem larger by the placement of enormous mirrors that cover the walls behind the beds.

HOTEL BAROCCO
Manager: Franco Caruso
Via della Purificazione 4, Piazza Barberini, 9
Rome 00187, Italy
Tel: (06) 48 72 001, Fax: (06) 48 59 94
37 rooms, Double: €207–€520
Open: all year, Credit cards: all major
Heart of city, facing Piazza Barberini
Region: Lazio, Michelin Maps: 430, 2038
www.karenbrown.com/italyinns/hotelbarocco.html

The splendid Duke Hotel reopened recently after a complete and thorough renovation supervised by brother-sister team Marco and Rosa Visocchi, who learned the art of hospitality from their father and grandfather. They have integrated these high standards and attention to detail and quality in the daily running of The Duke Hotel, located in the residential Parioli neighborhood. As yet undiscovered by international tourists and with a prevalently Italian guest list, the hotel's general ambiance is authentically Italian. The reception area leads to a cozy reading room and the heart of the hotel, the Polo Lounge and bar area with its colorful celestial-blue stained-glass skylight, fireplace, and English-club ambiance. Light lunches or dinners can be served in this multi-use area as well as tea in the afternoon or aperitifs with piano bar in the evening. Rosa personally assists with menu planning at the hotel's restaurant, following particular gastronomic themes according to the season. The polished and elegant classical style of decor continues throughout the luminous bedrooms, with warm beige, red, and forest-green schemes. Some rooms have balconies or terraces. The extraordinary feature of this hotel is its customized guest care including twice-daily maid service, courtesy shuttle service to the city center, museum and concert ticketing, tour guides, transfers, and immediate response to guests' every need.

❄ ☕ 💳 ☎ 🛗 🚶 🍴

THE DUKE HOTEL   ***New***
Owners: Marco & Rosa Visocchi
Via Archimede, 69
Rome 00197, Italy
Tel: (06) 36 72 21, Fax: (06) 36 00 41 04
78 rooms, Double: €280–€372
Open: all year, Credit cards: all major
Parioli neighborhood near Villa Borghese
Region: Lazio, Michelin Maps: 430, 2038
www.karenbrown.com/italyinns/duke.html

For location, the Gregoriana is superb: it is situated on Gregoriana Street, which runs into the Piazza Trinita dei Monti at the top of the Spanish Steps. In spite of the perfect location, when I first saw the Gregoriana I just did not see how I could include it in our book because it has no antique ambiance: in fact, the decorating style might be classified as Chinese with a mish-mash of art deco. However, after staying at this hotel, I just did not see how I could not include it—it is such a well-run small hotel and has such a sparkle of personality that it brightens the otherwise often impersonal city of Rome. As a guest here, you will not be just one of the thousands of tourists in Rome—upon arrival, the concierge will probably already know you by name and will continue to greet you personally as you come and go. Instead of feeling like a face that goes with a key hanging on the wall, you will experience a warmth and intimacy as if you were a guest in a private home. The bedrooms are simple and spotlessly clean. Those at the rear are especially quiet and some enjoy a balcony with a view over the rooftops of Rome. Only breakfast is served. However, there is a concierge on duty 24 hours a day to cater to your special needs. *NOTE:* If you are traveling with a family, ask about the exceptionally spacious suites.

HOTEL GREGORIANA
Owner: Maria Novella Panier-Bagat
Via Gregoriana, 18
Rome 00187, Italy
Tel: (06) 67 94 269, Fax: (06) 67 84 258
19 rooms, Double: €206–€216
Open: all year
Near the top of the Spanish Steps
Region: Lazio, Michelin Maps: 430, 2038
www.karenbrown.com/italyinns/gregoriana.html

The charming Hotel Hassler (once a wealthy Medici palace) stands out as Rome's premier deluxe hotel—still family-owned and family-managed. Its location at the top of the Spanish Steps is unsurpassed: the majority of Rome's monuments and chic boutiques are close by, and for guests who want to explore Villa Borghese Park, complimentary bikes are available. The fact that the proprietor, Roberto Wirth, is on the premises shines forth: you almost feel like a guest in a private home. Every detail reflects loving care. When the Hassler was renovated, Astrid Wirth, Roberto's wife, even tracked down the old-established manufacturer who was able to reproduce the original fabrics for the walls. The decorating theme is classical with hues of warm reds and ochres prevailing, the same rich colors used in many palazzi across Rome. At the heart of the Hassler is a romantic inner garden courtyard, a superb oasis with stone walls laced with vines, statues, flowers, cozy little tables, and a bar. The rooftop restaurant at the Hassler is also spectacular, boasting one of the finest views in Rome: the entire panorama of the city surrounds you as you dine. All of the guestrooms are splendid, but if money is no object, reserve one of the Hassler's magnificent suites, some with enormous terraces and a view so spellbinding that you will never want to set foot from this beautiful hotel.

HOTEL HASSLER
Manager: Roberto E. Wirth
Trinita dei Monti, 6
Rome 00187, Italy
Tel: (06) 69 93 40, Fax: (06) 67 89 991
85 rooms, Double: €648–€860
Open: all year, Credit cards: all major
At the top of the Spanish Steps
Region: Lazio, Michelin Maps: 430, 2038
www.karenbrown.com/italyinns/hotelhassler.html

The Inn at the Spanish Steps is divine. Surprisingly, there are few exceptional accommodation choices in the historic center, but this property, half a block from the world's most famous staircase, is truly remarkable. The dream of the Di Rienzo brothers, owners of several large hotels in Rome, was to create an intimate, almost club-like ambiance with all the trimmings for a few privileged guests in an unbeatable location, so they took over an historical, 17th-century private residence (Hans Christian Andersen lived here for years), striving to maintain its origins as a home. The inn now offers a minuscule reception room on the ground floor, 24 bedrooms spread out among the three upper floors, and a marvelous rooftop garden where guests can have an ample buffet breakfast or sunset drink, either in the cozy veranda or out on the flower-laden terrace, complete with bird's-eye view of the steps and the fashionable Via Condotti. Doubles are divided into two categories: superiors at the back and luxury doubles and junior suites at the front. Rooms with wood floors and antique furnishings include every possible amenity. Upholstered walls and coordinated drapes accent original features such as frescoed or beamed ceilings. Guests who remain more than three nights receive the bonus of an airport transfer or guided tour of the city. Nothing else compares.

THE INN AT THE SPANISH STEPS
Manager: Silvio Catalano
Via dei Condotti, 85
Rome 00187, Italy
Tel: (06) 69 925 657, Fax: (06) 67 86 470
24 rooms, Double: €235–€750
Open: all year, Credit cards: all major
At the Spanish steps
Region: Lazio, Michelin Maps: 430, 2038
www.karenbrown.com/italyinns/spanishsteps.html

One would only expect superlative hospitality from a hotel owned by the President of the Italian Tourism Board, but at the Lord Byron, guests receive much more: discreet and distinguished host Amedeo Ottaviani offers guests every imaginable service. The former patrician villa with pristine white exterior is hidden away on a cobblestone street in the city's most exclusive residential neighborhood. The peaceful but central location and highly personalized guest care are the successful ingredients in creating the intimate ambiance of a private home. An inviting lounge and library, just beyond the reception area, are decorated in line with the entire hotel in sleek art-deco style with lacquered black pieces and gold or red accents in carpeting, drapes, and upholstery all set off by stark white walls. The host's delightful private collection of portrait paintings displayed throughout softens the ambiance. Sumptuous bedrooms and suites on three top floors have the same attention to detail, with vintage marble bathrooms and views over stately villas and a lush park. Downstairs is the attractive, club-like Salotto bar and lounge, where you can enjoy light lunches and wine tastings from the award-winning cellars. Not to be missed is a meal in the elegant dining room, Sapori del Lord Byron, where the house chef creates his renowned dishes with total respect to traditional Italian cuisine and ingredients—exceptionally distinctive.

HOTEL LORD BYRON
Owner: Amedeo Ottaviani
Via G. de Notaris, 5
Rome 00197, Italy
Tel: (06) 32 20 404, Fax: (06) 32 20 405
36 rooms, Double: €300–€950
Open: all year, Credit cards: all major
On the edge of Villa Borghese Park
Region: Lazio, Michelin Maps: 430, 2038
www.karenbrown.com/italyinns/lordbyron.html

The Hotel Majestic Roma, located on the famous Via Veneto, exudes a refined, tasteful, old-world ambiance. As with other luxury hotels in Rome, the rates are high, but so are the outstanding ambiance and the service. From the moment you enter through the circular revolving doorway into the spacious, high-ceilinged lobby with a few well-chosen antiques and bouquets of fresh flowers, the mood of quiet elegance is established. Instead of one large lounge, you find a series of intimate parlors where guests can gather. In each room there are beautifully upholstered chairs and opulent fabrics on the walls and richly draped windows. Be sure to peek in and see the fabulous frescoed ceiling of the 19th-century Salone Verdi, which is used for special banquets. A wonderful old-fashioned wrought-iron elevator with polished brass trim takes guests to the bedrooms, each with its own personality, as in a private home. All are elegant in decor and traditionally furnished in an old-world, opulent style. On warm days, an outdoor terrace with a view of the city is a perfect place to pause for a cool drink. There is also a beautifully decorated, formal dining room, La Veranda, where guests enjoy typical Mediterranean dishes, as well as Continental cuisine.

HOTEL MAJESTIC ROMA
Manager: Franco Sestini
Via Veneto, 50
Rome 00187, Italy
Tel: (06) 42 14 41, Fax: (06) 48 80 984
96 rooms, Double: €490–€4400*
*Breakfast not included: €23–€40
Open: all year, Credit cards: all major
In the heart of Rome on Via Veneto
Region: Lazio, Michelin Maps: 430, 2038
www.karenbrown.com/italyinns/majesticroma.html

La Residenza was recommended to us by several readers who claimed it to be their favorite place to stay in Rome. And, after a personal visit, I can certainly understand why they like it so much. This former villa really is quite different—appearing to be more like a private residence (which once it was) than a hotel. Its façade looks very Italian, with typical brown-shuttered windows, greenery, and flowers behind a small paved courtyard where guests may park their cars (based on availability of space). As for location, it just couldn't be better—just off the Via Veneto with Rome's poshest hotels for neighbors. The front hall has been converted into a reception area flanked by several guest lounges. On our original visit, these public rooms lacked much style, but on our last inspection we were amazed at the changes. Now, instead of dated grass cloth, the walls in the lounges are splendidly covered with traditional striped fabric in rich pinks, creams, and greens. To complement the newly covered walls, the overall decor has also been upgraded and the ambiance is one of comfortable sophistication with lovely antiques, potted plants, and handsome paintings. The breakfast room has also had a face-lift and it is much prettier than before. This four-star hotel is one of the best buys in Rome.

LA RESIDENZA
Manager: Casaburo Vincenzo
Via Emilia, 22
Rome 00187, Italy
Tel: (06) 48 80 789, Fax: (06) 48 57 21
27 rooms, Double: €180–€223
Open: all year, Credit cards: all major
Between Via Veneto and the Spanish Steps
Region: Lazio, Michelin Maps: 430, 2038
www.karenbrown.com/italyinns/residenza.html

Sarah Townsend, artist, painter, decorator, landscape designer, and overall connoisseur of life's best offerings, can only be described as the Renaissance woman. She has astounded everyone with the magnificent restoration project of Palazzo Terranova, her greatest challenge after selling her previous bed and breakfast, Il Bacchino. Accessed by a steep, winding road, the 18th-century rectangular palazzo, which dominates the northern Tiber valley and seemingly all of Umbria, is softened by surrounding terraced gardens filled with roses, lavender, cascading geraniums, and magnolia trees. The stylish home is a showplace for the family's own precious heirlooms and paintings brought over from England, combined with the best artisans' creations that Umbria has to offer. Each masterpiece of a bedroom, with its stenciled and painted designs, holds some enchanting feature and, just as in the creation of a painting, utmost attention has been given to color scheme, composition, and lighting. The palatial Traviata suite, on a floor of its own, off one of the many sitting rooms open to guests, has it all—a king-sized wrought-iron poster bed, custom lace linens, solid marble bath, and stunning views. Delightful staff is on hand to satisfy any whim. If you cannot get a room, do reserve a meal prepared at their excellent restaurant. *Directions:* Sarah can send you detailed directions.

PALAZZO TERRANOVA
Owners: Sarah & Johnny Townsend
Localita: Ronti
Ronti, Morra (PG) 06010, Italy
Tel: (075) 85 70 083, Fax: (075) 85 70 014
12 rooms, Double: €420–€775
Open: all year, Credit cards: all major
80 km N of Perugia
Region: Umbria, Michelin Map: 430
www.karenbrown.com/italyinns/terranova.html

The Villa Il Poggiale has its grand opening planned for spring 2003 and we were privileged to be invited to a "sneak preview." This elegant Tuscan country villa dating to the Renaissance period had such illustrious proprietors as noble families Corsini, Martini, and Ricasoli-Rucellai, and has been in the Vitta family for the past 50 years. Brothers Johanan and Nathanel have brought the family residence back to its former glory, transforming it from a private country home to an exclusive inn, with no expense spared on comfort and modern conveniences. On the ground floor you find the grand main salon plus two smaller ones off which six of the generous bedrooms and suites with antique furnishings and lovely new bathrooms are found. Soft-peach, olive-green, and pale-yellow color schemes are displayed in fine fabrics used for bedspreads, draperies, and upholstery. Other frescoed bedrooms upstairs are nicely spaced apart by three additional sitting rooms, the most desirable being those away from the main road. A full buffet breakfast using special recipes from the Renaissance is served overlooking the garden, which leads down to the swimming pool with its extraordinary views of the picture-perfect Tuscan landscape. Light lunches are served downstairs in La Cantinetta cellar. All very promising. *Directions:* Drive through San Casciano following signs for Empoli. After 2 km, Villa Il Poggiale is on the left-hand side of the Via Empolese.

❄ ☕ 🧹 CREDIT ☎ 🐕 🏌 ♈ P 🍽 ≈ 🖼 🍇

VILLA IL POGGIALE   *New*
Owners: Johanan & Nathanel Vitta
Via Empolese, 69
San Casciano Val di Pesa (FI) 50026, Italy
Tel: (06) 69 92 52 25, Fax: (06) 69 92 52 27
22 rooms, Double: €130–€270
Open: Mar to Nov, Credit cards: all major
17 km S of Florence
Region: Tuscany, Michelin Map: 430
www.karenbrown.com/italyinns/poggiale.html

The Rosa Alpina hotel is an oasis of luxury, comfort, and elegance in the very heart of the majestic Dolomite mountains. Although San Cassiano dates back to 1780, the area has recently been invaded with new construction and accommodation as a result of the growing popularity of this ski and summer resort. The Pizzininis were a fundamental part of the development of the area and besides running the hotel in the pre-World War II years, they built the first ski lift and power plant for the village. For three generations the Pizzinini family has dedicated itself to the art of hospitality and performs this art with extreme naturalness, warmth, and efficiency, which is seemingly innate to the people in this Val Badia area. Although presenting a simple, typical chalet-style exterior from the street, the hotel expands to the side and back with mountain views and private gardens. Rooms and suites reflect the colors of surrounding nature, with primarily soft-cream hues accented with meadow greens and rust reds. The hotel incorporates many special features such as four restuarants, one with a one-star Michelin rating. Here chef Norbert Niederkofler works wonders based on regional recipes and leads off-season cooking classes. Daniela Pizzinini directs the full-spa center. *Directions:* Exit from the A22 at Val Gardena and drive through Ortisei, Selva, Corvara, and La Villa to San Cassiano. The Rosa Alpina is on the main road in town.

ROSA ALPINA
Owner: Paolo Pizzinini
Strada Micura de Ru, 20
San Cassiano in Badia (BZ) 39030, Italy
Tel: (0471) 84 95 00, Fax: (0471) 84 93 77
50 rooms, Double: €160–€397
Closed: mid-Sep to Dec & Apr to Jun, Credit cards: all major
29 km W of Cortina, 6 km SE of Badia
Region: Trentino-Alto Adige, Michelin Map: 429
Relais & Châteaux
www.karenbrown.com/italyinns/rosaalpina.html

Finding the appealing Golf Hotel brought us an unexpected bonus: we discovered a niche of Italy that hugs the border north of Trieste, an absolutely gorgeous region of wooded hills, rolling fields, and vineyards. The Castello Formentini, superbly positioned on a hillock overlooking the countryside, has belonged to the Counts of Formentini since the 16th century. For many years there has been a restaurant within the castle, serving excellent meals and a medieval banquet on select Saturdays. Just outside the castle walls, one of the historic buildings of the castle complex has been converted into a small, charming luxury inn. The attractive, gracious owner, Isabella Formentini, says that all of the magnificent antique furnishings in the hotel are family heirlooms: in fact, she says the furniture is more valuable than the castle. Everything is authentic, even the wonderful prints and paintings. From the intimate lobby to each of the spacious guestrooms, everything is decorator-perfect and exudes a delightful country-manor ambiance. Only four of the rooms are within the castle, but all guests can stroll through the gate and into the castle grounds where the swimming pool lies invitingly in the shaded lawn. Guests also enjoy a tennis court and a nine-hole pitch-and-putt golf course. The hotel is open in the winter for groups of 10 to 20 persons.

❋ ⬛ 🎿 CREDIT ☎ 🏠 🍴 🏇 ⵂ P 🍴 ≈ 🏃 🖼 🔔 🍇

GOLF HOTEL
Owner: Contessa Isabella Formentini
San Floriano del Collio (GO) 34070, Italy
Tel: (0481) 88 40 51, Fax: (0481) 88 40 52
14 rooms, Double: €155–€295
Open: Mar to Nov, Credit cards: all major
40 km N of Trieste, 7 km N of Gorizia
Region: Friuli-Venezia Giulia, Michelin Map: 429
www.karenbrown.com/italyinns/golfhotel.html

Without a doubt, San Gimignano is one of the most picturesque places in Tuscany: a postcard-perfect hilltop village punctuated by 14 tall towers. During the day, the town bustles with activity, but after the busloads of tourists depart, the romantic ambiance of yesteryear fills the cobbled streets. For the lucky few who spend the night, there is a jewel of small inn, the Hotel L'Antico Pozzo. What a pleasure to see a renovation with such excellent taste and meticulous attention to maintaining the authentic character of the original building. The name of the hotel derives from an antique stone well (pozzo), which is softly illuminated just off the lobby. The fact that only the most affluent families could afford the luxury of a private well indicates that this 15th-century townhouse was once a wealthy residence. A timeworn stone staircase leads up to the air-conditioned bedrooms, tucked at various levels along a maze of hallways. Each one of the quietly elegant rooms has its own personality with thick stone walls, terra-cotta floors, and beautifully framed antique prints, plus satellite television. One of my favorites, number 20, has the palest of pastel-peach-colored walls, windows opening onto the terrace, and a fabulous domed ceiling painted with ancient Roman designs. Number 14 is also outstanding—a very large room with a canopy bed. Another advantage of L'Antico Pozzo is that this is a long-time family-run hotel.

HOTEL L'ANTICO POZZO
Manager: Emanuele Marro
Via San Matteo, 87
San Gimignano (SI) 53037, Italy
Tel: (0577) 94 20 14, Fax: (0577) 94 21 17
18 rooms, Double: €125–€155
Open: all year, Credit cards: all major
55 km SW of Florence, 38 km N of Siena
Region: Tuscany, Michelin Map: 430
www.karenbrown.com/italyinns/anticopozzo.html

San Gimignano is one of the most fascinating of the medieval Tuscany hilltowns. As you approach, this looks like a city of skyscrapers: come even closer and the skyscrapers emerge as 14 soaring towers—dramatic reminders of what San Gimignano must have looked like in all her glory when this wealthy town sported 72 giant towers. Most tourists come just for the day to visit this small town, but for those lucky enough to be able to spend the night, San Gimignano has a simple but very charming hotel, La Cisterna. The hotel is located on the town's main square and fits right into the ancient character of the surrounding buildings with its somber stone walls softened by ivy, arched shuttered doors, and red-tile roof. Inside La Cisterna, the medieval feeling continues with lots of stone, vaulted ceilings, leather chairs, and dark woods. The bedrooms are not fancy, but pleasant, and some have balconies with lovely views of the valley. Renovations added air conditioning in the restaurant and satellite TV (for European channels and CNN). La Cisterna is probably more famous as a restaurant than as a hotel and people come from far and wide because not only is the food delicious, but the dining rooms are delightful. Especially charming is the dining room with the brick wall, sloping ceiling supported by giant beams, and picture windows framing the gorgeous hills of Tuscany.

LA CISTERNA
Owner: Salvestrini family
Piazza della Cisterna, 24
San Gimignano (SI) 53037, Italy
Tel: (0577) 94 03 28, Fax: (0577) 94 20 80
50 rooms, Double: €88–€124
Open: Mar 10 to Jan 10, Credit cards: all major
55 km SW of Florence, 38 km NW of Siena
Region: Tuscany, Michelin Map: 430
www.karenbrown.com/italyinns/cisterna.html

La Collegiata is the perfect choice for those who want to explore the wonders of the Tuscan countryside beginning with the medieval town of San Gimignano. Celebrating 400 years of existence, the stone convent was transformed into a private residence by the Contessa Guicciardini one hundred years ago, then after a six-year restoration project it opened as a hotel. Achieving a masterpiece of architectural engineering, all possible efforts were made to conserve original features while incorporating modern conveniences. On the main road just outside town, the fortress-like structure is surrounded by a botanical park, a rose garden, and a swimming pool. The downstairs sitting rooms, library, and elegant dining rooms are situated around a stone courtyard with a stone well that is a miniature of the famous cisterna in the piazza of San Gimignano. The hotel features vaulted or paneled ceilings, unique antique pieces, portrait paintings, and terra-cotta floors. Individually styled bedrooms, all with views, have antique furnishings, rich blue or green draperies, and beautiful travertine marble bathrooms. The bi-level suite within the tower has the only element out of context with the rest of the Renaissance ambiance—a large Jacuzzi right in the middle of the room surrounded by windows taking in the magnificent views.

LA COLLEGIATA
Manager: Silva Perko
Localita: Strada 27, San Gimignano (SI) 53037, Italy
Tel: (0577) 94 32 01, Fax: (0577) 94 05 66
20 rooms, Double: €340–€850*
*Breakfast not included: €20
Closed: Jan & Feb, Credit cards: all major
2 km W of San Gimignano
Region: Tuscany, Michelin Map: 430
Relais & Châteaux
www.karenbrown.com/italyinns/lacollegiata.html

Staying at the Villa Arceno is truly like staying with friends in a sumptuous Italian villa. Although a luxurious property with stunning decor and impeccable service, the hotel exudes the warmth and charm of a small inn. The manager, Gualtiero Mancini, makes everyone feel at home. The mood of grandeur is set as you approach by a seemingly endless private road that winds through lovingly tended vineyards to a classic, three-story, ochre-colored villa. At one time the summer home of royalty, this 17th-century Palladian villa has been masterfully restored, both outside and within. The public rooms are more like lounges in a private home with a sophisticated, yet comfortable, elegance. The individually decorated guestrooms in the main villa are gorgeous—even the standard rooms are enormous and splendidly decorated. All the rooms are so outstanding it is difficult to choose, but I think my favorites are suites 104 and 204, both with sweeping vistas of vine-covered fields. In addition to just reveling in the utter peace and quiet, sightseeing in nearby Siena, or exploring the wonders of Tuscany, you can enjoy bicycles, a swimming pool, a tennis court, and, best of all, a park. Here you can stroll for hours along romantic lanes shaded by imposing rows of centuries-old cypress trees or meander on paths through the forest, passing almost-hidden statues and small temples, down to an idyllic, secluded lake.

HOTEL VILLA ARCENO
Manager: Gualtiero Mancini
San Gusmè (SI) 53010, Italy
Tel: (0577) 35 92 92, Fax: (0577) 35 92 76
16 rooms, Double: €310–€470
Open: mid-Mar to mid-Nov, Credit cards: all major
22 km NE of Siena, 9 km NW of Castelnuovo
Region: Tuscany, Michelin Map: 430
www.karenbrown.com/italyinns/hotelvillaarceno.html

If you are looking for a place to stay in the heart of Tuscany that is moderately priced, yet does not sacrifice one ounce of charm or quality of accommodation, the family-run Hotel Belvedere di San Leonino is unsurpassable. Ceramic pots of geraniums, trellised grapevines, and climbing roses soften and add color to the weathered stone buildings, which were originally a cluster of 15th-century farmers' cottages. Off the central patio area you find a small reception area, a living room blandly decorated with contemporary furniture, and an attractive dining room with tiled floors, rustic beamed ceiling, and appropriately simple wooden tables and chairs. When the weather is warm, meals are served outside in the garden. Because the rooms are tucked into various parts of the old farmhouses, they vary in size and shape. They also differ in decor, but all have an antique ambiance with wrought-iron headboards, beautiful old armoires, and pretty, white curtains. What adds the icing to the cake is the setting of the Belvedere, nestled in the very heart of the Chianti wine region, surrounded by stunning scenery—in every direction you look there are idyllic, sweeping vistas of rolling hills dotted with vineyards, olive groves, and pine forests. Hotel Belvedere is conveniently located only a short drive from the freeway.

HOTEL BELVEDERE DI SAN LEONINO
Manager: Signora C. Orlandi
San Leonino (SI) 53011, Italy
Tel: (0577) 74 08 87, Fax: (0577) 74 09 24
28 rooms, Double: €120–€130
Meals for guests only (closed Tues)
Open: mid-Mar to mid-Nov, Credit cards: all major
16 km N of Siena, 65 km S of Florence
Region: Tuscany, Michelin Map: 430
www.karenbrown.com/italyinns/hotelbelvedere.html

The Residence San Sano is a very special small hotel in San Sano—a picturesque hamlet in the center of the Chianti wine-growing region. We were charmed by the hotel, which is incorporated into a cluster of 16th-century stone houses. The exceptionally gracious owners, Giancarlo Matarazzo and his German wife, Heidi, were both schoolteachers in Germany prior to returning to Italy to open this small hotel. They have done a splendid job in the renovation and in the decor. A cozy dining room serves guests excellent meals featuring typically Tuscan-style cooking. Each of the bedrooms is delightfully furnished in antiques and each has a name incorporating some unique feature of the hotel, the name evolving from the time during reconstruction when Heidi and Giancarlo remembered each room by its special feature. One is called the Bird Room: here birds had claimed the room for many years and had nested in holes that went completely through the wall. With great imagination, the holes were left open to the outside, but on the inside were covered with glass. Another room is named for a beautiful, long-hidden Romanesque window that was discovered and incorporated into the decor and another for an antique urn uncovered during renovation. On our latest visit, a swimming pool and several spacious new rooms overlooking the vineyards had been added.

HOTEL RESIDENCE SAN SANO
Owners: Heidi & Giancarlo Matarazzo
San Sano (SI) 53010, Italy
Tel: (0577) 74 61 30, Fax: (0577) 74 61 56
14 rooms, Double: €120–€140
Meals for hotel guests only (closed Sun)
Minimum nights required: 5
Open: mid-Mar to Nov, Credit cards: all major
60 km S of Florence, 9 km S of Radda
Region: Tuscany, Michelin Map: 430
www.karenbrown.com/italyinns/residencesansano.html

The marvelously scenic Langhe wine country, rivaling Chianti but without all the tourists, was crying out for an upscale property in a historical residence and the San Maurizio has now come to the rescue. This super inn poised up on a hill looking over vineyards and olive groves opened in 2002 after a courageous and lengthy total renovation. Originally a Cistercian monastery, the massive U-shaped building around a lovely rose garden has 32 elegantly appointed rooms (most are suites), created from the monks' cells, each equipped with all amenities and technological conveniences. Many architectural features have been enhanced by the restoration including soaring ceilings with frescoes, original wood or brick floors, arched doorways, plus a chapel and vaulted wine cellars dating to the 17th century. Guests can lounge in one of a series of grand sitting rooms, appointed with antiques, Oriental carpets, and gold-framed paintings, or outdoors in the surrounding gardens with walks. The formal restaurant, in the very capable hands of renowned chef Guido di Costigliole, concentrates on the best regional cuisine, accompanied of course by the rich selection of local wines. Outings on horseback, golf, and guided historical visits of castles and wineries can be organized. A swimming pool and beauty center are right on the premises. *Directions:* From San Stefano Belbo, follow signs for Valdivilla. After 2 km turn right at the sign for the inn.

RELAIS SAN MAURIZIO   **New**
Owner: Cesare Pavese
Localita: San Maurizio, 39
San Stefano Belbo (CN) 12058, Italy
Tel & fax: (0141) 84 06 78
32 rooms, Double: €205–€320
Open: all year, Credit cards: all major
22 km SE of Asti
Region: Piedmont, Michelin Map: 428
www.karenbrown.com/italyinns/maurizio.html

The 16th-century Locanda San Vigilio has been in Guarienti Di Brenzone's family for over 400 years. This small hotel, nestled next to a miniature private cove that in days of yore offered shelter to fishing boats, has a prime location directly on Lake Garda. There is not much action here. If you want to see and be seen by the rich and famous, choose the glamorous Villa d'Este on Lake Como as your hub, but if you desire utter tranquillity, the Locanda San Vigilio makes a good choice. Here you will find understated luxury, nothing commercial at all. Only a small sign marks the tree-lined entrance just a few kilometers north of the town of Garda. The entrance to the hotel also serves as access for a public park and at first you might think you have the wrong turn, but tell the attendant at the gate that you have a reservation at the hotel and he will let you pass. The lane runs through the picnic grounds to the parking area for the Locanda. After parking your car in the designated area, you walk past the family's private villa and then down a path to the hotel, a sturdy stone building so close to the water that waves gently lap the walls. The dining room is especially inviting and if you are lucky, you can dine at one of the cozy tables overlooking the lake. The guestrooms vary in size, some being much more spacious than others. The prize bedrooms are the more expensive ones upstairs with windows overlooking the lake.

LOCANDA SAN VIGILIO
Owners: Agostino & Guarienti Di Brenzone
Manager: Christine Kössler
San Vigilio–Lake Garda (VR) 37016, Italy
Tel: (045) 72 56 688, Fax: (045) 72 56 551
14 rooms, Double: €232–€646
Open: Mar to Dec, Credit cards: AX, VS
154 km W of Venice, 3 km N of Garda
Region: Veneto, Michelin Maps: 428, 429
www.karenbrown.com/italyinns/locandasanviglio.html

The refreshingly unspoiled village of Santa Maria di Castellabate sits beside the sea at the southern tip of the Bay of Salerno. Just steps away from this cluster of colorful houses and brightly painted fishing boats, the Palazzo Belmonte nestles in utter tranquillity within its own 5-acre park, hidden from view by high stone walls. There is not even a discreet sign at the massive gates to hint that you have arrived at a hotel. The palazzo is the home of your charming host, Prince Belmonte, who opens both his home and his heart to a few lucky guests. Amazingly, the property has remained in the prince's family since it was built in the 17th century as a hunting lodge where the kings of Italy and Spain came to play. Today you too will feel like royalty. The magic begins the moment you enter through the vaulted portal into the central stonewalled courtyard where the scent of jasmine, roses, and honeysuckle perfumes the air. Prince Belmonte has his private residence on the top floor of the palazzo but the remainder houses 21 deluxe guestrooms. Thirty new luxurious rooms were opened in 2002 in the private park. A path through the garden leads to a beautiful swimming pool and beyond to a small green "secret" gate which leads down to the palazzo's private sandy beach. The food is outstanding and usually served on the terrace—to dine by candlelight under the stars looking out to the sea is truly memorable.

PALAZZO BELMONTE
Owner: Prince Angelo di Belmonte
Manager: Angela Wilkinson
Santa Maria di Castellabate (SA) 84072, Italy
Tel: (0974) 96 02 11, Fax: (0974) 96 11 50
51 rooms, Double: €186–€351
Meals for hotel guests only
Open: May to Nov, Credit cards: MC, VS
72 km S of Salerno, on S edge of town
Region: Campania, Michelin Map: 431
www.karenbrown.com/italyinns/palazzobelmonte.html

Santa Maria di Castellabate is a picturesque village hugging the sea at the southern tip of the Bay of Salerno. I fell in love with this exceptionally colorful, unspoiled, fishing hamlet several years ago. The Hotel Villa Sirio had been in the Tortora family for many generations, but was sold early in the 20th century. Luckily for you and me, Alfonso Tortora bought back his family home and with his wife, Rosalinda, took several years restoring the building, opening it in 1997 as a charming, small hotel. They are fantastic hosts who treat guests as friends, extending their hearts to all who come through the door. The handsome building is painted a rich yellow with white trim around the windows and dark-green shutters. The mood is set as you enter the intimate reception area where oil paintings decorate the walls and give a welcoming, homelike ambiance. The color scheme throughout is a happy one and all of the guestrooms are lovingly decorated in fine taste. The rooms facing the sea are in pretty hues of blue and yellow, while those facing the village are in green and yellow. Ask for one of the rooms facing the sea with a balcony—these are especially romantic. What fun to sleep with the waves lapping beneath your window! The food is excellent and served in a beautiful dining room under a coved ceiling with giant arches where the fishing boats used to be brought into the house for safekeeping.

HOTEL VILLA SIRIO
Owners: Rosalinda & Alfonso Tortora
Via Lungomare de Simone
Santa Maria di Castellabate (SA) 84072, Italy
Tel: (0974) 96 01 62, Fax: (0974) 96 05 07
14 rooms, Double: €176–€207*
*Includes breakfast & dinner
Closed: mid-Jan to mid-Mar, Credit cards: all major
72 km S. of Salerno, in center of village
Region: Campania, Michelin Map: 431
www.karenbrown.com/italyinns/villasirio.html

Sardinia's lovely beaches and inlets of turquoise water are outstanding, but not to venture inland from the coast means missing wonderful scenery and rich archaeological sites. The perfect solution is to combine the two—after a holiday by the sea, plan to stay for several days at the Hotel Su Gologone. Here you can experience all the best the countryside has to offer: delightful rural landscape, rustic country charm, excellent meals featuring Sardinian specialties, and even sightseeing excursions. The Hotel Su Gologone is set in a high valley among gently rolling hills dotted by grazing sheep. Adding drama to the tranquil scene is a backdrop of granite mountains whose jagged peaks reach to the sky. The exterior of the hotel exudes a country charm with stark white walls accenting Mediterranean-blue shutters and doors, red-tiled roof, and flowers, flowers, flowers. Inside, the ambiance of a country hotel is set from the moment you enter the lobby. All of the furnishings have a rustic flair with the extensive use of local handicrafts including hand-woven rugs, pretty fabrics, and simple wooden furniture. Although there are 65 guestrooms, the hotel seems much smaller because many of the rooms are in small cottages scattered about the property. Although the room rate is amazingly low, the Su Gologone offers the amenities of a resort hotel with a pool, tennis, mini golf, excursions, bikes, horseback riding, and a new spa.

HOTEL SU GOLOGONE
Manager: Luigi Crisponi
Sorgente Su Gologone
Sardinia–Oliena (NU) 08025, Italy
Tel: (0784) 28 75 12, Fax: (0784) 28 76 68
65 rooms, Double: €135–€280
Open: Christmas & Mar to Nov, Credit cards: all major
6 km NE of Oliena, on road to Dorgal, Island of Sardinia
Region: Sardinia, Michelin Map: 433
www.karenbrown.com/italyinns/hotelsugologone.html

The Pitrizza is a tiny jewel of a hotel located on the Emerald Coast of the island of Sardinia—the playground of the Aga Khan and the jet set of the world. From the moment you enter through the front gate, marked only with a discreet sign, you are in a world of tranquillity and absolute beauty. There is a central clubhouse that has a beautiful lounge, a delightful dining room with hand-hewn wooden chairs, a card room, and a bar. A small, protected patio extends from the dining room where meals are served when the weather is warm. French doors from the lounge open onto the terrace, which leads down to a most unusual swimming pool, cleverly designed into the natural rock. Once in this outstanding pool, you have the impression that you are swimming in the sea, not a pool, because the water level matches that of the bay. The bedrooms are all spacious and beautifully decorated—everything is of the very finest quality. They are tucked away in small cottages whose sod roofs covered with flowers blend into the landscape. If your idea of a vacation is a frenzy of activity and things to do, then the Pitrizza is definitely not for you. There are no planned activities, no sports director, no loud music—only lovely peacefulness, gourmet food, a beautiful pool, a beauty and fitness spa, and a delightful small white-sand beach. Although extremely expensive, the Pitrizza is truly special and lives up to every expectation of excellence.

❄ ⚓ ☕ 💳 ☎ 🏃 🎿 👫 🐎 ⅄ P 🍴 🚭 🏊 🖼 🏌 🎣 💃

HOTEL PITRIZZA
Manager: Pierangelo Tondina
Sardinia–Porto Cervo 07020, Italy
Tel: (0789) 93 01 11, Fax: (0789) 93 06 11
52 rooms, Double: €1180–€1700*
*Includes breakfast & dinner
Open: early May to mid-Oct, Credit cards: AX, MC
NE tip of Island of Sardinia
Region: Sardinia, Michelin Map: 433
www.karenbrown.com/italyinns/pitrizza.html

Sardinia is a large island, making it difficult to settle in just one place and visit all the sights. Therefore, we felt it important to find a hotel recommendation for those who want to explore in depth the area around Alghero. After looking without success for a charming place to stay in the city itself, we chose instead the Hotel El Faro, a large hotel situated 12 kilometers away on the tip of a small peninsula. Both an ancient round stone tower and a lighthouse mark the strategic spot. The hotel too has a mock lighthouse as a symbol of its name "El Faro." The white-stuccoed hotel spreads out over the peninsula and because there is water on three sides, all of the guestrooms have a sea view (and a balcony from which to enjoy it). Some of the vistas are more spectacular than others, so ask for a room in front overlooking the bay, such as number 159 or one of its neighbors. The mattresses are a bit soft for our taste, but the large bathrooms are topnotch, and the furniture attractive—mostly good-quality wicker with fabric-covered cushions. Terraced below the hotel are a large sun deck, then on a still lower level, a circular swimming pool, and lower still (snuggled in the rocks) a third pool. The ambiance is of a modern, first-class resort-style hotel—not much to distinguish it from those you would find anywhere in the world, but a friendly, well-kept place to stay.

HOTEL EL FARO
Manager: Yvan Bezzi
Sardinia–Porto Conte (SS) 07041, Italy
Tel: (079) 94 20 10, Fax: (079) 94 20 30
98 rooms, Double: €165–€774
Minimum nights required: 3
Open: May to end of Sep, Credit cards: all major
12 km from Alghero, Island of Sardinia
Region: Sardinia, Michelin Map: 433
www.karenbrown.com/italyinns/hotelelfaro.html

Having heard about a lovely little chalet tucked among the pines high in the Italian Alps near the French border, I was beginning to wonder what awaited me as the road wound through the ski town of Sauze d'Oulx with its unattractive jumble of modern concrete ski hotels. However, the road soon left the resort town and continued as a track, twisting higher and higher into the mountains until suddenly Il Capricorno came into view, nestled in the forest and surrounded in winter by ski runs. This is a wonderful place to enjoy a skiing holiday or perfect for summer walking along mountain trails. Just as you enter the hotel there is a tiny bar and, beyond, a cozy dining room enhanced by dark wooden chalet-style chairs, rustic wooden tables, and a stone fireplace with logs stacked neatly by its side. The bedrooms, too, are simple but most pleasant, with dark-pine handmade furniture, neat little bathrooms, and, for a lucky few, balconies with splendid mountain views. However, the greatest assets of this tiny inn are the owners, Mariarosa and Carlo Sacchi. Carlo personally made most of the furniture and will frequently join the guests for skiing. Mariarosa is the chef, a fabulous gourmet cook. *Directions:* Exit the A32 at Oulx (signpost Sauze d'Oulx) and follow the road up into the mountains and through the town. In winter you are collected by snowmobile from the town.

IL CAPRICORNO
Owners: Mariarosa & Carlo Sacchi
Les Clotes
Sauze d'Oulx (TO) 10050, Italy
Tel: (0122) 85 02 73, Fax: (0122) 85 00 55
7 rooms, Double: €170
Meals for hotel guests only
Open: Dec to May & mid-May to mid-Sep, Credit cards: VS
2 km E of Sauze d'Oulx, 60 km W of Turin
Region: Piedmont, Michelin Map: 428
www.karenbrown.com/italyinns/ilcapricorno.html

The Masseria San Domenico opened its doors to guests in 1996. Not that the building is new—quite the contrary—the lovely old farmhouse (masseria) dates back to the 17th century. The age is immediately reconfirmed as you drive up to the hotel—both sides of the lane are bordered by groves of centuries-old olive trees with thick gnarled trunks and silvery-green leaves. Typical of the region, the large farm complex has a Moorish look, with white walls gleaming in the sunlight. However, the fact that this is no longer a rustic farm is quickly apparent: an enormous, lake-like swimming pool lies snuggled next to the hotel; there are two tennis courts; the food is outstanding; the beautifully decorated guestrooms are all spacious, with large tiled bathrooms. The decor in all the bedrooms is similar, with marble floors, crisp-white walls, cheerful floral drapes and matching bedspreads, stenciled designs accenting the ceilings, and fanciful, painted wrought-iron headboards. The sea is 500 meters from the hotel and some of the rooms capture the bright blue of the Adriatic sparkling in the sun across an expanse of olive trees. The hotel also offers a new golf club and full spa. The Masseria San Domenico makes the perfect choice if you are looking for a hotel offering every amenity, yet so superbly managed that you feel like a pampered guest in a small, family-run hotel. *Directions:* The hotel is on the right as you drive south from Savelletri di Fasano.

MASSERIA SAN DOMENICO
Manager: Viola Melpignano
Savelletri di Fasano (BR) 72010, Italy
Tel: (080) 482 79 90, Fax: (080) 482 79 78
52 rooms, Double: €245–€1950
Closed: Jan 10 to Jan 30, Credit cards: MC, VS
2 km S of Savelletri on coastal road
Region: Apulia, Michelin Map: 431
www.karenbrown.com/italyinns/sandomenico.html

The Maremma, a beautiful area in the coastal foothills of southern Tuscany, quite undiscovered by tourists, offers a wealth of sightseeing possibilities: walled villages, Etruscan ruins, archaeological sites, and lovely landscapes. Until recently there were few places to stay that offered much charm, but happily this problem was solved when the Pellegrini family converted a 200-year-old stone farmhouse into a small hotel. Here you will find true Tuscan hospitality. The dining room is the heart of the inn and has tables set in a beamed-ceilinged room, which is filled with sunlight from large French doors opening onto a terrace where meals are served on warm days. The bedrooms in the original house are quite small, but 13 new, very spacious guestrooms and four suites have been built in an annex. There is also a new swimming pool. Another real bonus is the food: it is wonderful—everything is homemade under the direction of Signora Pellegrini, including marvelous pastas prepared by local housewives, and the hotel even produces its own wines which are served with the meals. Specialties of the inn are Signora Pellegrini's cooking classes and trekking (horseback riding). In the corral below the hotel, horses are groomed each day for guests' use: in fact, special room rates are offered which include riding in the Maremma countryside. *Directions:* From Scansano, take S.S. 322 toward Manciano. The hotel is on the left.

ANTICO CASALE DI SCANSANO
Owners: Massimo Pellegrini & family
Scansano (GR) 58054, Italy
Tel: (0564) 50 72 19, Fax: (0564) 50 78 05
32 rooms, Double: €95–€174
Open: Mar to mid-Jan, Credit cards: all major
30 km S of Grosseto, 2 km E of Scansano
Region: Tuscany, Michelin Map: 430
www.karenbrown.com/italyinns/anticocasale.html

The Villa Soranzo Conestabile is a splendid, three-story, 16th-century mansion that was built as a summer residence by one of the wealthiest Venetian families who were direct descendants of the powerful Doge, Giovanni Soranzo (the genius who originated the concept of Venice as a great sea power). Although located in the center of Scorzè, a small agricultural and commercial town, the house is secluded within its own 3-hectare park, which is especially romantic with a small pond, a stream, lovely gardens, centuries-old trees, and seven spectacular magnolias, which must be some of the largest in the world. Today the Villa Soranzo Conestabile is owned by the Martinelli family. The property was bought by the grandfather whose restaurant in Cortina was a favorite hangout for Hemingway (notice the wonderful old photos of Hemingway and granddad on the wall). My favorite guestroom, number 2, is a spacious, high-ceilinged corner room with antique furniture and windows capturing lovely views of the park. If you are on a budget, choose one of the less expensive bedrooms on the top floor. Although smaller and less grand, they are also decorated with antiques and are very attractive (my favorite is number 18). The Villa Soranzo Conestabile is an excellent value, especially when compared with hotel prices in Venice. It is possible to commute to the city center by the frequent bus service from in front of the house (a 45-minute trip).

❄ ⚓ ☕ 🧺 CREDIT ☎ 🐕 🏇 🏇 P 🍴 ⛷ 🐾 🍇

VILLA SORANZO CONESTABILE
Owner: Martinelli family
Manager: Lorenz Martinelli
Via Roma, 1
Scorzè (VE) 30037, Italy
Tel: (041) 44 50 27, Fax: (041) 58 40 088
20 rooms, Double: €105–€170
Open: all year, Credit cards: all major
24 km NW of Venice
Region: Veneto, Michelin Map: 429
www.karenbrown.com/italyinns/villasoranzo.html

This is one of the most scenic areas of the Dolomites and Sesto is one of the most attractive of the mountain towns. Just beyond town you find the delightful Berghotel Tirol, a lovely hotel built in typical Dolomite chalet style. Inside, the tasteful decor continues the delightful Alpine style, with one lovely room with beams and light-pine furniture leading to another. However, the special features of the Berghotel Tirol are its marvelous location on the hillside looking over this lovely valley with towering mountains as a backdrop and the warmth of welcome from Kurt Holzer, his wife Resi, and their son Walter. Many of the rooms have large balconies, which capture the view and the warmth of the mountain sun. The adjacent "residence" has lovely apartments (for two to four persons) with tiny kitchens, which can be rented for weekly stays or on a half-board basis. A network of trails in every direction tempts everyone into the crisp mountain air. When you return at night to the hotel, it is rather like a house party: table-hopping is prevalent as guests share their day's adventures. Below the hotel are a fitness center with sauna, panoramic swimming pool, whirlpool, and massage rooms, a children's room with billiards and football, and a large parking garage. *Directions:* Arriving in Sesto from Dobbiaco, go through town to the suburb of Moos where you turn left for the hotel.

BERGHOTEL TIROL
Owner: Holzer family
Sesto (Sexten) (BZ) 39030, Italy
Tel: (0474) 71 03 86, Fax: (0474) 71 04 55
46 rooms, Double: €110–€220*
*Includes breakfast & dinner
Open: Christmas to Easter & late May to Oct
2 km SE of Sesto toward Moos, 44 km NE of Cortina
Region: Trentino-Alto Adige, Michelin Map: 429
www.karenbrown.com/italyinns/berghoteltirol.html

When you wake up at the Hotel Helvetia and look out your window at the tiny crescent bay where colorful houses reflect in the still waters and fishing boats bob in the harbor, you might think for a moment you are in Portofino. Sestri Levante is not quite as picture-perfect—but almost—and here you will find less congestion and much more reasonable prices. In the beautiful section called Baia del Silenzio sits a jewel of a small hotel, the Helvetia, pressed snugly into the hillside, at the far end of the bay with a stunning view. This appealing small hotel is not fancy or pretentious, but just exactly right, and its prices provide an exceptional value. The decor is bright and pretty, with a few antiques for accent and masses of fresh flowers. All the rooms have been renovated and have excellent modern bathrooms. Opt for one of the lovely deluxe rooms with a view of the sea and a balcony—these are worth every penny. The final touch of perfection to this delightful establishment is that the owners, Signor and Signora Pernigotti, personally manage the property. *Directions:* Exit the A12 at Sestri Levante, following signs to the town center. At the roundabout in the center of town, go around the circle and take the road that runs along the park. Turn left when you come to the beach, left in front of the white church with tall columns, then immediately left again. At this point, follow signs to Hotel Helvetia.

HOTEL HELVETIA
Owner: Signor L. Pernigotti
Via Cappuccini, 43
Sestri Levante (GE) 16039, Italy
Tel: (0185) 41 175, Fax: (0185) 45 72 16
24 rooms, Double: €110–€160
Open: May to Nov, Credit cards: all major
34 km SE of Portofino, 59 NW of La Spezia
Region: Liguria, Michelin Map: 428
www.karenbrown.com/italyinns/helvetia.html

The Foresteria Baglio della Luna is a charming hotel within a few minutes' drive of Agrigento's jewel—the Valley of the Temples. The oldest part of the complex is a 13th-century square tower. Later, more buildings were added, and in the 18th century the property became a private countryside estate, which today has been cleverly converted into an appealing inn. You enter from a quiet lane through high walls into an attractive inner courtyard with an ancient well in the center. At the far end of the courtyard a doorway through the stone wall leads down to beautiful terraced gardens. The spacious, deluxe suites (all with Jacuzzi tubs) are located in the tower, but even the standard guestrooms are very comfortable and prettily furnished with antique headboards, tiled floors, handmade rugs, and attractive, color-coordinated fabrics on the drapes and bedspreads. Along one side of the courtyard are the public rooms: a cozy bar, a pretty lounge with lots of paintings on the walls and comfortable leather sofas, and the restaurant, which specializes in regional Sicilian and Italian dishes. The attractive, formal restaurant is one of the best in Sicily, managed by chef Damian Ferraro. The restaurant opens onto one of the most outstanding features of this intimate hotel—a delightful indoor-outdoor dining room with walls of glass that fold back completely so that the room is totally open to the cool breezes.

FORESTERIA BAGLIO DELLA LUNA
Manager: Ignazio Altieri
Contrada Maddalusa-Valle dei Templi
Sicily–Agrigento 92100, Italy
Tel: (0922) 51 10 61, Fax: (0922) 59 88 02
24 rooms, Double: €225–€490
Open: all year, Credit cards: all major
128 km SE of Palermo, 212 km SW of Taormina
Region: Sicily, Michelin Map: 432
www.karenbrown.com/italyinns/bagliodellaluna.html

Agrigento is home to Valle dei Templi, justifiably the most visited archaeological site in Sicily. If you want to savor these stunning temples to their fullest, secure a room at the Villa Athena. If you are looking for a hotel with personal warmth, beautiful furnishings, and special charm, this will not be a good choice since neither the public rooms nor the guestrooms exude much allure and there is a dated ambiance throughout. However, if you want to stay right next to the ruins, this is the only option for accommodations and the location is absolute perfection. Behind the hotel, the gardens extend to the very edge of the archaeological site. If you enjoy walking, there is no need for a car—just steps from the hotel a path leads in one direction to the temples and in the other to the museum where many of the fabulous artifacts from the site are beautifully displayed. In front of the hotel, in a separate building opposite the parking area is the hotel's restaurant—a popular luncheon stop for tour groups. In the summer, when the weather is good, dinner is served outside on a terrace where you dine under the stars with the temples softly illuminated on the nearby hill. What is special about the Villa Athena is its location and awesome views. This is one place you must splurge: request one of the rooms overlooking the ruins. *Directions:* The Villa Athena adjoins Valle dei Templi. Follow signs to the archaeological site to find the hotel.

❄ ⚓ ☕ 💳 P 🍴 ≈ 🖼 🏄

VILLA ATHENA
Owner: D'Alessandro family
Via dei Templi, 33
Sicily–Agrigento 92100, Italy
Tel: (0922) 59 62 88, Fax: (0922) 40 21 80
40 rooms, Double: €180–€208
Open: all year, Credit cards: all major
128 km SE of Palermo, 212 km SW of Taormina
Region: Sicily, Michelin Map: 432
www.karenbrown.com/italyinns/villaathena.html

Hugging the crest of a rocky coastal mountain rising 750 meters above Trapani, Erice's authentic testimony to yesteryear is broken only by several tall communication towers just outside the ancient walls. This appealing town of twisting cobbled streets makes a convenient overnight stop when visiting the Greek temple and theater at Segesta. As you wind up the hill toward Erice, watch for the parking area near Porta Trapani: park here and walk through the arched stone entrance and up the Via Vittorio Emanuele to the Hotel Moderno. The intimate reception area is very inviting, with fresh flowers and attractive prints on the walls. A hallway leads to a lounge accented by chairs grouped around small round tables where guests can just relax or enjoy a cold drink from the adjacent bar. A stone staircase leads up to the guestrooms, all of which are immaculately clean and fresh with whitewashed walls and white-tiled floors. Some bedrooms are decorated with light knotty-pine furniture; others have an antique motif. One of my favorites, room 35, has a handsome king-sized iron bed with brass trim and an antique armoire. About half of the rooms are located just across the street in another very old building which has been renovated—these rooms are similar and equally pleasant. My favorite in the annex is number 71, an especially spacious room with a king-sized bed with a handsome French-style headboard.

HOTEL MODERNO
Owner: Giuseppe Catalano
Via Vittorio Emanuele, 63
Sicily–Erice 91016, Italy
Tel: (0923) 86 93 00, Fax: (0923) 86 91 39
41 rooms, Double: €103–€114
Open: all year, Credit cards: all major
15 km NE of Trapani, 96 km SW of Palermo
Region: Sicily, Michelin Map: 432
www.karenbrown.com/italyinns/moderno.html

Tenuta Gangivecchio is far off the beaten path. Not only will you discover a jewel of a small inn, but the adventure of finding Gangivecchio leads you through Sicily's beautiful Madonie region. The Tornabene family began by converting a room in their home (a 13th-century Benedictine monastery of great character) into a restaurant, serving a set-menu lunch based upon fresh produce from the farm. The excellence of the simple yet delicious meals soon brought guests from as great a distance as Palermo, a two-hour drive away. Happily for the traveler who loves to stay in the countryside, the enterprising Tornabene family have now renovated the stables of the monastery into ten tastefully decorated guestrooms, appealing in their simplicity, with rustic red-tile floors, fresh whitewashed walls, hand-loomed scatter rugs, dark-wood accents, rough-hewn beamed ceilings, attractively framed old prints on the walls, and sweet cotton floral bedspreads. Delicious home-cooked meals are served to guests in a pretty dining room on the ground floor of the inn. Plan to arrive on a weekend for a lunch prepared by Signora Wanda and her daughter Giovanna, served in the dining room of the monastery. *Directions:* Drive east through Gangi on S.S. 120. Just outside of town turn right at a signpost for Gangivecchio. Go about 1 km and turn left at the tiny yellow sign. Continue 5 km up the hill and the Tenuta Gangivecchio is on your right.

TENUTA GANGIVECCHIO
Owner: Paolo Tornabene
C. da Gangivecchio Vanda Tornabene
Sicily–Gangivecchio 90024, Italy
Tel & fax: (0921) 68 91 91
10 rooms, Double: €120*
*Includes breakfast & dinner
Closed: 1 or 2 weeks end of Jun, Credit cards: AX, VS
130 km SE of Palermo, 127 km NW of Catania
Region: Sicily, Michelin Map: 432
www.karenbrown.com/italyinns/gangivecchio.html

The more adventurous traveler will be greatly rewarded with a stay at the Eremo, a 15th-century convent-turned-inn near the sea, conveniently located for exploring the baroque cities of Ragusa, Noto, and Modica. The noble Nifosi family restored the historic building with the desire of offering unique accommodation to travelers. The combination of professions in the family (antique collector, architect, and chef) made the project a natural. The typical baglio fortress with white-stone courtyard dominates the flat plain. An arched reception area was once part of the church and is striking with its contrast of white stone walls and black tiled floors, guarded by a knight in armor. The refined decor throughout is soothingly simple, in keeping with the building's medieval origins, and bedrooms, fashioned from friars' cells, are appointed with wrought-iron beds, white bedspreads, and antique armoires. Particular attention has been given to the traditional Sicilian cuisine, accompanied by a long list of Sicilian wines and served in either what was once the vaulted refectory or the crypts below. Fascinating itineraries are organized by boat, bike, jeep, or even by the owner's private plane, including overnight trips to the islands or Tunisia. Shuttle service is available from cities or airports. *Directions:* From N115, turn southwest toward the coast. Nine km before Marina di Ragusa, turn right and follow the signs to the Eremo della Giubiliana.

❄ ⚓ ☕ ♨ 💳 📷 🏠 🚶 🐎 P 🍴 ≋ 🔥 🐕 ♿ 🍇

EREMO DELLA GIUBILIANA
Manager: Salvatore Mancini
S.P. per Marina di Ragusa Km 7.5
Sicily–Marina di Ragusa 97100, Italy
Tel: (0932) 66 91 19, Fax: (0932) 66 91 29
11 rooms, Double: €240–€520
Open: all year, Credit cards: all major
On the southern coast of Sicily
Region: Sicily, Michelin Map: 432
www.karenbrown.com/italyinns/eremogiubiliana.html

If you want to stay in the heart of Palermo, the Centrale Palace Hotel has an absolutely superb location—on one of Palermo's most colorful main streets with the city's prime sightseeing targets just steps away. Within minutes you can be at the spectacular cathedral, or the museums, or the theater. However, it is not location alone that makes the Centrale Palace so special—this well-run, friendly hotel would be a winner anywhere. The building dates back to the 17th century, at which time it was the home of a noble family. Its grand past is still alive in the soaring ceilings, beautiful polished tile floors, marble columns, ornate chandeliers, frescoed ceilings in the conference rooms, handsome mirrors, fine oil paintings, and many precious antiques. The attractive guestrooms maintain the old-world ambiance with traditional furnishings and color-coordinating fabrics. One of the most endearing features of the hotel is its lovely roof garden overlooking the city, where breakfast and dinner are served in warm weather. Palermo is such an impossibly congested metropolis that our suggestion is to pick up a rental car as you leave the city. However, if you do drive, ask the hotel to send you directions, then mark the location on your map. Happily, once you arrive, the receptionist will have a porter take your car to their parking area. This, I assure you, is a blessing. The hotel has plans underway to add more bedrooms in the near future.

❄ ⏣ ☕ ♨ 💳 ☎ 🛗 🏋 🏇 🍸 P 🍴 🖼 ⚓ 🔔 🐾 ♿ 🍇 🍷

CENTRALE PALACE HOTEL
Manager: Pietro Cascino
Corso Vittorio Emanuele, 327
Sicily–Palermo 90134, Italy
Tel: (091) 33 66 66, Fax: (091) 33 48 81
63 rooms, Double: €216–€500
Open: all year, Credit cards: all major
On the northern coast of Sicily
Region: Sicily, Michelin Map: 432
www.karenbrown.com/italyinns/centralepalace.html

The Villa Igiea Grand Hotel is an oasis of blissful tranquillity, insulated from the frantic traffic and congestion of Palermo. With all the fabulous archaeological sites, quaint towns, and outstanding cathedrals in the area, it is wonderful to have such a splendid hotel to come home to at night. The approach to the villa is not scenic, but from the moment you enter the gates you are in another world: a world of spacious lobbies, sweeping verandas, formal dining rooms, handsome antiques, and generously sized, well-furnished bedrooms with large modern bathrooms. Many of the bedrooms have private balconies overlooking the gardens to the sea. There is a museum-like quality to the hotel, yet it has all the comforts of a deluxe hotel. It is called a villa, but has more of the ambiance of a small castle. The hotel, situated on a low bluff overlooking the sea, is surrounded by greenery. In addition to tennis courts, a lovely free-form swimming pool nestles on a ledge that overhangs the water. Next to the pool the hotel has its very own ancient Greek temple—now how many hotels can top that? The most outstanding attributes of the hotel are its gardens that envelop the building in a nest of beautiful pines and masses of gorgeous flowerbeds intertwined with twisting pathways. Altogether, a most delightful spot. *Directions:* The Villa Igiea is situated on the bay at the western edge of town, just before the mountain.

VILLA IGIEA GRAND HOTEL
Manager: Maurizio Viviani
Salita Belmonte, 43 (Acquasanta)
Sicily–Palermo 90142, Italy
Tel: (091) 63 12 11, Fax: (091) 54 76 54
115 rooms, Double: €181–€607
Open: all year, Credit cards: all major
On the northern coast of Sicily
Region: Sicily, Michelin Map: 432
www.karenbrown.com/italyinns/igiea.html

Although often missed by tourists, Syracuse has a fascinating ancient center located on the island of Ortygia, where the Greeks founded the city of Syracuse. However, you hardly realize you are on an island since it is linked to the modern town by just a short bridge. This historic old part of Syracuse is definitely where you want to be and, without a doubt, the Grand Hotel Siracusa is the place you want to stay. The hotel has a ideal setting: across the street from the dock where colorful fishing boats are pulled up and just a pleasant stroll away from the beautiful Duomo, the Piazza Archimede, and the Temple of Apollo. The Grand Hotel Siracusa, housed in a handsome yellow building with white trim, has a pleasing old-world ambiance. Inside, you are greeted by an old-fashioned elegance with marble columns, marble floors, high ceilings, potted plants, portraits on the walls, huge Venetian-glass chandeliers, and accents of antique furniture. The bedrooms are tastefully decorated with traditional-style furniture, pretty, muted wallpapers, and color-coordinating bedspreads and draperies. Ask for one of the rooms with a view to the sea—it is fun to look out your window and watch the fishing boats reflecting in the clear blue water. A glass-enclosed elevator takes you up to the attractive rooftop restaurant where you dine romantically in front of walls of windows overlooking the waterfront and the town.

GRAND HOTEL SIRACUSA
Manager: Fernando Bambara
Viale Mazzini, 12
Sicily–Syracuse 96100, Italy
Tel: (0931) 46 46 00, Fax: (0931) 46 46 11
58 rooms, Double: €217–€372
Open: all year, Credit cards: all major
On the eastern coast of Sicily
Region: Sicily, Michelin Map: 432
www.karenbrown.com/italyinns/siracusa.html

With a glorious, unobstructed view to the sea, the Hotel Belvedere can definitely lay claim to one of the prime positions in the picturesque town of Taormina. Of course this location is not just luck because, undoubtedly, the site was carefully chosen when the Belvedere (one of the first hotels in town) was constructed at the turn of the last century. The gentleman who originally built the hotel is the grandfather of the present owners—a continuity that adds greatly to the care and warmth of welcome given to the guests. From first glance, the hotel is immediately appealing—a pale ochre-colored villa laced with ivy and accented by wrought-iron balconies. Flowers abound on the walkways and a romantic garden terraces down below the hotel, providing quiet shady nooks for guests to enjoy the view. On one of the lower terraces, a large swimming pool is practically hidden by a lush blanket of shrubs, shade trees, and towering palms. This cool oasis is a favorite gathering spot for guests, and although there is no formal restaurant, light refreshments including pasta, sandwiches, and cold drinks are available by the pool. The lounges of the hotel are pleasantly decorated with contemporary furniture accented by some family antiques. The guestrooms are modern, with built-in beds. However, it is not the decor that captures the hearts of guests who return each year, but rather the friendliness of the staff and the superb setting.

HOTEL BELVEDERE
Owner: Claude Pecaut
Via Bagnoli Croci, 79
Sicily–Taormina 98039, Italy
Tel: (0942) 23 791, Fax: (0942) 62 58 30
47 rooms, Double: €157–€183
Poolside snack bar open daily
Open: mid-Mar to Nov, Credit cards: MC, VS
On the eastern coast of Sicily
Region: Sicily, Michelin Map: 432
www.karenbrown.com/italyinns/belvederesicily.html

There is no doubt that the Timeo is the new shining star of Taormina. Its location alone is worth special mention, being positioned just under the main attraction of Taormina's historical center, the Greek-Roman amphitheater, dramatically illuminated at night. Since there is no street traffic it is a particularly peaceful spot as well. The discreet entrance and reception lead to the veranda living room, with parquet floors and highlighted by selected antiques. A cozy winter-garden bar with painted trellis is found off a long hallway lined with windows leading to the restaurant. Two contrasting dining rooms, one with arches and original dark mahogany panels and the other luminous and airy with surrounding full-length windows, are where exquisite meals based on fresh seafood are served. The true center of the hotel is the expansive terrace which all the common rooms overlook, divided into outdoor dining area and sitting areas with plump wicker sofas from which to enjoy the breathtaking sea views. An elegant, neo-classical style prevails throughout the bedrooms, which are situated above and below the main building and in the adjacent peach-colored villa, most with terraces or balconies. A shuttle to a private beach is provided. Since our last visit the hotel restored an annex building now called the Villa Flora which allowed them to add 30 rooms. *Directions:* Follow signs to the Teatro Greco—the hotel is on the way.

GRAND HOTEL TIMEO & VILLA FLORA
Via Teatro Greco, 59
Sicily–Taormina 98039, Italy
Tel: (0942) 23 801, Fax: (0942) 62 85 01
87 rooms, Double: €238–€850
Open: all year, Credit cards: all major
On the eastern coast of Sicily
Region: Sicily, Michelin Map: 432
www.karenbrown.com/italyinns/timeo.html

The Villa Sant'Andrea is a four-star deluxe hotel snuggled along a tiny bay that lies below Taormina, our favorite, very old, Sicilian town, which has a breathtaking position on a cliff above the sea. A cable car (within an easy walk of the hotel) can swiftly whisk you up the hill to Taormina to see its splendid Greek theater, browse through the quaint streets, or have lunch in a trattoria. Then, when your excursion is over, you can take the cable car back to the tranquillity of the beautiful Villa Sant'Andrea, which exudes the ambiance of an English home—which is not surprising as the hotel was originally built in 1830 as a private residence for a wealthy English family. Of course, the building has been added on to over the years, but it still has an intimate appeal. Commanding a superb waterfront setting, the villa is built in levels that step down the hill, ending right on the beach where, surrounded by palm and banana trees, the hotel has its own section with lounge chairs reserved exclusively for guests. On a level just above the beach there is a charming terrace—a favorite nook for breakfast. The decor of the public rooms has a refined, homelike elegance with many lovely antiques and period paintings. Good taste also prevails in the guestrooms, some of which have a lovely view of the sea, enhanced by the dramatic rocks that jut above the clear blue waters. *Directions:* On S114, the road that runs along the sea below Taormina.

VILLA SANT'ANDREA
Manager: Ninni Occhipinti
Via Nazionale, 137
Sicily–Taormina 98030, Italy
Tel: (0942) 23 125, Fax: (0942) 24 838
80 rooms, Double: €214–€479*
*Breakfast not included: €16.50
Open: Apr 3 to Nov 8, Credit cards: all major
On the eastern coast of Sicily
Region: Sicily, Michelin Map: 432
www.karenbrown.com/italyinns/andrea.html

The Grand Hotel Continental Siena, an elegant small hotel that opened in early 2002, is one of the most exciting properties to come on the scene in Siena in many years. Although there are lovely places to stay on the periphery, there has never been an outstanding hotel in the heart of Siena, within steps of all of its fabulous sights. To say that this need for an exceptional property has now been fulfilled is an understatement: the Grand Hotel Continental Siena is an absolute dream and would be a sensation anywhere in the world. Located just off the Piazza del Campo, the building dates back to 1600 when it was designed as a magnificent palace for the noble Chigi family. After years of labor by countless artisans, the palace has been returned to its original splendor. The grandeur and opulence of the rooms are breathtaking. Fine fabrics, exquisite furnishings, and priceless antiques create a setting of unsurpassed grandeur. At the heart of the palace a central courtyard, protected by a glass roof, allows the sunlight to fill the hotel with sunshine. Off the courtyard the various parlors and ballrooms are gorgeous. A sweeping, wide staircase leads upstairs to the sumptuous bedrooms and suites, some of which feature magnificent, museum-quality, frescoed ceilings. There is a shuttle service to the "sister" property, the Park Hotel, where guests can take advantage of its various amenities, including golf, tennis, and swimming.

GRAND HOTEL CONTINENTAL SIENA
Manager: Enzo Cadirni
Banchi di Sopra, 85
Siena 53100, Italy
Tel: (0577) 56 011, Fax: (0577) 56 01 555
51 rooms, Double: €255–€1140*
*Breakfast not included: €26
Open: all year, Credit cards: all major
In heart of Siena, steps from Piazza del Campo
Region: Tuscany, Michelin Map: 430
www.karenbrown.com/italyinns/hotelcontinental.html

Siena is a fascinating walled, hilltop city filled with a wealth of fabulous museums, intriguing squares, and breathtaking churches. If you want to stay within walking distance of the all the major sights and your budget precludes a splurge at the deluxe Grand Hotel Continental, the Palazzo Ravizza pensione makes an excellent choice. The brick exterior of the hotel looks quite plain but inside, the beauty of this once-grand 17th-century palace is immediately revealed. Belonging to the same family for 200 years, the mansion exudes the warmth of a home, with an intimate parlor, card room, music lounge, cozy bar, handsome ceiling frescos, old family portraits, and fresh flowers on polished antique tables. The Palazzo Ravizza is a simple hotel and some of the fabrics show a well-worn look, but overall it is well kept and appealing and for the price, it is an excellent choice. The individually decorated bedrooms vary in size, but all are furnished with antiques. The choice rooms are those that overlook the back garden—I especially liked rooms 14 and 11 (a junior suite). The most outstanding feature of the Ravizza is its splendid large garden. This is the heart of the hotel where guests enjoy a cold drink at one of the tables on the terrace, relax on one of the benches strategically placed for capturing a sweeping view of the Tuscany hillside, or dine on the terrace in balmy weather. *Directions:* Near the Porta San Marco gate. Ask hotel for exact directions.

PALAZZO RAVIZZA   New
Owner: Francesco Grottanelli
Pian dei Mantellini, 34
Siena (SI) 53100, Italy
Tel: (0577) 28 04 62, Fax: (0577) 22 15 97
40 rooms, Double: €200–€300*
*Includes breakfast & dinner
Open: all year, Credit cards: all major
15-minute walk to Piazza del Campo
Region: Tuscany, Michelin Map: 430
www.karenbrown.com/italyinns/ravizza.html

The Park Hotel Siena, a splendidly renovated 16th-century villa, is perched on a hillside on the outskirts of Siena, close to the wonders of this fabulous city, yet with space for tennis, a swimming pool, and even a golf course. Guests can easily slip into the heart of Siena for sightseeing since a shuttle bus runs between the Park Hotel Siena and its "sister" property, the Grand Hotel Continental Siena, just steps from the Piazza del Campo. As soon as you step through the doors into the elegantly appointed reception hall decorated with fine antiques, you will be surrounded by an ambiance of quiet grandeur. Although a deluxe property, the Park Hotel Siena exudes the feeling of a private home, with intimate groupings of finely upholstered sofas and chairs, carved stone fireplaces, handsome oil paintings, and magnificent chandeliers. My favorite room is the lovely dining room, with its tall windows opening onto the terrace. Pastel-colored walls, high, vaulted ceilings, soft lighting, handsome chandeliers, beautiful tiled floors, high-backed dining chairs, and tables set with fine linens and crystals create a mood of gentle romance. As you would expect, the individually decorated, spacious guestrooms are beautifully appointed and furnished with antiques. *Directions:* From the Siena-Florence highway, take the Siena Nord exit. As you follow the road into Siena, there is a sign to the hotel on your right.

PARK HOTEL SIENA
Manager: Maurizio Romani
Via di Marciano, 18
Siena 53100, Italy
Tel: (0577) 44 803, Fax: (0577) 49 020
69 rooms, Double: €230–€672*
*Breakfast not included: €24
Closed: Nov 15 to Mar 15, Credit cards: all major
2 km NW of town center
Region: Tuscany, Michelin Map: 430
www.karenbrown.com/italyinns/parkhotelsiena.html

The Locanda dell'Amorosa, a charming small hotel with great warmth and excellent management, makes a super base for exploring Tuscany and Umbria. From the Locanda dell'Amorosa it is an easy drive to such sightseeing delights as Siena, Pienza, Orvieto, Todi, and Assisi. The Locanda dell'Amorosa is actually a tiny town located a few kilometers south of Sinalunga. You approach along a cypress-lined road that cuts through fields of grapes. Park your car and enter through the gates into the walled 14th-century medieval village where you are greeted by an enormous courtyard with its own little church—exquisite inside with its soft pastels and its lovely fresco of the Madonna. A rustic wine bar next to the church features a selection of the estate's wines and can provide guests a light meal when the restaurant is closed. On the right side of the courtyard are the stables, which have been converted to a stunning restaurant whose massive beams and natural stone-and-brick walls arc tastefully enhanced by arched windows, thick wrought-iron fixtures, and wooden tables. The guestrooms, located in a separate building, are tastefully appointed with a few antiques and matching bedspreads and draperies. The rest of this tiny village spreads out behind the main square and the buildings are used for the production of wine. *Directions:* Exit the A1 at Sinalunga. Just before town turn left toward Torrita. After 2 km, the hotel is on your right.

❄ ☕ 💳 ☎ 🏃 🍸 P 🍴 ≈ 🖼 🍷

LOCANDA DELL'AMOROSA
Managers: Carlo Citterio & Alessandra Chervatin
Sinalunga (SI) 53048, Italy
Tel: (0577) 67 72 11, Fax: (0577) 63 20 01
20 rooms, Double: €234–€660
Closed: Jan 6 to Mar 6, Credit cards: all major
80 km S of Florence, 45 km E of Siena
Region: Tuscany, Michelin Map: 430
www.karenbrown.com/italyinns/dellamorosa.html

There is no better budget-priced hotel in our guide than the Hotel Grifone, and happily it is nestled idyllically on the edge of Lake Garda in Sirmione, one of Italy's fairy-tale villages. Naturally, you cannot expect luxury in this officially-rated two-star hotel, but if you are searching for a simple, clean bedroom with a world-class location, look no further! The Hotel Grifone and Restaurant Grifone share the same quaint stone building facing the castle and the lake. Both have been run for many years by the Marcolini family. The younger generation now operates the business—charming Christina oversees the hotel while her brother, Nicola, manages the restaurant. The delightful small restaurant abounds with charm and has a stunning glass-enclosed terrace above the lake where guests love to dine when the weather is warm. The entrance to the hotel is on the street behind the restaurant. There is a simple lobby where you check in and to the left is a little sitting room, which opens onto a private patio overlooking a miniature sand beach. The guestrooms, with modern furnishings, are all upstairs. These are small but immaculately clean and tidy, and each has a private bathroom with a shower in the corner. Best of all, every room has a view. *Directions:* Turn right immediately after coming through the gates of Sirmione. After a short walk, you will see the restaurant facing the castle.

HOTEL GRIFONE
Owner: Nicola Marcolini
Via Bocchio, 4
Sirmione–Lake Garda (BS) 25019, Italy
Tel: (030) 91 60 14, Fax: (030) 91 65 48
16 rooms, Double: €55*
*Breakfast not included
Open: Easter to Oct
In historic center, 127 km E of Milan, 35 km W of Verona
Region: Lombardy, Michelin Maps: 428, 429
www.karenbrown.com/italyinns/hotelgrifone.html

There are several hotels within Sirmione's walled city, but most of the moderately priced ones lack any charm. One exception is the Hotel Sirmione, which occupies an interesting 200-year-old building in the heart of town. As you cross over the moat, you can see the hotel to your left, which doesn't look like a hotel at all from this view, but more like a series of pretty houses, each individually painted with colors that reflect into the water. You need to walk into town to access the hotel, which is comprised of two buildings which face each other as you walk to the boat dock—a marvelously strategic location. The reception part of the hotel is in the appealing yellow building accented by green shutters to your right. Inside there is a contemporary look, but everything is done with good taste. Just off the bar, there is a large dining room that is a particularly inviting, extremely cheerful room with windows on three sides. There is also a delightful outdoor dining terrace, shaded in summer with a vine-covered trellis. In the annex just across the street, there is a second hotel that has 54 completely renovated new bedrooms, a wellness area with sauna, whirlpool, thermal swimming pool, and bar overlooking the marina. As we have revisited Sirmione over the years, it has been fun to watch the Hotel Sirmione evolve from a simple hotel into one that will satisfy anyone.

HOTEL SIRMIONE
Manager: Ferme family
Piazza Castello, 19
Sirmione–Lake Garda (BS) 25019, Italy
Tel: (030) 91 63 31, Fax: (030) 91 65 58
101 rooms, Double: €130–€250
Open: Mar to Nov, Credit cards: AX, VS
In historic center, 127 km E of Milan, 35 km W of Verona
Region: Lombardy, Michelin Maps: 428, 429
www.karenbrown.com/italyinns/sirmione.html

What a sense of impending grandeur you experience as you wait for the giant iron gates of the Villa Cortine Palace to swing open. Inside, the road winds and curves impressively past fountains and statues, flower gardens and mighty trees, until it reaches the summit where the Villa Cortine Palace majestically reigns. This beautifully situated villa has been expanded so that it now boasts a new section, which appears to have more than doubled the original size. Throughout the hotel, the guestrooms are undergoing well-deserved renovation. The newly upgraded rooms have much more charm than those that still retain the rather dated rattan furniture. Some of the rooms are in the original part of the villa, which is to the left as you enter the lobby. This section displays a truly old-world grandeur with incredibly ornate furniture, soaring ceilings, and stunning paintings. What leaves absolutely nothing to be improved upon are the gardens—they are awe-inspiring. The villa is surrounded by graveled walkways that wind in and out amongst the fountains, ponds, statues, and glorious rose gardens, all overlooking the lovely Lake Garda. A path leads down to the lake where there is a private pier for swimming. The hotel also has a swimming pool and tennis court.

VILLA CORTINE PALACE HOTEL
Manager: Roberto Cappelletto
Sirmione–Lake Garda (BS) 25019, Italy
Tel: (030) 99 05 890, Fax: (030) 91 63 90
54 rooms, Double: €400–€650
Minimum nights required: 3
Open: Mar 28 to Oct 20, Credit cards: all major
On Lake Garda, 127 km E of Milan, 35 km W of Verona
Region: Lombardy, Michelin Maps: 428, 429
www.karenbrown.com/italyinns/villacortinepalace.html

The sleepy village of Solomeo, located between Perugia and Lake Trasimeno, had been almost completely abandoned until a well-known cashmere company bought and restored most of the town to its original charm, using the individual houses and apartments for offices and workshops. Pier Luigi Cavicchi, an import/export consultant, and his friendly wife Donatella (who runs the family's not-so-distant farm) inherited a turn-of-the-last-century villa, located right in the heart of town. Pier Luigi (who had spent many happy summers at the villa) and his wife thoroughly renovated the property and opened it as an inn. Their wish was to maintain the original character of the beloved residence while adding all possible amenities (including air conditioning). The result is a compact and quaint hotel that has it all. The 12 English-style country bedrooms are named after flowers and this theme is followed through in stenciled borders, bedspread fabrics, and bathrooms. Preserved stencil work on walls and ceilings in the entrance, tea room, and upstairs sitting room were done by the same artist who decorated the town's church across the street. The bright breakfast room downstairs has stone walls and beams and leads to terraces overlooking the countryside where a garden, swimming pool, exercise room with sauna and solarium, meeting room, and two garden bedrooms are situated. In the immediate area are a golf club and horseback-riding facilities.

LOCANDA SOLOMEO
Owners: Pier Luigi & Donatella Cavicchi
Piazza Carlo Alberto dalla Chiesa, 1
Solomeo (PG) 06070, Italy
Tel: (075) 52 93 119, Fax: (075) 52 94 090
12 rooms, Double: €114–€116
Open: all year, Credit cards: all major
10 km W of Perugia
Region: Umbria, Michelin Map: 430
www.karenbrown.com/italyinns/locandasolomeo.html

Located about an hour's drive south of Milan's Linate airport, the Locanda del Lupo makes a convenient stop if you plan to drive directly south toward Florence. Soragna is a sleepy little town in the countryside whose main point of interest is a walled, medieval fortress. Around the central plaza buildings of great character are interspersed with modern construction. The Locanda del Lupo, built in the 18th century by the noble Meli Lupi family, is just a block off the plaza and easy to find. The inn is best known as a gourmet restaurant: there is a series of beautiful dining rooms with gleaming copper hanging from whitewashed walls, terra-cotta floors, dark-beamed ceilings, antique clocks, and 17th-century oil paintings. To the left of the reception area is a cozy bar and, beyond, a formal living room furnished in antiques. A flight of stairs leads to the guestrooms whose old-world ambiance is enhanced by beamed ceilings, tiled floors, and thick walls. Each bedroom is individually decorated and exudes a refined, country-house atmosphere. Authentic antique furnishings (including fine wooden chests and wrought-iron bedsteads) impart a feeling of quality. *Directions:* From the Milan-Bologna A1 expressway, take the Fidenza exit and follow signs to Soragna. Go to the central square (Piazza Garibaldi) where you find Via Garibaldi running off the square.

LOCANDA DEL LUPO
Manager: Enrico Dioni
Via Garibaldi, 64
Soragna (PR) 43019, Italy
Tel: (0524) 59 71 00, Fax: (0524) 59 70 66
46 rooms, Double: €104–€165*
*Breakfast not included: €8
Open: all year, Credit cards: all major
100 km S of Milan, 118 km N of Bologna
Region: Emilia-Romagna, Michelin Map: 429
www.karenbrown.com/italyinns/locandadellupo.html

The 15th-century Villa Bogoni, a large rustic farmhouse, is located in the rich, flat plains that stretch between Verona and Mantua. Although for many years home to noble families, its greatest glory came during the 16th century when Murzio Gonzaga, son of the Duke of Mantua, restored the house and embellished it with the frescoes of Giulio Romano, famous student of Raffaello. As the centuries passed, the once-elaborate house was divided into small apartments where farmers lived with their families. Your charming, exuberant hostess, Adriana Bogoni, who was born here at the estate, discovered the frescoes when she was a child and later, when the property became hers, she was able to bring them back to life. Today Adriana, ably assisted by her daughter, Lara, and son, Simone, has renovated the house and opened it to guests. Bedrooms vary in size and decor. All are brightly painted in colors such as pink or green, but number 1 is my favorite, a larger bedroom with a handsome antique wooden bed. Throughout there is a homey, comfortable, lived-in ambiance, but what makes a stay here special is the warmth of the Bogoni family who open their hearts as well as their home to guests. Adriana is also wonderful in the kitchen, and upon prior request will prepare dinner for her guests. *Directions:* From the A22, take the Mantova Nord exit. Go east 9 km to Castel d'Ario and turn north to Sorgà. The Villa Bogoni is at the far end of town.

VILLA BOGONI
Owner: Adriana Bogoni
Via Vittorio Veneto 19/A
Sorgà (VR) 37060, Italy
Tel & fax: (045) 73 70 129
6 rooms, Double: €104–€118
Dinner by prior request
Open: all year, Credit cards: all major
18 km NE of Mantova, 25 km S of Verona
Region: Veneto, Michelin Map: 429
www.karenbrown.com/italyinns/bogoni.html

The Grand Hotel Excelsior Vittoria has a superb location high on the cliff overlooking the port and bay of Sorrento and surrounded by an orange grove and park of about 4 acres with a swimming pool. You enter the hotel, a grand old villa with a real old-world atmosphere, through a formal gate, which is just a short stroll from the center of town. The furnishings, for the most part, continue the antique mood. The Excelsior Vittoria is a good place to splurge and reserve one of the superior rooms with a view of the sea. The ceilings in some of the reception rooms and in the marvelous airy dining room have gorgeous frescoed designs. The terraces and gardens surrounding the hotel offer wonderful views, as do the bedrooms that face the bay. When we first saw the Grand Hotel Excelsior Vittoria, there was a gracious, though faded, elegance to the hotel, giving it a slightly worn look. However, this magnificent villa has since been lovingly restored under the guidance of Lidia Fiorentino, the owner's wife, carefully retaining the unique turn-of-the-last-century mood alongside modern air conditioning. Staying here will certainly delight anyone who loves the feeling of reliving the grandeur of days gone by in a villa by the sea.

GRAND HOTEL EXCELSIOR VITTORIA
Owner: Fiorentino family
Piazza Torquato Tasso, 34
Sorrento (NA) 80067, Italy
Tel: (081) 80 71 044, Fax: (081) 87 71 206
*105 rooms, Double: €268–€1366**
**Breakfast not included: €22*
Open: all year, Credit cards: all major
48 km S of Naples, 250 km S of Rome
Region: Campania, Michelin Map: 431
www.karenbrown.com/italyinns/excelsiorvittoria.html

It was love at first sight as I drove up the long graveled road through forest and vineyard and suddenly caught my first glimpse of the Borgo Pretale, a tiny cluster of weathered stone buildings nestled next to their medieval watchtower. My first impression was more than justified—this small inn is truly paradise. There are absolute serenity and beauty here with nothing to mar the perfection. Civilization seems far away as the eye stretches over a glorious vista of rolling hills forested with oaks, juniper, and laurel, interspersed with square patches of vineyards. But although this small village is seemingly remote, it is only a short drive south of Siena, thus a perfect hideaway from which to enjoy the magic of Tuscany. The rooms in the tower are showplaces of fine country antiques and splendid designer fabrics, blended together with the artful eye of a skilled decorator. Every piece is selected to create a sophisticated yet rustic elegance. The rooms in the surrounding cottages are furnished in a more "country" style, though maintaining standards of elegance and comfort. The lounge beckons guests to linger after dinner by the roaring fire. A path leads to a groomed tennis court and farther on to a swimming pool on a hillside terrace. *NOTE:* The closest town on most maps is Rosia, which is about 5 kilometers southeast of Borgo Pretale. To reach the hotel, go through Rosia and follow signs to Borgo Pretale.

BORGO PRETALE
Manager: Daniele Rizzardini
Sovicille–Pretale (SI) 53018, Italy
Tel: (0577) 34 54 01, Fax: (0577) 34 56 25
35 rooms, Double: €205–€240
Open: Apr to Nov, Credit cards: all major
18 km SW of Siena on Rte 73
Region: Tuscany, Michelin Map: 430
www.karenbrown.com/italyinns/borgopretale.html

The walled hilltown of Spoleto is a must on any trip to Umbria. What Spoleto has that is so outstanding is its Bridge of Towers (Ponte delle Torri), an absolutely awesome feat of engineering. Built in the 13th century on the foundations of an old Roman aqueduct, this bridge, spanning a vast crevasse, is supported by ten Gothic arches that soar into the sky. The Hotel Gattapone (a mustard-yellow building with dark-green shutters) is built into the hillside and provides a box-seat location to admire this architectural masterpiece. As you enter, there is a cozy reception area. To the left is a bright, sunny lounge with modern black-leather sofas, a long black-leather bar, very pretty deep-blue walls, large pots of green plants, an antique grandfather clock, and, best of all, an entire wall of glass which provides a bird's eye view of the bridge. To the right of the reception area, steps sweep down to another bar and lounge where breakfast is served. This room is even more starkly modern, with deep-red wall coverings. The newer wing of the hotel houses the superior-category bedrooms, each with a sitting area and large view windows. In the original section of the hotel the bedrooms are smaller, but also very attractive and every one has a view. Although most of the hotels in this guide have more of an antique ambiance, the Gattapone is highly recommended—a special hotel offering great warmth of welcome and superb vistas.

HOTEL GATTAPONE
Owner: Dr. Pier Hanke Giulio
Via del Ponte, 6
Spoleto (PG) 06049, Italy
Tel: (0743) 22 34 47, Fax: (0743) 22 34 48
15 rooms, Double: €140–€230
Open: all year, Credit cards: all major
130 km N of Rome, 48 km S of Assisi
Region: Umbria, Michelin Map: 430
www.karenbrown.com/italyinns/hotelgattapone.html

Le Logge di Silvignano, a stunning castle of creamy-beige stone, embraces one side of a tiny 12th-century village with a population of about 85 people tucked high in the hills north of Spoleto. It is not surprising to learn the building was originally a strategic lookout to guard against enemy attack since the setting is breathtaking, with a sweeping view of the narrow valley far below. Although termed a "castle" the structure is not in the least foreboding, but rather a splendid edifice with a handsome, open, arched gallery supported by ornately carved, octagonal pillars stretching across the front. There are six beautiful, individually decorated suites, all extremely attractive with medieval stone floors accenting handsome furniture which is either antique or handcrafted locally of wood or wrought iron. The fine bed linens and fabrics are woven locally from the Montefalco looms. A huge terrace, magically transformed into a romantic, manicured garden enhanced by fragrant, colorful roses, spreads in front of the castle to the edge of the bluff. Although Le Logge would be a winner by any standards, it is the genuine warmth and charm of your lovely hosts that make a stay here so outstanding. For dinner, guests can prepare a light meal in their own kitchenette or dine in a local restaurant. Breakfast, which features pastries cooked by a woman in the village, is included in the room rate. *Directions:* Ask for detailed driving instructions when you make reservations.

LE LOGGE DI SILVIGNANO   **New**
Owners: Diana & Alberto Araimo
Frazione Silvignano, 14
Spoleto (PG) 06049, Italy
Tel: (0743) 27 40 98, Fax: (0473) 27 05 18
6 suites, Double: €185–€210
Closed: Jan 10 to Feb 10, Credit cards: all major
130 km N of Rome, 48 km S of Assisi
Region: Umbria, Michelin Map: 430
www.karenbrown.com/italyinns/silvignano.html

Spoleto is always a favorite with tourists, not only during the music festival (end of June until mid-July), but throughout the year. Due to its popularity, there used to be a shortage of charming places to stay within the walled city but happily that problem was solved with the opening of the Hotel San Luca in 1995. The family-owned San Luca is a splendid small hotel—very polished, very sophisticated, yet exuding great personal warmth and friendliness. Built within a 19th-century tannery, the hotel (which is painted yellow and has a traditional red-tiled roof) only hints at its past. The renovation has been so extensive that much of what you see today is of new construction, but the ambiance is old-world. From the moment you enter, there is a fresh, luminous atmosphere with pastel walls reflecting light streaming in through large arched windows opening onto a central courtyard. The reception lounge is especially appealing, with comfortable chairs upholstered in cheerful peach fabric grouped around a large fireplace and a few choice antiques adding greatly to the homelike feeling. A pair of canaries in an antique birdcage repeats the color scheme. The spacious, pastel-colored, completely soundproofed guestrooms are all equally attractive and well equipped with lots of closets, excellent lighting, and large, exceptionally modern bathrooms. And the surprise is that the price for such high quality is amazingly low.

❄ �"⚏ 🍵 CREDIT ☎ 🏠 ♿ 🚶 🐴 🍸 P 🍴 🚭 👥 ♿ 🍇

HOTEL SAN LUCA
Manager: Daniela Zuccari
Via Interna delle Mura, 21
Spoleto (PG) 06049, Italy
Tel: (0743) 22 33 99, Fax: (0743) 22 38 00
35 rooms, Double: €150–€300
Open: all year, Credit cards: all major
In historic city center, 130 km N of Rome, 48 km S of Assisi
Region: Umbria, Michelin Map: 430
www.karenbrown.com/italyinns/hotelsanluca.html

Italy abounds with romantic places to stay, but none can surpass the outstanding beauty of the Villa Milani. This stunning property, on a hill overlooking Spoleto, just about has it all: enchanting architecture, breathtaking 360-degree view, splendid decor, gorgeous antiques, and owners who shower their guests with kindness. The villa was built in 1880 by one of Rome's most famous architects, Giovanni Battista Milani, the great-grandfather of your hostess Giovanna Milani Capobianchi. Milani obviously poured both his talent and heart into his countryside retreat, embellishing his home with splendid ceilings, fireplaces, columns, marble statues, romantic gardens, and ancient Roman artifacts. The result is splendid. The current owners lived for many years in Rome then changed their lifestyle completely and moved to Spoleto, where they tenderly restored the home to its original splendor, adding beautiful bathrooms to each bedroom and a fantastic pool, perched on a terrace looking out to the soft wooded hills of Umbria. Giovanna must have inherited some of her grandfather's talent, for she has decorated each room to perfection. The smallest room is also the most romantic, located in the tower with windows on four sides. *Directions:* Coming from the north on S.S.3, turn right at the second exit after the Spoleto tunnel (opposite the Monteluco road). At the first intersection turn left and go uphill following signs to the villa.

VILLA MILANI
Owners: Giovanna & Luigi Capobianchi
Localita Colle Attivoli, 4
Spoleto (PG) 06049, Italy
Tel: (0743) 22 50 56, Fax: (0743) 49 824
11 rooms, Double: €201–€663
Meals for hotel guests
Open: all year, Credit cards: all major
3 km E of Spoleto, 124 km N of Rome
Region: Umbria, Michelin Map: 430
www.karenbrown.com/italyinns/villamilani.html

As you twist up the steep, narrow road from Spoleto toward Monteluco, you will see on your left an appealing, ochre-colored villa. The setting looks so fabulous that you will hope this is your hotel. It is, and you won't be disappointed. The Eremo delle Grazie is an astounding property—truly a living museum, with history simply oozing from every nook and cranny. The property has been the home of the Lalli family for many years, but its roots hark back to the 5th century when a small grotto where religious hermits came to live occupied the site. The grotto still exists, but now serves as a wine cellar behind the bar. From its humble beginnings the importance of this grotto grew, becoming so well known that one of Italy's important cardinals, Camillo Cybo, lived here (his bedroom is now one of the guestrooms). The cardinal enjoyed his comfort so instead of residing in the small damp grotto, he slept in a lovely bedroom, which he had painted to look like a cave. One of my favorite places in Eremo delle Grazie is the tiny, incredibly beautiful, vaulted chapel with beautifully preserved 15th-century paintings of the life of Mary. Another favorite is the splendid terrace with a sweeping view of the glorious Umbrian landscape. According to Signor Lalli, Michelangelo was once a guest here. In his letter to Vasari, Michelangelo wrote that he left part of his heart at Eremo delle Grazie—as you will, too.

EREMO DELLE GRAZIE
Owner: Professor Pio Lalli
Spoleto–Monteluco (PG) 06049, Italy
Tel: (0743) 49 624, Fax: (0743) 49 650
11 rooms, Double: €207–€362
Open: all year, Credit cards: MC, VS
3.5 km E of Spoleto, 124 km N of Rome
Region: Umbria, Michelin Map: 430
www.karenbrown.com/italyinns/eremodellegrazie.html

The road to the Pensione Stefaner winds up a tiny mountain valley in the heart of the Dolomites. The road is spectacular. As we rounded the last curve before San Cipriano (St. Zyprian), the valley opened up and there spread before us was a sweeping vista of majestically soaring mountains. Across soft-green meadows painted with wildflowers and dotted with tiny farm chalets soared an incredible saw-toothed range of gigantic peaks. A tiny church with a pretty steeple added the final touch of perfection to the already idyllic scene. There are many places to stay in this region—none are glamorous resorts, but generally small, family-run pensions. One of our favorites is the Pensione Stefaner, an attractive, chalet-style hotel with flower-laden balconies—easily found as it is on the main highway through town. There is a smattering of antiques, but most of the furniture is new. The hotel is efficiently and warmly managed by the attractive Villgrattner family. Mathilde is a gracious hostess and her husband Georg creates wonderful home-cooked meals for the guests (everyone also loves their friendly German Shepherd). The simple bedrooms (very '60s in their decor) all have en-suite shower rooms, and some have balconies with mountain views. *Directions:* From the Verona-Brennero autostrada, exit at Bolzano Nord and follow signs for Tires. Go through town to San Cipriano and the Pensione Stefaner is on your left.

PENSIONE STEFANER
Owners: Mathilde & Georg Villgrattner
Tires–San Cipriano (BZ) 39050, Italy
Tel: (0471) 64 21 75, Fax: (0471) 64 23 02
15 rooms, Double: €86–€110*
*Includes breakfast & dinner, Meals for hotel guests only
Closed: mid-Nov to mid-Dec
NE Italy in Dolomites, 17 km E of Bolzano
Region: Trentino-Alto Adige, Michelin Map: 429
www.karenbrown.com/italyinns/stefaner.html

Tucked into the hills above Rome where cool breezes freshen the air, Tivoli has been a retreat for Roman nobility since the 2nd century and today tourists flock here each day by the busload to visit the gardens at Villa d'Este. Until 1995, when the Hotel Sirene opened its doors after total renovation, there was no good place to spend the night in Tivoli but that has definitely changed. Now you can stay in the Sirene, just a pleasant ten-minute walk to the Villa d'Este. The hotel's most outstanding feature is its breathtaking view of the Temple of Vesta, a tiny, romantic, Corinthian-columned temple, so perfect it looks like a stage set across the ravine. Hotel Sirene was built in 1865 as a private villa by an English lady, Isabelle (the restaurant is named in her honor). The villa was later converted into a hotel and at the time was truly up to date—it was the first hotel in Italy to have electric lights. Today, the hotel not only has electric lights but they come on magically by automatic eye as you walk down the halls. The lobby of the hotel is dramatic, with marble floors and a galleried, two-story atrium highlighted by a large crystal chandelier. The guestrooms are all pleasant with color-coordinated drapes, upholstered headboards, and matching bedspreads. The ambiance is not antique, but rather of a modern, well-run, family-owned hotel. Splurge and request a room (such as 405) with a terrace overlooking the temple.

HOTEL SIRENE
Owner: Lady Nadia Faroni
Piazza Massimo, 4
Tivoli (RM) 00019, Italy
Tel: (0774) 33 06 05, Fax: (0774) 33 06 08
40 rooms, Double: €136–€166
Open: all year, Credit cards: all major
36 km NE of Rome, facing Temple of Vesta
Region: Lazio, Michelin Map: 430
www.karenbrown.com/italyinns/hotelsirene.html

Tivoli is best known for the gardens of Villa d'Este where hundreds of fountains lure travelers from far and near. However, in our estimation, Tivoli's most astounding attraction is 6 kilometers away where Hadrian built the most awesome villa in the ancient world. Set in a garden to the right of the entrance to Hadrian's villa is the pretty sienna-colored Hotel Restaurant Adriano. The emphasis here is definitely on the restaurant, which serves some of the finest food in Italy. The kitchen serves wonderful hand-made pasta dishes, recipes that have been passed down through the family for generations. The restaurant has hosted such notables as President Kennedy and Queen Elizabeth! The Adriano is run by the young Cinelli family (Umberto, Patrizia, and Gabriella) who personally supervise both the kitchen and the hotel. Patrizia is also an artist whose watercolors decorate the walls and whose flair for design is evident in the lovely fresh flower displays and pretty decor. The Adriano is basically a restaurant, with just a few guestrooms—not a fancy hotel. However, the bedrooms, although simple, are attractively decorated and each has its private bathroom. If you are looking for deluxe accommodations, this might not suit you, but if the charm and friendliness of a wonderful "restaurant with rooms" appeals to you, this is truly a winner.

HOTEL RESTAURANT ADRIANO
Owner: Cinelli family
Adriana, 194
Tivoli–Villa Adriana (RM) 00010, Italy
Tel: (0774) 38 22 35, Fax: (0774) 53 51 22
10 rooms, Double: €115–€160
Open: all year, Credit cards: all major
6 km S of Tivoli, 30 km NE of Rome
Region: Lazio, Michelin Map: 430
www.karenbrown.com/italyinns/adriano.html

Crowning the top of a small hill near the enchanting walled village of Todi (which you can see in the distance), the Relais Todini has a breathtaking, 360-degree view of wooded hills, soft valleys, manicured fields, vineyards, and tiny villages. You will be captivated at first sight of this charming, 14th-century stone hotel with architectural roots going back to the Etruscan-Roman period. Although built of rustic, tan-colored stone, there is nothing rustic about this hotel. From the moment you walk through the manicured gardens and into the beautiful frescoed lobby, you are surrounded by elegance and luxury. You register at an intimate table rather than a hotel-like counter before being shown to your room. All the guestrooms are beautifully decorated and the suites are especially opulent, with fine antique furniture and lush fabrics. The public rooms are also handsomely furnished, particularly the dining room with its tall-back chairs upholstered in tapestry and charming chandeliers embellished with clusters of grapes. One wall has windows of glass that open out to a terrace and beyond to a large swimming pool. On the estate tennis, biking, horseback riding, walking, and swimming are just a few of the options available to guests. *Directions:* From Rome, take the A1 north, exiting at Orte. Follow E45 toward Perugia. Exit at Casigliano-Collevalenza and follow signs toward Todi. Turn left at the junction Rosceto Scalo to the hotel.

RELAIS TODINI
Manager: Clementi Paolo
Todi–Collevalenza (PG) 06050, Italy
Tel: (075) 88 75 21, Fax: (075) 88 71 82
12 rooms, Double: €175–€268
Meals for hotel guests only (closed Mon-Wed)
Open: all year, Credit cards: all major
12 km SE of Todi, 9 km S of Perugia
Region: Umbria, Michelin Map: 430
www.karenbrown.com/italyinns/todini.html

The elegant Le Tre Vaselle is located in Torgiano, a small wine village not far from Assisi. The interior reflects the ambiance of a graceful country manor with sophisticated furnishings and exquisite taste displayed in every detail. The hotel belongs to the Lungarotti family who are famous for their production of superb wines and who own all of the vineyards surrounding Torgiano for as far as the eye can see. Excellent meals, accompanied by fine Lungarotti wines, are served in the beautiful dining room. The guestrooms are attractively decorated and offer every amenity of a deluxe hotel. Le Tre Vaselle also has outstanding conference rooms furnished in antiques with adjacent dining rooms. The Lungarotti family has thought of everything—to keep the wives happy while their husbands are in meetings, cooking classes are sometimes offered. Other diversions include an outdoor swimming pool, an indoor pool with whirlpool and jet-tech swimming, a sauna, a gym, and even a small outdoor amphitheater. The Lungarottis also have a private wine museum that would be a masterpiece anywhere in the world. Not only do they have an incredible and comprehensive collection of anything pertaining to wine throughout the ages, but the display is a work of art. If you are interested in the production of wine, the museum alone would be worth a detour to Le Tre Vaselle. *Directions:* The hotel is well marked in the center of town.

❄ ☕ ♨ 💳 ☎ 🛗 🧍 🍴 🐴 ♈ P 🍴 ≈ 🖼 🔔 🍇

LE TRE VASELLE
Owner: Lungarotti family
Via Garibaldi, 48
Torgiano (PG) 06089, Italy
Tel: (075) 98 80 447, Fax: (075) 98 80 214
61 rooms, Double: €185–€240
Open: all year, Credit cards: all major
17 km SW of Assisi, 158 km N of Rome
Region: Umbria, Michelin Map: 430
www.karenbrown.com/italyinns/letrevaselle.html

The Hotel Gardesana, housed within a grand 15th-century building, is a treasure: an intimate, family-managed, lakeside hotel, romantically snuggled above the colorful inner harbor of Torri del Benaco, a delightful fishing village which is so incredibly picturesque that it looks like a stage set. The four-story, rich-salmon-colored building has an arched portico stretching across the front and a rustic terra-cotta roof. You step inside into a pleasingly decorated lounge and reception accented by antiques and bouquets of fresh flowers. One floor up is the dining room with doors opening onto a wisteria-clad terrace, which looks across the tiny harbor with its colorful bobbing boats reflecting in the water to the impressive turreted walls of the medieval castle. The scene oozes romance but, best of all, the food is superb (the restaurant has earned many honors). The comfortable guestrooms are decorated in a traditional style and, like the rest of the hotel, reflect the refined good taste of the owners. All of the bedrooms are nice, but request one with a view of either the harbor or the lake and, if you want to really splurge, see if one of the rooms with a balcony is available. The Hotel Gardesana is not an opulent, super-deluxe hotel, but is instead a wonderful, friendly place to stay in one of Italy's quaintest towns. *Directions:* In the center of Torri del Benaco on the west side of Lake Garda.

HOTEL GARDESANA   **New**
Owners: Annalisa & Giuseppe Lorenzini
Piazza Calderini, 20
Torri del Benaco–Lake Garda (VR) 37010, Italy
Tel: (045) 72 25 411, Fax: (045) 72 25 771
34 rooms, Double: €104–€138
Minimum nights required: 3
Closed: Nov, Credit cards: all major
150 km W of Venice, 73 km S of Trento
Region: Veneto, Michelin Map: 429
www.karenbrown.com/italyinns/gardesana.html

When the Porto Pirgos first opened its doors to guests in 1999, it redefined the meaning of luxury. A refined, intimate elegance reigns supreme, with cozy nooks, comfortable chairs, soft lighting, awesome antiques, bouquets of fresh flowers, wrought-iron fixtures, beamed ceilings, thick walls, oil paintings, gorgeous antiques, and richly hued Oriental carpets accenting antique terra-cotta floors. Adding to the romance are the sea views framed by every window. You cannot help falling in love with this superb small hotel built on a slope of a hill that stretches down to a pristine white-sand beach gently lapped by the crystal sea. Built upon the foundations of a private villa, the hotel today continues to exude the ambiance of an exquisite, fine home. The guestrooms are also furnished with antiques and, like the rest of the hotel, everything is of the highest quality and good taste. A large swimming pool is set in the garden by the hotel and a second pool nestles under towering pine trees next to the beach. Breakfast and dinner are included in the price of the room and not only is the food exceptionally delicious, but the setting is outstanding. The main dining room has a stunning mosaic floor that looks as if it came right out of an old Roman villa. When the weather is balmy, guests eat out on the terrace where, as the sun sets and the stars begin to appear, you can see the volcano of Stromboli on the horizon.

PORTO PIRGOS
Owner: Adolfo Salabe
Manager: Caterina Messina
Localita: Marina di Bordila, S.S. 522
Tropea–Parghelia (CZ) 89861, Italy
Tel: (0963) 60 03 51, Fax: (0963) 60 06 90
18 rooms, Double: €500, Includes breakfast & dinner
Open: mid-May to Oct, Credit cards: all major
5 km E of Tropea, Southern Italy–near tip of toe
Region: Calabria, Michelin Map: 431
www.karenbrown.com/italyinns/portopirgos.html

The moderately priced Stella d'Italia is located in San Mamete, a tiny, picturesque village nestled along the northern shore of Lake Lugano, just a few minutes' drive from the Swiss border. Mario and Dolores Ortelli are the most cordial of hosts and son Franco, the fourth generation of the family to run the Stella d'Italia, works in the restaurant. The heart of the hotel is a 17th-century villa with thick-walled rooms, painted ceilings, and large French windows opening to views of the lake. The same panoramic lake view is enjoyed by all the guestrooms. Equally spacious rooms are found in the wing renovated in 1999—these have not only space and views but also terraces and top-of-the-line bathrooms. Quite the nicest feature of the hotel is the superb little lakefront garden—a green lawn, fragrant flowers, lacy trees, and a romantic vine-covered trellised dining area make this an ideal spot for wiling away the hours. Steps lead down to a small pier from which guests can swim. Another interesting feature for golf enthusiasts is that there are several golf courses within an easy drive of the hotel—one of these (near the town of Grandola) is among the oldest in Italy. The ferry dock for picking up and dropping off passengers is adjacent to the hotel. *Directions:* From Lugano (Switzerland) head east towards St. Moritz. Cross the border in Valsolda and San Mamete is the next village. Park beside the hotel.

STELLA D'ITALIA
Owner: Ortelli family
San Mamete
Valsolda–Lake Lugano (CO) 22010, Italy
Tel: (0344) 68 139, Fax: (0344) 68 729
35 rooms, Double: €111–€142
Open: Apr to Oct, Credit cards: all major
8 km E of Lugano, 100 km N of Milan
Region: Lombardy, Michelin Map: 428
www.karenbrown.com/italyinns/stelladitalia.html

If you are searching for a tiny yet super-luxurious hotel in the heart of Venice, an excellent choice is the Hotel Al Ponte dei Sospiri, which exudes an ambiance of opulence yet has just eight rooms—all junior suites. Because there are so few rooms, the friendly, professional staff is able to give personal attention to each guest, caring for them as if in a private home. Once a palace, it was lovingly brought back to its former glory and emerged in 2000 as a tiny hotel hugging the edge of a small canal, only steps from Piazza San Marco. There is a pretty awning-accented entrance on the street, but by far the most theatrical way to arrive is by boat, docking at the private pier marked by cute red-and-white-striped "barber" poles. All of the guestrooms are decorated opulently, with walls richly covered with fine fabrics, tall windows accented by swagged draperies, and accents of antique furniture, a style that reflects the splendor found in palaces in the 17th century. However, amenities such as satellite TV, mini bars, topnotch bathrooms, and Internet connections in each room add all the modern touches. Breakfast is normally served in the guestroom although if guests prefer, they can have it at one of the small tables in the bar. Although this is officially rated a four-star hotel, its amenities rival those found in many five-star properties. Room rates drop considerably in July and August, making this a great value.

HOTEL AL PONTE DEI SOSPIRI
Manager: Laura Demarco
Calle Larga San Marco, 381
Venice 30124, Italy
Tel: (041) 24 11 160, Fax: (041) 24 10 268
8 rooms, Double: €180–€619
Open: all year, Credit cards: all major
Vaporetto stop: San Zaccaria, also private dock
Region: Veneto, Michelin Map: 429
www.karenbrown.com/italyinns/sospiri.html

In 2001 we just happened upon this delightful hotel, which had been open for only five days. The gracious owner, Mariella Bozzetto, showed us over this exceptionally beautiful palazzo, home in the 12th century to one of the most powerful men in Venice, the Doge Marino Falier. Mariella, a talented architect, designed the hotel conversion with a passion that every detail be perfect—and it is. The result is stunning. You enter into a charming entry hall with pastel-peach- and cream-colored walls softly illuminated by Murano glass wall sconces, an inlaid marble floor, and large oil paintings of old Venice. Upstairs you find a pretty room set with small tables where a rich buffet breakfast is served each morning with fine linens, fresh flowers, and lovely silverware. The guestrooms, splendid with lush draperies, color-coordinating fabric walls, and beautiful bedspreads, have all the latest modern enhancements, including TVs, air conditioning, hairdryers, and even Internet connection outlets. Each room is individual in décor, yet has the same opulent elegance. If possible, splurge on the suite—it is more expensive, but one of the best values in Venice. It is splendidly decorated with rich fabrics, antique chandelier, romantic canopy bed, antique mirror, Oriental carpet on gleaming hardwood floor, bathroom with Jacuzzi tub, and a little balcony overlooking the canal. This hotel is a fantastic bargain for the quality received.

HOTEL ANTICO DOGE
Owner: Mariella Bozzetto
Cannaregio, 5643
Venice 30131, Italy
Tel: (041) 24 11 570, Fax: (041) 24 43 660
11 rooms, Double: €170–€330
Open: all year, Credit cards: all major
Vaporetto stop: Ca d'Oro
Region: Veneto, Michelin Map: 429
www.karenbrown.com/italyinns/anticodoge.html

After three years of intense renovation, the Hotel Colombina reopened in 1999 as one of Venice's jewels. This perfectly delightful small hotel exudes the charm and elegance of the 15th century when it was built as the private mansion of a wealthy Venetian. The location is superb—in the historical heart of Venice, only 100 meters from Saint Mark's Square, yet on a quiet canal where the gentle singing of gondoliers will lull you to sleep at night. When redoing the hotel, the owner, Odino Polo, spared no expense to ensure that every detail is of the highest quality and that the furnishings reflect the grandeur of Venice. Manager Andrea Doria not only takes an intense personal interest in the hotel's perfection but also welcomes guests as friends. All of the bedrooms are decorated in the elegant Venetian style, with similar decor in each: beautiful fabric walls, lush draperies, fine fabrics, antique-style furnishings, and, in the rooms with high ceilings, massive Venetian glass chandeliers. Just the colors of the fabric-covered walls vary from one delightful room to the next. Much smaller than the others, but especially romantic is a room tucked under the rafters with its own little rooftop terrace. There is a cheerful breakfast room with scenes of Venice. For other meals, a limitless number of quaint places to eat are just steps away.

HOTEL COLOMBINA
Owner: Odino Polo
Manager: Andrea Doria
Calle del Remedio-Castello, 4416
Venice 30122, Italy
Tel: (041) 27 70 525, Fax: (041) 27 76 044
33 rooms, Double: €180–€390
Open: all year, Credit cards: all major
Vaporetto stop: San Zaccaria, also private dock
Region: Veneto, Michelin Map: 429
www.karenbrown.com/italyinns/colombina.html

The Hotel Flora is reached down a tiny lane, just off one of the main walkways to St. Mark's Square: a secluded hideaway, protected from the bustle of the city yet conveniently close to all the action. At the end of the tiny alley the doors open into a small lobby, beyond which is an enchanting small garden, an oasis of serenity with white wrought-iron tables and chairs surrounding a gently tinkling fountain. Potted plants, small trees, and lacy vines complete the idyllic scene. The hotel encloses the garden on three sides: doors open to the right to a dear little bar and the breakfast room. The lounges are Victorian in mood with dark furniture. The bedrooms vary greatly in their size and decor, but all have antique furnishings and Victorian-style wallpaper covers many of the walls. There is definitely an old-world atmosphere. There is no restaurant at the hotel, which is absolutely no problem since Venice abounds with wonderful places to dine. Breakfast, of course, is served to guests. Signor Romanelli, who owns this small hotel, personally sees that his guests are well taken care of. The Hotel Flora is a favorite of many travelers to Venice. Although it is a relatively simple hotel and would not appeal to those looking for deluxe accommodations, the Hotel Flora is a rare find for those who want a relatively inexpensive place to stay in the heart of Venice that combines a superb location, warmth of welcome, and charm.

HOTEL FLORA
Owner: Ruggero Romanelli
Calle Larga 22 Marzo, 2283/a
Venice 30124, Italy
Tel: (041) 52 05 844, Fax: (041) 52 28 217
44 rooms, Double: €180–€240
Open: all year, Credit cards: all major
Vaporetto stop: Vallaresso
Region: Veneto, Michelin Map: 429
www.karenbrown.com/italyinns/hotelflora.html

If you love opulent elegance, and if cost is of no consequence to you, the Gritti Palace is an excellent choice for your hotel in Venice. The location is marvelous—just a short walk from St. Mark's Square yet far enough removed to miss the city's noise and summer mob of tourists. With careful planning, you can be entirely insulated in a private and very special world from the moment you arrive until you reluctantly depart. If you take a private motor launch from the airport or the Piazza Roma, you can descend stylishly at the deluxe little private pier in front of the hotel where porters will be waiting to whisk you to your room to be pampered and spoiled. All at a price, of course. The Gritti Palace is expensive—but then what would you expect when staying in the 15th-century palace of the immensely wealthy Venetian Doge, Andrea Gritti? The Gritti Palace has a charming terrace on the bank of the Grand Canal where you dine in splendor and watch the constant stream of boat traffic. The lobby and lounge areas open off the terrace and are grandly decorated with antiques. The bedrooms are large and very fancy in decor, and those that face the canal are presented with a 24-hour show. *NOTE:* The Gritti Palace offers cooking courses, each lasting from Monday through Friday and specializing in a particular aspect of the preparation fine food. If you are interested, contact the hotel for details.

HOTEL GRITTI PALACE
Manager: Massimo Feriani
Campo Santa Maria del Giglio, 2467
Venice 30124, Italy
Tel: (041) 79 46 11, Fax: (041) 52 00 942
91 rooms, Double: €589–€3692*
*Breakfast not included: €50
Open: all year, Credit cards: all major
Vaporetto stop: Santa Maria del Giglio, also private dock
Region: Veneto, Michelin Map: 429
www.karenbrown.com/italyinns/gritti.html

The Hotel Lisbona, a small, rose-colored villa with brown shutters, is tucked down an arcaded walkway, yet only a hundred meters from Saint Mark's Square. The location is excellent and we had stopped by many times, but thought the decor too simple. However, in 1998 we had a pleasant surprise: the Lisbona had just completed a total renovation, with all new carpets, wall coverings, and draperies. The intimate reception area, which also serves as the lounge, has an old-fashioned look with a terrazzo floor accented by an Oriental carpet, chairs covered in turquoise velvet, brocade walls, and a Venetian glass chandelier. The bedrooms too had a total face-lift. Each is similarly decorated, with either a pastel-pink or light-blue damask material covering the walls, matching draperies, and color-coordinating bedspreads. Each room has air conditioning, a mini bar, satellite TV, direct-dial phone, and even a safe deposit box. The side of the hotel faces onto the San Moisé Canal, and from most of the bedrooms you can watch the action of gondolas and small boats as they ply the waterway (which can be a bit noisy). Like many of the smaller hotels in Venice, the Lisbona is managed by the owner, the gracious Cristiano Fogliata, who is usually at the front desk to personally greet his guests. The Hotel Lisbona is not a deluxe hotel, but a good-value, moderately priced place to stay in the heart of expensive Venice.

HOTEL LISBONA
Owner: Cristiano Fogliata
San Marco, 2153
Venice 30124, Italy
Tel: (041) 52 86 774, Fax: (041) 52 07 061
15 rooms, Double: €285
Open: all year, Credit cards: all major
Vaporetto stop: San Marco
Region: Veneto, Michelin Map: 429
www.karenbrown.com/italyinns/lisbona.html

Named after the famous musician, Antonio Vivaldi, the Locanda Vivaldi, a charming hotel that reflects its rich heritage as a 16th-century palace, first opened for guests in 1999. A mood of refined elegance is set from the moment you enter. There is no formal counter bustling with people waiting to check in. Instead, guests sit in quiet comfort in front of an antique table to register. The reception area extends to a most appealing small lounge that looks like a lovely room in a private home: prettily slipcovered sofas, a gorgeous antique desk, a handsome mirror, and bouquets of fresh flowers create a refined, understated elegance. One side of the lounge opens to a romantic garden, and at the other end of the room is an intimate bar. The guestrooms are all very similar in decor. Fabric-covered walls, handsome headboards with ornate gilt trim, and lovely bedspreads and draperies create sumptuous, old-world elegance. Some of the rooms even have shower saunas. The more expensive rooms face the lagoon and, if you want to splurge, the finest room also has a small balcony. Another real bonus of the Locanda Vivaldi is that on the third floor you find a terrace that captures a stunning view of Venice. If you arrive by boat, you enter the hotel through a beautiful, perfectly manicured garden. The hotel owns the building that encloses one side of the garden and plans are underway to add a few more guestrooms there.

LOCANDA VIVALDI
Manager: Claudio Vecchiato
Riva degli Schiavoni, 4150/52
Venice 30122, Italy
Tel: (041) 27 70 477, Fax: (041) 27 70 489
22 rooms, Double: €240–€620
Open: all year, Credit cards: all major
Vaporetto stop: San Zaccaria, also private dock
Region: Veneto, Michelin Map: 429
www.karenbrown.com/italyinns/locandavivaldi.html

Readers frequently share a discovery in some remote hideaway, but we rarely receive recommendations for well-known hotels in popular tourist spots. However, we heard from many readers who urged us to include the Londra Palace in our guide, and they were right—the Londra Palace is indeed very special. It enjoys a choice location, just a few minutes' walk from Saint Mark's Square, right on the waterfront, and boasts of 100 windows facing the lagoon. In addition, there is a snug rooftop terrace, which captures an incredible panorama of magical Venice. The guestrooms are splendidly decorated, each with at least one authentic, 19th-century piece of Biedermeier furniture. In addition to antiques, each room has fine original paintings and sumptuous fabrics, creating an ambiance of refinement and elegance. The bathrooms too are special—all are tiled with pink Carrara marble. Since 1992 the hotel has undergone a total renovation and the final phase of this eight-million-dollar renovation was completed in March 1999. During this final phase, the hotel's lobby, restaurant, bar, public areas, and façade have been brilliantly transformed. The hotel is gorgeous. The extra seating in the restaurant will be a bonus for chilly days, but when the weather is balmy, there is no more romantic spot to dine than the excellent Do Leoni, a terrace restaurant in front of the hotel, facing the lagoon.

LONDRA PALACE
Manager: Mauro Zanotti
Riva degli Schiavoni, 4171
Venice 30122, Italy
Tel: (041) 52 00 533, Fax: (041) 52 25 032
53 rooms, Double: €270–€790
Open: all year, Credit cards: all major
Vaporetto stop: San Zaccaria
Region: Veneto, Michelin Map: 429
www.karenbrown.com/italyinns/londrapalace.html

The Luna Hotel Baglioni not only holds the honor of being Venice's oldest hotel, but also holds one of the finest locations in town, in the heart of Venice overlooking the San Marco lagoon and the island of San Giorgio. This aristocratic hotel has a rich history, beginning in 1108 when the Knights Templar stayed in a building on this site. By the 16th century, the hotel was well established then was further enhanced in the 18th century when the sumptuous Marco Polo Room was embellished with stunning frescoes. From the moment you enter into the spacious reception hall, you cannot help being awed by the magnificence of the soaring ceilings, huge chandeliers, antique furniture, fresh flowers, and fine oil paintings. Everything is on a grand scale. Each public room is outstanding, from the ornately imposing lounge with its splendid Oriental carpet to the serenely attractive Canova restaurant, renowned for its fine cuisine. However, nothing can surpass the elegance of the Marco Polo Room with its enormous paintings, beautiful mirrors, soft lighting, and massive Murano glass chandelier hanging from the sensational frescoed ceiling. A beautiful buffet breakfast is served here each morning and this has to be the most magnificent place in Venice to have breakfast. As would be expected, the guestrooms are all splendidly decorated with period-style furnishings and many also have balconies overlooking the Grand Canal.

LUNA HOTEL BAGLIONI
Manager: Stefano Bàccara
San Marco, 1243
Venice 30124, Italy
Tel: (041) 52 89 840, Fax: (041) 52 87 160
115 rooms, Double: €192–€678
Open: all year, Credit cards: all major
Vaporetto stop: San Marco, also private dock
Region: Veneto, Michelin Map: 429
www.karenbrown.com/italyinns/baglioni.html

For all of you who have been to Venice and fallen in love with both the Hotel Flora and its incredibly kind owners, the Romanelli family, we are delighted to let you know that they purchased a second building just a few minutes' walk from the Flora and have renovated it into another small hotel, called Novecento. The hotel occupies two very old residences—one side of the building is rosy peach, the other soft ochre. Green shutters enhancing stone windows and a wrought-iron fixture overhanging the street add to the appeal of the building. The interior differs from the Flora in that it incorporates the once-popular decorating style of Fortuny, who incorporated motifs from exotic places such as Africa, Egypt, and Morocco into his designs. Although it doesn't have a central courtyard like the Flora, the Novecento has a pretty garden in the back where guests can relax. The same Romanelli father-son team who so expertly and with such heart manage the Hotel Flora also personally oversee their second hotel. The Hotel Flora has been in our guide since its first edition many years ago and remains one of our very favorites. It is also the favorite of many other travelers, so space is always at a premium but, happily, there will now be a second choice to experience the gracious hospitality of the Romanelli family.

NOVECENTO
Owner: Romanelli family
Calle del Dose 2683/84
Venice 30124, Italy
Tel: (041) 24 13 765, Fax: (041) 52 12 145
9 rooms, Double: €160–€240
Open: all year, Credit cards: all major
Vaporetto stop: Santa Maria del Giglio
Region: Veneto, Michelin Map: 429
www.karenbrown.com/italyinns/novecento.html

The Pensione Accademia is enchanting—a romantic Venetian villa with charming gardens and an idyllic setting on a small piece of land that is nestled between two canals. You enter into a sweet "secret garden" enclosed by walls that are heavily draped with ivy. If you look closely, you will discover black iron gates that open to steps leading down to the villa's private dock. As you leave the garden and enter the wisteria-covered palazzo, you come into a spacious lobby, which opens at the other end onto another garden. A staircase leads to some of the guestrooms that are located in the original villa. Other bedrooms are connected by a hallway to a portion of the hotel borrowed from an adjacent building. In 1998 all of the rooms throughout the villa were renovated. Some of the bedrooms have canal views, but from these you can hear some of the noise of passing motor boats. If you want a quiet room, ask for one overlooking the rear garden. The only hitch to this picture of perfection is that your chances are slim of snaring a room in this romantic hideaway—the hotel is so special that loyal guests reserve their own favorite room for the following year as they leave. Spring and fall are most heavily booked—your chances are better in July and August when the prices are even a little lower.

PENSIONE ACCADEMIA
Owner: Giovanna Salmaso
Dorsoduro, 1058
Venice 30123, Italy
Tel: (041) 52 10 188, Fax: (041) 52 39 152
26 rooms, Double: €128–€270
Open: all year, Credit cards: all major
Vaporetto stop: Accademia, also private dock
Region: Veneto, Michelin Map: 429
www.karenbrown.com/italyinns/accademia.html

The owner of one of the finest small hotels in France—whose opinion I value highly—recommended the Hotel Metropole as his favorite place to stay in Venice. Now, after being a guest, I can understand his choice—the Romantik Hotel Metropole has great heart. On entering, I was immediately aware of an aura of hospitality that is usually encountered only in intimate, very small hotels—everyone seems to take personal responsibility that your stay will be a happy one. It appears that the owners, the Beggiato family, who personally manage the hotel, have imbued the staff with their own warmth of welcome. Many employees have been with them since the hotel first opened in 1971 and seem to care about the hotel as if it were their own. The Beggiatos are passionate about antiques and have over 2,000 pieces displayed in the hotel, including a fascinating collection of very old corkscrews, small mother-of-pearl boxes, cradles, silver teapots, crucifixes, and intricate wrought-iron locks. All of the spacious bedrooms are individually decorated as in a private home and have fine antique furniture. In 2001 the hotel finished a total renovation and exudes an ambiance of refined elegance throughout. Another great bonus is the romantic garden, a favorite place for lunch or dinner. Some of the bedrooms overlook this pretty garden while others have a beautiful view of the lagoon, as the Hotel Metropole has a marvelous waterfront setting.

ROMANTIK HOTEL METROPOLE
Owner: Beggiato family
Riva degli Schiavoni, 4149
Venice 30122, Italy
Tel: (041) 52 05 044, Fax: (041) 52 23 679
70 rooms, Double: €350–€750
Open: all year, Credit cards: all major
Vaporetto stop: San Zaccaria, also private dock
Region: Veneto, Michelin Map: 429
www.karenbrown.com/italyinns/hotelmetropole.html

The Hotel Violino d'Oro faces a small canal on one side and the Piazza San Moisé on the other. This hotel opened in 2000 and offers an excellent choice of accommodations for those looking for a small-hotel atmosphere with friendly service in a great location near San Marco. Two sisters, Federica and Cristina, bought a mansion that had most recently been used as an office building, totally renovated it, decorated the rooms in the style of the 18th century, and opened it as a hotel. Each bedroom is very similar, with fabric on the wall behind the bed and color-coordinated draperies and bedspreads. Murano glass chandeliers continue the mood of Venice's romantic heritage. There is a typical hotel setup in each room with desk and chair, luggage stand, satellite TV, mini bar, and direct-dial phone. The marble bathrooms mostly have showers, although some bathtubs are available. All of the bedrooms are attractive. My personal favorite is 203, a bright and sunny corner room that overlooks the canal and San Moisé. The breakfast room is very appealing, with sunny walls painted yellow, soft lighting, and a painted ceiling. Another real plus for the hotel is a rooftop terrace where guests may relax and enjoy the scene of Venice below. The hotel is totally non-smoking—a feature that will certainly appeal to those who remember entering guestrooms where the smell of smoke still lingers.

HOTEL VIOLINO D'ORO
Manager: Cristina Boscolo Chio
Venice 30124, Italy
Tel: (041) 27 70 841, Fax: (041) 27 71 001
26 rooms, Double: €100–€350
Open: all year, Credit cards: all major
Vaporetto stop: Vallaresso, also private dock
Region: Veneto, Michelin Map: 429
www.karenbrown.com/italyinns/violino.html

The Hotel Cipriani was founded by the late Giuseppe Cipriani, who during his lifetime became almost a legend in Venice. This beloved man, who founded the internationally famous Harry's Bar in Venice, had a dream of building a fabulous hotel within easy reach of St. Mark's Square and yet far enough away to guarantee seclusion and peace. He bought 3 acres on the island of Giudecca and with the financial assistance of some of his prestigious friends, such as Princess Briget of Prussia and the Earl of Iveagh (head of the Guinness brewing company in Dublin), he accomplished his dream—an elegant Venetian palace-style hotel. The Cipriani is the perfect hotel for those of you who must have a pool, for it is the only hotel with a pool in Venice. And what a pool it is: Olympic-size and surrounded by beautiful gardens. The splendor continues inside where the lounges are tastefully decorated in whites and beiges and the bedrooms are large and elegant. In addition to the hotel rooms and suites, there are seven super-deluxe apartments (some overlooking St. Mark's Square), which are located next to the hotel in the renovated Palazzo Vendramin. You truly have the best of all worlds at the exquisite Cipriani—you are at a deluxe resort yet only minutes from the heart of Venice in the private launch that waits to whisk you, any time of the day or night, to St. Mark's Square.

HOTEL CIPRIANI
Manager: Dr. Natale Rusconi
Isola della Giudecca, 10
Venice–Isola della Giudecca 30133, Italy
Tel: (041) 52 07 744, Fax: (041) 52 03 930
103 rooms, Double: €813–€6000
Open: all year, Credit cards: all major
Vaporetto stop: Zitelle, also private dock
Region: Veneto, Michelin Map: 429
www.karenbrown.com/italyinns/hotelcipriani.html

Torcello is a tiny, sleepy island about 50 minutes from Venice by boat. For those who want to be close to Venice yet feel worlds away, the Locanda Cipriani Torcello is a superb, romantic hideaway owned by the Cipriani family. Your charming host, Bonifacio Brass, still remembers his famous grandfather who founded one of the world's most renowned pubs, Harry's Bar in Venice. The magical Locanda Cipriani Torcello is popular with knowledgeable gourmets as a fantastic restaurant. Many arrive every day from Venice just to dine, and then depart, never knowing that this restaurant also has exceptionally charming guestrooms upstairs. The inn looks like a simple farmhouse, but has been renovated with great charm and exudes a gentle, understated elegance with an abundance of beautiful country antiques enhanced by lavish displays of fresh flowers. You enter into a rustic, cozy dining room, but when the weather is warm, almost all of the guests prefer to dine outside on the beautiful terrace overlooking the splendid, beautifully manicured gardens that in summer offer a fantasy of color. There are only five bedrooms—all are delightful and decorated in a simple, charming decor. Many famous guests have already discovered this oasis, including Ernest Hemingway, a close friend of Cipriani's, who came here to write. I think you will share his belief that the Locanda Cipriani Torcello is a very special place.

❄ ⊥ 🖴 🖳CREDIT 📠 ☎ 🍴 🍸 🍴 ⚓ ✒

LOCANDA CIPRIANI TORCELLO
Owner: Carla Cipriani
Manager: Bonifacio Brass
Venice–Isola Torcello 30012, Italy
Tel: (041) 73 01 50, Fax: (041) 73 54 33
5 rooms, Double: €230–€330
Closed: Jan 5 to Feb 10, Credit cards: all major
Island location, Vaporetto stop: Torcello
Region: Veneto, Michelin Map: 429
www.karenbrown.com/italyinns/locandacipriani.html

If the idea of being close to Venice and yet near a beach and casino appeals to you, then perhaps you should consider a hotel located on the Lido, a small island opposite St. Mark's Square. A 15-minute boat ride and a short taxi trip bring you to the Albergo Quattro Fontane, a charming inn that reminds me more of a French country home than an Italian villa. It has a white-stucco exterior with gabled roof, green shutters, and vines creeping both over the door and around some of the small balconies. To the left of the main building is a lovely courtyard whose privacy is established by another wing of the hotel, giving the garden a cozy, walled-in effect. Inside the hotel there is an ambiance of a country home with antiques cleverly used throughout the lounges. The beach is only a short distance away and the Albergo Quattro Fontane can make arrangements for you to reserve a private beach cabana when you arrive at the inn. The cost per day will vary, depending both upon the location and the comparative luxury of the cabana you choose. The beach is wide and the water inviting and clear, although the sand is not as fine and white as we have seen on some of the beaches in southern Italy. It is quite an experience to sample the interesting hierarchy of the Italian beach system.

ALBERGO QUATTRO FONTANE
Manager: Bente Bevilacqua
Via 4 Fontane
Venice–Lido 30126, Italy
Tel: (041) 52 60 22 7, Fax: (041) 52 60 72 6
68 rooms, Double: €230–€340
Open: Apr to mid-Nov, Credit cards: all major
Vaporetto stop: Lido
Region: Veneto, Michelin Map: 429
www.karenbrown.com/italyinns/quattrofontane.html

The Hotel Gabbia d'Oro, ideally located in the heart of Verona, is truly a gem that captures the romance of this fascinating city. From the moment you step inside you are surrounded by a relaxed, understated elegance. Although this is a deluxe hotel, there is no hint of stiff formality—the welcome is genuinely warm and friendly in this superbly managed small hotel. Just off the spacious reception area is a cozy lounge with massive beamed ceilings, ancient stone walls, fine antiques, and handsome old prints in gold frames. Beyond the lobby is an intimate bar where wood paneling—richly mellowed with the patina of age—sets off to perfection chairs upholstered in cherry-red fabric. There is also a charming, sun-filled inner courtyard, called L'Orangerie, where you can savor a cup of tea or sip a glass of champagne while relaxing after a day of sightseeing or while enjoying a well-chosen assortment of reading material such as books on travel, fashion, interiors, and flowers. The guestrooms continue the ambiance of loving care. All are individually decorated, reflecting exquisite taste: antiques abound and handsome color-coordinating fabrics are used throughout. Nothing has been spared to make each room beautiful. The standard bedrooms are very pretty, but if you want to splurge, opt for a junior suite. It is such a pleasure to see a hotel that reflects so beautifully the authentic rich heritage of the original building.

HOTEL GABBIA D'ORO
Manager: Camilla Balzarro
Corso Porta Borsari, 4/A
Verona 37121, Italy
Tel: (045) 80 03 060, Fax: (045) 59 02 93
27 rooms, Double: €232–€351*
*Breakfast not included: €23
Open: all year, Credit cards: all major
In the heart of Verona
Region: Veneto, Michelin Map: 429
www.karenbrown.com/italyinns/gabbiadoro.html

The entrance to the Hotel Victoria is starkly modern—almost with a museum-like quality. The white walls, white ceiling, white floors, and an enormous skylight are softened by green plants. At first glance I was disappointed since I had heard so many glowing reports of the merits of this small hotel. However, the mood begins to change as you enter the reception area with its Oriental carpets and by the time you arrive in the lounge area, there is a definite move toward an antique ambiance. Here you find original heavy ancient wooden beams and one of the original stone walls exposed, leather chairs, and some lovely antique tables. The bedrooms are extremely modern and beautifully functional with good reading lights, comfortable chairs, Internet connections, and excellent bathrooms. The Victoria actually dates back centuries and the new hotel is built within the shell of an ancient building. The architect incorporated some of the archaeologically interesting finds of the site into a museum in the basement level. When the hotel is not full and all of the tables are not needed, special "windows" open up on the floor of the bar and coffee lounge and the museum below is lit so that you can study the artifacts as you enjoy an aperitif or your breakfast.

HOTEL VICTORIA
Manager: Giusy Loro
Via Adua, 8
Verona 37121, Italy
Tel: (045) 59 05 66, Fax: (045) 59 01 55
66 rooms, Double: €190–€420
Open: all year, Credit cards: all major
In the heart of Verona
Region: Veneto, Michelin Map: 429
www.karenbrown.com/italyinns/hotelvictoria.html

As you drive into the simple town of Vescovana, you will be amazed at the treasure that awaits you secreted behind high walls—the splendid 16th-century, three-story Villa Pisani and its magnificent gardens. The home is so huge it seems to stretch forever along the terrace. Inside, the feeling of the villa's immense size and grandeur continues with a seemingly endless number of exquisitely decorated, antique-filled rooms blending one into the other. Adorning walls and ceilings are incredible frescoes—it has taken over 30 years to restore them to their original beauty. Each of the ornately decorated bedrooms is filled with family heirlooms and stunning art collections. Your surroundings are so sensational that if it weren't for the exceptional warmth of your charming hostess, Mariella Bolognesi Scalabrin, you might feel as if you were staying in a museum. As grand as the home is, just as spectacular are the estate's vast, perfectly groomed gardens, which were designed to combine the formality of those in Italy with the charm of those in England. The result is breathtaking: clipped hedges forming intricate designs, trellises draped with flowers, whimsical fountains, and handsome statues. *NOTE:* Because of the many delicate antiques, the villa is not appropriate for children. *Directions:* Leave the A13 at Boara and turn left for Padova. After 2 km turn left at the stop light in Stanghella to Vescovana. The villa is on your right.

VILLA PISANI
Owner: Mariella Bolognesi Scalabrin
Via Roma, 19
Vescovana (PD) 35040, Italy
Tel & fax: (0425) 92 00 16
8 rooms, Double: €145–€250
Open: all year, Credit cards: all major
43 km N of Ferrara, 85 km SW of Venice
Region: Veneto, Michelin Map: 429
www.karenbrown.com/italyinns/villapisani.html

With great finesse and determination, Lucia and Paolo, an editor and art collector, managed to purchase Villa Campestri, a magnificent Renaissance villa—no easy feat, considering the 400-acre property had been in one family for 700 years. The cream-colored villa with handsome lawns and surrounding cypress woods commands a spectacular view over the immense valley and Mugello mountain range. A swimming pool among the trees enjoys this same view. This is the area north of Florence known for its concentration of Medici villas. The guestrooms in the villa have been restored to their original splendor, with high Florentine woodworked ceilings, carefully selected antiques, and delightful blue-and-white-tiled bathrooms. The honeymoon suite features a grand gold-crowned red canopy bed. A sitting room adorned with rich paintings leads to the elegant, stencil-painted dining rooms where original combinations of fresh local produce, cited in several noted restaurant guides, are served with great attention to detail, accompanied by an excellent selection of wines. Equally characteristic rooms are located in the side wing and small independent house. In the vicinity are golf, tennis, and riding stables. Villa Campestri offers refined and romantic accommodations with professional and cordial hospitality given by daughter, Viola. *Directions:* Exit A1 at Barberino di Mugello and follow signs for Borgo San Lorenzo then to Vicchio then to Campestre.

VILLA CAMPESTRI
Owners: Lucia & Paolo Pasquali
Localita: Campestri 19/22
Vicchio di Mugello (FI) 50039, Italy
Tel: (055) 84 90 107, Fax: (055) 84 90 108
21 rooms, Double: €145–€181
Open: Mar to Nov, Credit cards: all major
35 km NE of Florence
Region: Tuscany, Michelin Maps: 429, 430
www.karenbrown.com/italyinns/villacampestri.html

Volterra, a walled medieval hilltown, is not as well known as its ever-popular neighbor, San Gimignano, but it too exudes great authentic medieval character. Although not quite as colorful, it benefits from fewer tourists and offers a wealth of museums and many boutiques selling items made of alabaster, for which the town is renowned. Conveniently located within the walled city, very near the gate called Porta Florentina, the Hotel La Locanda is intimate and very attractive. The exterior is a pretty pinkish-beige color with arched doorway, flowerboxes at the windows, green shutters, and a wrought-iron light sconce. You enter into a small foyer with gorgeous parquet floors and fresh flowers accenting the antique reception desk. Just beyond are a small lounge and then the cheerful room for breakfast, the only meal served (the restaurant for the hotel, under the same ownership, is the Etruria, just a short walk up the street). Throughout the hotel you find original art, with the work of local artists on display in all of the rooms. An elevator leads up to three floors of guestrooms, all as fresh and pretty as can be. Each level has its own color scheme—green, red, or blue—established by the carpeting and the richly hued, handsome coordinating fabrics used for draperies and bedspreads. The marble bathrooms are excellent and the suites even have Jacuzzi tubs. *Directions:* Inside the city walls, on the street leading to, and close to, Porta Florentina.

HOTEL LA LOCANDA   **New**
Owner: Assenza Andrea
Via Guarnacci, 26-28
Volterra (PI) 56048, Italy
Tel: (0588) 81 547, Fax: (0588) 81 541
19 rooms, Double: €115–€150
Open: all year, Credit cards: all major
76 km S of Florence, 50 km NW of Siena
Region: Tuscany, Michelin Map: 430
www.karenbrown.com/italyinns/locanda.html

Regions of Italy

Hotels by Region

Apulia

Alberobello, Hotel dei Trulli
Marina di Pulsano, Tenuta del Barco
Monopoli, Il Melograno
Savelletri di Fasano, Masseria San Domenico

Basilicata

Maratea, La Locanda delle Donne Monache
     Santavenere Hotel
Maratea–Acquafredda, Villa Cheta Elite

Calabria

Cittadella del Capo, Palazzo del Capo
Tropea–Parghelia, Porto Pirgos

Campania

Amalfi, Hotel Santa Caterina
Capri
     Casa Morgano
     Grand Hotel Quisisana
     Hotel Luna
     Hotel Punta Tragara
     La Scalinatella
     Villa Brunella

Positano
     Albergo Casa Albertina
     Buca di Bacco
     Hotel Palazzo Murat
     Hotel Villa Franca
     Hotel Poseidon
     Punta Regina
     Il San Pietro di Positano
     Le Sirenuse Hotel

Ravello
     Hotel Palumbo
     Palazzo Sasso
     Villa Cimbrone
Santa Maria di Castellabate
     Hotel Villa Sirio
     Palazzo Belmonte
Sorrento, Grand Hotel Excelsior Vittoria

Emilia-Romagna

Bologna, Hotel Corona d'Oro 1890
Brisighella, Relais Torre Pratesi
Castel Guelfo, Locanda Solarola
Ferrara
     Duchessa Isabella Hotel
     Hotel Principessa Leonara

Ferrera (continued)
    Locanda della Duchessina
Mantova, Albergo San Lorenzo
Montegridolfo, Albergo Palazzo Viviani
Ravenna, Albergo Cappello
Soragna, Locanda del Lupo

Friuli-Venezia Giulia

Rivarotta, Villa Luppis
San Floriano del Collio, Golf Hotel

Lazio

Anguillara Sabazio, Country Relais I Due Laghi
Bracciano, Hotel Villa Clementina
Farnese–Voltone, Il Voltone
Frascati, Hotel Flora
Grottaferrata, Park Hotel Villa Grazioli
Ladispoli–Palo Laziale, La Posta Vecchia
Poggio Mirteto, Hotel Borgo Paraelios
Ponza (Isola di), Gennarino a Mare
Rome
    Hotel Gregoriana
    Hotel Hassler
    Hotel Lord Byron
    Hotel Majestic Roma
    La Residenza
    Hotel Barocco
    The Duke Hotel
    The Inn at the Spanish Steps
Tivoli, Hotel Sirene

Tivoli–Villa Adriana, Hotel Restaurant Adriano

Liguria

Camogli, Hotel Cenobio dei Dogi
Chiavari a Leivi, Ca'Peo
Finale Ligure, Hotel Punta Est
Levanto, Hotel Stella Maris
Monterosso al Mare–Cinque Terre
    Hotel Pasquale
    Hotel Porto Roca
    Hotel Villa Steno
Portofino
    Hotel Eden
    Hotel Splendido
    Splendido Mare
Sestri Levante, Hotel Helvetia

Lombardy

Argegno–Lake Como, Albergo Villa Belvedere
Azzate, Locanda dei Mai Intees
Bellagio–Lake Como
    Grand Hotel Villa Serbelloni
    Hotel Florence
    La Pergola
Cernobbio–Lake Como, Villa d'Este
Erbusco-Lake Iseo, L'Albereta
Gardone Riviera–Lake Garda, Villa Fiordaliso
Gargnano–Lake Garda, Grand Hotel Villa Feltrinelli
    Hotel Villa Giulia

Lombardy (continued)

Gargnano–Villa–Lake Garda
    Baia d'Oro
    Lake Garda, Hotel du Lac
Limone sul Garda–Lake Garda, Hotel Le Palme
Luino, Camin Hotel Luino
Mandello del Lario, Relais Villa delle Rose
Milan
        Antica Locanda dei Mercanti
        Four Seasons Hotel Milano
        Grand Hotel et de Milan
        Hotel de la Ville
Milan–Vizzola Ticino, Hotel Villa Malpensa
Sirmione–Lake Garda
        Hotel Grifone
        Hotel Sirmione
        Villa Cortine Palace Hotel
Valsolda–Lake Lugano, Stella d'Italia

Marches

Portonovo, Fortino Napoleonico

Piedmont

Alba, Palazzo Finati
Belgirate, Villa Dal Pozzo d'Annone
Cannero Riviera, Cannero Lakeside Hotel
Cioccaro di Penango, Locanda del Sant'Uffizio
Monforte d'Alba, Villa Beccaris

Orta San Giulio–Lake Orta
    La Contrada dei Monti
    Villa Crespi
Pescatori–Lake Maggiore, Hotel Verbano
San Stefano Belbo, Relais San Maurizio
Sauze d'Oulx, Il Capricorno

Sardinia

Sardinia–Oliena, Hotel Su Gologone
Sardinia–Porto Cervo, Hotel Pitrizza
Sardinia–Porto Conte, Hotel El Faro

Sicily

Sicily–Agrigento
    Foresteria Baglio della Luna
    Villa Athena
Sicily–Erice, Hotel Moderno
Sicily–Gangivecchio, Tenuta Gangivecchio
Sicily–Marina di Ragusa, Eremo della Giubiliana
Sicily–Palermo
    Centrale Palace Hotel
    Villa Igiea Grand Hotel
Sicily–Syracuse, Grand Hotel Siracusa
Sicily–Taormina
    Grand Hotel Timeo & Villa Flora
    Hotel Belvedere
    Villa Sant'Andrea

Trentino-Alto Adige

Bressanone (Brixen), Hotel Elephant
Castelrotto (Kastelruth), Hotel Cavallino d'Oro
Corvara, Romantik Hotel La Perla
Fiè (Völs), Romantik Hotel Turm
Merano
      Hotel Castello Labers
      Hotel Castle Fragsburg
Pergine, Castel Pergine
Rasun di Sopra, Ansitz Heufler Hotel
San Cassiano in Badia, Hotel Rosa Alpina
Sesto (Sexten), Berghotel Tirol
Tires–San Cipriano, Pensione Stefaner

Tuscany

Campiglia Marittima, Castello di Magona
Carmignano–Artimino, Paggeria Medicea
Castellina in Chianti
      Locanda Le Piazze
      Romantik Hotel Tenuta di Ricavo
Castelnuovo, Hotel Relais Borgo San Felice
Castiglion Fiorentino, Relais San Pietro
Cetona, La Frateria di Padre Eligio
Cortona
      Hotel San Michele
      Il Falconiere Relais e Ristorante
      Villa Marsili
Elba–Ottone, Hotel Villa Ottone

Florence
      Grand Hotel Villa Cora
      Hotel Curtatone
      Hotel Helvetia and Bristol
      Hotel Il Guelfo Bianco
      Hotel Lungarno
      Hotel Regency
      Marignolle Relais & Charme
      Mario's
      Palazzo Magnani Feroni
      Relais Uffizi
      Torre di Bellosguardo
      Villa Montartino
Florence–Candeli, Hotel Villa La Massa
Florence–Fiesole
      Hotel Villa Fiesole
      Pensione Bencista
      Villa San Michele
Gaiole in Chianti
      Castello di Spaltenna
      L'Ultimo Mulino
Lucca
      Albergo San Martino
      Locanda L'Elisa
      Palazzo Alexander
Montebenichi, Castelletto di Montebenichi
Montefiridolfi, Il Borghetto Country Inn
Montefollonico, La Chiusa

Tuscany (continued)

Montepulicano
    La Dionora
    Montorio
    Mueblé Il Riccio
    Villa Poggiano
Monteriggioni, Hotel Monteriggioni
Orbetello, San Biagio
Panzano in Chianti, Villa Le Barone
Petrignano, Relais alla Corte del Sole
Pienza, Hotel Relais Il Chiostro di Pienza
Pienza–Monticchiello, L'Olmo
Pietrasanta, Albergo Pietrasanta
Porto Ercole, Il Pellicano
Porto Santo Stefano, Hotel Torre di Cala Piccola
Radda in Chianti, Relais Fattoria Vignale
Reggello–Vaggio, Villa Rigacci
San Casciano Val di Pesa, Villa Il Poggiale
San Gimignano
    Hotel L'Antico Pozzo
    La Cisterna
    La Collegiata
San Gusmè, Hotel Villa Arceno
San Leonino, Hotel Belvedere di San Leonino
San Sano, Hotel Residence San Sano
Scansano, Antico Casale di Scansano
Siena
    Grand Hotel Continental
    Palazzo Ravizza
    Park Hotel

Sinalunga, Locanda dell'Amorosa
Sovicille–Pretale, Borgo Pretale
Vicchio di Mugello, Villa Campestri
Volterra, Hotel La Locanda

Umbria

Armenzano, Hotel "Le Silve di Armenzano"
Assisi
    Hotel Umbra
    Il Palazzo
    La Fortezza
    Residenza d'Epoca San Crispino
Bevagna, L'Orto degli Angeli
Canalicchio di Collazone, Relais Il Canalicchio
Città delle Pieve, Relais dei Magi
Colle San Paolo, Hotel Villa di Montesolare
Gubbio, Relais Ducale
Montefalco, Villa Pambuffetti
Montone, La Locanda del Capitano
Orvieto
    Hotel Palazzo Piccolomini
    La Badia
Ronti, Palazzo Terranova
Solomeo, Locanda Solomeo
Spoleto
    Hotel Gattapone
    Hotel San Luca
    Le Logge di Silvignano
    Villa Milani
Spoleto–Monteluco, Eremo delle Grazie

Umbria (continued)

Todi–Collevalenza, Relais Todini
Torgiano, Le Tre Vaselle

Valle d'Aosta

Breuil Cervinia, Hotel Hermitage
Champoluc, Villa Anna Maria
Cogne, Hotel Bellevue
Cogne–Valnontey, Hotel Petit Dahu

Veneto

Arcugnano, Villa Michelangelo
Asolo
    Albergo al Sole
    Hotel Duse
    Villa Cipriani
Cortina d'Ampezzo
    Hotel de la Poste
    Hotel Menardi
Costermano, Locanda San Verolo
Follina, Villa Abbazia
Gargagnago, La Foresteria Serègo Alighieri
Mira, Romantik Hotel Villa Margherita
Montagnana, Hotel Ristorante Aldo Moro
Pedemonte, Hotel Villa del Quar
Quarto d'Altino, Hotel Villa Odino
San Viglio–Lake Garda, Locanda San Viglio
Scorzè, Villa Soranzo Conestabile
Sorgà, Villa Bogoni

Torri del Benaco–Lake Garda, Hotel Gardesana

Venice
    Hotel Al Ponte dei Sospiri
    Hotel Antico Doge
    Hotel Colombina
    Hotel Flora
    Hotel Gritti Palace
    Hotel Lisbona
    Hotel Violino d'Oro
    Locanda Vivaldi
    Londra Palace
    Luna Hotel Baglioni
    Novecento
    Pensione Accademia
    Romantik Hotel Metropole
Venice–Isola della Giudecca, Hotel Cipriani
Venice–Isola Torcello, Locanda Cipriani Torcello
Venice–Lido, Albergo Quattro Fontane
Verona
    Hotel Gabbia d'Oro
    Hotel Victoria
Vescovana, Villa Pisani

Key Map

Map 1

BELLUNO

FRIULI

Follina

Vittorio Veneto

UDINE

A23

56

13

San Floriano del Collio

Rivarotta

VENETO

Asolo

248

348

A27

A23

A4

SLOVENIA

Castel Franco

47

53

53

Cavasagra

TREVISO

A4

13

Quarto d'Altino

TRIESTE

VICENZA

47

Scorzè

Torcello

Arcugnano

PADUA
(Padova)

Dolo

Mira

VENICE (Venezia)

Lido

Rome

● Places to Stay

○ Orientation/
  Sightseeing

a	b	Quadrants
c	d	

Map 2

AUSTRIA

AUSTRIA

38

A22

49

● Rasun di Sopra

49

MERANO

Lana ○

BOLZANO
(Bolzen)

38

● Bressanone
(Brixen)

San Cassiano
in Badia ●

51

Sesto
(Sexten) ●

● Castelrotto
● Fiè (Völs)
● Tires (Tiers)

● Corvara

48

48

● CORTINA d'AMPEZZO

51

42

42

○ Obereggen

○ 48
Cavalese

ALTO ADIGE

51

Rome ●

● Places to Stay

○ Orientation/
  Sightseeing

a	b
c	d	Quadrants

A22

BELLUNO ○

TRENTO ○

● Pergine

47

Feltre ○

50

Map 3

Map 4

SWITZERLAND

Locarno

Valsolda -
San Mamete

Cannero Riviera

LUGANO

Lake Como

Verbania

Lake Maggiore

Luino

Lake Lugano

Argegno

Stresa

Isola dei
Pescatori

Bellagio

Mandello
del Lario

Belgirate

Orta
San
Giullo

Lake Orta

Varese

Cernobbio

LECCO

Azzate

Montone

COMO

Malpensa
Airport

A9

A8

Milan-
Vizzola Ticino

BERGAMO

A26

A4

LOMBARDY

A4

Novara

MILAN
(Milano)

Linate
Airport

Rome

● Places to Stay

○ Orientation/
Sightseeing

| a | b | Quadrants |
| c | d | |

A7

A1

Maleo

Cremona

PIACENZA

A21

Map 5

Martigny

SWITZERLAND

Chamonix

Mont Blanc

Breuil Cervinia

Champoluc

Courmayeur

A5

AOSTA

Rome

● Places to Stay

○ Orientation/Sightseeing

Gran Paradiso
National Park

Cogne

Lake
Maggiore

Valnontey

VALLE D'AOSTA

Tunnel

a | b
c | d

Quadrants

FRANCE

PIEDMONT

A5

to MILAN →

A26

A4

Vercelli

A 26/4

A26

25

TURIN
(Torino)

590

Casale

457

Moncalvo

Sauze d'Oulx

Cioccaro di
Penango

457

A21

Monforte d'Alba

Alba

457

ASTI

A21

ALESSANDRIA

San Stefano Belbo

408

Map 6

Map 7

Soragna
Fidenza
Vescovana
EMILIA-ROMAGNA
FERRARA
MODENA
ADRIATIC SEA
Rome
A1
BOLOGNA
A13
A14
Castel Guelfo
RAVENNA
Places to Stay
Orientation/ Sightseeing
Faenza
a b
c d
Quadrants
Brisighella
Forlì
A1
A12
Pietrasanta
Borgo San Lorenzo
Vicchio di Mugello
Portico di Romagna
Rimini
Monsummano
Pistoia
67
A11
LUCCA
A11
Carmignano
Montegridolfo
Artimino
FLORENCE (Firenze)
Rufina
TUSCANY
PISA
A1

410

Map 8

Fiesole

FLORENCE
(Firenze)

Candeli

Empoli

67

A1

Reggello

Nord San Casciano
San Casciano
Sud San Casciano

Incisa

Vaggio

Bargino

Montefiridolfi

222

Tavernelle

Rome

Greve
in Chianti

429

San Donato

Panzano
in Chianti

Valdarno

● Places to Stay

○ Orientation/
   Sightseeing

◎ Exit from Expressway

Barberino
Val d'Elsa

406

TUSCANY

A1

| a | b |
| c | d | Quadrants

2

Poggibonsi

Radda
in Chianti

429

San Gimignano

Le Piazze

Castellina
in Chianti

Gaiole
in Chianti

Arezzo

68

Colle d'Val d'Elsa

San
Sano

Volterra

San Leonino

222

Monteriggioni

406

Montebenichi

Badesse-Nord

San Gusmè

Castelnuovo
Berardenga

Badesse-Sud

San Felice

Pievescola di
Casole d'Elsa

SIENA

73

Monte
San Savino

541

Sovicille-
Pretale

Serre di Rapolano

Val d'Chiana

73

73

Sinalunga

Rosia

Elba

TUSCANY

Map 9

TUSCANY

← to Florence A1

73

AREZZO

Polvano

Monte Savino

Castiglion Fiorentino

SIENA

326

A1

Val d'Chiana Bettolle

CORTONA

Montanare

15

Sinalunga

Petrignano

Montefollonico

Pienza

Montepulciano

Monticchiello

Chiusi Chianciano

Panicale

Cetona

Colle San Paolo

Città delle Pieve

SPINA

Fabro

A1

Orvieto exit

220

ORVIETO

Lake Bolsena

Lake Trasimeno

Solomeo

Citta dei Costello

E45

Ronti

Spedalicchio

Umbertide

Montone

GUBBIO

UMBRIA

E45

PERUGIA

Pianello

ASSISI

Armenzano

Torgiano

Spello

Foligno

Bevagna

Montefalco

Trevi

Collevalenza

TODI

Lake Corbara

SPOLETO

Monteluco

to Rome A1

2

73

3

3

3

15

Rome

● Places to Stay

○ Orientation/ Sightseeing

◎ Exit from Expressway

a	b
c	d

Quadrants

Fossombrone

73

Map 10

MARCHES

TUSCANY

UMBRIA

ANCONA ● Portonovo

ADRIATIC SEA

Sovicille Pretale
SIENA
Sinalunga
● Petrignano
Pianello
Solomeo
PERUGIA
ASSISI
Porto S. Giorgio

Campiglia Marittima
Montefollonico
Pienza
Monticchiello
Montepulciano
Cetona
Canalicchio di Collazone
Torgiano
Armenzano

Piombino
Portoferráio
Ottone
GROSSETO
Orvieto
Montefalco
Bevagna
Trevi
Silvignano
SPOLETO
Ascoli Piceno

ELBA
Scansano
Todi
Terni
Monteluco
Civitella del Tronto

Porto S. Stefano
Orbetello
Farnese
Rieti

Cala Piccola
Porto Ercole
Poggio Mirteto

Lake Bracciano
Bracciano
CIVITAVECCHIA
Anguillara Sabazia
Tivoli

Ladispoli
Palo Laziale
Leonardo da Vinci Airport
ROME (Roma)
Frascati
LAZIO

FIUMICINO
Ostia
Grottaferata

TYHRRENIAN SEA

Anzio

223
E1
74
A1
3
E7
3
313
E1
A24
A25
A1
E1/A2
148

Rome

● Places to Stay
○ Orientation/Sightseeing

| a | b | Quadrants |
| c | d | |

413

Map 11

LAZIO

Rome

● Places to Stay
○ Orientation/
   Sightseeing

| a | b | Quadrants
| c | d |

to Rome

○ Gaeta

Ponza

Formia

A2

A30

A16

A16

A30

Ventotene

NAPLES
(Napoli)

POMPEII
○

Ischia

BAY OF NAPLES

A3

SALERNO
○

Ravello
●

SORRENTO

Positano
●   ● AMALFI

CAPRI

BAY OF SALERNO

Paestum
○

Santa Maria
di Castellabate
●

Map 12

CAMPANIA

Barletta

BARI

APULIA

Monopoli

NAPLES

POMPEII

Fasano

Sorrento • Ravello Salerno

Savelletri di Fasano

CAPRI

Potenza

Matera

Alberobello

BRINDISI

Positano

AMALFI

Paestum

Pisticci

Marina di Pulsano

Santa Maria di Castellabate

Acquafredda

TARANTO

LECCE

BASILICATA

Avetrana

Galatone

Maratea

Cittadella del Capo-Bonifati

TYHRRENIAN SEA

CALABRIA

CROTONE

Parghelia

TROPEA

Sicily

REGGIO

Rome

● Places to Stay

○ Orientation/ Sightseeing

| a | b | Quadrants |
| c | d | |

415

Sicily

Map 13

Sardinia

PORTO CERVO

OLBIA

Porto Tores

SASSARI

597

Porto Conte   ALGHERO

131

NUORO

131

Oliena

Home

537

131

ORISTANO

● Places to Stay

○ Orientation/Sightseeing

a	b
c	d

Quadrants

CARBONIA

CAGLIARI

Santa Margherita   ○ Pula
di Pula

Map 14

Index

P

Enhance your Guides—Visit us Online

www.karenbrown.com

- Hotel specials
- Color photos of hotels and B&Bs
- 20% online discount for book purchases
- Discount airfare, both business and coach class
- Direct links to individual property websites and e-mails
- Up-to-the-minute phone, fax, and e-mail information
- Rental cars, travel planning, trip insurance, itineraries, maps, and more

Become a Member of the Karen Brown Club

- Additional specials and offers from our travel partners
- Exclusive access to "new discoveries" from our current research
- An additional 20% savings on purchases from our online store

A complete listing of member benefits can be found on our website

Don't delay, join online today!

www.karenbrown.com

Any of the accommodations in this guide can be reserved through **Hidden Treasures of Italy**, a specialized travel service for independent travelers.

*Together with your accommodation reservations, **Hidden Treasures** can also provide additional services such as:*

- *Individual itinerary recommendations (trains / car rentals / chauffeured transfers)*
- *Ground transportation arrangements*
- *Private guides / museum and concert tickets*
- *Special interest activities (food and wine tours / cooking classes / golf programs / organized dinners in private historical villas / private garden visits / chartered sailing itineraries to islands / and many others).*

***Hidden Treasures** also represents a unique "Limited Collection" of personally selected villas available for unforgettable vacations, special events, family reunions, weddings, or other personalized programs.*

Service fees apply.

HIDDEN TREASURES OF ITALY, INC.
665 West Sheridan Road
Chicago, IL 60613
U.S. Toll Free Tel: (888) 419-6700

U.S. Tel:	(773) 871-0500
Fax:	(773) 871-2970
e-mail:	info@htitaly.com
Web Site:	www.htitaly.com

Hidden Treasures of Italy also Specializes in Complete On-Site Wedding / Honeymoon Planning.

Personalized consultation and arrangements for civil or religious wedding ceremonies and reception in the city of your choice. Complete local organization of all legal, administrative, and logistical details to help make your wedding in Italy truly memorable and hassle-free.

From a private romantic ceremony for two, to a complete traditional wedding package in any of the most enchanting historical sites Italy has to offer.

Hidden Treasures *can also assist in organizing customized trips for groups of friends, extended family, or business associates.*

Whether for a once in a lifetime family occasion, or as a special incentive for your best employees, **Hidden Treasures** *provides the highest expression of quality, service, and hospitality in the most charming locations throughout all of Italy.*

www.htitaly.com

KB Travel Service

❖ **KB Travel Service** offers travel-planning assistance using itineraries designed by *Karen Brown* and published in her guidebooks. We will customize any itinerary to fit your personal interests.

❖ We will plan your itinerary with you, help you decide how long to stay and what to do once you arrive, and work out the details.

❖ We will book your airline tickets and your rental car, arrange rail travel, reserve accommodations recommended in *Karen Brown's Guides,* and supply you with point-to-point information and consultation.

Contact us to start planning your travel!

800-782-2128 or e-mail: info@kbtravelservice.com

Service fees do apply

KB Travel Service
16 East Third Avenue
San Mateo, CA 94401 USA
www.kbtravelservice.com

Independently owned and operated by Town & Country Travel
CST 2001543-10

Seal Cove Inn

Located in the San Francisco Bay Area

Karen Brown Herbert (best known as author of Karen Brown's Guides) and her husband, Rick, have put 23 years of experience into reality and opened their own superb hideaway, Seal Cove Inn. Spectacularly set amongst wildflowers and bordered by towering cypress trees, Seal Cove Inn looks out to the distant ocean over acres of county park: an oasis where you can enjoy secluded beaches, explore tide-pools, watch frolicking seals, and follow the tree-lined path that traces the windswept ocean bluffs. Country antiques, original watercolors, flower-laden cradles, rich fabrics, and the gentle ticking of grandfather clocks create the perfect ambiance for a foggy day in front of the crackling log fire. Each bedroom is its own haven with a cozy sitting area before a wood-burning fireplace and doors opening onto a private balcony or patio with views to the park and ocean. Moss Beach is a 35-minute drive south of San Francisco, 6 miles north of the picturesque town of Half Moon Bay, and a few minutes from Princeton harbor with its colorful fishing boats and restaurants. Seal Cove Inn makes a perfect base for whale watching, salmon-fishing excursions, day trips to San Francisco, exploring the coast, or, best of all, just a romantic interlude by the sea, time to relax and be pampered. Karen and Rick look forward to the pleasure of welcoming you to their coastal hideaway.

Seal Cove Inn • 221 Cypress Avenue • Moss Beach • California • 94038 • USA
tel: (650) 728-4114, fax: (650) 728-4116, website: www.sealcoveinn.com

Travel Your Dreams · Order Your Karen Brown Guides Today

Please ask in your local bookstore for Karen Brown's Guides. If the books you want are unavailable, you may order directly from the publisher. Books will be shipped immediately.

_____ *Austria: Charming Inns & Itineraries* $19.95

_____ *California: Charming Inns & Itineraries* $19.95

_____ *England: Charming Bed & Breakfasts* $18.95

_____ *England, Wales & Scotland: Charming Hotels & Itineraries* $19.95

_____ *France: Charming Bed & Breakfasts* $18.95

_____ *France: Charming Inns & Itineraries* $19.95

_____ *Germany: Charming Inns & Itineraries* $19.95

_____ *Ireland: Charming Inns & Itineraries* $19.95

_____ *Italy: Charming Bed & Breakfasts* $18.95

_____ *Italy: Charming Inns & Itineraries* $19.95

_____ *Mexico: Charming Inns & Itineraries* $19.95

_____ *Mid-Atlantic: Charming Inns & Itineraries* $19.95

_____ *New England: Charming Inns & Itineraries* $19.95

_____ *Pacific Northwest: Charming Inns & Itineraries* $19.95

_____ *Portugal: Charming Inns & Itineraries* $19.95

_____ *Spain: Charming Inns & Itineraries* $19.95

_____ *Switzerland: Charming Inns & Itineraries* $19.95

Name _____ Street _____

Town _____ State_____ Zip _____ Tel _____

Credit Card (MasterCard or Visa) _____ Expires: _____

For orders in the USA, add $5 for the first book and $2 for each additional book for shipment. Overseas shipping (airmail) is $10 for 1 to 2 books, $20 for 3 to 4 books etc. CA residents add 8.25% sales tax. Fax or mail form with check or credit card information to:

KAREN BROWN'S GUIDES
Post Office Box 70 · San Mateo · California · 94401 · USA
tel: (650) 342-9117, fax: (650) 342-9153, e-mail: karen@karenbrown.com, www.karenbrown.com

KAREN BROWN wrote her first travel guide in 1976. Her personalized travel series has grown to 17 titles, which Karen and her small staff work diligently to keep updated. Karen, her husband, Rick, and their children, Alexandra and Richard, live in Moss Beach, a small town on the coast south of San Francisco. They settled here in 1991 when they opened Seal Cove Inn. Karen is frequently traveling but when she is home, in her role as innkeeper, enjoys welcoming Karen Brown readers.

CLARE BROWN was a travel consultant for many years, specializing in planning itineraries to Europe using charming small hotels in the countryside. The focus of her job remains unchanged, but now her expertise is available to a larger audience—the readers of her daughter Karen's country inn guides. When Clare and her husband, Bill, are not traveling, they live either in Hillsborough, California, or at their home in Vail, Colorado, where family and friends frequently join them for skiing.

JANN POLLARD, the artist responsible for the beautiful painting on the cover of this guide, has studied art since childhood, and is well known for her outstanding impressionistic-style watercolors, which she has exhibited in numerous juried shows, winning many awards. Jann travels frequently to Europe (using Karen Brown's Guides) where she loves to paint historical buildings. Jann's original paintings are represented through The Gallery, Burlingame, CA, 650-347-9392 or www.thegalleryart.net. Fine-art giclée prints of the cover paintings are also available at www.karenbrown.com.

BARBARA TAPP, the talented artist who produces all of the hotel sketches and delightful illustrations in this guide, was raised in Australia where she studied in Sydney at the School of Interior Design. Although Barbara continues with freelance projects, she devotes much of her time to illustrating the Karen Brown guides. Barbara lives in Kensington, California, with her husband, Richard, their two sons, Jonothan and Alexander, and daughter, Georgia.

Icons Key

This year we have introduced the icons listed below in the guidebooks and on our website (*www.karenbrown.com*). These allow us to provide additional information about our recommended properties. When using our website to supplement the guides, placing the cursor over an icon will in many cases give you further details.

❄	Air conditioning in rooms	🍴	Restaurant
☕	Breakfast included in room rate	🏊	Swimming pool
	Children welcome	🎾	Tennis
	Cooking classes offered		Television
CREDIT	Credit cards accepted		Wedding facilities
	Dinner served upon request	♿	Wheelchair friendly
☎	Direct-dial telephone in room		Golf course nearby
	Dogs by special request		Hiking trails nearby
	Elevator		Horseback riding nearby
	Exercise room		Skiing nearby
	Mini-refrigerator in room		Water sports nearby
🚭	Non-smoking rooms		Wineries nearby
P	Parking available		